RENEWALS 458-4574

DATE DUE

OCT 2 4			
MAY 1 2			
GAYLORD			PRINTED IN U.S.A

Texts and Textuality

WITHDRAWN
UTSA Libraries

WELLESLEY STUDIES IN CRITICAL THEORY, LITERARY HISTORY, AND CULTURE
VOLUME 13
GARLAND REFERENCE LIBRARY OF THE HUMANITIES
VOLUME 1891

Wellesley Studies in Critical Theory, Literary History, and Culture

William E. Cain, *General Editor*

Texts and Textuality
Textual Instability, Theory, and Interpretation

Edited by
Philip Cohen

Garland Publishing, Inc.
New York and London
1997

Library of Congress Cataloging-in-Publication Data

Texts and textuality : textual instability, theory, and interpretation / edited by
    Philip Cohen.
        p.   cm. — (Garland reference library of the humanities ; vol.
    1891. Wellesley studies in critical theory, literary history, and culture ; vol. 13)
        Includes bibliographical references and index.
        ISBN 0-8153-1956-8 (alk. paper)
        1. Literature—History and criticism—Theory, etc.   2. Literature—
    Philosophy.   3. Criticism.   I. Cohen, Philip G.   II. Series: Garland refer-
    ence library of the humanities ; vol. 1891.   III. Series: Garland reference
    library of the humanities. Wellesley studies in critical theory, literary history,
    and culture ; vol. 13.
    PN81.T424   1997
    809—dc20   96-23047
                                                                    CIP

Printed on acid-free, 250-year-life paper
Manufactured in the United States of America

General Editor's Preface

The volumes in this series, Wellesley Studies in Critical Theory, Literary History, and Culture, are designed to reflect, develop, and extend important trends and tendencies in contemporary criticism. The careful scrutiny of literary texts in their own right of course remains a crucial part of the work that critics and teachers perform: this traditional task has not been devalued or neglected. But other types of interdisciplinary and contextual work are now being done, in large measure as a result of the emphasis on "theory" that began in the late 1960s and early 1970s and that has accelerated since that time. Critics and teachers now examine texts of all sorts—literary and non-literary alike—and, more generally, have taken the entire complex, multifaceted field of culture as the object for their analytical attention. The discipline of literary studies has radically changed, and the scale and scope of this series is intended to illustrate this challenging fact.

Theory has signified many things, but one of the most crucial has been the insistent questioning of familiar categories and distinctions. As theory has grown in its scope and intensified in importance, it has reoriented the idea of the literary canon: there is no longer a single canon, but many canons. It has also opened up and complicated the meanings of history, and the materials and forms that constitute it. Literary history continues to be vigorously written, but now as a kind of history that intersects with other histories that involve politics, economics, race relations, the role of women in society, and many more. And the breadth of this historical inquiry has impelled many in literary studies to view themselves more as cultural critics and general intellectuals than as literary scholars.

Theory, history, culture: these are the formidable terms around which the volumes in this series have been organized. A number of these volumes will be the product of a single author or editor. But perhaps even more of them will be collaborative ventures, emerging from the joint enterprise of editors, essayists, and respondents or commentators. In each volume, and as a whole, the series will aim to highlight both distinctive contributions to knowledge and a process of exchange, discussion, and debate. It will make available new kinds of work, as well as fresh approaches to criticism's traditional tasks, and indicate new ways through which such work can be done.

William E. Cain
Wellesley College

I would like to dedicate this book to future opera singer or Supreme Court justice or both, my daughter Caitlin Marie Cohen.

Contents

Acknowledgments

In commissioning and editing this volume, I have incurred many debts. As always, Noel Polk has offered both suggestions and encouragement. With the encouragement of editors Jackson Bryer and Carla Mulford, a different version of my introduction and some of the essays in this collection appeared in a special issue of *Resources for American Literary Study* (Vol. 20, No. 2) that I edited. I am grateful to the editors of *RALS* and to The Pennsylvania State University Press for permission to reprint these essays. (Copyright 1994 by The Pennsylvania State University Press and reproduced by permission of The Pennsylvania State University Press.) I am especially grateful to Richard Kopley, the associate editor at *RALS*, for his painstaking editorial work. His suggestions, questions, and comments improved this volume immeasurably. Robert Cook, the Director of the University Media Services Center here at UT-Arlington, worked indefatigably to produce both the index and camera-ready copy. I am also grateful to Nancy Wood for providing me with the release-time that enabled me to complete this project.

Philip Cohen
Arlington, TX

Textual Instability, Literary Studies, and Recent Developments in Textual Scholarship

Philip Cohen

I begin with neither a literary theorist nor a literary critic but that well-known bibliographer and textual scholar, Smedley Force, specifically from his seminal "Prologomena to Any Future Study of *Winnie-the-Pooh*." Professor Force asserts that

> Criticism must be postponed until the text has been definitively established, the *lacunae* surrounded (but not replaced) with a sufficiently broad range of conjectured readings, the variorum footnotes, appendices, bibliographies, and concordances compiled. When we turn from the current stream of drivel on *Winnie-the-Pooh* and ask ourselves how much of this indispensable groundwork for useful study of the book has been laid, we discover . . . that nothing of merit has even been begun. (Crews 141)

Rumor has it that Frederick Crews had in mind the magisterial tone and scholarly emphasis of the late Fredson Bowers, a primary exponent of the Anglo-American editorial tradition, when he penned Force's essay for his wonderfully malicious and satirical casebook *The Pooh Perplex*. Parody, of course, ridicules by exaggeration, and there is in textual scholarship, the scholarly study of the genesis, transmission, and editing of texts, a venerable tradition of the sort of essay that Crews skewers so ably in Force's "Prologomena." Typically, essays in this genre were writ-

ten from well within the modern Anglo-American editorial tradition of eclectically constructing a single text that approximates
ideally what an author finally intended to appear before his audience. Coming out of a tradition first articulated by W. W. Greg
and subsequently elaborated by Bowers and G. Thomas Tanselle,
these essays quite naturally focused on the importance for critics
of selecting an established text as the object of scholarly and critical scrutiny. In such pieces, authors bewail the textual naivete of
literary critics who are in other respects quite sophisticated, and
they call for a change in this distressing state of affairs. Some
authors may suggest we redouble our efforts to persuade our
reluctant colleagues of the relationship of textual and bibliographical issues to larger issues of literary theory, interpretation,
and pedagogy. More typically, however, authors simply declare
that colleagues should be more willing to familiarize themselves
with this relationship.

In this introduction to a collection of essays on the relevance of a recently revivified, retheorized textual scholarship to
literary study, I want to offer a revised version of the old exhor-
tation. Like those of my predecessors, my homily begins with
recognizing the fact of textual instability, with recognizing that
the texts of written and printed and electronic works often exist
in different versions. Over time, texts are subject to welcome and
unwelcome, intended and unintended changes by authors,
friends, editors, and publishers. Chance also accounts for some
measure of transmissional variation. Contemporary textual
scholars diverge sharply, however, from some of the implications that have traditionally been drawn from this commonplace
but no less crucial fact. Anglo-American textual scholars have
gone on to stress the paramount necessity of stabilizing the text
by purging transmissional corruption and emending a copy-text
with later authorial substantive revisions unless it can be shown
that an author also revised the base text's punctuation and
spelling. Descending from Greg's seminal "Rationale of Copy-
Text," this different treatment of what are known as substantives
and accidentals derives from the observation that non-authorial
corruption is more likely to affect the latter than the former.
Contemporary textual scholarship, however, has come to view
such an editorial operation upon the material and historical reality of textual instability as an interpretive act that privileges from
the start final authorial and single-text orientations toward texts

over other possible textual orientations. Consequently, I want to sketch out some rather different lessons than earlier commentators have about how an awareness of textual instability should affect our activities as scholars and teachers of literature.

Early on in the game, Bowers himself provided the apotheosis of this particular genre in his "Textual Criticism and the Critic":

> It is still a current oddity that many a literary critic has investigated the past ownership and mechanical condition of his second-hand automobile, or the pedigree and training of his dog, more thoroughly than he has looked into the qualifications of the text on which his critical theories rest. (5)[1]

The critic is urged throughout this polemical essay "for the humility of his soul . . . to study the transmission of some appropriate text" (4). Or again, before the critic "expatiates upon subtle ambiguities . . . he had better check his facts, that is to say his text" (34).

Now I was trained as a graduate student by an eminent editor who is very much a proponent of authorial texts, authorial intentions, and authorial meanings. Thus it did not occur to me when I first read this essay that Bowers was so firmly entrenched within debatable authorial, intentionalist, and positivist notions about texts that he stressed only what literary critics could learn from textual scholarship. The theoretical naivete of his rhetorical strategy may remind us that the relative consensus over the assumptions, aims, and methods of literary study it reflects has long since passed from the academic scene. From our position in the 1990s, Bowers's stance and tone now seem unfair at best. That the avenues between textual scholarship, literary theory, interpretation, and pedagogy are now open to two- and three- and even four-way traffic is evidenced by the zest and diversity found in the numerous challenges to the Anglo-American editorial tradition mounted during the past decade in the theoretical and practical work of scholars as diverse as Jerome McGann, D.F. McKenzie, Peter Shillingsburg, D.C. Greetham, Hershel Parker, and Hans Walter Gabler.[2] Such work indicates that a paradigm shift in textual scholarship has been under way for some time now. Indeed, many recent editorial proposals and discussions share a restriction or rejection of authorial intention as a means of

discriminating among authorial versions and a skepticism about
the validity of creating an eclectic best text that never existed historically.[3] As Paul Eggert observed at the 1993 Society for Textual
Scholarship Conference, the eclectic approach rests on the dubious construct of "a single author who was in perfect possession
of a complete text of the work" (4). More importantly, much
recent textual work has been influenced by poststructuralism's
heightened theoretical self-consciousness and recognizes that
constituting any text or group of texts out of the available historical versions is a profoundly theoretical and interpretive task
rather than an objective and mechanical one. One conclusion
often drawn from this decentering of the text is that scholarly
editions should stress presenting in some coherent fashion the
fluid process represented by a work's textual manifestations
rather than some finished textual product.

It may be objected that the best eclectic editors from Greg
to Tanselle have always stressed the inescapably interpretive and
evaluative aspects of editorial work. But they have done so only
within authorial and single-text orientations toward their textual
materials. Literary judgment must play a part in recovering an
author's intentions, but there is no doubt in the classic statements
of the eclectic editorial position about what the textual scholar
must try to recover. Thus Bowers again in an essay on "Textual
Scholarship" for a 1963 MLA volume on modern linguistic and
literary scholarship unequivocally states that a critical edition
"that pursues and recovers the author's full intentions . . . and
correctly associates them in one synthesis, is clearly the only suit-
able edition that is complete and accurate enough to satisfy the
needs of a critic" (25). Eighteen years later, Tanselle echoes this
position in a similarly-titled essay for a similar MLA volume: "Of
the various directions that editorial intervention could take, the
one of scholarly interest is that which leads toward the text
intended by the author" (37). In contrast, D.C. Greetham's
"Textual Scholarship," written in 1992 for the most recent MLA
volume, legitimizes non-authorial and multiple-text orientations:

> Instead of postulating a single, consistent, authorially
> sponsored text as the purpose of the editorial enter-
> prise, [contemporary editorial proposals] suggest
> multiform, fragmentary, even contradictory, texts as
> the aim of editing, sometimes to be constructed ad hoc

by the reader. In general, then, the characteristic feature of textual scholarship in the closing years of this
century is its democratic pluralism: there is no longer,
in Anglo-American editing, at least, any single ortho-
doxy among textual scholars. (112)

Greetham's essay reverses the earlier relationship
between the authorial textual orientation and literary theory,
placing the former squarely within the boundaries of the latter.
Just as critics now routinely explore the related institutional and
social discursive and non-discursive assumptions and practices
that constitute different hermeneutical schools and their rhetorical strategies, so some textual scholars now view any conception
of textuality as similarly situated rather than absolute. Thus the
texts of literary works, as well as their interpretations, may be
regulated by larger constraints. In short, the texts of literary
works, like interpretations of them, are constituted rather than
given, multiple rather than singular. I hasten to add that text-
constitution is constrained not only by critical, institutional, and
social practices, but also by the relevant documents that are
extant or can be inferred. Still, it is one thing to think of the
authorial orientation as a scholarly constant, but it is quite another to view the author as a Foucauldian function, as only one of a
number of possible strategies for constituting, organizing, and
using texts. In his thoroughly enjoyable *The Death of Literature*,
Alvin Kernan argues, for example, that the authorial orientation
and the stable, closed text are less absolutes than the results of
print technology, *laissez-faire* economics, and the
Romantic/Modernist myth of the autonomous, creative artist.[4]
The fixed conception of textuality as fixed derives from print
technology and so differs from classical and medieval conceptions. With the transition from print to electronic means of generating, transmitting, storing, and accessing information will
come, Kernan predicts, the development of yet another conception of textuality as "the electronic database destabilizes the text"
(109).

Following the imperialist tendency of English studies in
general over the last twenty years, textual scholarship today is
moving towards a broader conception of what counts as a text, a
textual medium, and a textual form: no longer is a text conceptu-
ally limited to abstract sequences of words and punctuation rep-

resented by material signs contained in manuscripts, typescripts, and printed books as has been stipulated in the otherwise very different Anglo-American, French, and German editorial traditions.[5] Now texts may be verbal or nonverbal or a mixture of both, and forms are not restricted to marks on paper. We are learning that the cinematic medium can create a text consisting of images produced by projecting light through frames of film and accompanied by amplified sounds. Increased interest in the productions or performances of various oral traditions centers on another type of text and another type of medium: the highly unstable linguistic sequences delivered through the medium of the human voice. Although we should not allow this conceptual broadening of texts and textuality to blur the many significant differences between verbal texts— whether embodied in papyrus or manuscript or print—and nonverbal texts such as visual images or sculptures, the medium, to paraphrase Marshall McLuhan, has nevertheless become a text. In *The Textual Condition*, for example, Jerome McGann has argued that the physical form containing a linguistic text is also a text, albeit one coded bibliographically or spatially rather than linguistically. Thus the layout, typography, binding, paper, and ornamentation of a book work in concert with or in opposition to the linguistic text they convey. Such a textualizing of what has traditionally been treated as the physical form containing a text renders analytical bibliography an even more interpretive discipline than it has been heretofore, suggesting the possibility that editors translate texts into new contexts rather than recover them.[6]

The fluidity and variability of contemporary conceptions of text and medium are best represented by the hypertext produced by electronic writing and contained in the memory of a computer. In different ways, Alvin Kernan, George Landow, Richard Lanham, and Jay David Bolter have all recently explored how blocks of text in a hypertextual network may contain images and linguistic and numerical symbols that may be linked together in any number of ways. Indeed, hypertext presents the supreme challenge to traditional theories of textuality, whether autonomous or communicative, that have been shaped by earlier means of textual production such as manuscript and print technology. In the web of a computer hypertext, lexias or blocks of text may be linked in any number of ways by an active, writerly reader (Landow 22). The open, writerly virtual text flickering on one's monitor is worlds away from the closed, readerly text that evolved during the Romantic/Modernist period, and corresponds to poststructuralist conceptions of textuality. From our vantage point in what scholars of electronic writing like to call the late age of print, the appearance of the hypertexts of electronic information technology are only now starting to contribute to current discussions of textual authority a heightened awareness of how the different material conditions of textual production—for example, manuscript or print or electronic technology—help constitute different theories of textuality.

In terms of actual scholarly editions, we are only now starting to see the practical consequences of the new pluralist, even poststructuralist editorial paradigm. Beginning with Gabler's well-known and controversial synoptic edition of Joyce's *Ulysses* in 1984, a handful of scholarly editions premised upon a fundamental rethinking of the editorial task have appeared in English. Another example that comes to mind is Stanley Wells and Gary Taylor's decision in their 1986 Oxford Shakespeare to edit the texts of the bard's plays according to the social criteria of performance rather than the authorial criteria of Shakespeare's intention and to print two texts of *King Lear*, one based on the Quarto and one based on the Folio. More recently, Jerome McGann's *New Oxford Book of Romantic Period Verse* (1993), an anthology rather than a scholarly edition, is the product of his argument "for a socialized concept of authorship and textual authority" in *The Critique of Modern Textual Criticism* (8). This innovative anthology generally features the first printed versions of poems with printers' errors corrected and with emendations from earlier manuscript versions only when these first printed versions are clearly in error.[7] McGann's collection thus makes available not the texts that authors finally wanted to appear before their audience but rather the texts that appeared before their original audiences.

The length of time involved for this reconceptualizing of editorial theory to bear fruit in the form of material editions may stem from textual scholarship's status as one of the more conservative branches of literary study. Then again it may simply reflect the length of time required either to produce a scholarly edition or to assimilate fully the consequences for textual scholarship of electronic information technology.[8] And more poststructuralist editions are on the way. In her penetrating *Shakespeare Verbatim*, new historicist and textual scholar Margreta de Grazia has recently performed the first full-scale ideological reading of a significant edition—in this case, Malone's edition of Shakespeare in the late eighteenth-century. This landmark edition initiated the empirical, historical, and psychological bent of modern Shakespeare studies in that it

> was the first to emphasize the principle of authenticity in treating Shakespeare's works and the materials relating to them; the first to contain a dissertation on the linguistic and poetic particulars of Shakespeare's period; the first to depend on facts in constructing Shakespeare's biography; the first to include a full chronology for the plays, and the first to publish, annotate, and canonize the 1609 Sonnets. (2)

Although Malone believed he was sorting through documents, records, and earlier editions in order to uncover the authentic, historical Shakespeare and to stabilize his texts, de Grazia argues that Malone's apparatus constructed the text according to an Enlightenment rather than a Renaissance textual orientation. Under the guise of discovering the man who *was* Shakespeare, Malone *created* Shakespeare as a modern liberal bourgeois subject with a rich, fully interiorized psychological life. In short, he constructed an eighteenth-century Shakespeare, and his text and apparatus reflect not a Renaissance reality, but the then-new requirements of modern literary studies. De Grazia is currently preparing an edition of the Sonnets based upon her new historicist deconstruction of this seminal forerunner of modern scholarly editions of the bard. One wonders how successfully her scholarly imagination will be able to come to grips with the intractable difficulties of translating theoretical conceptions into material editions.[9]

    Scholars are confronted, then, by different texts and different versions of texts that have mutely survived the ravages of time and history, sometimes rather the worse for wear. In the Anglo-American tradition of textual scholarship, editors conflated authorial and historical orientations and believed that they had no intellectual and ethical choice but to stabilize the text and restore to it the purity of its author's intended voice. The reality of textual instability and the antifoundationalist impact of much poststructuralist literary theory upon textual scholarship, however, have combined to decenter not only a text's meaning, but also its very constitution. In this new theoretical context, the mutability of texts now suggests that no single ontology of the literary text, let alone the literary work, or methodology for its constitution exists. Indeed, searching for a single ontology—whether single or multiple, unitary or fragmented, centered or decentered, essential or contextual—now seems like chasing vainly after a chimera. The plethora of pre- and postpublication materials extant for many nineteenth- and twentieth-century literary works has helped some textual scholars, especially those influenced by the growing interdisciplinary movement known as the history of the book, to argue that ontological convictions about literary texts and works are really extensions of larger networks of cultural and political relations masquerading as naturalized philosophical facts.[10] This perception is a pragmatic or rhetorical rather than an essentializing view of textuality, text-constitution, and text-interpretation, the sort of stance that Steven Mailloux advocates in his excellent *Rhetorical Power.* Traditional editors often appealed to centered notions of textuality, to *a priori* Platonic conceptions of a text, in order to justify their particular way of altering and combining texts from different documents. But what they were really doing was naturalizing or mystifying their own textual orientation.

As teachers and students of literature, we are becoming more and more theoretically sophisticated. We seem willing to concede that theories and methodologies constrain as well as enable their users, that they help frame the terms of the debates about specific works by first determining the range of questions that can legitimately be asked of texts and then generating the contours of the possible answers. Ideological critics have made us aware of how our far from neutral questions and answers may be related to larger interests. In recent MLA job lists, an emphasis on various approaches towards literary and non-literary discursive practices has been sharing top billing with, and gradually replacing, the previous organization of the discipline according to the various periods of literary history. A quick comparison of the paper titles of recent conventions of our professional organizations with those of past meetings duly recorded in the dusty volumes deposited in one's campus library reveals the same transformation. The course descriptions contained in the humblest of departmental catalogues and bulletins and the prefaces and introductions of books produced by the most prestigious scholarly presses all attest to this heightened theoretical literacy. Stanley Fish's well-known titular question *Is There a Text in This Class?* may have seemed provocative in 1983, but the answer he gave then may strike many now as unexceptionable:

> The answer this book gives . . . is "there is and there isn't." There isn't a text in this or any other class if one means by text what E.D. Hirsch and others mean by it . . . but there is a text in this and every class if one means by text the structure of meanings that is obvious and inescapable from the perspective of whatever interpretative assumptions happen to be in force. (vii)

But this emphasis on the reception of texts is only half of the story. Because of the influence of literary theory on textual scholarship in the 1980s, even the often tedious, always staid job of text-constitution is much more contentious than it has hitherto been. In *Scholarly Editing in the Computer Age*, Peter Shillingsburg usefully makes just this point, that editors perform interpretive activities based on various assumptions as they minister to texts, and no more so than in their adherence to one or several of various possible orientations—for example, aesthetic, historical, sociological, and authorial—toward texts, works, and authority. Since he believes that no one orientation is logically superior to the others, Shillingsburg argues that editors and readers must forsake the search for the "right" text and become cognizant instead of how theoretical, institutional, and social practices produce their different orientations, leading to different principles governing the selection of copy-text, the editing of copy-text, and the presentation of textual information in an apparatus (29-30).

Coming out of graduate school ten years ago, I had a skepticism concerning critical theory based less on any actual knowledge of its primary texts than on my stubborn empiricism. Like many a traditional scholar who condemned the invasion of theory from a distance, I found a great deal to admire and to learn from once I actually went about the task of becoming more theoretically literate. By the same token, a condescension toward textual scholarship based on little more than ignorance may often be found among the ranks of the theoretically literate. Students of literary theory and interpretation have yet to pay attention to the conclusions that the recent rethinking of editorial theory and practice has produced. An anecdote illustrates my point. Recently, I was in my department's coffee-room, chatting with one of our humanities doctoral students about her dissertation. Her project is to develop an integrated theory and pedagogy for the teaching of reading and writing inspired, in part, by the essays of a major twentieth-century British novelist. I casually mentioned that she might look at the scholarship on her writer's actual composition and revision processes and at the editions and facsimiles of her manuscripts, typescripts, and published work. Looking at me with just the slightest trace of condescension, she asked, "That's what you do, isn't it?" It had clearly never occurred to her that consulting her author's actual experience of composition was an activity relevant to her work. Moreover, now that I had raised the issue, it seemed equally clear that she found the suggestion somewhat quaint. Still, it was refreshing to see that blindered consciousnesses are not limited to those on the side of empiricism. As McGann observes, "contemporary theory and hermeneutics" has "largely avoided a serious engagement with the problem of facticity and positive knowledge" ("The Case of *The Ambassadors*" 151).

That texts are intrinsically unstable, frequently consisting of a series of determinate historical versions has consequences for all students of literature because different versions of a literary work frequently help shape different readings independently of the interpretive paradigms brought to bear upon them. And pondering the textual instability of the works we interpret is relevant to our grappling with one of the thorniest issues in contemporary literary studies: how are the meanings of texts generated? Textual literacy will not necessarily lead us to endorse the claims of intentionalists such as E.D. Hirsch or Hershel Parker. The latter, for example, asserts that the only valid meaning is authorial meaning, that "authorial is built into the words of a literary work during the process of composition" (23), and that it is recoverable by historical, biographical, and bibliographical analysis. Textual instability may just as easily lead one to conclude that meaning is more fluid than fixed. Rather than immanent in the text or the product of an author's intentions, meanings, in this alternative view, arise from the relations produced when *particular* texts are viewed from *particular* contexts: as textual versions and contexts change, so may the range of possible meanings. Thus the essence of texts may be their ability to be re-ontologized and re-interpreted endlessly as different textual versions and contexts are employed.

The fact of textual instability, then, points less to the need to stabilize a text than to the need to investigate and account for its various permutations. Textual instability is the very real, very material counterpart of the instability of interpretive practices. The mutability of textual meaning, its decentered quality, is no longer only the result of different institutionalized critical approaches but also that of different conceptions of textuality that scholars bring to the editorial function. Both sides of the equation, textual production and textual reception, help make some interpretations possible and persuasive while barring others. Because text-production, as well as text-reception, has been decentered so that the literary work is now envisioned by some as manifesting itself in a series of texts from the roughest of manuscripts to the most recent edition, scholars should become just as interested in the work in *all* of its textual splendor, in the relationships between different versions, as in the relationships between different features of a single text.

An acceptance of textual instability might well contribute to the ongoing effort to historicize and socialize literary study, with all of its attendant controversies. To remember that texts are not immune from the flow of history, that they are composed, revised, expurgated, improved, defaced, restored, emended, and circulated as a matter of course, is to help check the formalist thrust of much twentieth-century literary theory and practice. Because the dream of a pure and organically unified form divorced from context or meaning has had an especially seductive appeal for artists and critics alike ever since the Romantic period, formalism, like the Hydra of Greek myth, has had many heads. As soon as one manifestation, like the New Criticism, is lopped off, another, such as structuralism or the American brand of deconstruction, appears in its place. By insisting on tracing out the connections between texts and broader, extra-literary concerns such as gender and power, the new Marxism, feminism, and historicism have all been actively engaged in a seemingly endless Herculean combat. But textual instability is a powerful if often overlooked weapon in our arsenal. I say "powerful" because the empirical data of textual mutability may not necessarily presuppose a commitment to one brand of literary theory over another and "overlooked" because poststructuralists rarely concern themselves with such tedious matters as text transmission and constitution. But it is the very data of text transmission and constitution, swirling around the central fact of textual instability, that help make implausible the modernist quest for pure form by providing a constant reminder that texts are products of conflicts as well as resolutions, conflicts between commerce and art, between authors and friends and colleagues, and between aspects of the self.

The reality of textual instability not only makes formalism less tenable, but also complicates terribly any reductive or unified notion of authorial intention for traditional biographical and historical critics. Anglo-American textual scholarship once concerned itself primarily with discovering an author's final intention. When one begins paying attention to all the different authorial versions of a text and the complex of motivations and circumstances that produced them, one becomes more receptive to Shillingsburg's contention that only an author's intention "to record on paper, or in some other medium, a specific sequence of words and punctuation" can be recovered more or less conclusively (*Scholarly Editing* 36). Far less objectively recoverable is an author's intention to prefer one authorially intended sequence over another or to mean something by that sequence. Textual instability encourages us to view the texts of literary works as the sites of various conflicts— conflicts not only between authors and publishers and editors and collaborators, but also between the conscious and unconscious domains of an author's psyche. As Parker in *Flawed Texts and Verbal Icons* and, more recently, Jack Stillinger in *Multiple Authorship and the Myth of Solitary Genius* have shown, these conflicts are often the norm rather than the exception and make formalist arguments about unity, whether organic or mechanical, seem mistaken. Consequently, textual instability can lead those critics who were trained in traditional modes of literary scholarship to become as suspicious as any poststructuralist hermeneut about the objective recuperability of authorial intention or the formal unity of literary works. Although traditional textual scholarship and poststructuralism have evolved out of radically different, even antithetical, intellectual assumptions and traditions, the empirical evidence of textual instability provided by the former buttresses the latter's rejection of unity and belletristic formalism as *a priori* aesthetic criteria. The many textual transformations of a work that occur as it wends its way down through history and time through its documentary forms toward us suggest that it can be stabilized only though the external imposition of some particular orientation, some particular theoretical notion of textuality.

Before closing, I would like to comment on how an awareness of textual instability may affect one's practice in the classroom, that locus of theory, criticism, and pedagogy. In this respect, it is instructive to remember that successful movements in literary studies are not always the result of intellectually superior arguments and methodologies. Often academic success in our discipline is fueled, in part, by an attention to pedagogy, to how well the practitioners of a particular school of textual study communicate their concerns and goals to their students, both undergraduate and graduate. Unfortunately, even those scholars already interested in the genesis and transmission of texts often skip over such a concern in the classroom on the grounds that their work is too esoteric. During a 1994 Australian conference on textual scholarship in different disciplines and different media, I was surprised by how little attention was given to the subject of pedagogy. Only after a paper concerning two new controversial editions of *King Lear* and *Doctor Faustus* did one discussant mention students and only then to lament the decline of reading skills that would enable them to read one, let alone two versions of *Lear*. As everyone who has written an article or presented a paper on textual matters knows, moreover, it is all too easy for speaker and audience to flounder and drown in a sea of minutiae. Still, textual scholars must adapt their rhetoric and occasionally arcane terminology to audiences in both the classroom and the conference session because examining the implications of the textual histories of literary works can be just as productive as discussing old and new readings of them. My undergraduate and graduate students alike have often been fascinated and challenged by pondering the textual histories of literary works and the many issues that they raise. Perhaps textual history appeals to students' stubborn empiricism in a way that convoluted discussions of a Byzantine authorial intention or intricate displays of critical ingenuity do not.

By advocating the study of the textual history of literary works, I do not mean to suggest reducing literary study to an exercise in the accumulation of facts. Rather, the study of textual history can be an excellent way of sparking debate over some of the important theoretical and interpretive controversies within our discipline. In *Professing Literature*, Gerald Graff critiques the incoherent theoretical foundations of most university departments of literature. From the start, these departments have been painfully torn asunder by one conflict after another over what constitutes the canon of literature and how it should be taught. Graff is not discouraged by the fact that these conflicts are not amenable to a logical resolution. On the contrary, he finds it troubling "how little of the potential educational value of such conflicts the professional system has been able to turn into part of what it teaches and studies" and argues that organizing the typical English department curriculum by fields has had the unintended effect of hiding these conflicts from our students (Graff 6). Much is lost since "students learn not just by exposure to individual instructors, but by sensing how the teaching aggregate hangs together or divides" (Graff 9). Graff's well-known solution, set forth most recently in *Beyond the Culture Wars*, is to teach the conflicts rather than attempt to resolve them since a resolution is impossible in a democratic academy and society. Investigating textual instability can provide a point of entry for teaching the conflicts, one that combines an intellectual understanding of the conflicts with an awareness of their material consequences.

In some of my classes, students and I now routinely discuss the composition, revision, and publication history of significant texts. The discussions often broaden outward to include the particular and general interpretive consequences of particular textual histories. Along with literary histories, anthologies, and criticism, for example, we look at commercial and scholarly editions of various American authors in a course on canon-formation and development in American literary studies in order to examine the mechanisms and material means by which the discipline constructs and deconstructs various canons. In an introductory class for first-year graduate students and in a seminar on textual scholarship and the humanities, we explore how traditional and contemporary textual and twentieth-century literary theories have grappled with the same essential questions about textual meaning and interpretation. Some students really do become interested in how textual scholarship and literary theory interpenetrate each other, in how it is possible to theorize different textual ontologies as well as textual hermeneutics, and in how the theorizing affects textual meaning. Such concerns open up discussions of critical theory by emphasizing its more material manifestations, its practical consequences in terms of text-constitution. Indeed, comparing Gabler's synoptic edition of *Ulysses* to almost any recent edition approved by the MLA's Center for Scholarly Editions makes theory's impact literally visible.[11]

Each essay in this volume attempts to bring a different theoretical orientation to bear upon a different textual situation or history in order to explore one or both of the following subjects: 1) how different textual situations and their material means of production help generate different theories of textuality and 2) how different conceptions of textuality help generate an understanding of different textual situations and their material means of production. By exploring the connections between textual instability and textual theory, interpretation, and occasionally pedagogy, the contributors take as their collective subject the condition of textuality itself, the various ontologies, epistemologies, and hermeneutics of verbal texts, of sequences of words and punctuation conveyed by different media. They ponder the dialectical relationship between texts and textuality by bringing some of the textual theories that compete with each other today into contact with a broad range of primarily literary—in the broadest sense—textual histories. My hope is that the relatively unusual focus of this collection on textual instability and theories of textuality will help contribute to a better understanding of the consequences that the complex and reciprocal relations between the production, transmission, and reception of texts have for their study.

In the opening essay, "Oral Tradition into Textuality," John Miles Foley observes that the history of making folklore texts is a problematic one of reducing performance-events in traditional contexts to detached, relatively self-sufficient libretti and instead applies oral theory and the performance-centered perspective, two prominent folklore approaches, to the editing of ancient Greek, medieval English, and Serbo-Croatian oral traditional events. In "Reading in and around *Piers Plowman*," poststructuralist David C. Greetham examines the editing of "a poem written in an archaic metrical system and (probably) in a relatively obscure dialect" to illustrate that medievalists too are currently interrogating such issues as intention, textual dissemination, eclecticism, affect, socialization, and indeterminacy. Anthropologist James C. Faris's "Context and Text: Navajo Nightway Textual History in the Hands of the West" explores how Euro-Americans began securing the extended nine-day healing practice of the Navajo people of the American Southwest over one hundred years ago. In so doing, he discusses the narratives' epistemological character; their generation vis-a-vis Western notions of authenticity, authorship, and textuality; and their specific pertinence to Navajo healing. New Historicist Christopher D. Felker applies procedures derived from the history of the book school to the publication history of Wheatley's 1773 *Poems on Various Subjects, Religious and Moral* in "'The Tongues of the learned are insufficient': Phillis Wheatley, Publishing Objectives, and Personal Liberty," while from a cultural feminist perspective, Johanna M. Smith's "'Hideous Progenies': The Texts of *Frankenstein*" discusses the questions concerning authorship and textual and interpretive instability raised by the two manuscript versions of Mary Shelley's novel, two early editions, and the numerous play and movie adaptations.

Returning to American writers, Tim Morris's "'My thought is undressed': Some Theoretical Implications of the Texts of Dickinson's Poems" argues that the critical abandonment of the received texts of Emily Dickinson's poems for successively closer approximations to her manuscripts introduces new theoretical problems, since many of the manuscripts exist as "variorum" texts with alternate readings provided by the author. Their irresolvably indefinite nature thus challenges two opposed and influential approaches to the poetics of textuality: Kristevan organicism and Derridean deconstruction. Rhetorician Michael Feehan's "Multiple Editorial Horizons of *Leaves of Grass*" discusses the difficulties involved in constituting a text for Walt Whitman's work, which appeared nine times during the poet's life, each time with new poems and often with revisions of earlier poems. Feehan argues for the usefulness of a model of textuality that combines Jerome McGann's emphasis on the material and social contexts of literary production and reproduction with Kenneth Burke's dramatistic theory for understanding the internal structure of each version of *Leaves* and the relations among all nine versions. James Murphy proposes in his "A 'Very Different Dance': Intention, Technique, and Revision in Henry James's New York Edition" a new model of how authorial intention relates to the revision of literary texts. Drawing on Searle's distinction between prior intentions and intentions in action, he examines James's revisions for his New York Edition to demonstrate how a single authorial vision does not unify both revisions and unchanged passages in an individual work. Rather, a marked similarity exists among all the revisions regardless of which works they appear in. Quarreling with some literary theorists' pervasive substitution of authorial analysis with social discursive analysis, Paul Eggert's "Discourse versus Authorship: The Baedeker Travel Guide and D.H. Lawrence's *Twilight in Italy*" also attempts to re-figure the intentionalist paradigm by mapping out the complex authorial intertextual relationships between Lawrence's travel book and his life and other work from the same period. In my own intentionalist essay, "'The Key to the Whole Book': Faulkner's *The Sound and the Fury*, the Compson Appendix, and Textual Instability," I discuss the relevance of the text's instability both for interpreting the novel and for thinking about some of the theoretical concerns currently bedeviling editorial theory. That editions containing Faulkner's appendix with its many revisions, simplifications, and evaluations of the novel shaped numerous succeeding critical responses suggests that an author can indeed re-write or at least re-contextualize a novel merely by framing it.

Moving into the realm of electronic texts and textuality, Jay David Bolter's "The Rhetoric of Interactive Fiction" is concerned with the theoretical questions raised by the increasing presence of interactive texts designed to be read on a computer screen. Using Stuart Moulthrop's interactive fiction "Victory Garden" as his text, he develops an inventory of the traditional and poststructuralist rhetorical strategies that are useful for reading hypertextual fiction. In a similar vein, Susan Lang's "Converging (or Colliding) Traditions: Integrating Hypertext into Literary Studies" tempers somewhat the emerging consensus that hypertext and the digital revolution in literary studies promise to reconfigure our notions of textuality, text, reader, and author. As an example of this modified reconfiguration, she demonstrates how the convergence in the classroom of a linear printed text, Jane Austen's *Northanger Abbey*, and hypertext technology gives rise to different readings and how converging technologies and conceptions of textuality, particularly hypertextual and information theory, may alter the ways in which texts are taught.

I want to conclude this introduction by noting that every aspect of my updated homily on textual instability would have been labelled heresy by that most devoted and perspicacious of Pooh critics, Smedley Force. Intent on authoritatively establishing the definitive texts of the Pooh books, Professor Force serves to remind us of where textual scholarship has been rather than where it is going, of its positivistic past rather than its more theorized future. I take my leave of him, therefore, as he waits, in vain, for replies to his questions: "Why are there no watermarks in *Winnie-the-Pooh*? Why are there no chain lines? No signature? No cancelland or cancellans?" (Crews 145).

NOTES

[1]Another much-quoted example of this genre is Bruce Harkness's "Bibliography and the Novelistic Fallacy," while a more recent book-length example in this vein is Hershel Parker's provocative *Flawed Texts and Verbal Icons*.

[2]Readers may consult works by these authors cited in my bibliography and individual essays by them—with the exception of McKenzie and Parker—in my *Devils and Angels: Textual Editing and Literary Theory*.

[3]For more commentary on and alternatives to the Anglo-American editorial tradition, see essays by Michael Groden, Donald Reiman, Gerald McLean, Paul Eggert, D. C. Greetham, and Hans Walter Gabler.

[4]Other useful discussions of the origin and development of the modern notion of the autonomous, fully individuated author and of the discourse of authorship that it represents include Rose, Saunders, and Woodmansee.

[5]Readers may consult essays by Hans Walter Gabler and Hans Zeller for introductions to German textual scholarship and Louis Hay's "Genetic Editing, Past and Future" for a discussion of French genetic criticism.

[6]For a shrewd and well-illustrated demonstration of how the inter-relationships between the bibliographical aspects of documents and the linguistic texts they contain may affect meaning, see George Bornstein's "What Is the Text of a Poem by Yeats?" To McGann's bibliographical and linguistic codes

Bornstein adds a third contextual code in which meanings are shaped as well by the placement of texts in relation to other texts in a volume.

7When a work exhibits a process of close and steady development, however, McGann substitutes a later printed version for an initial one.

8Indeed, many of the participants in an Internet bulletin board dedicated to electronic scholarly editions currently seem to agree that electronic hypertext critical editions and electronic authorial archives with sophisticated user-friendly software for constructing everything from clear reading texts to eclectic texts to synoptic texts may well replace print editions for serious scholars and critics. Of course, this possible transformation of the editorial product in no way means that the discipline of textual scholarship will be eclipsed: much of the work needed to produce and contextualize a print edition for a scholarly audience will be needed to produce an electronic edition or archive. In "The Electronic Text & the Death of the Critical Edition," Charles Ross concurs, contending that "the birth of the reader-as-editor must be at the cost of the death of the Critical Edition" and that such a print edition is a prestructuralist form (1).

9Also on the horizon are a hypertext edition of *The Piers Plowman Archive* currently being planned by the University of Virginia's Hoyt Duggan and others and an electronic edition of Chaucer's *Canterbury Tales* being prepared by Oxford University's Peter Robinson. Oxford's Electronic Publishing division has also produced electronic editions of Shakespeare, Locke, and Hume. The University of Virginia's Jerome McGann is currently constructing the Dante Gabriel Rossetti Archive.

10For especially helpful general essays on the social and cultural history of the book, see Davidson's introduction and Darnton's "What Is the History of Books?" in the former's *Reading in America*.

11Gabler himself has since retreated somewhat from his synoptic presentation of *Ulysses* by means of an integral apparatus. Each page of his recent edition of Joyce's *Dubliners* contains some of the edited text followed by part of the apparatus at the bottom. The rest of the editorial apparatus—textual notes and emendations and the historical collation—follows the edited text. Gabler, however, emphasizes "following the constant interaction of text and apparatus," categorically asserting that the latter is "not an adjunct to the text, but an integral element of the edition" (24, 31).

WORKS CITED

Bolter, Jay David. *Writing Space: The Computer, Hypertext, and the History of Writing.* Hillsdale, NJ: Lawrence Erlbaum, 1991.

Bornstein, George, ed. *Palimpsest: Editorial Theory in the Humanities.* Ann Arbor: U of Michigan P, 1993.

_____. "What Is the Text of a Poem by Yeats?" In Bornstein, 167-93.

Bowers, Fredson. "Textual Criticism." *The Aims and Methods of Scholarship in Modern Languages and Literatures.* Ed. James Thorpe. 1963. 2nd and rev. ed. New York: MLA, 1970. 29-54.

_____. "Textual Scholarship and the Literary Critic." *Textual Scholarship and Literary Criticism.* Cambridge: Cambridge UP, 1959. 1-34.

Cohen, Philip, ed. *Devils and Angels: Textual Editing and Literary Theory.* Charlottesville: UP of Virginia, 1991.

Crews, Frederick C. *The Pooh Perplex.* New York: E. P. Dutton, 1965.

Darnton, Robert. "What Is the History of Books?" *Daedalus* 111 (Summer 1982). Rpt. in *Reading in America: Literature and Social History.* Ed. Cathy Davidson. Baltimore: Johns Hopkins UP, 1989. 27-52.

Davidson, Cathy N. Introduction. *Reading in America: Literature and Social History.* Baltimore: Johns Hopkins UP, 1989. 1-26.

de Grazia, Margreta. *Shakespeare Verbatim: The Reproduction of Authenticity and the 1790 Apparatus.* Oxford: Oxford UP, 1991.

Eggert, Paul. "Finding Editorial Bearings: Discourse or Authorship." Paper presented at the April 1993 Society for Textual Scholarship Conference, New York, NY.

_____. "Textual Product or Textual Process: Procedures and Assumptions of Critical Editing." In Cohen, 57-77.

Fish, Stanley. *Is There a Text in This Class?* Cambridge: Harvard

UP, 1983.

Gabler, Hans Walter. "Textual Studies and Criticism." *New Directions in Textual Studies*. Ed. David Oliphant and Robin Bradford. Austin, TX: U of Texas P, Harry Ransom Humanities Research Center, 1990. 151-165.

_____, with Walter Hettche, eds. *Dubliners*. By James Joyce. New York: Garland, 1993.

_____, with Wolfhard Steppe and Claus Melchior, eds. *"Ulysses": A Critical and Synoptic Edition*. By James Joyce. 3 vols. New York: Garland, 1984.

_____. "Unsought Encounters." In Cohen, 152-66.

Graff, Gerald. *Beyond the Culture Wars: How Teaching the Conflicts Can Revitalize American Education*. New York: Norton, 1992.

_____. *Professing Literature: An Institutional History*. Chicago: U of Chicago P, 1987.

Greetham, D.C. "Editorial and Critical Theory: From Modernism to Postmodernism." In Bornstein, 9-28.

_____. "Literary and Textual Theory: Redrawing the Matrix." *Studies in Bibliography* 42 (1989): 1-24.

_____. "The Manifestation and Accommodation of Theory in Textual Editing." In Cohen, 78-102.

_____. "Textual Scholarship." *Introduction to Scholarship in Modern Languages and Literatures*. Ed. Joseph Gibaldi. New York: MLA, 1992. 103-37.

_____. *Textual Scholarship: An Introduction*. New York: Garland, 1992.

Greg, W. W. "The Rationale of Copy-Text." *Studies in Bibliography* 3 (1950-51): 19-36. Rpt. in *Art and Error: Modern Textual Editing*. Ed. Ronald Gottesman and Scott Bennett. Bloomington: Indiana UP, 1970. 17-36.

Groden, Michael. "Contemporary Textual and Literary Theory." In Bornstein, 259-86.

Harkness, Bruce. "Bibliography and the Novelistic Fallacy." *Studies in Bibliography* 12 (1959): 59-73. Rpt. in *A Mirror for Modern Scholars: Essays in Methods of Research in Literature*. Ed. Lester A. Beaurline. New York: Odyssey Press, 1966. 56-71.

Hay, Louis. "Genetic Editing, Past and Future: A Few Reflections by a User." *TEXT* 3 (1987): 117-34.

Kernan, Alvin. *The Death of Literature*. New Haven: Yale UP, 1990.

Landow, George P. *Hypertext: The Convergence of Contemporary Critical Theory and Technology.* Baltimore: Johns Hopkins UP, 1992.

Lanham, Richard A. *The Electronic Word: Democracy, Technology, and the Arts.* Chicago: Chicago UP, 1993.

McGann, Jerome J. "The Case of *The Ambassadors* and the Textual Condition." In Bornstein, 151-66.

_____. *A Critique of Modern Textual Criticism.* Chicago: U of Chicago P, 1983.

_____. "Literary Pragmatics and the Editorial Horizon." In Cohen, 2-21.

_____, ed. *The New Oxford Book of Romantic Period Verse.* Oxford: Oxford UP, 1993.

_____. *The Textual Condition.* Princeton: Princeton UP, 1991.

McKenzie, D.F. *Bibliography and the Sociology of Texts. The Panizzi Lectures, 1985.* London: The British Library, 1986.

McLean, Gerald. "What Is a Restoration Poem? Editing a *Discourse, Not an Author." TEXT 3 (1987): 319-46.*

Mailloux, Steven. *Rhetorical Power.* Ithaca: Cornell UP, 1989.

Parker, Hershel. *Flawed Texts and Verbal Icons: Literary Authority in American Fiction.* Evanston, IL: Northwestern UP, 1984.

Reiman, Donald. *The Study of Modern Manuscripts: Public, Confidential, and Private.* Baltimore: Johns Hopkins UP, 1993.

Rose, Mark. *Authors and Owners: The Invention of Copyright.* Cambridge: Harvard UP, 1993.

Ross, Charles L. "The Electronic Text & the Death of the Critical Edition." Paper Presented at the December 1993 MLA Convention, Toronto.

Saunders, David. *Authorship and Copyright.* London: Routledge, 1992.

Shillingsburg, Peter. "The Autonomous Author, the Sociology of Texts, and the Polemics of Textual Scholarship." In Cohen, 22-43.

_____. "Polymorphic, Polysemic, Protean, Reliable, Electronic Texts." In Bornstein, 29-43.

_____. *Scholarly Editing in the Computer Age.* Athens: U of Georgia P, 1986.

_____. "Text as Matter, Concept, and Action." *Studies in Bibliography* 44 (1991): 31-82.

Stillinger, Jack. *Multiple Authorship and the Myth of Solitary Genius.* Oxford: Oxford UP, 1991.

Tanselle, G. Thomas. "Historicism and Critical Editing." *Studies in Bibliography* 39 (1986): 1-46.

_____. "Recent Editorial Discussion and the Central Questions of Editing." *Studies in Bibliography* 34 (1980): 23-65.

_____. "Textual Scholarship." *Introduction to Scholarship in Modern Languages and Literatures.* Ed. Joseph Gibaldi. New York: MLA, 1981. 29-52.

Wells, Stanley, and Gary Taylor, eds. *William Shakespeare: The Complete Works.* The Oxford Shakespeare. Oxford: Clarendon P, 1986.

Woodmansee, Martha. *The Author, Art, and the Market.* New York: Columbia UP, 1994.

Zeller, Hans. "A New Approach to the Critical Constitution of Texts." *Studies in Bibliography* 28 (1975): 231-64.

Oral Tradition into Textuality

John Miles Foley

I begin with two "epiphemes," the oral equivalent of epigraphs. Dennis Tedlock, who works with the living tradition of Zuni storytelling and the manuscript record of the once-living Mayan *Popol Vuh*, has observed that "to have the alphabetically written text of an ancient performance is one thing, and to hear a full voice in that text is another" ("Hearing a Voice" 141).[1] Consider also the words of Dell Hymes, another Native Americanist and another architect of Ethnopoetics, an interpretive project that aims to understand traditional oral works in their own, native terms: "One can believe, I do believe, that about the dry bones of print, words heaped up in paragraphs, something of the original spirit lingers. That spirit need not be lost to comprehension, respect, and appreciation. We are not able to revive by singing, or stepping over a text five times, but by patient surrender to what a text has to say, in the way it has to say it, something of life can again become incarnate ("Custer" 11). Here then is our central challenge for the present essay: What becomes of oral traditions committed, in myriad ways, to textual form? How does this textuality — "incipient" in that it represents either a historical culture's initial known attempt at such codification or a relatively rare document adrift in a sea of living oral tradition — deal with and convey the textless world that preceded it or exists alongside it? Another way to put the same question is to ask how a given text continues the tradition of reception.

NATIVE AMERICAN TRADITIONS

Let us begin with Native American traditions and texts, an area that has seen substantial activity over the last two decades as many of the most forward-thinking linguists and folklorists have turned to this body of traditions in attempting to come to grips with the ungraspable phantom of faithful textual representation. The approach often called Ethnopoetics has been at the forefront of this discussion: in particular, Hymes and Tedlock have pointed the way toward modes of representation that recall the event-centered, oral/aural reality of the works they are examining and making ever more available to others. The common thread connecting their highly individualistic versions of Ethnopoetics is a concern that the endemic expressive structure of the narratives be recovered and made the fundamental basis upon which Native American verbal art is presented and interpreted. Instead of forcing these narratives into an essentially irrelevant form under the patently false premise that western European (and fundamentally Greco-Roman) poetics constitutes a universal set of categories, they have insisted on tradition-dependent identities for the works they study.

Since the core assumptions and theorems of both varieties of Ethnopoetics, as well as the questions of how and why these two investigators make their texts as they do, have been treated elsewhere,[2] let us concentrate here on the implications of Tedlock's and Hymes's methods for the transformation of performance to libretto. Tedlock's procedure with the Zuni stories consists of mapping the oral event onto an augmented textual surface designed to bear more and different kinds of meaning than can the conventional printed page. His criteria for this encoding derive entirely from the unique event of performance and reflect traditional strategies of expression only to the extent that the individual event is representative of the performance tradition. The thrust of his text-making, then, is by usual standards a kind of overdetermination of the reader's activity, a mandate to exit the silence and convention of the usual process and to give (or restore) voice to the "dead letters" of the printed page. What he aims to preserve in this intersemiotic facsimile amounts to the set of cues — partially reflective of Richard Bauman's keys to performance (*Verbal Art* 15-25) or the metonymic signals that are the stock-in-trade of traditional referentiality (Foley, *Immanent Art* 38-60) — that shape the reader's reception of the work, only now with the reader also becoming a listening audience. In short, Tedlock has transformed the heard reality of the oral traditional event into a visual, textual rhetoric, specifically a set of typographic cues, with the express intention of mitigating the displacement caused by textualization of that event, that is, of making the text speak.

Tedlock's subsequent move toward what he calls "ethnopaleography," which consists of "taking the Popol Vuh text back to those who continue to speak the language in which it was written" ("Hearing a Voice" 143), illustrates yet more radically the thrust of his overall interpretive program. Instead of attempting an analytical parsing of the textual document, he advocates restoring its voice, breaking the silence to which time and script have condemned it by direct appeal to an ongoing speech tradition. The success of this appeal depends on at least two crucial factors: (1) some degree of continuity between the ancient text and the modern oral traditions that are to be its comparands, and (2) what we might understand as at least a rough match in performance register: "The fieldworker will be seeking after contemporary speeches, prayers, songs, and narratives, looking for patterns in the wording that have analogs in the ancient text and noting the ways in which such patterns are actualized in performance" (147). At its root, ethnopaleography offers another way to revivify the text, to privilege that which textuality has rendered rhetorical by reduction of experience to object, and to do so by reawakening the voice that makes it an event.

In the same spirit of causing texts to speak, Hymes has concentrated on editing into his editions and translations a set of native poetic features that includes lines, verses, versicles, stanzas, scenes, acts, and parts (see especially "Tonkawa Poetics"). All of these interlocking features are derived from, rather than imposed upon, the works he studies, and together they comprise a rhetoric that is instrumental in their reception. What is more, Hymes views this set of features as both traditional — in their institutionalized identity as rhetorical structures in not just one but all related performances and texts — and individually deployed — in the sense of a single author's license to create within their general purview. For example, in his analysis and presentation of Charles Cultee's "Salmon's Myth," he distinguishes between Tedlock's emphasis on pause and other intonational features on the one hand and the kinds of performance structures in which he is interested on the other ("Language, Memory" 395-96, emphasis added):

> Dennis Tedlock's admirable insistence on the vocal realization of texts has given rise to the impression in some quarters that pauses alone, not other kinds of

> markers as well, let alone interdependence of signals
> with content and function, are the foundation of units
> in a text. . . . But pause or any other feature of sound
> is *in itself* a physical, not a cultural phenomenon. It
> becomes an aspect of structure only in terms of the
> basic principle of "practical structuralism," contrast
> and repetition, the use of form/meaning covariation
> to establish what counts as the same and what as dif-
> ferent. In a single case, one cannot be sure what fea-
> tures are accidental, what are conventional in the style
> of one narrator, what are conventional in the commu-
> nity.

Hymes's ethnopoetics is, then, essentially an immanent poetics: strategies and categories for expression constitute aspects of a register that provides for a high degree of communicative economy within a well defined performance arena. The uniqueness of the narrator's individual realization of a given tale resonates against and within that larger cultural poetics.

With this distinction in mind, it is not difficult to see how Hymes can derive from the "dry bones" of early dictated texts an ethnopoetically faithful libretto, without necessary recourse to ethnopaleography. If performance rhetoric inheres in works of verbal art as a coherent set of signals that in their dedicated form tap into dedicated channels of meaning, then even the most prosaically configured written record of a tale can be reconfigured and made to speak. Of course it cannot be forced back into the event from which it was extruded; plain common sense must tell us that there are endemic limits on extrapolation from silence. But for Hymes some important aspects of Native American narrative poetics persist as performance modulates to text, and although the intersemiotic translation must make recovery less than complete, recognition of what amounts to a traditional rhetoric opens the now-written work to more faithful interpretation.

SOUTH SLAVIC TRADITIONS INTO TEXTS

Although South Slavic oral traditions share with the Native American the temporal accidents of being both living (or in some cases recently living) and much studied over the past few decades, their histories of edition and analysis vary quite dramatically. Insofar as epic narrative is concerned, the Serbian and Croatian traditions were from their first extensive collection and publication closely linked with the western European hegemony established by the Homeric poems and seconded by medieval vernacular works such as the Old French *chansons de geste* and Anglo-Saxon *Beowulf* (cf. Murko). For this and other reasons the classic texts, such as those collected, edited, and published by Vuk Stefanović Karadžić in the mid-nineteenth century, have always exhibited standard poetic lineation of their decasyllabic or *bugarštica* verses (cf. Stolz, Miletich), but have lacked entirely any encoding of the kind of paralinguistic or rhetorical features like those highlighted in the text-making of Tedlock and Hymes.

This leveling may have focused attention on those aspects of poetics that happened to have precedent in the western European model, but they just as certainly obscured those features that did not enjoy such precedent. The decasyllabic line, for instance, an archaic and complex metrical structure, was only too easily misinterpreted as a trochaic pentameter, with the obvious consequence of deflecting analysis from the real nature of the meter-phraseology symbiosis that informed the traditional idiom (Foley, *Traditional Oral Epic* 85-106). For another example, the instrumental and vocal music that accompanied the performance of most Moslem and some Christian epics was in effect "written out" of the textual transcriptions; to date it has never received the attention it deserves as a full partner in the performance event. More generally, the native Serbian and Croatian scholarship, largely laboring under the same typically modern, unexamined predisposition that "oral tradition is usually a book and not a memory" (Parks 58), has concentrated almost exclusively on the individual artistry of the singers of tales, seeking to discover literary values in their performed narratives and downplaying (if even considering) their traditional resonances.[3]

Karadžić, an ethnographer, linguist, and lexicographer very much ahead of his time, felt the widespread nineteenth-century European urge to lay bare his culture's roots and yet managed to introduce or refine contemporary methods of textual representation. Unlike many scholars of that period, most infamously the Grimms (cf. especially Ellis), he interfered little with the received transcriptions of oral performances during editing, making very few if any changes in the dictated texts. Even when he did intervene to modify, or much more rarely to add, a line or

part-line, he consistently turned to patently traditional diction as
the source for his emendations.[4] Furthermore, he not seldom
included multiple variants or versions of a given collected narrative, customarily by a different poet from a different geographical area, placing the two (rarely more) contiguously in the volume and labeling the subsequent version(s) "Opet to isto"
("Again the same"). In addition, Karadžić attempted to create
natural settings for the poems within individual volumes of his
published collection, either by genre (e.g., the "various women's
songs" of volume one being separated from the "oldest heroic
songs" of its sequel) or by principal characters or events (e.g.,
groupings centered around the beloved Serbian hero Marko
Kraljević or the historically and mythically epochal Battle of
Kosovo of 1389). By these latter two strategies Karadžić the editor was able to simulate something of the (extratextual) traditional context, presenting alternate realizations of some songs
while encouraging a reception of each poem/performance
against a larger, more resonant background. To a remarkable
extent, given what other contemporary investigators licensed
themselves to do, he demonstrated a respect for these narratives
on their own terms and tried to fashion a mode of textual presentation in which at least some of the performance rhetoric was
inscribed.

    The collection and publication project undertaken by
Milman Parry and Albert Lord, from the 1933-35 fieldwork in
then-Yugoslavia through the ongoing series *Serbo-Croatian Heroic
Songs* (1953-), brought the pragmatics of textual representation of
this tradition to a new level. In concert with the theory behind the
Parry-Lord field methods, the first two volumes of *SCHS* presented multiple versions of the same tale by the same and different singers from the region of Novi Pazar. Lord described the
publication plans for the series as follows ("General
Introduction" 16; cf. *Traditional Oral Epic* 178-96, 288-327):

> In investigating an oral epic tradition, it is nec-
> essary to begin with a study of the songs of an
> individual singer and then to proceed to a con-
> sideration of the other singers in the same dis-
> trict. One thus sees the singer both as an indi-
> vidual and in relation to the community of
> singers to which he belongs. For that reason our

> selected texts will be published by districts, and
> within each district the songs of a single singer
> will be grouped together.

By reading through the different performances of *The Captivity of Djuljić Ibrahim* for example, one can gain some sense of the multiformity of oral epic tradition. Although this series also has some drawbacks (run-on prose translations, concentration on textual aspects of performance, and so on),[5] it does offer the reader a chance to escape many of the drawbacks of editions that epitomize individual versions at the expense of context.

ANCIENT AND MEDIEVAL TRADITIONAL TEXTS

In moving on to ancient and medieval texts that constitute our only entrée to long-extinct oral traditions, with respect to which the complexities associated with the persistence of traditional forms only multiply, it may be well to recall our central focus: to ascertain as well as possible *how a given text continues the tradition of reception*. In those simplest of situations where, as is often the case with living traditions, we are confronting a transcription of an oral performance, the question, though demanding, is clear: to what extent does the text contribute meaningfully to the faithful reconstrual of the experience, with all of the implications inherent in an understanding of the work as a performed event? We have considered the opinions and strategies offered by Tedlock and by Hymes for Native American and by Karadžić and by Parry and Lord for South Slavic and have noted both advantages and shortcomings in each approach to representation of oral tradition in the textualized format. But now we must consider texts about whose genesis we may know very little. What is more, for ancient and medieval texts we must acknowledge the strong possibility or probability that writing may have been employed at any or all levels of their composition or transmission or both, so that the relatively simpler problem of transcriptions made according to incompletely understood rules and assumptions will not be the only complication. For such transitional documents, passed down through an unrecorded series of rewritings, the picture of compositional identity becomes very murky indeed. Elaborate hypotheses painstakingly formulated to explain the probable act or acts of composition may founder if pressed to account for even this or that small alternative in the chain of composition and transmission.

Among the pitfalls awaiting the classicist or medievalist will be the potentially quite misleading matter of whether or not writing was "available" to the poets and audiences of the so-called Dark Ages of Greece and England. As folklorists have long known, the mere presence of some kind or level of literacy, established perhaps by an inscription on an artifact, means next to nothing as evidence for or against oral or written communication in a given mode or situation. Late twentieth-century North Americans, many of them deeply engaged in intensely literate pursuits for most of their waking hours, also participate in oral traditions that may never have been textualized.[6] We will thus need to keep firmly in mind the fact that verbal activities involve registers of discourse that may or may not be immediately or eventually textualized, according to the demands of the codicils to the sociolinguistic contract in force in a given culture. The past decade has seen awareness of the importance of social function emerge among classicists and medievalists as well, with scholars like William V. Harris and Rosalind Thomas offering realistically complex views of the various uses of oral and written media in the ancient world, and with Franz H. Bäuml, Katherine O'Brien O'Keeffe, and A.N. Doane, among others, productively complicating our perspective on the false dichotomy of medieval orality and literacy.

For such reasons it seems best to stipulate that our understanding of the "original composition" of the Homeric epics and *Beowulf*—if indeed that phrase is strictly applicable—is likely to remain uncertain and to focus instead on what can be inferred about the reception of these works from the persistence of traditional forms as a textual rhetoric. This emphasis entails a reversal of the usual heuristic perspective: instead of trying to gauge how much has been preserved or lost, we need rather to ask what the documents can tell us about how they should be read. Our authority for posing the analytical query in this way rests on the evidence for a prior (and perhaps ongoing) oral tradition accompanying the generation of texts, on comparative evidence from other oral traditions, and not least on the principles of word-power and metonymy.[7]

ANGLO-SAXON TEXTS

Recent research has done much to demystify the process

underlying the textual transmission of Anglo-Saxon poetry, especially to modify what was long perceived as an absolute gap into a complex spectrum of oral-to-textual transmission.[8] Foremost among scholars pursuing a reevaluation of the model for writing and reading manuscripts from this period have been Katherine O'Brien O'Keeffe and A.N. Doane, both of whom have sought to reconcile the textual record presented in Old English poetic manuscripts with the traditional oral environment from which they stem and to which they remain linked in significant ways. Through careful examination of texts that appear in multiple copies, O'Keeffe has concluded that "early readers of Old English verse read by applying oral techniques for the reception of a message to the decoding of a written text" (*Visible Song* 191). Her method entails an exacting analysis of poetry as various as Cædmon's *Hymn*, *Solomon and Saturn I*, the "Metrical Preface" to Alfred's *Pastoral Care*, and poems from the *Anglo-Saxon Chronicle*, with special attention to the mechanics of copying as an index of the mix of residual orality and literacy not only indicated but also prescribed by the document in question.

O'Keeffe finds not a static but a developing literacy in these texts and interprets this variance as evidence of differing expressive and perceptual contracts. In distinguishing between our modern, monolithic notion of literacy and this more realistic, situated conception of the various modes of literacy in Anglo-Saxon England, she thus "refer[s] not to the numbers of individuals who might be judged to have been able to read in Anglo-Saxon England, but, more significantly, to the very practice of reading, the decoding strategies of readers, their presuppositions, visual conventions and understanding of space" (6-7). She goes on to argue that "the manuscript records of Old English poetry witness a particular mode of literacy, and examination of significant variants and of developing graphic cues for the presentation of verse (such as mise-en-page, spacing, capitalization and punctuation) provide strong evidence of persisting residual orality in the reading and copying of poetry in Old English" (7). Even as Anglo-Saxon scribes were writing out their manuscripts, and even as these manuscripts were copied and recopied, it was not our contemporary model of literate behavior that was informing the commission to writing and apprehension by reading. It was rather the expressive and perceptual strategies of oral tradition that would play a major role in "post-oral" reception of the poetry, only now in a form that survived the transformation from performance to text.

Doane's perspective also sheds considerable light on the transition or continuum between oral tradition and text in Anglo-Saxon poetry. As an editor who advocates "making an informed, principled, definitive, and declared decision about a given text's relation to writing and orality" ("Oral Texts" 76), he posits four kinds of interfaces. The first three are familiar from earlier scholarship: (1) the scribal transcription of a performed event, (2) the oral "autograph" poet who serves as his or her own scribe, and (3) the literate poet who knows the tradition well enough to emulate an oral performance in writing. Interestingly, however, his fourth scenario entails a scribe who may be thought of as composing in the oral traditional manner, an act he calls "reperformance": "Whenever scribes who are part of the oral traditional culture write or copy traditional oral works, they do not merely mechanically hand them down; they rehear them, 'mouth' them, 'reperform' them in the act of writing in such a way that the text may change but remain authentic, just as a completely oral poet's text changes from performance to performance without losing authenticity" (80-81). While not concurring with O'Keeffe at all points, Doane shares her commitment to dissolving the old typology of text-making as distinct from composition, and in doing so he emphasizes the ways in which the multiformity that is the lifeblood of oral tradition still nourishes the ongoing process of textualization.[9]

These insights obviously have important implications for our discussion of the persistence of traditional oral forms as textual rhetoric. First, a continuity of reception across the supposed gulf between oral traditional performance and manuscript record means that mere commission to writing entails neither the final fossilization nor the wholesale shift in poetics that earlier studies in oral tradition had assumed as matters of course. In the simplest of cases, in which an Anglo-Saxon scribe might, not unlike a nineteenth- or early twentieth-century fieldworker, have taken down an oral poem from a poet's dictation, O'Keeffe's and Doane's conclusions lead us to view the visual spatialization of the utterance as rife with residual orality, as representing the performed event in at least some of its pre-textual identity. Do all oral traditional signals survive the transformation? Certainly not, but their theses would hold—in an interesting parallel to Tedlock's ethnopoetic vision of a text being made to encode its performance—that some of the signals do in fact survive and that they are foregrounded when one has multiple texts of a poem to compare.

But what of the more complicated (and almost certainly much more numerous) cases, those involving Anglo-Saxon poems not simply taken down from dictation but actually composed in writing? This is precisely the distinction made by Larry Benson in his much discussed but ultimately reductive article on "The Literary Character of Anglo-Saxon Formulaic Poetry," in which he showed that the formulaic content of Old English verse probably composed in writing was approximately equivalent to that of poems that some scholars had assigned to oral tradition and then went on to hold that the hypothesis of orality was thus untenable.[10] What the new evidence teaches us is that even the "least oral" of links in the chain of composition and transmission—the textual record itself—retains significant traces of a mode of expression and reception associated in its origin with oral tradition. And if this least oral part of the process, what we normally conceive of as an end-product or objective fact far removed from the process of oral tradition, can maintain such signals and help to determine its own reception within what was once construed as a medium entirely antithetical to oral tradition, then clearly some reconsideration of the interpretive issues involved in its composition and reception is in order. To put it telegraphically, this new view of textual dynamics at the level of the manuscript representation of Old English poetry dovetails snugly with the investigation of word-power and metonymy in the form of textual rhetoric.

THE HOMERIC TEXTS

The theme of supposedly mute texts, heretofore edited into submission, teaching twentieth-century readers to interpret them also finds expression in Homeric studies, especially in the work of Richard Janko and Gregory Nagy.[11] In a 1990 article on editing practices and the text of the *Iliad*, Janko observes that "to delete verses, emend, or postulate multiple authorship is the natural reaction of scholars trained in a literate and literary culture, whether ancient or modern, but it is the wrong response" (326). Instead of "correcting" the received text, an editorial program that in effect forces it into agreement with a mythical standard and in the process deletes all evidence of its true provenance, he advocates an edition that reflects the inherent diversity of the surviving texts, with full attention to the apparent contradictions that especially the Parry-Lord studies have shown are a natural feature of extended oral narrative.[12] By aligning the recently published evidence of early contact between the Greeks and the Near East with his own investigations of ancient Greek poetry from a diachronic point of view, Janko then concludes that the Homeric poems were, in origin, oral dictated texts that can be seen as arising in a "plausible cultural context" sometime during the eighth century B.C. (330).

For Janko the thesis of oral dictation offers a waystation on the road from an entirely unlettered oral tradition to the textual heterogeneity that exists in the extant manuscripts. The importance of his argument reaches beyond an explanation of the surviving evidence, however, to the core of our attempt to come to grips with the Homeric texts as libretti. For if Janko is correct, the texts themselves present a picture not unlike that described by O'Keeffe and Doane for the Old English manuscripts: a group of residually oral (or oral-derived) documents that in effect preserve the multiformity that amounts to the tradition's bequest to a now-written or -textualized poetry. If this is a realistic assessment of the texts as they stand, then we are not only licensed but also required to confront the implications of their multiformity. That responsibility will mandate, among other things, an attention to the specialized Homeric register, together with the (rhetorical) performance arena it helps to create and the communicative economy it inherently fosters.

Nagy envisions a quite different cultural context for the fixation of the Homeric poems, one that expressly does not involve writing as the crucial dynamic. Rather he nominates the phenomenon of Panhellenism—a nationalistic and normalizing sociohistorical reality that shaped the *polis* and the Olympic Games, for instance— as the leveling factor that proved most important in streamlining a diverse set of Homeric traditions to an epitomized, unified tradition. Through the increased social mobility of the poet, who as *dêmiourgos* ("artisan in the community") could more and more move from one locale to another and experience the tradition in its multiformity, the variety inherent in a collection of insular situations gradually started to lessen and a more uniform single situation began to gain ascendancy. Eventually this process would lead to *rhapsodes*, performers who did not themselves compose, and a fixed text would be created without the primary impetus of writing technology.

The fundamental textuality behind the conventional (literary) ideas of "canon" and "author" is called into question by Nagy's reconstrual of the evolution of ancient Greek poetry. Canon comes to name not that which critics have sifted out of documents with clear individual pedigrees but rather that which the internally driven process of fixation has presented as poetic epitomes. The composer also becomes an idealized figure, as the Panhellenic process erodes or eliminates opportunities for both recomposition in performance and self-identification of the poet.[13] For such reasons Nagy contends that

> the evolution of an ancient Greek canon in both poetry and song need not be attributed primarily to the factor of writing. Granted, writing would have been essential for the ultimate preservation of any canon once the traditions of performance were becoming obsolete; still I argue that the key to the actual evolution of a canon must be sought in the social context of performance itself. (84)

This emphasis on performance brings us back to the question of the interrelationship of event and text. Whereas Janko relates the two by interposing an oral dictated text, a written document that preserves Homeric multiformity and deserves to be understood for that very lack of uniformity, Nagy constructs a model that avoids this initial quantum leap to another medium and proposes instead a different kind of fixation—in essence an incipient textuality without texts. Drawing from the work of J.L. Austin and Barbara Johnson, Nagy explains that he views composition and performance as inextricably linked: "If indeed performance 'takes on meaning only by referring to the instance of its utterance,' then this instance, this occasion, must be the basis for the intent of the utterance, for its rhetoric. If, further, the occasion should ever be lost or removed, then the intent of the utterance is destabilized. We may say that the very notion of genre serves as a compensation for the "lost occasion" (9). With this model he is in effect providing a rationale for the textual rhetoric that persists in an oral-derived traditional text (whether actually written or fixed without writing through Panhellenization). The destabilization he envisages as "compensated for" by the idea of genre can be extended to apply to the reduction of a performance to the cenotaph of a manuscript: in this case it is not only the genre but all of its associated rhetorical strategies that assume the expressive responsibility. To make possible reentry of the performance arena and to reengender some vestige of the communicative economy that was the natural yield of that situation, textual artifacts must counteract the destabilizing influence of the lost occasion by recourse—institutionalized and traditional recourse—to the submerged rules of genre and rhetoric that now bear the responsibility for keying performance.[14]

TRANSFORMATION(S)

The range of opinions and perspectives on the nature of oral traditional works that survive in textual form is, as we have seen, quite various. Each tradition or genre encounters textualization differently, and theories of how that process proceeds even within the same tradition and genre themselves vary (see, e.g., Lord, "The Merging"). We can, however, locate at least two common emphases in recent scholarship having to do with this question.

First, the old model of the Great Divide between orality and literacy has given way in most quarters, pointing toward the accompanying demise of the absolutist dichotomy of performance versus document. One of the preconditions for this shift from a model of contrasts to one of spectra has been the exposure of writing and literacy as complex technologies that are certainly neither monolithic nor deserving of unqualifed reduction across cultures, but which, as generalized abstractions, harbor virtually innumerable differences according to tradition, genre, function, and the like (cf. especially Finnegan, *Oral Poetry*, *Literacy and Orality*; also Street). Consequently, text can no longer be separated out as something different by species from the oral tradition it records or draws upon; the question becomes not whether but how performance and document speak to one another.

The second shared emphasis, particularly evident among the works by O'Keeffe, Doane, Janko, and Nagy mentioned above, amounts to a corollary of the first. If what we have in the oral-derived document is in some sense an active remembrance of oral tradition, then our interpretive strategies must address that continuation in its fullest rhetorical implications. We are thus led to ask—without primary deferral to a history of composition that can perhaps never be compiled—how a given text continues the tradition of reception. The responsibility for attention to this question does not derive from our knowledge or hypothesis that the work under consideration reaches us as a first-generation transcription of an oral performance but from the evidence of an oral tradition in its background and some demonstration of the work's continuing dependence upon that oral tradition. Prima facie evidence for such continuing dependence would take the form of rhetorical transformations of the expressive and receptional strategies variously called metonyms (*Immanent Art*) and keys to performance (*Verbal Art*). Whether we are dealing with living traditions like the Native American or South Slavic, or with works like the Old English and Homeric poems that survive only as manuscripts, the question will remain the same: how does the text teach us to read it, to sense its word-power in the context of performance and tradition?

IMPLICATIONS OF CONTEXT: PERFORMANCE ARENA

In respect to *performance arena*, it should be emphasized that a very simple difference must inform everything that can be said about the word-power of an oral-derived *text* as opposed to live performance: the "place" where the work is experienced by a reader, the event that is re-created, must be summoned solely by textual signals. The phenomenological present conferred by actual performance context—the Rajasthani *bhopo*'s episode before his illustrated cloth "map," the folk preacher's retelling of a Biblical tale before his or her congregation, the South Slavic *bajalica*'s whispered spell in her client's ear[15]—vanishes, and along with it the unique and enriching primal connection between this particular visit to the performance arena and the traditional sense of having been there before. The face-to-face interaction, not only between performer and audience but also among audience members, cannot be played out in a written text, no matter how multi-channeled that document may be. Nothing can wholly replace the personal exploration of an oral traditional performance by a person steeped in the significative geography of the event.

In the case of a work that one cannot automatically assume to be a first-generation transcription of a performance, a similar caveat is necessary. The ideal preparation for faithful reception of such a work is prior immersion in the oral tradition from which it derives, that is, familiarity not only with the descriptive or analytically measurable parameters of a culture but, much more importantly, with what Hymes has named its "ways of speaking." Knowing how to use the idiom in which a work presents itself is an accepted (if silently acknowledged) sine qua non for literary studies, so it should come as no surprise that interpretation of a traditional oral form requires as thorough as possible an understanding of its particular, dedicated register. Of course, as composition in writing becomes more and more the rule, and native artists themselves move further and further away from actual performance, the special valence of the register that gains intelligibility precisely from its employment within the performance arena will begin to wane. This diminution of illocutionary force will be a problem first for the involved culture, which may resort to strategies such as "textual communities" (cf. Stock 90-92) to preserve intelligibility, and then, at much greater distance and correspondingly more severely, for the modern reader who attempts to decode what present themselves as decontextualized (in Nagy's term, "destabilized") messages. A textual rhetoric of traditional, performance-derived forms will keep the delicate umbilical of metonym and meaning in place temporarily, but as textuality develops its own significative dynamics, that umbilical will wither and eventually lose its function as a conduit of extratextual meaning.

Standing at the far end of the process, at a point far beyond the rhetorical transformation of traditional oral forms, latter-day readers of ancient Greek, Old English, and other oral-derived works must first set realistic goals for entry of the performance arena, which itself may have been rhetorical (but still powerfully determinative) even when the extant texts were created. It will of course not be possible to bring to the interpretive encounter anything approaching the ideal — an intimate intracultural knowledge of the prior and informing oral tradition. Nor can one assume, without fear of jeopardizing the viability of the entire enterprise, that the work as it survives represents what was without doubt an oral performance. Whatever is attempted as a methodology, and whatever emerges as a reading, must be assessed against this background.

But let us not focus exclusively on what cannot be recovered. With a realistic calibration, a latter-day reader can indeed hope to make some gains in understanding by entering the performance arena as a partial if inevitably not a full participant in the specialized communicative exchange. With Hymes (especially "Tlingit Poetics"), I find the idea of a partial but finite gain — particularly one that can be made in no other way — worthy solace for the certain impenetrability of the barriers of both culture and history. Limited access to the arena becomes an option open to the reader of both transcribed performances and works with roots in oral tradition, on the condition that one is willing to concentrate on the dedicated system of signification that bears institutionalized, metonymic meaning, on the keys to performance that survive transformation to text. Even against the inevitable loss that accompanies textualization, we can still sense a work's empowering relationship to the enabling event of performance (real or rhetorical) and the enabling referent of tradition.

In other words, the continuity of reception of a work that stems from oral tradition but which survives only as a text will depend on the reader's ability to recognize the rhetorical signals that are the bequest of performance and tradition, and then to credit these signals with the institutionalized meanings they carry as a dedicated register of verbal communication. Only when the text has been made to yield the kind of augmented discourse that mirrors a traditional oral performance in its highly focused mode of signification can the message be faithfully received. In addition to the meaning-laden signals, and perhaps less obviously, it will also be the gaps of indeterminacy in such texts that reach out beyond the confines of the document and conventional literary modes of reference to the extratextual event of performance and the referent of tradition. Not only the value-added signals — whether special formulas or other verbal strategies that encode so much more than the sum of their denotative parts — but just as crucially the "blank spots" or logical cruces within a text will require the reader to configure the work of verbal art on the basis of his or her active presence in the performance arena.[16]

That signals and gaps comprise a topography visible and resolvable only from the vantage point available within the performance arena proves important for texts throughout the spectrum from transcribed performances to "literary" works with roots in oral tradition. At one end of the spectrum, the transcribed performance obviously requires engagement of the tradition's rules for generating meaning in performative context: what is committed to writing or print has its primary allegiance to what remains unwritten, and cannot be successfully addressed as something it is not. In a broadly defined middle area, where the signals and gaps have been transformed into a textual rhetoric and employed by a writer, the reader's responsibility is not dissimilar. Augmenting the discourse will still require, albeit to a lesser extent and with a variant dynamics, activation of the network of signification that derives from oral tradition; performance, even in this altered mode, will still have to be keyed if the work is to be made intelligible.[17] At the far end of the spectrum, as textuality asserts its primacy over the word-power that depends on oral tradition, the metonymic meaning of signals may become muted (or at least the signals may become more limited in range and analytical in focus[18]), and those gaps that both result from and depend on an implied referent may become fewer or non-existent. As much recent scholarship has shown, however, even those works we consider most highly textual still resonate with traditional oral meaning — if we can learn to identify it.

NOTES

Parts of this essay derive from Chapter 3, "The Rhetorical Persistence of Traditional Forms," in *The Singer of Tales in Performance*, with revision aimed at presenting the core ideas in an economical fashion.

[1]For the purposes of the present essay, text designates either the written objective record of an oral performance or an authored work that had no pretextual existence as an oral performance.

[2]See Foley, *Singer*, ch. 1. Many of the strands of argument that constitute the present essay are drawn out at full length in "The Rhetorical Persistence of Traditional Forms," ch. 3 of the same volume.

[3]Cf. Svetozar Koljević, perhaps the most evenhanded of native scholars, who complements his acknowledgement of the

traditional background with the following statement: "But there are also occasions when [the singer's] spiritual needs make him step beyond history and push through the limits of existing social morality. It is not surprising that in such instances his basic formulas sometimes fail him: his utterance has to be unique, or formulopoeic, not because he cares for originality, but because he has to compel the language to do what it has never done before" (viii).

[4]Cf. especially Foley, "Literary Art" 192-94. Examples of Karadžić's intervention are the syllabic expansion of *belu* to *belinu* to yield the formally metrical decasyllabic line "Te on seje belinu pšenicu" ("And he sowed white wheat"); and the much rarer kind of substitution represented in the modification of "Mitar skoči, *u planinu podje*" ("Mitar jumped up, he headed for the mountain") to "Mitar skoči *na noge lagane*" ("Mitar jumped up to his light feet"). This latter intervention, constituting the substitution of a phrase more traditional and metonymically resonant than the dictated text reading (cf. the discussion of this and similar phrases at Foley, *Immanent Art* 83-87), illustrates the sureness of Karadžić's grasp of the register. An interesting comparison is provided by Elias Lönnrot's "editing" of the Finnish *Kalevala*, on which cf. especially DuBois.

[5]I have experimented (e.g., "Editing") with electronic "hypertext" editions of songs in multiple versions, in order to avoid privileging (in essence textualizing) one version and, complementarily, to deepen the resonance of each variant and multiform.

[6]Two among myriad examples are folk preaching (e.g., Rosenberg) and oral narratives such as "tall tales" (e.g., Bauman, *Story*).

[7]On traditional referentiality as a special mode of signification, see especially *Immanent Art* and *Singer*. The latter book argues most fundamentally that word-power in oral tradition and in oral-derived texts arises from the enabling event of performance and the enabling referent of tradition. By concentrating on the issues associated with performance arena (real or rhetorical), register (or specialized idiom), and communicative economy, we can gain insight into the textual coda to the event: the rhetorical transformation of traditional oral signals.

[8]In what follows I make no attempt to reconstrue what is known or hypothesized about the actual transmission or dating

of Old English texts; for a summary of relevant scholarship on *Beowulf*, see *Traditional Oral Epic* 31-39. The general thrust of what has been called the New Philology points in a complementary direction, away from a collection of hierarchically arranged objects and toward a plurality of witnesses that demand interpretation in social context.

[9]Cf. Doane's ("Ethnography" 420) commitment to understanding "the nature of [scribal] writing in a culture in which speech has not yet lost its primacy," and where the role of the scribe is to respond to the voice, "obeying as he works many of the same somatic imperatives voice imposes," where text is "as much act, event, gesture, as it is thing or product, with its origins not just in prior texts, but in memory and context."

[10]Two major problems with Benson's approach are his failure to take account of the tradition-dependent nature of Old English phraseology (he effectively searches for Homeric formulas in Anglo-Saxon texts) and an exclusive focus, typical of the early period of scholarship, on the product rather than the process of composition.

[11]For summaries of what is known about the history and transmission of the Homeric poems, see Foley, *Traditional Oral Epic* 20-31 and Janko, *The Iliad* 20-38.

[12]An annotated bibliography of the Oral Theory, also known as the Parry-Lord approach, is available in Foley, *Oral-Formulaic Theory* (with updates in the journal *Oral Tradition*); for a historical and methodological survey, see Foley, *The Theory*.

[13]Cf. especially his three stages of fixation (80), wherein the identity of the poet gradually becomes effaced, with only the generic aspects being preserved: ". . . the Panhellenic tradition of oral poetry appropriates the poet, potentially transforming even historical figures into generic ones who represent the traditional functions of their poetry. The wider the diffusion and the longer the chain of recomposition, the more remote the identity of the composer becomes. Extreme cases are Homer and Hesiod."

[14]Cf. the oral-dictated text theory advanced by Barry Powell, who argues that the scribe who cooperated with Homer in fashioning the massive *Iliad* and *Odyssey* was also the person who adapted Phoenician letter-forms and invented the Greek alphabet.

[15]On the Rajasthani *bhopo*, see Smith; on folk preaching, Rosenberg; on South Slavic charms, chapter 4 of Foley, *Singer*.

[16]For examples of how this can be accomplished to a limited but still substantial extent, see *Immanent Art,* chs. 4-6; and *Singer,* chs. 4-6.

[17]One thinks here of the "translations" of Latin works into the Old English poetic idiom, some closer or more literal than others (cp. the two parts of *Genesis,* for example) but all of them employing the register of Old English poetic diction, an oral-derived traditional idiom that projects a certain mode of reception. See the discussion of "indexed" translation in the Old English *Andreas* in chapter 6 of Foley, *Singer.*

[18]Cf. the rhetorical handbooks so common in the later Middle Ages, and especially the *topoi* discussed authoritatively by E.R. Curtius (79-105 and 145-66).

WORKS CITED

Austin, J.L. *How to Do Things with Words.* Oxford: Clarendon, 1962.

Bauman, Richard. *Verbal Art as Performance.* Prospect Heights: Waveland Press, 1977.

———. *Story, Performance, and Event: Contextual Studies of Oral Narrative.* Cambridge: Cambridge UP, 1986.

Bäuml, Franz H. "Varieties and Consequences of Medieval Literacy and Illiteracy." *Speculum* 55 (1980): 237-65.

———. "Medieval Texts and the Two Theories of Oral-Formulaic Composition: A Proposal for a Third Theory." *New Literary History* 16 (1984-85): 31-49.

Benson, Larry D. "The Literary Character of Anglo-Saxon Formulaic Poetry." *Publications of the Modern Language Association* 81 (1966): 334-41.

Curtius, Ernst Robert. *European Literature and the Latin Middle Ages.* Princeton: Princeton UP, 1953.

Doane, A.N. "Oral Texts, Intertexts, and Intratexts: Editing Old English." *Influence and Intertextuality in Literary History.* Ed. Jay Clayton and Eric Rothstein. Madison: U of Wisconsin P, 1991. 75-113.

———. "The Ethnography of Scribal Writing and Anglo-Saxon Poetry: Scribe as Performer." *Oral Tradition* 9 (1994): 420-39.

DuBois, Thomas. "From Maria to Marjatta: The Transformation of an Oral Poem in Elias Lönnrot's *Kalevala*." *Oral Tradition* 8 (1993): 247-88.

Ellis, John M. *One Fairy Story Too Many: The Brothers Grimm and Their Tales*. Chicago: U of Chicago P, 1983.

Finnegan, Ruth. *Oral Poetry: Its Nature, Significance, and Social Context*. Cambridge: Cambridge UP, 1977.

———. *Literacy and Orality: Studies in the Technology of Communication*. Oxford: Blackwell, 1988.

Foley, John Miles. "Literary Art and Oral Tradition in Old English and Serbian Poetry." *Anglo-Saxon England* 12 (1983): 183-214.

———. "Editing Oral Epic Texts: Theory and Practice." *Text* 1 (1984): 75-94.

———. *Oral-Formulaic Theory and Research: An Introduction and Annotated Bibliography*. New York: Garland, 1985.

———. *The Theory of Oral Composition: History and Methodology*. Bloomington: Indiana UP, 1988. Rpt. 1992.

———. *Traditional Oral Epic: The Odyssey, Beowulf, and the Serbo-Croatian Return Song*. Berkeley: U of California P, 1990. Rpt. 1993.

———. *Immanent Art: From Structure to Meaning in Traditional Oral Epic*. Bloomington: Indiana UP, 1991.

———. *The Singer of Tales in Performance*. Bloomington: Indiana UP, 1995.

Harris, William V. *Ancient Literacy*. Cambridge, MA: Harvard UP, 1989.

Hymes, Dell. *"In vain I tried to tell you": Essays in Native American Ethnopoetics*. Philadelphia: U of Pennsylvania P, 1981.

———. "Language, Memory, and Selective Performance: Cultee's 'Salmon's Myth' as Told to Boas." *Journal of American Folklore* 98 (1985): 391-434.

———. "Tonkawa Poetics: John Rush Buffalo's 'Coyote and Eagle's Daughter.'" *Native American Discourse: Poetics and Rhetoric*. Ed. Joel Sherzer and Anthony Woodbury. Cambridge: Cambridge UP, 1987. 17-61.

———. "Tlingit Poetics." *Journal of Folklore Research* 26 (1989): 236-48.

———. "Custer and Linguistic Anthropology." *Journal of Linguistic Anthropology* 1 (1991): 5-11.

Janko, Richard. "The *Iliad* and its Editors: Dictation and Redaction." *Classical Antiquity* 9 (1990): 326-34.

———. *The Iliad: A Commentary*. Volume IV: Bks. 13-16. Cambridge: Cambridge UP, 1992.

Johnson, Barbara. *The Critical Difference: Essays in the Contemporary Rhetoric of Reading*. Baltimore: Johns Hopkins UP, 1980.

Koljević, Svetozar. *The Epic in the Making*. Oxford: Clarendon, 1980.

Lord, Albert B. "General Introduction." *Serbocroatian Heroic Songs (Srpskohrvatske junačke pjesme)*. Coll., trans., and ed. Milman Parry and Albert B. Lord. Cambridge, MA and Belgrade: Harvard UP and the Serbian Academy of Sciences, 1953. vol. 1, 1-20.

———. "The Merging of Two Worlds: Oral and Written Poetry as Carriers of Ancient Values." *Oral Tradition in Literature: Interpretation in Context*. Ed. J.M. Foley. Columbia: U of Missouri P, 1986. 19-64.

Miletich, John S. Ed., *The Bugarštica: A Bilingual Anthology of the Earliest Extant South Slavic Folk Narrative Song*. Urbana: U of Illinois P, 1990.

Murko, Matija. "The Singers and Their Epic Songs." Trans. J.M. Foley. *Oral Tradition* 5 (1990): 107-30. Orig. French version 1929.

Nagy, Gregory. *Pindar's Homer: The Lyric Possession of an Epic Past*. Baltimore: Johns Hopkins UP, 1990.

O'Brien O'Keeffe, Katherine. *Visible Song: Transitional Literacy in Old English Verse*. Cambridge: Cambridge UP, 1990.

Parks, Ward. "The Textualization of Orality in Literary Criticism." *Vox intexta: Orality and Textuality in the Middle Ages*. Ed. A.N. Doane and Carol Braun Pasternack. Madison: U of Wisconsin P, 1991. 46-61.

Powell, Barry B. *Homer and the Origin of the Greek Alphabet*. Cambridge: Cambridge UP.

Rosenberg, Bruce A. "The Message of the American Folk Sermon." *Oral Tradition* 1 (1986): 695-727.

Smith, John D. *The Epic of Pabuji: A Study, Transcription, and Translation*. Cambridge: Cambridge UP, 1991.

Stock, Brian. *The Implications of Literacy: Written Language and Models of Interpretation in the Eleventh and Twelfth Centuries*. Princeton: Princeton UP, 1983.

Stolz, Benjamin A. "On Two Serbo-Croatian Oral Epic Verses: The *Bugarštica* and the *Deseterac*." *Poetic Theory / Poetic Practice*. Ed. Robert Scholes. Iowa City: Midwest Modern Language Association, 1969. 153-64.

Street, Brian V. *Literacy in Theory and Practice*. Cambridge: Cambridge UP, 1984.

Tedlock, Dennis. *The Spoken Word and the Work of Interpretation*. Philadelphia: U of Pennsylvania P, 1983.

———. "Hearing a Voice in an Ancient Text: Quiché Maya Poetics in Performance." *Native American Discourse: Poetics and Rhetoric*. Ed. Joel Sherzer and Anthony Woodbury. Cambridge: Cambridge UP, 1987. 140-75.

Thomas, Rosalind. *Oral Tradition and Written Record in Classical Athens*. Cambridge: Cambridge UP, 1989.

Reading in and around *Piers Plowman**

D. C. Greetham

Why *Piers Plowman*? Why choose as the exemplary medieval work to illustrate the current debate over text and textuality a poem written in an archaic metrical system and (probably) in a relatively obscure dialect;[1] a work not even included in the vernacular canon-forming publication program of William Caxton (see Doyle "Remarks" 47-48; Adams "Editing" 62) or his immediate successor Wynkyn de Worde; a work that was first printed only in 1550 (STC 19906 [*Vision*], by R. Crowley) as an anti-prelatical tract, part of the Reformation attempt to find zealous precursors in the Middle Ages; and a work whose basic documentary and literary configuration—into A, B, and C versions (if that is all there are[2])—was not properly discerned until Skeat's edition (*Vision*) in the nineteenth century? And yet *Piers Plowman* it must be, for as John Burrow has observed (*TLS*), it is surely no accident that *Piers* has in recent years virtually replaced Chaucer and *The Canterbury Tales* as the site for the most provocative, critical interrogation of such issues as intention, textual dissemination, eclecticism, affect, socialisation, and indeterminacy. It is true that Chaucer still outpolls *Piers* in coursework, critical studies, and editing projects (there is, for example, no equivalent in *Piers* textual scholarship for the ongoing Chaucer Variorum and Chaucer Library or the projected Chaucer Encyclopedia); but it is in the enormously difficult—and inviting—problems of the *Piers* text, and through the spirited, and sometimes polemical, writings of such distinguished contributors to the debate as Robert Adams, Charlotte Brewer, E. Talbot Donaldson, Hoyt N. Duggan, David C. Fowler, Ralph Hanna, Anne Hudson, George Kane, Anne Middleton, Lee Patterson, and Derek Pearsall (on whose writings most of what follows is dependent), that medievalists have in recent years confronted the same thorny, perhaps irresolvable textual questions which animate much of the rest of this collection. The text, and texts, of *Piers* are both inviting *and* problematic, and this essay will attempt to delineate, for those readers for whom *Piers* remains largely an unread monument rather than a living product of the imagination, just what those attractions and problems are. These problems are so fundamental as to make it virtually impossible for me to make any sweeping statements about such questions as authorship, structure, style, genre, transmission, and reception which could not be challenged by one or other contemporary *Piers* critic.[3] When we cannot even determine these basic matters beyond doubt, then clearly we are faced with a text whose attributes are still very open to speculation. About all that can be confidently said about the textual state of *Piers* is that most modern textual critics accept that it exists in these three redactions—A (probably composed first, about 1365, of 2500 lines, surviving in eighteen copies and one fragment); B (usually regarded as based on A, written in the mid or late 1370s, of 7700 lines, surviving in sixteen copies, plus the print of the first edition, based on another now lost B manuscript); and C (with a highly problematic relationship to A/B, written in the mid-1380s, about the same length as B, extant in eighteen copies, of which ten also count as A-text manuscripts).

Let us turn back to that first printing in 1550 and to the status of *Piers* as text. A text of what? History? literature? theology? philosophy? politics? And is it "classical," "medieval" or "modern" in its textual state(s), its representation of authoriality, and its reception history? These questions, even the simple one of genre, are not trivial to the textual debate (see Barney, "Allegorical Visions," Wenzel, "Medieval Sermons," and Yunck, "Satire" for accounts of three of the generic influences on *Piers*). On the one hand, such theorists as Fredson Bowers (through editing both literary and philosophical texts under basically the same textual principles[4]) and G. Thomas Tanselle (through his emphasis on the comprehensiveness and exportability of Greg's copy-text theory[5]) have tried to efface the generic distinction by treating all texts as if they were *écriture*, or "always already written." But on the other hand, there have been textual critics for whom the designation of the genre of writing determines the editorial method to be used and for whom history, literature, philosophy and so on are indeed different textual modes and demand different textual methods. For example, in deciding how to edit

Johnson's *Dictionary* as a genre, Anne McDermott and Marcus Walsh argue (after E. D. Hirsch, Jr.) that "in order to determine the meaning of a word sequence it is necessary to narrow the supposed genre of a text to such a degree that meanings are no longer doubtful" (Hirsch, *Validity* 178; qtd. McDermott and Walsh 40-41). And Stanley Wells and Gary Taylor determine that the Oxford Shakespeare will present Shakespeare's texts as *performed* not as *written* (i.e. as plays not literature, and thus as social artifacts not as authorially intended objects [introduction xxxvii], although it is difficult to envisage how any print medium could represent the flexibility and variance of actual performance, see Michael Warren, "Theatricalization").

And, for *Piers*, similarly *differing* determinants can have significantly different editorial, critical, and even pedagogical results. Thus, Anne Middleton makes a distinction between the usual reading (and thus teaching) of Chaucer as a "solidly canonical 'modern' [i.e. 'literary'] author"[6] and the very different reception history of *Piers*, which has, until recently, "attracted the kind of interest usually accorded a historical document rather than a literary work" (168). Certainly at the undergraduate level, it is the canonical, and literary, Chaucer who is the required author, who is still the "first fyndere of our faire langage" (Hoccleve, *Regement of Princes* 4978), the "well of English undefiled" (Spenser, *Faerie Queene* IV.ii.32), and "the first warbler, whose sweet breath / Preluded those melodious bursts that fill / The spacious times of great Elizabeth" (Tennyson, *A Dream of Fair Women* 5), whereas *Piers Plowman* is out of the main literary tradition, a "difficult" text with no major acknowledged heirs,[7] best left to specialists or even to researchers from other disciplines. As Middleton and other commentators recognise, these different critical traditions and reception histories are confronted by the Athlone editions of *Piers* produced by George Kane and E. Talbot Donaldson, who determinedly confer a "classical" authorial, literary status on the poem(s) by claiming that it is both theoretically possible *and* aesthetically desirable to reconstruct a putative "original" form for the A and B versions—while working with a documentary transmission of extreme variance that might seem to place the work under the auspices of McGann's "modern scriptures," a transmission of "distinct layers or iterations of authorial production and intentionality, interlaced almost impenetrably with several kinds and states of scribal practice and habit" (Middleton, "Life" 168, n2). The problem of making such fine distinctions—between the authorial and the scribal—and the ambiguous site of the Athlone editions between classical and modern scriptures confirm for me Middleton's general cultural diagnosis that

> one of the reasons that *Piers Plowman*'s challenge to the editor and the annotator is exemplary of the more general questions that attend contemporary textual studies is that it is a work massively both *of*, and even *about*, this interesting and provisional category of "modern scripture"—made, I would argue, in the era when the cultural formation of this category first presented itself to vernacular writers as a theoretical and practical possibility. ("Life" 168-169)

So, yes, genre and cultural status are clearly of major concern in an editor's response to the *Piers* texts. If the model is "modern" and "literary" then *Piers* moves closer to versionist, layered, multi-intentionalist works like Wordsworth's *Prelude*, with its history as the "growth of a poet's mind."[8] Indeed, the evidence for (at the very least) three distinct stages of ongoing composition over several decades (the A, B, and C versions) might suggest that, like *The Prelude*, the poem would inevitably be subject to revision while its author still lived, and that, again like *The Prelude*, its only possible compositional teleology would be the poet's death. The problem with the *Prelude* analogy, however, is that, as all textual critics of *Piers* have long recognised, the authorial is indeed "interlaced" with the scribal, for (unlike *The Prelude*) the poem survives in no autograph copies, and its transmission by no means ceased with its author's death. Thus editors are inevitably tempted to discriminate between corrupt, scribal, disseminated, socialised, belated readings, and those witnessing to an authorial, original presence—in fact, to reconstruct an authorial presence in despite of what may often be a uniform scribal attestation. In other words, editors convinced of the literary, canonical, and authorial nature of *Piers* will approach the work as if it were a "classical," not a "modern" scripture—and this is the undertaking of the Athlone editors.

Such an undertaking has, I believe, three major tasks. The first is to demonstrate that the "almost impenetrable" interlacing of scribal and authorial can indeed be penetrated, or unlaced, that the textual strands can in fact be unwoven; the second is to place the work so securely in what Michael Hoey has called a "discourse colony," a genre of utterance (see discussion in McDermott and Walsh 49-51), that the discrimination of authorial and scribal can have some perceptible cultural or aesthetic purpose, rather than remaining merely an academic or philological exercise; and the third is to provide strict evidentiary procedures whereby the success or failure of the first two requirements can be adjudicated. These three tasks, which are themselves "interlaced" and cannot, therefore, be dealt with completely separately, are the subject of the rest of this essay, together with the resulting fourth issue, of how the first three affect the teaching of *Piers*.

The strategy of the Athlone editors (for which see the textual introductions to the A and B versions, together with Kane's "Conjectural Emendation" and "The Text"), and presumably of all who seek to reconstruct the unknown from the known, the ideal from the corrupt, is to work outwards from the incontestable to the contestable; that is, to establish protocols of authorial usage in documentarily unambiguous circumstances and to export these protocols into less secure environments, in fact, into environments where there is no security or attestation whatever, where all extant witnesses fail to attest the editorially predicted or desired reading. The criticisms of David C. Fowler on the Athlone B-text have addressed this problem. For example, Fowler finds that the Kane-Donaldson emendation, unsupported by any B manuscript, from the line "And wepen whan I shulde slepe • þough whete bred me faille" (Skeat B vii. 120) to "And wepen whan I sholde [werche] þou3 whete bred me faille" (Athlone B-text vii. 125) is not admissible on the grounds cited by the editors. Kane and Donaldson, using one of the protocols derived from their study of unambiguous readings, demand a) that *slepe* must be "unoriginal" because the preceding context requires a verb "denoting 'labour'" and b) that a perfected alliterative line (on [*w*]) must dictate *werche* rather than the synonyms *trauaille* or *laboure* or *swynke*. Moreover, they account for the *scribal* lapse to *slepe* by postulating a "rhyming inducement" from the previous *wepen* or by the influence of the following Latin tag *lacrimae . . . nocte* at vii. 128a.

These arguments would seem to fulfil my third requirement of strict evidentiary support, but they do so only if we accept the editors' presumptions about authorial (as distinct from scribal) metrical regularity and consistent thematic development on the one hand and the blandishments of context on the other. That is, authors do one sort of thing; scribes do another. Within the context of Middle English alliterative verse as a corpus, Hoyt N. Duggan has provided evidence of regular metrics ("Alliterative Patterning," *Wars of Alexander* xvii-xxiv) in multiple-witness works where sources can help distinguish authorial from scribal readings (e.g., *The Wars of Alexander* and *The Siege of Jerusalem*), and has also argued that the authorial alliterative system of *Piers* is similarly more regular than that in any of the extant witnesses ("Authenticity"), although he does accept that "from time to time Langland chose to have his say as precisely as possible and let the alliteration go." As Duggan sees it, in arbitrating the specific dispute between Fowler and Kane-Donaldson at B vii.120 the debate can be put in terms of an "Anglo-American form of empiricism [Fowler] that will always opt for what is written over any kind of mere probability" (Correspondence, 23 February 1994). The problem, of course, is to determine how one may identify those moments when Langland "let the alliteration go" and how "mere" must the probability be before it yields to empiricism.[9] If a different model of authorial performance in this crux (and by retrospective formulation, in authorial intention) were employed, then, as Fowler remarks, while "[t]he meaning developed in A does indeed suggest labour . . . this does not prohibit the B reviser from changing this to an emphasis on ascetic practices, a tendency quite evident throughout the B text" ("New Edition" 31). But to Kane and Donaldson, for whom the corruption of the B archetype is an article of editorial faith, attestation from B manuscripts as to "tendencies" of authorial change is inherently suspect, and a contextual reference provided by A is frequently promoted over the universal agreement of B witnesses.

This manoeuvre has been seen by some critics as a deliberate (and necessary) strategy of self-defence on the part of the Athlone editors, for after having already edited the manuscripts of A without reference to the manuscripts of B (or C)—a procedure he later regretted[10]—Kane came later to the editing of the B version not only with a text whose authorial, aesthetic features had been delineated, but also with a monistic view of the integrity of the A version against which divergencies in the deficiently witnessed B (Fowler's "changes" made by the B reviser) could be measured and found wanting. This conviction of versional integrity, with A, B, and C seen as impervious integers in the construction of the total utterance that is the *Piers* poem, rejects a theory of continuous poetic experimentation (what is usually called "rolling revision") and lays all blame for any blurring of the three categories on the inaccurate or meddlesome activities of scribal copyists, who failed to appreciate the triune formal properties that Kane-Donaldson insist upon.

But the severity of the textual taxonomy, combined with the use of different collational contexts at different stages in the construction of the Athlone edition (A alone, B in reference to A), leads to a logical impasse never fully acknowledged by the editors. As Derek Pearsall notes, "any readings from A used in B are suspect because they may be the product of just the processes of scribal corruption the recognition of which was made possible by the decision to exclude manuscripts of the B and C traditions from the study of variants" ("Theory and Practice" 121). It is the very precedent formulation of an authorial aesthetic in the A edition (a precedence that may or may not replicate a similar primary stage in the actual composition and dissemination of the poem) that determines for the Athlone editors both the formal properties to which B ought to aspire—in despite of its putative corrupt archetype—and the consequent inadequacy of the actual evidentiary status of B witnesses. Charlotte Brewer puts the charge very directly: "differences between the readings of Kane's [A] text and of the B manuscripts are construed by Kane and Donaldson as indicating corruption in the B archetype rather than authorial revision between A and B" ("Authorial" 78). The logical impasse in this strategy is, however, that precisely because A was edited by Kane as a hermetically sealed documentary and compositional unit, whereas B is edited in a series of speculative conjunctions with A, the editorial principles of the two volumes of the Athlone edition produced so far are remarkably different even on this evidentiary level, and it remains to be seen whether the Athlone C edition (in preparation by G. H. Russell) will similarly be edited in the light of A.

To put it very bluntly: would Kane's view of the authorial protocols (of metricality, thematics, and so on) have been different if he had edited A in the light of B rather than vice versa, and would he and Donaldson in editing B have been less eager to dismiss the "changes" of the B reviser without the control already established by A? Fowler has no doubts about the matter: "the main point is that there is no justification for this kind of harmonization of the A and B texts" (32), and that even if metricality can be established as a likely authorial resource, the imposition of perfect alliterative staves throughout the poem is an unwarranted constraint on authorial license and variance: "If he were told that [a reading] does not alliterate I suspect the author's response would be, 'It may not alliterate, but it's true!'" ("New Edition" 32).

Truth versus correctness, and (authorial) revision versus (scribal) corruption. How to resolve, or even articulate this conundrum? The method of determining correctness employed by Kane-Donaldson has commonly come to be known as "deep editing," with the implication that every textual segment (indeed, every morpheme) must be subjected to a stringent and deeply *critical* evaluation separately—on its own merits—for there can be no *prima facie* dependence on copytext or any other documentary forms, given the editors' hermeneutics of suspicion toward the scribal forms of witnesses. Thus deep editing denies the "presumptive" or "residual" authority of modern (Greg-Bowers) copytext, its status as "the text one falls back on at points where no . . . reason exists to dictate the choice among variants" (Tanselle "Classical, Biblical, and Medieval" 65). Presumptive authority must be rejected by deep editing, for to the deep editor there *should* always be a "reason" to "dictate the choice": variants cannot have equal, or indeterminate, authorial status. The conundrum of such discriminations is basic to the debate. Thus, Kane's attack ("'Z Version'") on the editors of the so-called Z text (Brewer and Rigg, see below) is based on his charge that they mistake scribal for authorial forms—that is, they have found "presumptive" authority where they should have practised deep editing—and is countered by Brewer's review ("Textual Principles") of the reissue of Kane's A text, in which she declares that in the complex, revisionary documentary traditions of A and B it may be impossible to identify authorial readings (i.e., correctness cannot be established, the variants are indeterminate, and therefore the editor must fall back on "presumptive" authority). One possible illumination in this murky debate may be via R. B. McKerrow's "contextuality principle." McKerrow argues that an editor should depart from "the originals . . . only where they appear to be certainly corrupt" (*Prolegomena* 20), defining such "certain" corruption as "any form which, in the light of our knowledge of the language at the time when the text in question was written, was 'impossible', that is, would not have been, in its context, an intelligible word or phrase" (21). For McKerrow, context is thus determinant at a very conservative linguistic level, a documentary conservatism enshrined in his edition of Nashe and in his program for the Oxford Shakespeare, later interrogated (and found wanting) by Greg (*Editorial Problem* esp. xxvii). But "impossibility" and "language" and "knowledge" can be very slippery concepts, and it is their slipperiness that can, I believe, account for the rival readings of Fowler and Kane-Donaldson—readings of authoriality, consistency, corruption, and, yes, "impossibility."

As we have seen, contextuality and impossibility are determined for Kane-Donaldson by their lack of faith in (scribal) text as historical document, that is, as testimony to authorial usage. Where such critics as Pearsall celebrate the role of medieval copyists elsewhere as "scribal editors [who] have participated most fully in the activity of a poem, often at a high level of intellectual and even creative engagement" ("Editing" 103), Kane and Donaldson most determinedly do *not* celebrate this Foucauldian "proliferation of meaning" but rather seek to use the other part of Foucault's formula—to cite the author as a "principle of thrift" (Foucault 118) to prevent such proliferation, and thus to close the phenomenological gap between text and intention by invoking both the "proper name" of the author and the "properties" by which the handiwork of this author may be known. They thus share James Willis's view of the medieval scribes as a sort of cultural "noise" (most "dangerous" in their "pernicious desire to do good" [3]), an *affect* of transmission that can only distort or flatten the highly individual defamiliarisation of language that the originary artist has wrought on the linguistic (and literary and metrical) raw materials. To this extent, the Athlone editors are quite orthodox subscribers to the formalist doctrine of "literariness," whereby the artist makes language "strange" and "forms difficult, to increase the difficulty and length of perception because the process of perception is an aesthetic end in itself and must be prolonged" (Shklovsky 741). Like the Russian Formalists, they find a distinction between scribal derivativeness and authorial originality quite unproblematic as a

principle, for to them "[a]rt is a way of experiencing the artfulness of an object" (Shklovsky 741), and artfulness is detected in
authorial originality and *making strange*. The problem is (merely)
in the satisfactory charting of the distinction between authorial
and scribal, and they insist that scribal presence can be determined by the degree to which a lection does or does not demonstrate the qualities of "compression, pregnancy, technical excellence, and . . . poetry" (B version 97) which they require for their
transcendent author. Homer never nods. Thus, the fact that they
adopt as a "main instrument" for their editing a belief in "the cor-
ruptness of the archetypal text of the B version of *Piers Plowman*"
(B version 97) frees Kane and Donaldson to disengage their criticism from documentary context as a primary witness to anything other than its own corruption and to recontextualise by an
appeal to the standards of authorial "compression, pregnancy"
and so on already established in Kane's A text. In the terms of
McKerrow's contextuality rule, Athlone thus inverts the values,
and the editorial performance, that the documentary conservative McKerrow had in mind by shifting the axis of "impossibility" (and "knowledge" and "intelligibility") from an alignment
with the context of the extra-poetic linguistic norm to an alignment with the putative idiosyncratic and non-replicable *ab*nor-
mality of poetic usage.

   This procedure has a perfectly respectable, well-attested
editorial history, a history that (again) is a product of the textual
criticism of "classical" rather than "modern" scriptures. Kane
and Donaldson construct a series of principles of editorial discrimination based on such classical dicta as the *lectio difficilior*
and the *lectio brevior* (the "more difficult" and "briefer" readings),
whereby an originary, authorial usage is more likely to be both
"hard" (because "pregnant") and "pithy" (because "com-
pressed") than is the typically bland and verbose or overemphatic language of the copyist. These principles seem like potentially
very effective tools in the intentionalist editor's job of rescuing
the author from the effects of transmission (leaving aside the possible absurdity of the authorial being identified with the unintel-
ligible—the "impossible"—and the scribal with the intelligible).

   But, as Robert Adams has effectively demonstrated,
what might seem an illuminating principle can in practice
become a very ambiguous procedure, since one thing (and one
editorial mistake) can lead to another:

> [I]f we have ill-advisedly chosen a very precise and vivid phrase as authentic, we will be strongly tempted to dismiss another plausible variant as scribal for its tendency toward blandness or flatness . . . . Conversely, if we have been taken in by an actual case of scribal censorship or euphemism, we will easily defend our choice by labelling its more striking competitor "overemphatic" and "lacking in subtlety" (43).

Adams illustrates his *caveat* by pointing to the Kane-Donaldson emendation of the famous crux in B passus 7 in which Piers determines to be less busy about either his *bilyue* (the Athlone emendation introduced into B from attestation in two A manuscripts) or his *bely ioye* (the universal reading in B manuscripts). Adams claims (and I admit to sharing his unease) that the Athlone determination to allow for only unidirectional revision or corruption avoids the issue of *authorial* rather than scribal intervention (and thus a dual authentic reading), a charge made by Anne Hudson in her critique of the same crux ["Middle English" 43-44]). Adams furthermore notes that the Athlone confidence in unidirectional revision also fails to recognise that "difficulty" (and compression and pregnancy) are not precise enough concepts to admit of only one resolution or one direction in variation: that the "easier reading" which Athlone sees in *bely ioye*—the product of scribal "tendencies of variation" (B version 85)—can be read in reverse as well: "[O]ne way of addressing the issue is to ask whether *bely ioye* seems overemphatic to us (hence the work of a vulgarizing scribe) or whether *bilyue* seems somehow euphemistic and vague (produced by the vulgarizing scribe's brother—the timid, flaccid scribe)" (43).

Adams's specific misgivings here are based on a recognition that "'hardness' may be of various kinds" (44), and may not only be of different types but of different degrees, so that "[h]arder readings must be distinguished not only from easier ones but from impossibly hard ones" (44). The problem even with this formulation is that, while it properly constructs a "three-value" not a "bipolar" system of logical discrimination (with the authorial safely in the middle as the "Goldilocks" option, the one that is neither too hot nor too cold, but "just right"), and while it thus replicates Kane's worry that a simpleminded or overly zealous pursuit of difficulty might lead an editor towards "nonsense" or "distorted grammatical complication" (A version 159) for its own sake, it is still faced, as Adams acknowledges, with the evidentiary problem of the epistemological rules whereby we may *know* the impossible for what it is. As he (almost despairingly) admits, "the categories of common scribal error help only to authenticate our decisions; they do not make them for us, except in the easy cases where we would not have needed them anyway" (44). That is, Kane and Donaldson, along with every editor who has tried to separate *usus auctoris* (the authorial usage or idiolect) from *usus scribendi* (the scribe's), inevitably read the textual phenomena backwards, or perhaps circularly, by citing error as the *fons et origo* of their editorial rationale, rather than as merely the phenomenological traces of their view of authoriality. Unable to follow Tanselle's advice that, to establish meaning and intention, an editor must look in "the work itself as the most reliable documentary evidence" ("Editorial Problem" 179)—precisely because the texts of the work itself are such a seductively inaccurate portrayal of authorial usage—the Athlone editors must paradoxically cite error as contextual negative evidence ("impossibility") for that discourse which is determinedly *not* present in the historical documentation, and yet use this defective evidence to validate a postulate which the documents do not, by the editors' own admission, support.

But none of this is unusual, for it is again the classical method of editing back from the known to the unknown, the corrupt to the ideal. Yes, it does involve circular reasoning, but no more than does the recension system of classical Lachmannian stemmatics or manuscript genealogy, the arrangement of witnesses into a family tree or "stemma," with the most authoritative (and error-free) on top and the derivative (and error-prone) on the bottom. The logical impasse in this system is that a manuscript is accorded status as a good or bad witness to authorial truth on the basis of its errors, and then (in situations where there is "indifferent variation" or no clear authority or error among variants) readings are established as authoritative or erroneous by their occurring in authoritative or derivative witnesses, an evidentiary short-circuit. While I might not fully agree with Lee Patterson's claim (in defence of the Athlone method) that the "process by which any edited text is achieved is inevitably and appropriately circular" ("Logic" 60), I do see in Kane-

Donaldson's impatience with, yet reliance on, the documentary record that same interrogation of textual criticism as a "science" of method rather than as "critique" of texts (what Vinaver called "a mistrust of texts" [352]) which Housman brought to his dismissive accounts of both best-text editing and the mathematical rigours of stemmatics:

> To believe that wherever a best MS. gives possible readings it gives true readings, and that only where it gives impossible readings does it give false readings, is to believe that an incompetent editor is the darling of Providence . . . . Chance and the common course of nature will not bring it to pass that the readings of a MS. are right wherever they are possible and impossible wherever they are wrong: that needs divine intervention; and when one considers the history of man and the spectacle of the universe I hope one may say without impiety that divine intervention might have been better employed elsewhere (36).

Housman, like Kane and Donaldson, thus shifts the axis of McKerrow's "impossibility" rule of context, preferring an unattested reading if that should persuasively reproduce an author's intention over a universally attested one whose fidelity to intention is indeterminate or suspect. Editing is, for both Housman and the Athlone editors, a *critical* task, and it involves enormous responsibilities, even (if you will) a divine "intervention" in the universe of the text to set it to rights. What Providence ought to do for the world, critical editors must do for the text. Like Housman, who maintains that best-text editing just "saves editors from working and stupid editors from thinking"—with the author paying the price for such "luxuries" (36)—-Patterson argues that a failure to acknowledge an originality for the authorial that "is qualitatively different from the unoriginality in which it is submerged," and a consequent failure to recognise that authorial meaning is "enacted in the language at every point," will leave us with the counsel of despair that "the only alternative is not to edit at all" ("Logic" 88).

But this formula is itself open to question. As Patterson acknowledges, the Athlone concentration on the original and authorial as different in nature from "culture" (or textual transmission) is a vestige of New Criticism and the belief in the "trans-historical" view of genius, and in poetry as that which must "transcend the empirical evidence" [70] to produce an organic work—a "well-wrought urn"—that is "never true to life, only to itself" [80]. These assertions can obviously be challenged, even if only at the level of Fowler's quite different view of poetic "truth," a truth which, as we have already seen, is linked by Fowler to a universal, constative truth and not simply or only to the aesthetic dictates (metricality, difficulty, and so on) that Patterson's model for the work demands and the Athlone editions enshrine.

The debate between Fowler and Kane-Donaldson over context thus invokes two different systems of Saussurean *langue* whereby the *parole* of text can be adjudicated. For the Athlone editors, the anomalies (in the Pergamanian sense of idiosyncratic disruptions to the norm of utterance) in the manuscript *parole* are not interpreted as evidence for authorial *langue*, the system of possible utterance, but as *negative* evidence of a quite different *langue* that cannot be directly recovered from the individual speech acts that constitute each documentary line of the poem. That different *langue* is the scribes' systematic reduction and misrepresentation of the signifying system intended by the author; it is almost as if we were trying to discern the possible codes of a language from a bad translation of that language or from utterances made by a non-native speaker. For Fowler, the *langue* is based on lexical and semantic correspondences discernible in text, and not on an entirely different grammaticality (of, for example, uniform metrics) that text cannot see. And the adjudicating *langue* of Fowler's criticism is much more attuned to the polemical, religious, and yes, *constative* reference inferable through *Piers* than to Patterson's formalist rejection of this referential quality in favour of truth to "itself" rather to "life."

The sublimity and anti-referentiality inherent in Patterson's specific for editing and for the work does, of course, confer an equal sublimity on the consciousness of the editor who has (re)constructed the "well-wrought urn," and this transcendental confidence can all too easily (claims Pearsall) decline into an exercise in self-gratification and self-promotion:

> The critical edition [of the Athlone type] becomes an extended exercise in literary taste, where the editor represents himself not as the practitioner of a science,

which is what recension claimed to be, but as a literary critic, making a multitude of fine judgements
about the value of particular readings, his opinion
being based on a larger judgement of his author,
which is derived from an accumulation of judgements
of just the kind he himself is making. There is a sublime notion of the author as someone whose words
will always be discerned to be superior among the
mass of scribal variants, and a sublime notion of the
editor as someone who alone will always be able to
discern them. The editor enters into a mystical com-
munion with his author, from which all others are
excluded. The edition is proclaimed and elevated as
the text, the text being understood to be a sacred
moment in the history of the act of composition, when
the author is delivered of his work and declares it to
be good. ("Theory" 109)

Pearsall's disdain for formalist organicism is not peculiar
to his criticism of *Piers Plowman* and of the Athlone editions. He
has long called for a loose-leaf edition of *The Canterbury Tales* (see
"Editing" 97) embodying what he views as the incomplete composition of the work (i.e., that Chaucer was *not* "delivered of his
work" and did *not* "declare it to be good"). And, as we have
already seen, he is much more hospitable to an acknowledged
scribal involvement in composition, a position that is obviously
anathema to a strict intentionalist or to a believer in the manifest
superiority of authorial readings. As I have pointed out elsewhere ("Textual Scholarship" 112), Pearsall's acceptance of
socialized text is emblematic of our post-formalist, deconstructive, culture-critical climate, and it clearly accords well with
McGann's theory of a social textual criticism. But in medieval
studies generally, and *Piers* studies specifically, Pearsall is not
alone.

Let us return briefly to the *bilyue / bely ioye* crux, and to
Anne Hudson's criticism of the Athlone emendation. Hudson's
case is similar to Adams's in her concern over editorial monism,
that "even if Langland did originally write *bilyue* in A, is it not
likely that he realised its unfortunate similarity in spelling with
the inappropriate noun *bileue*, 'faith', a potential confusion that
he sought to avoid by altering the word to a stronger synonym?
If this did happen, the editors have removed an authorial revision" ("Middle English" 43-44). Moreover, this acceptance of

variance and rejection of unidirectional corruption is just one element in Hudson's larger agenda to question the basic premisses of eclectic editing of the Athlone type. Thus, she is skeptical about the claims of both originalism and originality, denying both the assumption that "one form of the text has unique and unimpeachable authority" and the prescription that "nothing other than the author's original text . . . will be of any interest" (45). With such denials, where does authoriality now stand?

The attentive reader might have noticed that I have so far resisted using the name "Langland" (except in quoting from other critics) and have preferred the less-committal *Piers*. This is not a post-modern affectation, for the immediate reception history of *Piers* betrayed similar confusion, even imputing the poem to the character Piers, claiming Piers (not Langland) as model for the peasant uprising of 1381, or (like Puttenham) suppressing the title to authorship entirely by referring only to "that nameless malcontent." The best that the STC listing for the first edition (*Vision*) can come up with is "attributed to W. Langland." And I would guess that the other essays in this collection are not faced with this particular problem (except, of course, those dealing with folk or oral composition). Who is "Langland" in and around "his" poem, is he indeed the one *and only* poet,[11] and how might an answer to that question affect the reading and construction of texts of *Piers*? While Middleton has provocatively explored the cultural, aesthetic, and ontological significance of the name (and "signature") of the author of *Piers* ("William Langland's 'Kynde Name'"), the fact remains that, apart from a few allusive fifteenth-century annotations on C-text v. 36 in Trinity College Dublin MS D.4.1, of the name and author "we know nothing but what we can deduce to be relevant to the poet from the characterization of the dreamer in the poem" (Pearsall, *C-Text* 9), and Hanna acknowledges only "minimal evidence" for the life outside the poem (17).[12] Langland simply does not have the constative, historical presence outside his work that Chaucer, or Gower, or Hoccleve clearly have, and he does not seem to play with that constative identity in the way that, say, Chaucer does in *Sir Thopas* or Hoccleve does in the *Series* poems,[13] where the poet "named" in the actions of the poems plays against the role assigned for the character within the poems.

Langland is thus "only" a "proper name," but, as Foucault reminds us, authorial proper names are very powerful vehicles for textual understanding. Noting that the "author's name is not . . . just a proper name like the rest," Foucault speculates that "the fact that several texts have been placed under the same name indicates that there has been established among them a homogeneity, filiation, authentication of some texts by the use of others, reciprocal explication, or concomitant utilization" (106, 107). Kane-Donaldson would thus seem to be eminently Foucauldian in their "authentication" and "reciprocal explication," especially in the relations between the A and B texts. But problems arise in Foucault's insistence that, unlike the normal proper name, the authorial name "seems always to be present, marking off the edges of the text, revealing, or at least characterizing, its mode of being. The author's name manifests the appearance of a certain discursive set and indicates the status of this discourse within a society and a culture" (107).

As we have seen, for Patterson the discursive set marked off by "Langland" is a New-Critical, originalist ethic, whereas for Fowler it is constative and for Pearsall and Hudson social and even "non-authorial" (i.e., scribes may operate under the "name" of Langland to perpetuate and embroider a work "released" by Langland). And thus, for the editors of the "Z text" (MS Bodley 851), Charlotte Brewer and A. G. Rigg, this "work" is an authorial first draft, the most originary form of all, whereas for Kane it is a late scribal garbling of the author's name ("'Z Version'"). So Malcolm Godden, accepting the originary designation of Z, can artfully construct a spiritual autobiography for "Langland" based on a serial and progressive development from Z to A to B to C (*Making of Piers Plowman*), even though the serial composition of the three main versions is by no means irrefutably demonstrable.[14] Godden's biography of the name of "Langland" thus treats *Piers* as if it were indeed *The Prelude*, but would Wordsworth scholars be so brave if 1799, 1805, and 1850 (and all the intermediate stages) were not yet firmly placed in compositional order?

Godden's confusion (or conflation) of *Piers* with *The Prelude* is an emblem of the cultural problem Foucault speaks to: how the author's name "indicates the status of a discourse within a society and a culture." Simply transporting Langland into the nineteenth century will not do. But what will do? Under what cultural auspices can Langland's name be decoded? Will it be as a traditional *meaning-producing* "author" (in Barthes's sense of an originator "releasing a single 'theological' meaning (the 'message' of the Author-God)," or as a "scriptor," one whose textual production is a "multi-dimensional space in which a variety of writings, none of them original, blend and clash" ("Death of the Author" 146)? And for that question I have no answer, even though the very proliferation of blending and clashing readings in the dissemination of *Piers* manuscripts seems to fulfil Barthes's formula for the "scriptor" more than that for "author." But despite the work of such scholars as A. J. Minnis on concepts of authoriality, and of Jesse Gellrich on medieval ideas of the book, I am left with Middleton's enthusiasm for *Piers* precisely because that work, or text, or works, lies on a cultural cusp when the very "category" of "modern scripture" first becomes a possibility. Whether it is a possibility that is actualised either in the texts of *Piers* as we have them or in the putative authorial form behind these texts, or again, in the reciprocity between these two states, will depend on the activity of reading (and editing, as the most empowered form of reading): in other words by doing to *Piers* what Pearsall claims early scribal editors did to their texts.

And the problem of what to "do" to or with *Piers* is compounded when we try to teach the poem(s)—just as it is (or ought to be) when we try to teach *Lear* or *The Prelude* or *Ulysses*. The still-too-common prescription that "any text will do" will clearly not "do" for *Piers*, any more than it will for other versionist works from other periods. Teaching texts, and thus selecting texts, is almost as empowering as *making* them in editions, and every edition of *Piers* carries so much ideological freight that a pretended neutral reading through an edition will only ever be just that—a pretence. The Athlone editions, denying the value of active scribal intervention and privileging originary authority, are no less or more ideological than is, say, the Brewer-Rigg Z-text edition or even the Skeat parallel-text edition, in which the tripartite forms of the work first achieved embodiment. It is theoretically possible to read Kane-Donaldson against the grain, to destabilise the authorial text on top by reading, at the editors' invitation, from the rejected variants at the bottom, just as one can read the critical apparatus of any other scholarly edition. But given the criticisms of the apparatus voiced by Charlotte Brewer and others (see below), this process is not as evidentially secure as one might hope. And given that there is no text-only reading edition based on Athlone[15] (as there is, say, of the Gabler synoptic *Ulysses* and for many of the eclectic-text editions of American authors produced under the auspices of the Center for Editions of American Authors or its successor the Committee on Scholarly Editions), it is not even possible to accept unequivocally "as read" the formalist, New Critical, authorial text of Kane-Donaldson. One might try a best-text approach and assign an individual manuscript witness or an edition based on such a witness,[16] confident at least that this had at some time a verifiable documentary authority and historical existence, or one might capitulate by teaching from a modern English translation,[17] as long as one recognised, and made clear to students, that this compromise was in effect accepting the extra-literary significance of *Piers* (as social or historical or religious source, rather than as authorial or disseminated literary text). To my mind, the best way of teaching variance and (putative) authoriality is to resist such compromises by *doing* variance itself: that is, by assembling a kit of socially, aesthetically, or authorially *possible* readings for a particular section of the text (perhaps mining the apparatus of Kane-Donaldson for the evidence, as they suggest, or using the Skeat extracts from forty-five manuscripts [see n.16]), and testing the efficacy and ramifications of each variant in its context, using either Fowler's or Pearsall's or Kane-Donaldson's very different concepts of "context." This is a laborious process at the moment, but the planned hypertext archive for *Piers* (see Duggan *Piers Archive* and "Electronic") should make such travellings and reassemblings within the texts not only easier but also a better reflection of the documentary discourse(s) than any print edition could represent.

Duggan's electronic *Piers* archive thus has the possibility of replicating in the modern reader the medieval "scribal intervention" that Pearsall so values.[18] But if Pearsall's model of intervention (or even Kane-Donaldson's) is a medieval cultural norm; if medieval literature (according to a frequently-quoted dictum of Cerquiglini) "does not produce variance, it is variance [and] fluidity of discourse . . . its concrete alterity" (Cerquiglini 111-112, trans. and qtd. Fleischman 27, Nichols 1, re-qtd. Pearsall, "Theory" 124); if this *mouvance* in dissemination embodies a social standard of diffusion by which a text like *Piers* can be accorded its Foucauldian "status," then surely even the strictest of formalist/eclecticist critics would have to acknowledge that the explosion of variance in the composition/transmission of

Piers is itself testimony to that work's having been regarded, by author(s) and / or scribe(s), as (in Barthes's terms, in *S/Z* and elsewhere) a prototypically *scriptible* ("writerly") "text," a "network" or "tissue" which opens itself up to rewriting and recomposition, as opposed to a *lisible* "work," closed and complete. My experience on the text of Hoccleve's *Regement* (see "Challenges" esp. 61-62), a work that seems to have been as uninviting as possible to scribal adventurism, has at least given me a negative standard whereby to measure the textual hospitality of *Piers* and its variance. Where the *Regement* is, despite its wide attestation and dissemination, relatively fixed and invariant, *Piers* was just as clearly unfixed and variant, both while it was being composed and certainly after its composition: the *scriptible* work *par excellence*. Whether viewed as spiritual autobiography and / or as highly corrupt socialised text—two very different but not incompatible ontological models—*Piers* is thus the epitome of *mouvance*, and perhaps, therefore, the epitome of the medieval text.

Does this then mean that Kane and Donaldson have done a disservice to *Piers* by rendering it under such apparently monistic auspices—tight, secure versions without any leakage among them, firm principles for distinguishing between authorial and scribal usage, a faith in uni-directional variance? On the face of it, yes, the principles and practices of the Athlone editions do seem to foreclose debate. Some critics have even accused the editions of an editorial sleight of hand, of having deliberately hidden the evidence whereby the constructed text might be judged. Charlotte Brewer, for example, claims that the admittedly "conventional" procedure whereby only "manuscripts deviating from the edited text" are recorded in the apparatus might easily lead to an assumption that "a reading is attested by a manuscript which in fact omits this particular line," an especially serious problem when so many of Kane and Donaldson's readings "are very poorly attested" ["Authorial" 61]). But all multiwitness, fully evidentiary editions are difficult to read in some way, and the Athlone editions must be negotiated with the same care that one brings to, say, the synoptic apparatus of the Gabler *Ulysses* or to the transcriptions of the Cornell Wordsworth (see Parrish).

Another dissatisfaction directed against the Athlone editions' apparent foreclosing of criticism is the oft-expressed unease with the editors' claim that the success of the B text edition can be judged not by cavils about particular emendations but only by actually "reenacting" the editing itself (B version 220). Patterson supports this editorial claim by an act of interpretation, by reading the edition as organic, a totalising utterance in which no single element can be questioned (or changed) without addressing the formal ontology of the work as a whole: "As a system, the edition attempts to fit each individual reading into a coherent and self-consistent whole. What is perhaps most disappointing about the unfavorable reception the edition has received is that this systematic nature has been either ignored or devalued, with virtually all criticism being directed at the fitness of individual readings. But no specific criticism, however trenchant, can have relevance beyond its own singularity" (68-69). There is a paradox in this defence. If the edition is indeed organic, and if each reading is related to every other (a claim rebutted by Adams's pointing to "pre-computer" inconsistencies of specific emendations at different parts of the edition[19]), then any criticism (and change) of an individual reading will *ipso facto* change the "work" that it supports, just as Hans Zeller has claimed that *every* variant in a text makes a new "work" since "variation at one point has an effect on invariant sections of the text" (241).

But I appreciate the dissatisfaction voiced in Patterson's challenge to the Athlone's critics: play Kane and Donaldson's game by the same rules they have formulated or drop out of the contest. It's a large challenge, and one that most reviewers are not interested in, or able to meet. But while couched in deliberately dialectical, even antagonistic language, Kane and Donaldson's invitation to more editing is not different from the long history of textual criticism that has seen Johnson's Shakespeare rise to the challenge of Pope's, Erasmus' New Testament rise to the challenge of Jerome's Vulgate, and, yes, Kane and Donaldson's B-text rise to the challenge of Skeat. In such a *scriptible* environment, the Athlone editions are surely not the end of the road, and if the text(s) of the B version do indeed become even more *scriptible* by being encoded into Duggan's digital archive, the manipulation of this archive may—as I have suggested—allow the modern reader an interactive relation with *Piers* that may come close to replicating the first (scribal) editors' "intellectual and even creative engagement" with the ongoing poem.

*I am grateful to both Derek Pearsall and Hoyt N. Duggan, two of the most experienced *Piers* scholars (and representing very different critical and editorial positions on the poem) for having read a draft of this essay and given much valuable advice.

NOTES

[1]Langland's connection with, or retirement to, his original south-west Midlands (the Malvern hills specifically) rather than with the capital is argued by Samuels ("Langland's Dialect" 240), following Skeat, on the evidence of the relative dialectal consistency of the C-text manuscripts, as opposed to the greater complexity of dialectal features noted in B manuscripts, perhaps typical of London production. See further in Adams "Editing" 60-62 and Samuels, "Dialect and Grammar."

[2]Skeat's A, B, and C texts (an unfortunately named division, since it has also been generally taken as indicating a *sequence* of composition and production/publication as well as versioning, see note 16) is the taxonomic basis for the Athlone editions (A by George Kane, B by Kane and E. Talbot Donaldson), and, as this and other essays have suggested, also reinforces the formalist assumptions behind those editions. However, even those committed to the tripartite arrangement have, on occasions, admitted that the textual symptoms are often ambivalent. For example, Anne Middleton (who is part of the team annotating the Athlone B text) recognises that "[a]lthough by all the evidence [*Piers*] is in *intentio* a poem, its production apparently co-extensive with its author's writing life, it survives as three blurry snapshots of something that was in some sort of motion over about twenty years" ("Life": 174). And Donaldson, later wedded to a very firm view of the integrity of the B-text, had earlier doubts (in similar language to Middleton's) about the entire edifice: "I sometimes wonder whether the C-text, the B-text, and even the A-text are not merely historical accidents, haphazard milestones in the history of a poem that was begun but never finished, photographs that caught a static image of a living organism at a given but not necessarily significant moment of time" ("MSS R and F": 211). See further in Alford, "Design."

[3]See Middleton, "Critical Heritage," Baldwin, "Historical Context," Adams, "Langland's Theology," and Alford, "Design" for surveys of some of these issues.

[4]Bowers's eclectic, copytext principles were not only employed in various literary periods (from Marlowe and Dekker to Crane), but also in his edition of William James. Similarly, the editions of other philosophers (especially Jo Ann Boydston's of Dewey) have endorsed Bowers's textual principles.

[5]In such essays as "The Editing of Historical Documents" and "Greg's Theory of Copy-Text and the Editing of American Literature," Tanselle has championed the validity of Greg's theory in periods and disciplines outside the Renaissance drama for which Greg postulated his approach, and in general works like the *Rationale of Textual Criticism,* Tanselle has enlarged the reach of copytext/eclecticist concepts (with careful qualifications) into such fields as film, dance, music, and painting.

[6]Middleton follows Jerome J. McGann's formula for the "modern scripture" (see *Critique*: 10, 56-59) as that betraying "several distinct states and kinds of authorial intervention" (Middleton: "Life" 168, n2).

[7]Where *Piers* is regarded as part of a tradition or movement, it is as a satirical, polemical, or political tract, not as a source of poetic inspiration like Chaucer. See Helen Barr's edition of *The Piers Plowman Tradition* (*Pierce the Ploughman's Crede, Richard the Redeless, Mum and the Sothsegger,* and *The Crowned King*), and see Anne Hudson's account of "The Legacy of *Piers Plowman*."

[8]The analogy with Wordsworth and *The Prelude* has become almost a staple of *Piers* criticism (see Middleton, "Life" 174; Adams, "Editing," 53; Duggan, "Electronic" 64), and the artistic/textual premises of the analogy lie behind such comments as Pearsall's definition of *Piers* as "to all intents and purposes, Langland's whole known existence and his whole life's work" (C-text 9), and behind his citing of Guy Bourquin's opinion that the textual shape of *Piers* betrays a "renouvellement perpétuel de l'expression . . . en perpétuel devenir, à l'image de la vie spirituelle" (*Piers* 284, qtd. Pearsall "Editing" 100). The aesthetic link between development of *The Prelude* and *Piers* extends even to a critical dissatisfaction with the later text(s)—"reflecting a substantial diminution of poetic powers" (see Hanna 15 for a rebuttal but note that Russell ["Evolution," "Some Aspects"], editor of

the forthcoming Athlone C-text, believes that parts of C (specifically the Ophni-Finees episode in the Prologue) may not be the work of the poet of A and B). The collocation of Langland and Wordsworth is challenged in Seth Lerer's review "Medievalist Mayhem," specifically in regard to Malcolm Godden's *Making of Piers Plowman*.

[9]See Lawton, "Alliterative Style" for a survey of the critical issues relating to metrics.

[10]"The editor of *A* now considers that he allowed insufficient weight to readings from other versions in his editing, and that his earlier view of the situation . . . was mistaken" (Athlone B version 75, n15).

[11]While most modern commentators accept the single-author theory, David C. Fowler has ascribed the B-text to John Trevisa (*Literary Relations* 185-205) and, as noted above (n.8), Russell considers C to be partly of posthumous composition by another hand. See the earlier views of multiple authorship expressed by Manly "Authorship," rebutted by Donaldson in *Piers Plowman: The C-Text and Its Poet*.

[12]See his *William Langland* for a recent survey of the debate on authorship and for a full documentation of the (often contradictory) life-records.

[13]See Burrow "Autobiographical" and my "Self-Referential Artifacts."

[14]See Adams, "Editing,"59-63 for a discussion of the implications of this indeterminate and yet widely assumed order of composition and production, for example, the warning that "if the versions were not released in the same order in which they were composed, scribal perceptions of the relative authority of their divergent readings might well have differed from ours, and the direction of influence (i.e., for memorial as well as collational contamination) might not coincide with what we would expect from compositional order" (60). Adams cites, among other evidence, Doyle's paleographical evidence that the oldest extant manuscripts are B and C, not A (Doyle, "Remarks" 36, qtd. Adams, "Editing,"61).

[15]Although Schmidt's student's text, with a limited corpus of variants, is "based on" the Kane-Donaldson B-text.

[16]Examples of such single-witness editions are J. A. W. Bennett's *Piers Plowman* (1972), an edition of the B-text as found in Oxford Bodleian MS. Laud Misc. 581; Stella Brook's selections

from the same ms. (with facing-page modern English prose translation, 1975); and Elisabeth Salter and Derek Pearsall's selections from the C-text *Piers Plowman*, 1967 (based on Huntington HM 143—the base for both Pearsall's C-text of 1978 and the forthcoming Russell edition). Skeat's three-text version can also be used in this approach (with the A-text based on Oxford Bodleian MS. Eng. poet. a.1 [the Vernon MS, reproduced in full facsimile in A. I. Doyle, 1987]); the B-text on Oxford Bodleian MS. Laud Misc. 581; and the C-text on Huntington MS. HM 137. The 1505 Crowley first edition [*Vision* STC 19906], available on microfilm (ed. Bennett, 1976), may also be regarded as of independent status, since it was set from a lost B ms. A useful brief volume of parallel extracts from forty-five *Piers Plowman* mss was produced by Skeat for EETS in 1866 (*Parallel Extracts* repr. Greenwood, 1969), in which he first proposed the three- (rather than two-) text thesis for the poem. See also Pearsall's facsimile edition of MS Bodley Douce 104.

[17]For example, J. F. Goodridge's prose translation (Penguin, 1959, based on the Skeat B-text), which also includes the "autobiographical" passage from the C-text, or A. V. C. Schmidt's translation for World's Classics (1992), or Francis D. Covella's verse translation of the A-text. See also Brook's parallel-text edition (n16).

[18]Duggan acknowledges that no electronic archive can claim a "permanently definitive status" for a critical edition ("Electronic *Piers Plowman*" 75), for the new medium "advances the reconceptualization of text" (66) that will "permit readers to manipulate, search, compare, or concord" the digitised witnesses included in the archive, as no print edition can. However, he does assume (perhaps correctly) that for classroom use, "a more traditional printed version of the critical text" (72) will probably be preferred by most students and teachers; but this prejudice in favour of the codex may disappear within the next generation or two, as students are accustomed to screen-reading from their early years. Moreover, there are traces of other traditional print approaches in the methodology and aims of the *Piers* archive, for the eight manuscripts initially selected for digitisation are those "necessary to establish the B archetype" (n15), and it is only at a later stage of the project that full transcriptions of all witnesses will be included, extending to the two "spurious" and "unauthoritative" manuscripts (Huntington MS. HM 114 and Tokyo

Takamiya 23), which will "represent two kinds of reader response to the poem" (n10). These demurrals aside, the Duggan *Piers* archive will mark a major procedural and possibly pedagogical advance in our critical perception of the text of *Piers.* (Since this note was first written, the *Piers Archive* editors have decided to include a documentary edition of every extant manuscript, including the A-C splices. Moreover, Duggan notes that the color digital facsimiles "will make it possible for users to manipulate the digital image to see text now largely invisible or visible only with ultra-violet light" [Correspondence 23 February 1994]; and he is exploring the possibility of linking hypertextually the transcriptions to the facsimiles, notes, and bibliography.)

[19]For example, Adams notes that the formula "me it + transitive verb" (in the phrase "for kynde wit me it tau3te") is rejected as stylistically improper at B iii. 284 (just as Kane had rejected the analogous phrase in A), but that at B xviii. 351 exactly the same phrase is allowed as authorial, as is the general formula at other places in B where an analogy from Kane's A "offers no reading and thus no potential embarrassment" (50).

WORKS CITED

Adams, Robert. "Editing *Piers Plowman* B: The Imperative of an Intermittently Critical Edition." *Studies in Bibliography* 45 (1992): 31-68.

_____. "Langland's Theology." In Alford, *Companion.*

Alford, John A., ed. *A Companion to Piers Plowman.* Berkeley: U of California P, 1988.

_____. "The Design of the Poem." in Alford, *Companion.*

Baldwin, Anna P. "The Historical Context." In Alford, *Companion.*

Barney, Stephen A. "Allegorical Visions." In Alford, *Companion.*

Barr, Helen, ed. *The Piers Plowman Tradition.* London: Dent / Rutland: Tuttle, 1993.

Barthes, Roland. "The Death of the Author." *Image, Music, Text.* Trans. Stephen Heath. New York: Hill and Wang, 1977. 142-148.

_____. *S/Z: An Essay.* Trans. Richard Miller. New York: Noonday, 1974.

Bennett, J. A. W., ed. *Piers Plowman: The Prologue and Passus I-VII of the B Text as Found in Bodleian MS. Laud Misc. 581.* Oxford: Clarendon P, 1972.

_____, ed. *The Vision of Pierce Plowman.* (London: Crowley, 1550). STC microfilm. London, 1976.

Bourquin, Guy. *Piers Plowman*: Études sur la génèse littéraire des trois versions. Paris, 1978.

Bowers, Fredson, ed. *The Works of Stephen Crane.* Charlottesville: UP of Virginia, 1969-75.

_____, ed. *The Dramatic Works of Thomas Dekker.* Cambridge: Cambridge UP, 1953-61.

_____. *The Works of William James.* Cambridge: Harvard UP / New York: ACLS, 1975- .

_____. *The Complete Works of Christopher Marlowe.* Cambridge: Cambridge UP, 1973. 2nd ed. 1981.

Boydston, Jo Ann, ed. *The [Early / Middle / Later] Works of John Dewey 1892-1953.* Carbondale: Southern Illinois UP, 1967-90.

Brewer, Charlotte. "Authorial Vs. Scribal Writing in Piers Plowman." *Medieval Literature: Texts and Interpretation.* Ed. Tim William Machan. Binghamton: Medieval and Renaissance Texts and Studies, 1991. 59-89.

_____. "The Textual Principles of Kane's A-Text." *Yearbook of Langland Studies* 3 (1989): 67-90.

_____ and A. G. Rigg, eds. *Piers Plowman: The Z Version.* Toronto: Pontifical Institute of Medieval Studies, 1983.

Brook, Stella, ed. *Piers Plowman: Selections from the B-Text as Found in Bodleian MS. Laud Misc. 581.* Manchester: Manchester UP / New York: Barnes and Noble, 1975.

Burrow, John. *Times Literary Supplement* 22 December 1988: 1401-02 (reviewing Alford, *Companion to Piers Plowman*).

_____. "Autobiographical Poetry in the Middle Ages: The Case of Thomas Hoccleve." *Proceedings of the British Academy* 63 (1982): 389-412.

Cerquiglini, Bernard. *Éloge de la variante: Histoire critique de la philologie.* Paris: Seuil, 1989.

Chaucer Encyclopaedia. Gen. ed. Paul G. Ruggiers. Norman: U of Oklahoma P. In preparation.

Chaucer, Geoffrey. *The Variorum* Chaucer. Gen. ed. Paul G. Ruggiers. Norman: U of Oklahoma P / Folkestone: Wm. Dawson, 1979- .

Chaucer Library. Athens, Ga.: U of Georgia P. In progress.

Covella, Francis D., trans. *Piers Plowman A-Text: An Alliterative Verse Translation*. New York: Pegasus, 1992.

Donaldson, E. Talbot. *Piers Plowman: The C-Text and Its Poet*. New Haven: Yale UP, 1949. Repr. Hamden: Archon, 1966.

_____. "MSS R and F in the B-Tradition of Piers Plowman." *Transactions of the Connecticut Academy of Arts and Sciences* 39 (1955): 177-212.

Doyle, A. I. "Remarks on Surviving Manuscripts of Piers Plowman." *Medieval English Religious and Ethical Literature. Essays in Honour of G. H. Russell*. Eds. Gregory Kratzmann and James Simpson. Cambridge, 1986. 35-48.

_____, ed. *The Vernon Manuscript: A Facsimile of Bodleian Library, Oxford, MS. Eng. poet. a.1*. Cambridge: 1987.

Duggan, Hoyt N. "Alliterative Patterning as a Basis for Emendation in Middle English Alliterative Poetry." *Studies in the Age of Chaucer* 8 (1986): 73-106.

_____. "The Authenticity of the Z-Text of Piers Plowman: Further Notes on Metrical Evidence." *Medium Ævum* 56 (1987): 25-45.

_____. Correspondence, 23 February 1994.

_____. "The Electronic *Piers Plowman* B: A New Diplomatic-Critical Edition." *Æstel* 1 (1993): 55-75.

_____, et al. *The Piers Plowman Archive. Hypertext edition*. Ann Arbor: U of Michigan P, 1995- .

_____. and Thorlac Turville-Petre, eds. *The Wars of Alexander*. Early English Text Society, suppl. ser. 10. Oxford: Oxford UP, 1989.

Erasmus, Desiderius. *New Testament (Novum Instrumentum)*, 1516.

Fleischman, Suzanne. "Philology, Linguistics, and the Discourse of the Medieval Text." *Speculum* 65 (1990): 19-37.

Foucault, Michel. "What Is an Author?" *The Foucault Reader*. Ed. Paul Rabinow. New York: Pantheon, 1984. 101-120.

Fowler, David C. "A New Edition of the B text of *Piers Plowman*." *The Yearbook of English Studies* 7 (1977): 23-42.

_____. *Piers Plowman: The Literary Relations of the A and B Texts*. Seattle: U of Washington P, 1961.

Gabler, Hans Walter, ed., with Wolfhard Steppe and Claus Melchior. *Ulysses: A Critical and Synoptic Edition. By James Joyce*. New York: Garland, 1984. Corrected Text 1986.

Gellrich, Jesse M. *The Idea of the Book in the Middle Ages: Language Theory, Mythology, and Fiction*. Ithaca: Cornell UP, 1985.

Godden, Malcolm. *The Making of Piers Plowman*. Harlow: Longman, 1990.

Goodridge, J. F., ed. and trans. *Piers the Ploughman*. Harmondsworth: Penguin, 1959.

Greetham, D. C. "Challenges of Theory and Practice in the Editing of Hoccleve's Regement of Princes." *Manuscripts and Texts: Editorial Problems in Later Middle English Literature*, ed. Derek Pearsall. Cambridge: Brewer, 1987.

_____. "Self-Referential Artifacts: Hoccleve's Persona as a Literary Device." *Modern Philology* 86 (1989): 242-251.

_____. "Textual Scholarship." *Introduction to Scholarship in Modern Languages and Literatures*, ed. Joseph Gibaldi. New York: MLA, 1992. 103-137.

Greg, W. W. *The Editorial Problem in Shakespeare*. Oxford: Clarendon P, 1951. 2nd ed.

_____. "The Rationale of Copy-Text." *Studies in Bibliography* 3 (1950-51): 19-36.

Hanna, Ralph, III. *William Langland. English Writers of the Late Middle Ages*. Aldershot / Brookfield, VT: Variorum, 1993.

Hirsch, E. D., Jr. *Validity in Interpretation*. New Haven: Yale UP, 1967.

Hoey, Michael. "The Discourse Colony: A Preliminary Study of a Neglected Discourse Type." *Talking about Text*. Ed. Malcolm Coulthard. Birmingham, 1986. 1-26; qtd. in McDermott and Walsh.

Housman, A. E. "Preface to Manilus I." *Selected Prose*. Ed. John Carter. Cambridge: Cambridge UP. 23-44.

Hudson, Anne. "The Legacy of *Piers Plowman*. In Alford, *Companion*.

_____. "Middle English." *Editing Medieval Texts: English, French, and Latin Written in England*. Ed. A. G. Rigg. Conference on Editorial Problems, Toronto, 1976. New York: Garland, 1977. 34-57.

Jerome, Saint. *Biblia Sacra Iuxta Vulgatum Versionem*. Ed. B. Fischer, J. Gribomont, H. F. D. Sparks, W. Thiele, rev. R. Weber. Stuttgart: Württemburgische Bibelanstalt, 1969.

Johnson, Samuel, ed. *Works. By William Shakespeare*. London: 1765.

Kane, George. "Conjectural Emendation." In *Medieval Manuscripts and Textual Criticism*. U of North Carolina *Stud. in Romance Languages and Literature* 173. Ed. C.

Kleinhenz. Chapel Hill: U of North Carolina P, 1976.

_____, ed. *Piers Plowman: The A Version. Will's Visions of Piers Plowman and Do-well.* An Edition in the Form of Trinity College Cambridge MS R.3.14 Corrected from Other Manuscripts, with Variant Readings. London: Athlone P, 1960.

_____. "The Text." In Alford, *Companion.*

_____. "The 'Z Version' of Piers Plowman." *Speculum* 60 (1985): 910-930.

Kane, George, and E. Talbot Donaldson, eds. *Piers Plowman: The B Version. Will's Visions of Piers Plowman, Do-well, Do-better and Do-best.* An Edition in the Form of Trinity College Cambridge MS B.15.17, Corrected and Restored from the Known Evidence, with Variant Readings. London: Athlone P, 1975.

Lawton, David A. "Alliterative Style." In Alford, *Companion.*

Lerer, Seth. "Medievalist Mayhem." *Times Literary Supplement* 4 January 1991: 17.

Manly, J. M. "The Authorship of Piers Plowman." *Modern Philology* 7 (1909): 84-144. Repr. Early English Text Society, orig. ser. 139C (1910).

McDermott, Anne, and Marcus Walsh. "Editing Johnson's Dictionary: Some Editorial and Textual Considerations." *The Theory and Practice of Text-Editing: Essays in Honour of James T. Boulton.* Ed. Ian Small and Marcus Walsh. Cambridge: Cambridge UP, 1991. 35-61.

McGann, Jerome J. *A Critique of Modern Textual Criticism.* Chicago: U of Chicago P, 1983. Repr. Charlottesville: UP of Virginia, 1992.

McKerrow, R. B. *Prolegomena for the Oxford Shakespeare: A Study in Editorial Method.* Oxford: Clarendon, 1939. Repr. 1969.

_____, ed. *The Works of Thomas Nashe.* London: Bullen / Sidgwick and Jackson, 1904-10. Repr. with corrections and supplementary notes. Ed. F. P. Wilson. Oxford: Blackwell, 1958.

Middleton, Anne. "The Critical Heritage." In Alford, *Companion.*

_____. "Life in the Margins, or, What's an Annotator to Do?" *New Directions in Textual Studies.* Ed. Dave Oliphant and Robin Bradford. Austin: Harry Ransom Humanities Research Center/U of Texas P, 1990. 167-183.

_____. "Piers Plowman." In vol. 7 of *A Manual of the Writings in Middle English 1050-1500.* Gen. Ed. Albert E. Hartung.

Hamden: Shoestring P, 1986.

_____. "William Langland's 'Kynde Name': Authorial Signature and Social Identity in Late Fourteenth-Century England," in *Literary Practice and Social Change, 1350-1530*, ed. Lee Patterson. Berkeley: U of California P, 1990. 15-82.

Minnis, A. J. *Medieval Theory of Authorship: Scholastic Literary Attitudes in the Later Middle Ages*. London: Scolar P, 1984.

Nichols, Stephen G. "Introduction: Philology in a Manuscript Culture." *Speculum* 65 (1990): 1-10.

Parrish, Stephen, gen. ed. *The Cornell Wordsworth*. Ithaca: Cornell UP, 1975- .

Patterson, Lee. "The Logic of Textual Criticism and the Way of Genius: The Kane-Donaldson Piers Plowman in Historical Perspective." *Textual Criticism and Literary Interpretation*. Ed. Jerome J. McGann. Chicago: U of Chicago P, 1985. 55-91.

Pearsall, Derek. "Editing Medieval Texts: Some Developments and Some Problems." *Textual Criticism and Literary Interpretation*. Ed. Jerome J. McGann. Chicago: U of Chicago P, 1985. 92-106.

_____, ed. *Piers Plowman: A Facsimile of Bodleian MS Douce 104*. Cambridge: Boydell and Brewer, 1992.

_____, ed. *Piers Plowman: An Edition of the C-Text*. Berkeley: U of California P, 1978.

_____. "Theory and Practice in Middle English Editing." *TEXT* 7 (1994): 107-126.

Pope, Alexander, ed. *Works. By William Shakespeare*. London: 1740.

Russell, G. H. "The Evolution of a Poem: Some Reflections on the Textual Tradition of Piers Plowman." *Arts* 2 (1962): 33-46.

_____, ed. *Piers Plowman: The C Version (based on MS. HM143)*. London: Athlone P, forthcoming.

_____. "Some Aspects of the Process of Revision in Piers Plowman." In *Piers Plowman: Critical Approaches*. Ed. S. S. Hussey. London: 1969: 27-49.

Salter, Elisabeth and Derek Pearsall, eds. *Piers Plowman*. London, 1967.

Samuels, M. L. "Dialect and Grammar." In Alford, *Companion*.

_____. "Langland's Dialect." *Medium Æum* 54 (1985): 232-247.

Schmidt, A. V. C., ed. and trans., *Piers Plowman: A New Translation of the B-Text*. New York: Oxford UP (World's Classics),

1992.

———, ed. *The Vision of Piers Plowman: A Critical Edition of the B-Text*. London: 1978, 2nd rev. ed. 1982.

Shklovsky, Victor. "Art as Technique." Trans. Lee T. Lemon and Marion Reis. David H. Richter, ed. *The Critical Tradition: Classic Texts and Contemporary Trends*. New York: St. Martin's P, 1989.

Skeat, W. W., ed. *Parallel Extracts from Forty-Five Manuscripts of Piers Plowman*. Early English Text Society 1866. Repr. New York: Greenwood, 1969.

———, ed. *The Vision of William concerning Piers the Plowman, in Three Parallel Texts*. Oxford: Clarendon P, 1886. Rev. J. A. W. Bennett, 1954.

Tanselle, G. Thomas. "Classical, Biblical, and Medieval Textual Criticism and Modern Editing." *Studies in Bibliography* 36 (1983): 2168.

———. "The Editing of Historical Documents." *Studies in Bibliography* 31 (1978): 1-56.

———. "The Editorial Problem of Final Authorial Intention." *Studies in Bibliography* 29 (1976): 167-211.

———. "Greg's Theory of Copy-Text and the Editing of American Literature." *Studies in Bibliography* 28 (1975): 167-229.

———. *A Rationale of Textual Criticism*. Philadelphia: U of Pennsylvania P, 1989.

Vinaver, Eugène. "Principles of Textual Emendation." *Studies in French Language and Medieval Literature* Presented to Professor M. K. Pope. Manchester: U of Manchester P, 1930: 351-69.

The Vision of Pierce Plowman, now fyrste imprynted [Attributed to William Langland.] London: R. Crowley, 1550. [STC 19906].

Warren, Michael. "The Theatricalization of Text: Beckett, Jonson, Shakespeare." In *New Directions in Textual Studies*. Ed. Dave Oliphant and Robin Bradford. Austin: Harry Ransom Humanities Research Center/U of Texas P, 1990.

Wells, Stanley, and Gary Taylor, eds. *William Shakespeare: The Complete Works*. The Oxford Shakespeare. Oxford: Clarendon P, 1986.

Wenzel, Siegfried. "Medieval Sermons." In Alford, *Companion*.

Willis, James. *Latin Textual Criticism*. Urbana: U of Illinois P, 1972.

Yunck, John A. "Satire." In Alford, *Companion.*
Zeller, Hans. "A New Approach to the Critical Constitution of Literary Texts." *Studies in Bibliography* 28 (1975): 231-64.

Context and Text:
Navajo Nightway Textual History
in the Hands of the West[1]

James C. Faris

INTRODUCTION

This essay is an attempt to sketch an indigenous healing practice (prac-text) on its own terms as much as is possible in writing it down; outline the way (the other ways) the West has approached this practice; and consider what Barbara Johnson has called the "incommensurability of narrative registers" (xiii) to see if there is any possibility of mapping the shapes of Navajo conceptions without the traditional ratios.[2] If alterity is to have more than simple Western discursive relevance, then the unvalorable interval must be preserved.

The empirical material here will center on composite and generalized *vs.* specific Western descriptions of a Navajo healing ceremony, the Nightway, and on the evidences secured by the West of an authentic narrative text founding such a healing ceremony. The project makes no attempt to apprehend Navajo knowledges, save in the clumsy undertaking to describe them as would a Navajo speaking English. I hope that such knowledge is expressed in something like the kind of responses and exchanges which might occur in an extended philosophical discussion and conversation with a senior and knowledgeable practitioner—a Navajo Nightway medicine man. That is, this essay will explore the limits and pertinence and significance of Navajo Nightway knowledges and the possibilities of rendering them in writing, but this study will not question such knowledge in any sort of Western ontological—nor certainly epistemological—terms. While bizarre, I hope this discussion is within the bounds of Navajo propriety. This essay does not attempt to secure an

authentic, original, true, founding text—in my view, an obsession of the West. The unspoken "narrative," unspoken, of all
Nightway knowledge is, of course, considered true and founding
and authentic by Navajo. But it is also never uttered.[3]

THE NAVAJO NIGHTWAY

The Nightway Chant [*tł'ééjí hatáál*] is a Navajo healing
practice to reorder, harmonize, beautify a person whose state of
disorder, disharmony, and ugliness is usually manifest in physical symptoms about the head: blindness, deafness, some forms of
paralysis. Specifically, a leader [*hataałii*—"chanter"], commonly
known in English as a "medicine man" guides the afflicted person [*bik'i hatáałii*—"the one sung over"] through a nine-day series
of activities, activities designed to restore order, harmony, and
beauty [*hózhǫ́*—"holiness; everything in its place"]—to become
well.

The first half of this practice, consisting of four and one-
half days, involves a series of essentially exorcising activities such
as sweatbaths and "shock-rites." These activities are designed to
frighten or agitate the afflicted person to insure that the Nightway
is indeed the appropriate treatment and to begin the reordering,
and the activities are accompanied by hundreds of prayers and
songs and preparations and sacrifices (invitations) to attract holiness and the attendance of the Holy People (Navajo ancestors)
during the second half of the extended practice. The second half,
consisting of the final four and one-half days, involves affirming
rather than exorcising procedures, including hundreds of accompanying songs and prayers. Complex and intricate sand paintings
of great beauty—each commemorating incidents and events in
the journeys of an earth person [*diné*], known in English as "the
Dreamer," to the Holy People [*diné diyinii*] to acquire the knowledges and practices and activities necessary to the Nightway—
and flamboyant final night dancing by masked persons imper-
sonating the Holy People are central during this second half.
Should the affirming activities be conducted with sufficient care
and attention to detail—especially to proper order and
sequence—and sufficient piety on the parts of all concerned, then
hózhǫ́—"order, harmony, and beauty"—will be restored.

The disorder that is manifested in the physical symptoms is brought about by some violation, perhaps deliberate, per-

haps unknowing, of specific orders, harmonies, and beauties in the Navajo universe. These orders, harmonies, and beauties are evident in proper and appropriate Navajo social relations and in relations of people with a Navajo natural order. Causally, then, a person is largely responsible for her-/himself; violations of order result in the observed malady, in the manifested disorder. There are no longer otiose causal gods in the Navajo view. There is no heaven. There is no hell. The Holy People, who once ordered the world for its current inhabitants, no longer do so. Now invisible, they watch over humans from their current homes in the canyons, ruins, mountains and sacred sites of Navajo. They are attracted to affirm, to help engender, holiness if the Nightway practices have been done with sufficient care and are beautiful.[4] Indeed, the Holy People cannot resist attending when attracted by the beauty of the invitations and the sacrifices, but they have little causal role. If executed properly, the Nightway practices again bring about order and wellness just as violations of order automatically brought about the malady.

Behind the ceremony is a series of local histories that recount the adventures of the Dreamer in his visits to the Holy People to acquire the Nightway practices and bring them to benefit earth people. These histories are the formal "texts," the foundation for all practices of the Nightway: in their detail, they must obviously account for every activity, every song, every prayer, and every sand painting of any and all complete Nightway. In a distinct sense, there is nothing here outside the text. But any actual or specific practice of the Nightway replicates, to a partial extent only, the much more detailed or exact or full or complete history of the acquisition by the Dreamer—and hence by humans—of the Nightway. This history must contain all possibilities of all possible Nightway, only some of which will be manifest in any given Nightway. In this sense, the Nightway might be considered a "performance"—a performance of history—even if its "narrative" is perhaps unknown to the practitioners, the performers. It is indeed, then, a prac-text.

No circumstance exists, however, at which these texts, these histories, are actually or regularly transmitted orally as such, or certainly not in full concatenated detail. Apprentices to the "medicine men" learn first by practice—by watching, doing, and participating—and only then, if ever, do they learn the histories, the narratives themselves, or are they able to concatenate all the adventures that account for all the practices of all the variations and branches of the Nightway. This fact does not mean that the only competence is practice and not history, nor that apprentices are but engineers, nor indeed that the narrative and historical texts are unimportant. Nonetheless the success of a Nightway is in re-establishing order and beauty, in re-arranging and re-composing bent social relations—not in abstract authority, recondite references, and obtuse legitimacy, or in some arcane competencies in narrative accuracy. Deed precedes word, however much the former is dependent on the latter. And the texts, the histories, are not narrated, they are "practiced," performed in bits and pieces. They become active. Text becomes context, and context requires text.

Younger and less experienced Nightway practitioners may not know all the concatenated coherent histories that account for all Nightway practices, but only the practices themselves, their order, and the procedures necessary in using them for healing, for reordering, for rendering beauty.[5] Strangely, lay individuals will often know something of the narrative without knowing any of the practices necessary to the healing itself. Washington Matthews commented on this:

> In connection with the adventures of this hero [the Dreamer], an account of the rites should properly be given; but this is a part of the story which is often omitted. . . . I shall briefly state the reasons for this omission. The portions of the myth relating the adventures may be told to any one and may be easily understood and remembered by any one; hence many people who are not priests of the rite may be found who know the narrative portion of the myth only, and are ready to tell it. The ritual or esoteric portion of the myth is usually known only to a priest of the rite, who is rarely inclined to part with this knowledge. . . . If a layman, unacquainted with all the work of the rite, should hear the ritual portion of the myth, he would be apt to forget it, having little knowledge of the rite to assist his memory. ("Some Illustrations" 247)

The founding histories exist, in essence, only through the practices they are designed to inform: they are not normally used *as such* in empirical instruction. Further, I am unaware that these accounts were ever presented in any coherent circumstance or assembled in a totalizing whole prior to the insistence of Westerners interested in securing the "Nightway Myth."[6] In this case then, what, exactly, is the status of the histories? How can the accounts be said to exist in any necessary way if they normally come to be known only after the acquisition of the knowledge of the practices, transmitted through apprenticeships—practices that such histories brought to humans? Why is there any need to speak of founding texts or textuality for the Nightway practice? Are these artifactual? Do they exist, as positivists would argue natural laws of the universe exist, even if humans have not yet discovered them? Are they The Word?

These queries allow us to appreciate one of the apparent paradoxes of Navajo healing. Indeed, this paradox cannot be fully comprehended or resolved without reference to and maintenance of the differentiation between prac-text and textuality. This paradox can be expressed in this manner: every Nightway must be like every previous Nightway—there can be no innovations; however, no Nightway is empirically like any previous Nightway. In other words, although each practice, each specific text, must be perfect to effect healing and none of the practices is exactly like any one of them, all are derived from the same source, the same story, the same history.

NAVAJO KNOWLEDGE

It is critical here to point out that in the Navajo view all knowledge essential to humans was fixed at a point in time when the world was rid of monsters and humans had appeared and the ancestral Holy People had become invisible, henceforth to occupy the mountains, ruins, canyons, and sacred places of Navajoland (see Witherspoon 33; Yazzie passim; and Faris and Walters 13). Thus, human knowledge is neither expandable nor being created. The finite state of Navajo knowledge is a very important feature of the etiology, efficacy, and discourse of healing practices. Knowledge can be lost, however, and many Navajo healing practices are constantly impoverished by its loss.

In the case of the Nightway, this fact means that the instructions handed down are inviolable: they could not be changed under the sanction, perhaps, of not achieving their ends; they could not be added to. Details might, of course, be lost, but even this eventuality is an ultimate peril. In the performance of

Nightway, then, the medicine man attempts to follow as carefully as possible the learned appropriate rules, practices, and behavior so necessary to the healing. Accordingly, this means that every Nightway is and must be, in essence, like all other Nightway. Indeed, there must not be any deviation from this store of finite knowledge; there cannot be any innovation.

But here again is the paradox, for, in fact, there has never been a single Nightway exactly like any previous Nightway. In the Navajo view, as I understand it, this apparent paradox and contradiction is resolved by the consideration of context or practice, of circumstance, of a concrete instrumentalism that mirrors the means of acquisition of the knowledges as detailed in the Nightway narratives. In other words, it is the relationship of method to event, the relationship of textuality to practice [practext].[7]

NIGHTWAY AS PRACTICE

Any concrete circumstance may thus demand and involve more or less of specific learned practices: a concrete circumstance such as excessive snowfall or insufficient rainfall, or the medical history and gender of the afflicted person, or even the ability of a family to pay may dictate certain intricacies and complexities beyond the minimum necessary for an adequate Nightway. The more elaborate versions of critical sand paintings, for example, require more labor and time and hence require greater payment. The specific time of year, the number of previous Nightway in the specific season, the presence or absence of specific masks for Holy People impersonation in a medicine man's sacred bundle [jish] will all contribute to determinations of specific concatenations of Nightway practices. None of the versions are or can be wrong; none are or can be incomplete, since context is bounding and framing, and there is no possible deviation. But context is contingency, and contingency bears on the infinite ever-hanging details of ordinary life, for which any given Nightway is designed.

The issue is not so simple as it might seem. The variability of the Nightway has caused great confusion among commentators in the hundred years or so that the Nightway has been known to the West, not only at the level of narrative but also in the layers of practices. This can be noted in the disarray over composite versus specific descriptions of Nightway practices in

Western accounts, as well as in the two different complete narratives (the Nightway histories) recorded.

Four essential distinct substantive, *specific* descriptive accounts of concrete Nightway practices—Western accounts of Navajo contexts—exist: James Stevenson's account of a Nightway observed in 1884; Simeon Schwemberger's of a Nightway observed in 1905; Alfred Tozzer's of a Nightway observed in 1901; and Clyde Kluckhohn's of a Nightway claimed to have been observed in 1923. All of these specific descriptions are written in English and none is very adequate. They all were recorded, and three were published—the Schwemberger account exists as a manuscript in the Sharlot Hall Historical Library without much cognizance of the implications and complications noted above.[8] And three substantive *composite* descriptions of Nightway practices—Western accounts of Western [Navajo] contexts, (i.e., single descriptions combined from several different Nightway)—have been published: Washington Matthews's *The Night Chant*, Edward S. Curtis's *The North American Indian*, and Berard Haile's *Head and Face Masks*. Curtis's book is probably taken from an account written by a Euro-American trader's son and furnished to Curtis as all evidence suggests Curtis was not in Navajoland during a time when he might have witnessed an actual Nightway.[9] The material was written down and provided by Charles Day, who had seen many Nightway and was initiated into the Nightway, but Day was neither a Navajo nor a trained scholar, and he produced only a generalized composite description in response to Curtis's request.

The other two composite accounts by Washington Matthews and by Haile are the most extensive empirical material available, far better than the shorter specific descriptive accounts of Stevenson, Kluckhohn, Schwemberger, and Tozzer. And certainly Matthews, for one, was substantially aware of the implications of a composite account. Matthews states:

> I have witnessed the ceremonies of the Yebicai in whole or in part a dozen times or more and every time I have observed something new. . . . Half a dozen skilled observers each watching a different part of the work could not note all that pertains to the ceremony on one occasion, nor could they, without long study of the work have a suspicion of what they might have missed. In the myths this complexity of the ceremony

is well recognized, for we are told that the prophet [the Dreamer] after his first return home had to be again off for further instructions, he could not see it all at once. For these reasons I have not thought it expedient to describe the ceremonies as I observed them at any particular time, but to speak of them in general terms, as I now know them only after ten years of study and observation.[10] (WM: Matthews MS Roll 4, No. 516:3)

It is interesting that Matthews refers to the Dreamer's need to return to the Holy People to acquire additional instructions as sanction and justification for the presentation of an account of composite practices rather than accounts of a single and specific Nightway. Matthews recognizes that the Nightway as healing practice stems from an account of the acquisition of the details of the actual practices themselves by the Dreamer, but his use of the mythic authority is quite interesting. Is Matthews here suggesting his own behavior is somehow sanctioned by that of the Dreamer? This revealing passage suggests something of the dilemma of a man who was not a believer, but who at the same time was thoroughly acquainted with the narrative texts (he calls them "myths") as well as with the practices. Perhaps Matthews was even confused about the effectiveness of the practices—and hence the need to take the narratives seriously—while determined to make as clear and objective and secular a presentation of the Nightway as possible.

Nevertheless, the only appropriate Nightway is the concrete and specific ceremony designed for a specific person (or persons) by a specific medicine man with a specific genealogy of apprenticeship in a unique context. Any abstract, general, composite, or non-specific descriptions of practices are inadequate to the contextual determinations that dictate effective Nightway practices: that is, contexts—the concrete determining practices upon which narrative selection is made—are diluted, confused, or inadequately specified. Thus the quite deficient specific descriptions of Nightway by Stevenson, Schwemberger, Tozzer, and Kluckhohn are paradoxically more appropriate and strangely more adequate than the grand and detailed and scholarly composite accounts of Haile and Matthews, accounts that are constructed from the important experience of having seen many Nightway over several years of research. Despite Matthews's caveat quoted above, it is indeed strange that he did not give us a specific description.[11] The inadequate specific descriptions are, in the nomenclature adopted here, descriptive narratives of actual concrete Nightway; the grand expansive composite accounts are texts conflated from several concrete Nightway: that is, they have gone through a sorting and combining in the hands of non-Navajo (non-believers), an act with no meaning or precedence or relevance in Navajo causality. Matthews and Haile have made distinctly Western texts from Navajo contexts, curiously, by trying to "contextualize" them. By attempting to provide all situations or all conditions, they could only fail to specify the proper setting, the relevant context founding the texts. In relying on a Western notion of textuality to describe the ever-changing context, the text of the specific Nightway, they thereby disturbed the only reality possible in Navajo practice.

NIGHTWAY AS NARRATIVE

The recorded narrative texts of the Nightway, as the ostensible basis for descriptions of practices whether composite or specific, vary considerably in quality and adequacy. That their existence is distinctly artifactual to Western demands and obsessions has been commented upon. Here I want to consider those accounts that have been written down. Theoretically, the most adequate narrative is the narrative which accounts for the *totality* of possible Nightway practices by a careful description of *all* the adventures of the Dreamer during his times with the Holy People (for the purpose of acquiring Nightway).[12] But this consideration once again exposes the artifactual character of the concatenated narrative.

There are many written accounts of "The Nightway Myth" in a variety of sources, English and Navajo, the latter, of course, always written in one or another variety of Roman orthography. Very commonly these accounts are in small bits and in abstracted form.[13] Some of the more adequate of these episodic accounts, usually labeled by the "story" they specifically relate, are perhaps very much what apprentices learned: individual coherent episodes.

For the concatenated whole, however, there are but two essential accounts of substance. One of these accounts was collected in English and Navajo by Edward Sapir, Harry Hoijer, and interpreters Chic Sandoval and Berard Haile from Nightway medicine man Slim Curly in 1929 (Sapir and Hoijer 136-259). The other account was collected only in English by Franc Newcomb, interpreter Clyde Beyal and Mary Wheelwright from Nightway medicine man Hosteen Klah in 1928 (Faris, *The Nightway* 171-233). In this latter case, the Navajo was translated from the spoken Navajo into oral English, and only this English was recorded. These are the only two written narratives—concatenated series of episodes—that cover anything like the range of practices and actual possible events of a single Nightway. Specific ceremonial activities are linked only to specific episodes of the theoretically endless concatenation of possible narrative texts, each of which accounts for the gift of the concrete practice from the Holy People to Navajo. Sections were added together by the narrating medicine men to result in the curious totalizing documents sought/demanded by recorders who assumed there was but a single, bounded, authentic, and coherent "Nightway myth."

Each narrative episode may be labeled with an acknowledged name such as "The Whirling Logs," and each essentially details the acquisition of a new prayer stick, a new song, a new prayer, a new sand painting, some new healing procedure, or an example of a different circumstance that dictates a specific change. *None* of the narrative episodes, of course, is essential to the total narrative text or any part of it. No episode is necessary to plot construction, for the arrangement of the full text does not depend on plot construction. Except for internal correct sequence, which is *very* important in Nightway practices, neither a necessary order nor a developed plot line exists. Matthews, indeed, notes the loose character of the Nightway narrative. When discussing the narrative that binds some thirty of the forty-odd songs of House God known from all examples of the Nightway he encountered, Matthews remarks:

> Such is a Navaho song myth. It reminds one of certain plays which have recently come into vogue, in which the plot, if a plot can be found, serves no higher purpose than to hold together a few songs and dances.[14]
> ("Songs of Sequence" 194)

Obviously, virtuoso Nightway medicine men were encouraged by non-Navajo to relate more and more of these episodes. Indeed, a careful comparison of the two major extended recorded Nightway narratives, as well as of less extensive ones, does not reveal great basic differences, especially in structure; such a comparison demonstrates that each Nightway is episodically more or less rich than every other. The differences are basically accretive, linear, and of the same register; Nightway ceremonies are not substantially different in any qualitative measure. At least in these terms, each Nightway is therefore as "authoritative" as any other. There is an unspoken master narrative but no reference to a founding textuality, no ontological gesture. Only the existence of a successful healing performance establishes authority.

This "corpus" of all possible episodes that might be related is indeed related in the common received manner of Navajo oral discourse: "they say" ends every phrase of the only Nightway narrative we have that is precisely translated from the written Navajo as it was narrated, as if every medicine man is simply repeating from a possible store (see Sapir and Hoijer, passim). Although this recitation convention is common in other Navajo oral transmissions, its significance here should not be overlooked.

There are additional implications. As noted, at least theoretically, the most complete possible narrative text would describe all practices of all possible specific Nightway—and this includes the actual orally-transmitted practices, such as the hundreds of songs and prayers. The two existing narrative texts mention the acquisition of specific prayers and songs but do not actually record many of these in writing. The absence might be due in part to the facts that Sapir, Hoijer, Sandoval, and Haile were recording Nightway songs separately from the narrative and that Newcomb, Beyal, and Wheelwright were not prepared to write them all down, since songs and prayers are filled with redundancy and repetition. Whatever the reasons, the absence in the two most extensive written narrative texts we have of the Nightway of most of the actual orally-transmitted materials of any given Nightway, the prayers and songs, is indeed a peculiar situation.

SPECIFIC VERBAL PRACTICES: SONGS AND PRAYERS

It is certainly the case that apprentices learned songs and prayers as a part of specific Nightway practice prior to learning articulated narrative episodes that "account" for each activity. Sapir and Hoijer note the priority of the poetic texts, the songs and prayers: "It is the songs that the narrator has in mind and much in the story is constructed from them" (574). Thus it may be noted that, in its received form, the narrative, arguably an artifact of non-Navajo obsessions, is not as congruent or as well-formed or as precisely comparative as are those oral features of specific Nightway activities, such as the specific songs and prayers. A few anthropologists have been concerned with poetics and considered them quite as important as the derived and artificial narrative texts (cf. Gill; Frisbie, "An Approach" and "*Ritual Drama*"), but principally humanists have involved poetics or even attempted to treat the narratives as poetics (cf. Zolbrod, "From Performance to Print" and *Dinè bahané*). Unfortunately most anthropologists seem to have preferred the dry consolation, liminal determinations, and bounded closed projects of prose—treating prayers and songs as subversive to such comforts.[15] Unlike the recorded narratives, with their distorted importance to Western projects, activity, songs and prayers in actual Nightway practice are the textual practices most vitally significant to healing: the specific structural and formal mechanisms by which the verbal practices of song and prayer command and situate, constitute and reorder, is of greater importance.[16]

Comparative materials are difficult to assemble, and despite the hundreds of songs and dozens of prayers documented as characteristic of Nightway, there have been few rigorous systematic assemblages or comparative attempts. To be sure, this small number of assemblages can be attributed partly to the great reluctance of Nightway medicine men to allow the recording of specific Nightway practices; consequently, most of those song and prayer texts available in written form have been elicited outside Nightway practice itself. As such, they too sometimes have a distinctly artifactual character, without the determining contextual surroundings that might help readers or listeners comprehend their local function. The recording situation was thus artificial and contrived, and the song and prayer texts committed to written document lacked the indigenous stimuli and the social constitution by which they might be recognized by other medicine men. Indeed, there may have even been deliberate changes in such circumstances to avoid proper, pertinent, and appropriate verity, to avoid offending Holy People, to avoid actually supplicating and inviting in circumstances where no blessing is being asked or intended.

This artifactual character obviously complicates comparisons of poetic texts. But it is also important to remember the overwhelming contextual determinations of the Nightway: every one is different from every other one. It is unlikely that any Nightway medicine man could simply or easily recall or recite all Nightway songs and dozens of prayers without the many suggestions and contextual conditions an actual Nightway would provide.[17] Such texts are normally not learned outside these contexts, and to recount them in secular circumstances might be expected to yield some confusion, selection, and even deletion. Since we do not have any actual documentation or adequate complete contextual recording, we cannot determine the accuracy of these texts. But it does point out the difficulties of comparison.

Nonetheless, as textual practices, songs and prayers are specifically vital to the healing functions of Nightway. We can assume that if they are correct models and visions of order and beauty and of appropriate restored social relations, they will always be central and thus included in all successful variations and forms. Rather like complex algebraic expressions or the precepts of an intricate chemical formula, they are elaborate and baroque: ornaments and expressions within ornaments and expressions within ornaments and expressions.

Haile found the Nightway song materials recorded by Hoijer and George Herzog a great disappointment, for he had hoped the songs from Hosteen Klah would be "similar or identical" to those of Slim Curly, from whom Haile, Sapir, and Sandoval had also elicited a narrative text (Sapir and Hoijer). His great ambition, the creation of another Night Chant volume, was to founder. In a letter to Sapir dated 15 November 1935[?], Haile notes that "Curly would hardly recognize [Hosteen Klah's] songs."

Besides the lack of compatibility of the song texts from the two different Nightway medicine men, Haile had other problems, for he states in a letter to Sapir dated 20 October 1933, that "Strange to say, the wording of the songs seems to have very little connection with the chant legend, although we did not work out this point with Curly." This revealing statement implies he felt the songs were to be derived from, or at least bear some closer relationship to, narratives. But since the songs are specific appeals to the Holy People, it should not be surprising that they differ from an abstraction of no invitational importance and with no rhetorics of solicitation. It must be remembered, however, that both songs and prayer were given to earth people by the Dreamer, from the Holy People, whereas the concatenated narrative forms, the histories, are constructed by earth people from these events. Moreover, as the songs appeal to and invite specific Holy People, certain rhetorical techniques must be used; explicit reference to the narrative text is irrelevant or abandoned (or perhaps even unknown) by the singer in these circumstances.

Well aware that the function of the songs was to attract the Holy People, Matthews (*The Night Chant*) is more careful to note the rhetorical techniques to be found. He specifically mentions metathesis, antithesis, and epenthesis; commutation, synocopic, and paragogic techniques; and, of course, rhyme and prosody. He calls specific attention to euphony and homophony.[18] But since Matthews never considers the effectiveness of the Nightway practice, perhaps he never examines these rhetorics in terms of the specific types of orders to be corrected or the specific beauties to be reestablished: that is, he never considers the complementarity of gender relations and authority relations— the vital orders, the critical social relations—to be reinscribed by the practice of the Nightway. Each Nightway carefully constitutes gender distinctions with males marked, generation or age distinctions with the older marked, and "chiefs" with, interestingly, no unmarked contrast.

WRITING AND ANTHROPOLOGY: THE WEST IN WORD/ACT

The confounded and confused status of the Nightway "narrative" in terms of historical anthropology has been noted. The West's requirement for authentic text and the complications therein have been commented upon. Of course, there is an authentic founding text for Navajo as well; it is simply a narrative never realized as such in any known practice. Portions of this text come to exist only in specific Navajo practice, in situational and contextual Navajo healing. But this never-concatenated "narrative" represents the authority and absolute referent for Navajo, while even in—or especially in—its supposedly most authentic form, that of recorded text, it represents for the West an ignorance for which it has knowledge. This situation makes our obsessions with authenticity rather hollow and disingenuous. For in transforming Navajo "narratives" or this non-existent Navajo narrative into our own textuality, we not only change cultures, but we adopt the Nightway into our own registers for conceiving and adjudicating, into our own protocols. Then it can be classified, named, violated. It can be placed into our perfect language, our nonmetaphorical discourse, our direct means of apprehending, our timeless context. The Navajo Nightway narrative, never before concatenated in any form approximating totality and certainly never before written at all, can be written in English, assimilated to the language of the universe, the arrogant comprehension free of cultural experience. It then becomes the contextless text, and curiously, for the West, authentic and founding.

NOTES

[1]Apart from relevant analytical and theoretical expansions, some of the materials for this essay relate, in substantially reduced form, to Chapter Two ("The Nightway Recorded"), Faris, *The Nightway* 25-78.

[2]See Foucault (378) for discussion of the anthropological "perpetual ratio."

[3]Nightway texts as written documents are thus obviously a consequence of Western solicitation and anthropological behest, as Navajo did not have a traditional textual writing system. Aspects of this are considered below.

As Westerners were interested mostly in securing the material in English and almost no one spoke Navajo, the Nightway's stylistic aural rhetorical devices were usually not rendered in the written form. There is one concatenated Nightway history recorded in Navajo and rather rigorously translated—the Slim Curly version collected by Edward Sapir and Harry Hoijer and Berard Haile and Chic Sandoval (Sapir and Hoijer). It is rich in poetics and grand oral stylistic devices, but translated, its frequent repetitive phrases soon become tiresome, and it begins to sound like the song and prayer practices. Furthermore, as I have argued, the Nightway narrative form is not a body important in Navajo oral discourse, where such stylistic mechanisms would bear critical weight. Navajo loses, so to speak, in the specific exercise of the Nightway being solicited, written, and then closely translated. The rhetorics in the Slim Curly account strike me as hollow. Yet Navajo oral transmission always takes place with these rhetorics, and so even a narrative account normally not so transmitted is also structured with them in the Slim Curly transmission. This account contrasts with the Hosteen Klah account, collected by Franc Newcomb and Mary Wheelwright (Faris, *The Nightway*), which is written in English only (although Hosteen Klah delivered it in Navajo and it was simultaneously translated into English by Clyde Beyal).

[4]The use of the word "engendered" is deliberate, for it has been argued that the ordered social relations with which the Nightway is most concerned are social relations of gender and of authority. The person in ugliness has somehow violated or transgressed these sorts of social relations. The specification here of the types of social order in disarray is an analytical point, not a Navajo claim, and is argued in more detail in Faris and Walters.

[5]Significantly, in the Navajo view, knowledge, being limited, is very much an item of possession. One must pay to acquire it and any esoteric knowledges. Senior healers traditionally made their living on the dispensation of this knowledge, both in healing practice and in instructing apprentices. Those seeking to acquire it, normally apprentices, had to undertake the expense of attaining it. Today, however, transmitting this knowledge—or at least its sacred and esoteric details—is normally confined to Navajo apprentices and is not generally allowed for non-Navajo. When it is allowed, the knowledge must be paid for; anyone seeking to interview Navajo practitioners for their knowledge must properly observe this requirement. Because of this requirement, written texts, books, and tapes are sometimes considered inappropriate media for transmission as the medicine men have no control over their distribution. For these medicine men, there are, in these forms, no possible "royalties" or "residual rights."

[6]In the disbelieving and denigrating vocabulary of anthropology, of course, such histories, such foundational texts, are known as "myths," and the healing practices are "rituals" or "ceremonials." This semiotic is typical of attempts to both preserve alterity, usually for purposes of measure, while violating it by comprehension.

⁷Narrative / narratives, history / histories, refer to the fact that the Dreamer acquired knowledges sequentially. Some practices taught him by the Holy People were additions to earlier learned materials: additions of prayers here, songs there, appropriate to different contexts that any practitioner might encounter—e.g., the necessity to deter excessive snowfall at a Nightway. Some additions were appropriate to the specific history or the etiology of the malady of the person sung over. The Dreamer added on knowledge in his acquisition of the Nightway practices, and the totality of this knowledge is the totality of current practices, save those that have been more recently lost. In the existing written narratives, the quality of accretion is manifested: the narratives are episodic, and exist as sequences of events, each of these events a separate and sometimes unique practice.

That he is called "the Dreamer" [*bil' áhát'íní*—"with whom there is a vision"] suggests that his first attempts to communicate his experiences with the Holy People to his brothers were met with cynicism. Thus his experience was considered illusory and was not taken seriously until later when he and his commentary were finally accepted. Indeed, his first apprentices were his older brothers, those who had earlier doubted his communication of his experiences.

⁸See Faris (*The Nightway* 40-48) for the comparison and analysis of these specific descriptions, including evidence that much of Kluckhohn's account was plagiarized from Stevenson. Faris also contains bibliographical references to a number of partial accounts of specific Nightway, both published and unpublished. Of the four extended specific accounts, only Schwemberger and Kluckhohn record the identity of the medicine man.

⁹Curtis was in Navajoland during the spring and summer of both 1904 and 1906. The Nightway is a late fall and winter ceremonial only. In early 1905, Curtis was sent his Nightway "description" by Charles Day, a Euro-American trader's son who had facilitated his visits. After his 1904 visit and photography, Curtis wrote Day on 20 December 1904 requesting a Nightway description.

¹⁰There is another sense, however, in which any specific Nightway may not be quite "complete." See Faris, *The Nightway* 70.

¹¹See Faris, *The Nightway* 49; and "Some Observations"

for more detail of Matthews's Nightway research.

¹²The narrative that is complete would also presumably be in ways like the most adequate possible composite descriptive textual account of all possible practiced Nightway.

¹³See Faris, *The Nightway* 25-31, for a list of all these partial and piecemeal narrative wholes, and for detailed narrative segments.

¹⁴The Western obsession with plot or with some authentic core has had some curious yields. Having acquired the extensive Klah Nightway narrative, Wheelwright proceeded to publish it in her own dramatically shortened and adapted version (Klah, Tleji or Yehbichai Myth). She left out the very essence, the instructional detail that occurs in the concatenated episodes of the long narrative text (Faris, *The Nightway* 229). The text was abstracted to less than one-tenth its size, preserving a "plot," but not the valuable Nightway narrative detail that provides the specific instructions by the Holy People to the Dreamer for explicit healing and reordering purposes. It is as if having acquired the "plot," Wheelwright found the ceremonial detail irrelevant or superfluous. Wheelwright's little pamphlet indeed resembles the knowledge of Navajo laymen discussed by Matthews above.

¹⁵Paul Zolbrod is interested in the presentation of Navajo narrative as oral literature. He stresses the richness of nonalphabetic and nonprint dictated discursive projects, their stylization, prosodic detail, individualized features, and visual and aural impact. In the case of the Nightway, however, the narrative episodes are not essentially intended for oral delivery, indeed, for any delivery at all. Probably they cannot be considered in the same ways as some other Navajo narratives, such as creation histories, on which Zolbrod's *Dinè bahane'* focuses. See also "From Performance to Print."

¹⁶The extent to which the sand paintings, songs, and prayers are intimately linked and evoke one another was poignantly demonstrated to me when I took a copy of my *The Nightway*, which has extensive color plates of heretofore unpublished sand painting reproductions, to a very aged Nightway medicine man, Sei Naabageesz, whom I interviewed in the research (Faris, *The Nightway* 96). This 92-year-old Navajo was almost deaf and blind, but when I helped him see the color plates and he was able to recognize one of the sand paintings, he immediately broke out into song appropriate to that sand painting.

[17]Of course, linguists of the time probably were not interested in attending a complete nine-day Nightway with its two all-night sessions to see and hear and record the "contextualized" songs and prayers (especially if they could get a Nightway medicine man to give such songs and prayers in less rigorous circumstances). It must be remembered the Nightway is given only in the late fall and winter, at the altitudes of the Colorado Plateau. Here life outdoors for nine days, particularly in the two all-night sessions, may be anything but comfortable.

[18]Rhetorical figures operate at all levels. While I cannot be sure in my incompetent Navajo, I suspect there are numerous performance canons about the use of the Navajo language itself in explicit phonological and morphological terms, though perhaps not so much as in song. Certainly there are paromosisic techniques, parallelisms of sounds between clauses, and probably systolic or prosthetic mechanisms, alterations the length of a syllable in appropriate points. And any listener can hear anaphoric alliteration, at times strictly resolute, where each word in a clause begins with the same sound. (See Faris, *The Nightway* 64-65 for those rhetorical techniques that are recognizable in translation).

WORKS CITED

Curtis, Edward S. Letter to Charles Day. 20 December 1904. NAU: Day Family Collection. Series 4, Box 1, Folder 30. Northern Arizona University Library, Special Collections, Flagstaff.

_____. *The North American Indian*. Vol. 1. Cambridge: Harvard UP, 1907.

Faris, James C. *The Nightway. A History and a History of Documentation of a Navajo Ceremonial*. Albuquerque: U of New Mexico P, 1990.

_____. "Some Observations on the Ethical Integrity of Washington Matthews in Navajo Research." *Washington Matthews and the Beginning of Navajo Studies*. Ed. Katharine Halpern and Susan Brown McGreevy. Albuquerque: U of New Mexico P, 1995. Forthcoming.

_____, and Harry Walters. "Navajo History: Some Implications of

Contrasts of Navajo Ceremonial Discourse." *History and Anthropology* 5.1 (1990): 1-18.

Foucault, Michel. *The Order of Things: An Archaeology of the Human Sciences.* New York: Vintage Books, 1973.

Frisbie, Charlotte J. "An Approach to the Ethnography of Navajo Ceremonial Performance." *The Ethnography of Musical Performance.* Ed. Norma McLeod and Marcia Herndon. Norwood, PA: Norwood Editions, 1980.

_____. "Ritual Drama in the Navajo House Blessing Ceremony." *Southwest Indian Ritual Drama.* Ed. Charlotte J. Frisbie. School of American Research, Santa Fe. Albuquerque: U of New Mexico P, 1980. 161-98.

Gill, Sam. "Navajo Views of Their Origins." *Handbook of North American Indians.* Vol. 10. Ed. Alfonso Ortiz. Washington, DC: Smithsonian Institution P, 1981. 502-5.

Haile, Berard. *Head and Face Masks in Navaho Ceremonialism.* St. Michaels, AZ: St. Michaels P, 1947.

_____. Letter to Edward Sapir. 20 October 1933. UAZ: AZ/132/Box 3a. University of Arizona Library, Special Collections, Tucson.

_____. Undated Letter to Edward Sapir. Probably 15 November 1935. UAZ:AZ/132/Box 3a. University of Arizona Library, Special Collections, Tucson.

_____. Letter to Edward Sapir. 20 October 1933. UAZ:AZ/132/Box 16.6:13. University of Arizona Library, Special Collections, Tucson.

Hoijer, Harry, and George Herzog. Nightway songs of Hosteen Klah. Undated MSS. Probably 1927. WM:3-1-4. Wheelwright Museum of the American Indian, Santa Fe.

Johnson, Barbara. "Introduction." *Consequences of Theory.* Ed. Jonathan Arac and Barbara Johnson. Baltimore: Johns Hopkins UP. 1991. vii-xiv.

Klah, Hosteen. *Tleji or Yehbechai Myth.* Retold in Shorter Form from the Myth by Mary C. Wheelwright. Bulletin No. 1. Santa Fe: Museum of Navajo Ceremonial Art, 1938.

Kluckhohm[n], Clyde. "The Dance of Hasjelti." *El Palacio* 15 (1923): 187-192.

Matthews, Washington. *The Night Chant, A Navaho Ceremony.* Publications of the Hyde Southwestern Expedition. Whole Series Vol. 6 (Anthropological Series, Vol. 5). New York: Memoirs of the American Museum of Natural

History, 1902.

_____. "Some Illustrations of the Connection Between Myth and Ceremony." *Memoirs of the International Congress of Anthropology.* Vol. 22. Ed. C. Stansland Wake. Chicago: Schulte Publishing, 1894. 246-51.

_____. "Songs of Sequence of the Navajos." *Journal of American Folklore* 7.27 (1894): 185-194.

_____. Undated MSS. WM: Matthews MS Roll 4, No. 516:3. Wheelwright Museum of the American Indian, Santa Fe.

Sapir, Edward, and Harry Hoijer. *Navaho Texts.* Iowa City: Linguistic Society of America, 1942.

Schwemberger, Simeon. Nightway Description. Undated MSS. Probably 1905. SHH: Ref. Doc. Box 52, Folder 3. Sharlot Hall Historical Library, Phoenix, AZ.

Stevenson, James. "Ceremonial of Hasjelti Dailjis and Mythical Sand Painting of the Navajo Indians." *Bureau of American Ethnology Eighth Annual Report*, 1886-1887. Washington, DC: United States Government Printing Office, 1891. 229-85.

Tozzer, Alfred. "Notes on Religious Ceremonials of the Navaho." *Anthropological Essays Presented to Frederic Ward Putnam in Honor of his 70th Birthday.* Putnam Anniversary Volume. New York: G.E. Stechert, 1909. 299-343.

Witherspoon, Gary. *Language and Art in the Navajo Universe.* Ann Arbor: U of Michigan P, 1977.

Yazzie, Alfred. *Navajo Oral Tradition.* 3 vols. Rough Rock, AZ: Navajo Resource Center, Rough Rock Demonstration School, 1984.

Zolbrod, Paul. *Dinè bahane'. The Navajo Creation Story.* Albuquerque: University of New Mexico Press, 1984.

_____. "From Performance to Print: Preface to a Native American Text." *The Georgia Review* 35.3 (1981): 465-472.

"The Tongues
of the learned are insufficient":
Phillis Wheatley, Publishing Objectives,
and Personal Liberty

Christopher Felker

Eighteenth- and nineteenth-century reviews of Phillis Wheatley's first volume of *Poems on Various Subjects, Religious and Moral* (1773) describe her virtuosity for tracing the circumference of republican concerns. Those whose purposes it was to maintain the invisible center of a thriving Anglo-American economic culture celebrated her propriety in using ancient poetry, described her genius, valued as an "ornament" of Negro improvement, and noted her literary taste and piety.[1] The character of this "invisible center" is reflected in the debate between two of Wheatley's most influential readers—George Washington and Thomas Jefferson. For Jefferson, the publication of *Poems on Various Subjects* connected Wheatley's power to a cultural argument linking racism and progress. In an unabashedly critical judgment of Wheatley, Jefferson decried her assimilation by Yankee Protestantism and narrow mercantile interests. In his *Notes on Virginia* (Query XIV), Jefferson wrote:

> Misery is often the parent of the most affecting touches in poetry. Among the blacks is misery enough, God knows, but no poetry. Love is the particular oestrum of the poet. Their love is ardent, but it kindles the senses only, not the imagination. Religion, indeed, has produced a Phylis Whatley [sic]; but it could not produce a poet. The compositions published under her name are below the dignity of criticism. The heroes of the Dunciad are to her, as Hercules to the author of that poem. (2: 196)[2]

Jefferson regarded Wheatley as the worst product of a system of family slavery that culturally reprogrammed her so that in adulthood she willingly admitted that she had no memory of her African heritage other than the image of her mother pouring out water before the sun at its rising.[3] In restricting the range of her creativity to the realm of religion, Jefferson sought to contain her influence to that group of Anglo-American evangelicals— Whitefield and the Countess of Huntingdon—who, in Jefferson's view, co-opted any originality Wheatley might have had for "their enterprises of Christian benevolence and humanity" (Rawley 677). As Emory Elliott has explained, Wheatley was doubly afflicted since her main claim to originality besides her race and gender was her piety, and religion in general was greatly diminished as a force in the New Republic (37-45). Jefferson, with some satisfaction, could look upon those circumstances after the death of Wheatley's mistress—the decay of the Wheatley clan; the banishment of her booksellers Cox and Berry as royalist traitors; her marriage to the "improvident" and "shiftless gentleman" John Peters; her gnawing poverty and exile in Wilmington, Massachusetts; and her decline and death as a domestic in Boston's slums—as evidence that, though she was afforded an equal opportunity by liberal republican tendencies, she nevertheless fell victim to her corrupt origins.

Washington, on the other hand, celebrated Wheatley as an example of a culture feeding on consolidation. The volatility that Wheatley embodied was constructively redirected into channels of social growth. In a letter to his friend and military secretary, Colonel Joseph Reed, Washington recounts, "In searching over a parcel of papers the other day, in order to destroy such as were useless, I brought to light [a poem addressed to me by Mrs. or Miss Phillis Wheatley]; at first with a view of doing justice to her great poetical genius, I had a great mind to publish the poem, but not knowing whether it might not be considered rather as a mark of my own vanity than as a compliment to her, I laid it aside" (Reed 69). And later, displaying the maturity underlying the heroic image of our founding father, Washington wrote a letter directly to Wheatley that said:

> I thank you most sincerely for your polite notice of me, in the elegant lines you enclosed; and however undeserving I may be of such encomium and pane-

gyric, the style and manner exhibit a striking proof of your great poetical Talents. In honour of which, and as a tribute justly due to you, I would have published the Poem, had I not been apprehensive, that, while I only meant to give the World this new instance of your genius, I might have incurred the imputation Vanity. This and nothing else, determined me not to give it a place in the public Prints.

If you should ever come to Cambridge, or near Head Quarters, I shall be happy to see a person so favoured by the Muses, and to whom Nature has been so liberal and beneficent in her dispensations. (4: 360-61)

Between the responses of Jefferson and Washington lies the diffuse ideological terrain of personal liberty. Balancing, as she did, royalist and republican tendencies, African-American and mercantile self-interest, religious piety and evangelical ambition, Wheatley possessed a semiconcealed identity that consistently made her a valuable "currency" within an intracultural debate being waged with varying intensity by several parties. Though many are correct in claiming that Wheatley's value in mediating certain varieties of cultural respect represents a real and enduring power, I find the fact interesting because it implies a mechanism by which "minor" literature can be used to reterritorialize historical situations independently of prescriptive criticism about talent, tradition, individual reader-responses, and other awkward constructs.[4]

In describing the luxurious branching of an African-American woman's literary tradition stemming from Phillis Wheatley, Henry Louis Gates acknowledges that while she was "certainly the most reprinted and discussed poet in the tradition, [she] is also one of the least understood." In fixing Wheatley as "the most compelling example of a black woman's expanding consciousness in a racist Northern environment," Gates discovered that Wheatley's legacy, as transmitted through an extraordinary publication process, has produced an author who is a configuration of several, sometimes contradictory, personalities (11-12, 17).[5] The sense of Wheatley's reputation as the perplexing sum of her multiple social contacts (demonstrated repeatedly in the responses of her eighteenth-century readers) unites her literary efforts with the imaging of several distinct historical, theoretical, and literary possibilities in republican culture. The sequence of inquiries implied under the rubric "history of the book" (or reading) are highly effective in recovering these distinct possibilities. Larzer Ziff directs the attention of literary historians to the "pretexts" that explain the existence of books in the colonial and early national periods (6). Wheatley's poetry is one volume whose cultural work cannot be properly understood without a consideration of that pretext.

The work of contemporary Wheatley scholars continuously proves Foucault's claim that we "are in an epoch of juxtaposition, [an] epoch of the near and the far, of the side-by-side, of the dispersed . . . . our experience of the world is less that of a long life developing through time than that of a network that connects points and intersects with its own skein" (22). This description, drawn from our own times, also accurately describes Wheatley's immersion in late eighteenth-century Boston. "The words one reads on a printed page are the product of a complex process of transmission, reaching ultimately back to the author's mind," asserts G. Thomas Tanselle, and between the lines of Wheatley's reputation can be found the elements of a process affected by mechanical, social, and economic factors which gave her text its material embodiment (113). Understandably, scholars like John Shields and Houston Baker describe Wheatley primarily as the guiding agency of a rich African-American literary tradition originating in the early republic (Shields, Preface 28-29; Baker 6).[6] Other critics, interested in the feminist possibilities of her gender-specific negotiations with a paternalistic and vertically arranged society, view her work and life as offering an important genuine voice within a culture demanding her silent complicity.[7]

Typical of the blending of these two traditions in Wheatley scholarship is the commentary offered by John Shields in his notes to the Schomburg Library edition of Wheatley's collected works:

> Wheatley was the first black American author to publish a book . . . supported, both financially and intellectually, almost exclusively by other women. . . . With increasing frequency, Phillis Wheatley is justly being called the mother of black American literature. She may as well be considered the mother of American women writers; for, unlike those of her predecessor,

> Anne Bradstreet, whose poems were first seen
> through the press by male backers and exhorters,
> Wheatley's publication ventures were rendered possi-
> ble almost totally by the machinations of other
> women. (273)

Shields's comments make plain that Wheatley's literary identity
was profoundly dependent upon the several pretexts for her
writing. In the making of Wheatley's poetry, there can be no
meaning in the text without noticing its pretext; the woven fabric
of her poetry is made visible without a margin. *Texo* is Latin for
I weave—a text being words woven together even as textile is
cloth woven together—and *praetexo* means *I weave in front*, that is,
I weave a border. In this essay, I am less concerned with elaborat-
ing Wheatley's core identity—defined either as a newly liberated
servant attempting to profit from her entrance to a world of
equal opportunity (if not demonstrable social equality) or as an
artist struggling to nurse an infant muse—than I am with showing the ways in which Wheatley's 1773 publication venture
served to expose republican notions about personal liberty and
the diverse publishing objectives in the early republic. As Shields
underscores in the comment I cited above, one key to understanding Wheatley's impact on American culture is to focus on
the publication venture itself.

By addressing Wheatley's *Poems on Various Subjects* from
a "history of the book perspective" that is, as the combination of
several coordinated but distinct textual technologies, as a volume
which is a physical object, a sign system, the end product of
diverse arts and labors, and the starting point for intercultural
and intracultural communication—we may shed light on some of
the ways in which the printing of Wheatley's poems changed the
shape of early American culture. When I refer to eighteenth-century publishing practices, I am specifically addressing the basic
ensemble of relationships between capital, credit, and markets
and not, as might be the case in the nineteenth century, publishing as an artistic ideology. If one views Wheatley's volume of
poetry as a hybrid and divided cultural artifact isolating in one
space the competing and frictional combination of the interests
(both economic and political) framed by it, then it becomes possible to discover the ways in which Wheatley has been viewed as
a historically contingent figure. In turn, her scholarly appeal

depends upon the manifold ways she engaged those social processes informing republican print culture.[8] The crux of her engagement required the acceptance of a central entrepreneurial role, organizing and coordinating the trajectory of her own work within the socially imposed limits on her personal liberty.

As David Hall has repeatedly claimed, printing (and print culture) are best viewed as synonymous with information and consequently, books are a form of power to which some have greater access than others. Similarly, the ability to read and write and access the press itself are forms of empowerment that were unevenly available ("Report on the 1984 Conference" 111). By turning our attention toward those strategies that govern a text's cultural production and reception, we can remain sensitive to Wheatley's achievement while deepening our understanding of her situation in republican culture. Contemporary criticism, in its attempt to valorize Wheatley, has in many important respects sublimated this context in order to advance the presentist concerns of the critic.

With Wheatley's poetry, a republican readership in America tried to conceive itself in the work of an African female.[9] As a textual artifact, Wheatley's first volume of poetry "arranges" the aspects of republican culture. The text communicates by squarely implicating its author within the cultural forces that guided her production of a marketable text. Secondarily, in the advertising and reviews of the book, Wheatley's volume is used to represent the varieties of taste and responsibility expected of a cultivated readership. This reciprocity of author and reader, which is characteristic of Wheatley's verse, is rooted in the strategies of early American publishers who attempted to invent a native literature with the ability to exploit both old, familiar roles for readers, and new, potentially profitable ones.

I.

During the course of her career, Phillis Wheatley offered four proposals for book publishing. Two, which appeared in 1772 and 1779, were almost certainly written by Wheatley herself. Two other proposals, in 1784 and 1773, were probably written by others.[10] Wheatley's first proposal, for an "Octavo Volume" of "about 200 pages" to be published by Ezekiel Russell of Marlborough Street, appeared in the *Boston Censor* of 29 February, 14 March, and 11 April 1772. These four proposals exhibit two distinct trends. First, they show an author becoming increasingly aware of the marketplace. Wheatley's first proposals did not rely on overt patronage and claimed to present the work of a singular genius. By the time the 1779 proposal appeared, Wheatley sought the assistance of a great many "silent partners," and she understood that her own success depended on her direct affiliation with a bona fide celebrity like Ben Franklin. The fact that even with these calculations, Wheatley's poems did not meet with success should not be forgotten. Second, the proposals suggest that her reading public was progressively less interested in Wheatley's poetry as a form sensitive to definitive occasions of local history. Instead, the rhetoric of the 1779 proposal recognizes Wheatley as a minor figure whose creativity is notable because of the beneficence of her master's culture. More icon and less innate genius in this proposal, Wheatley saw her freedom within her culture as ambiguously defined, like the lives of those who read her work. Offering subscribers a glimpse at a curiosity, the later proposals engaged those grainy spaces in the imaginations of republican audiences much in the same way that the celebrated was equated with the fantastic at the profoundly heterotopic Peale's Museum in Philadelphia (1799).

In 1770, Ezekiel Russell published Wheatley's "Elegiac Poem." It was not a profound estimation of Wheatley's literary value that motivated this publication but rather the fact that Wheatley's exceptional youth and domestic station anticipated a great number of "curiosity sales." While his ventures into literature and political magazines formed a part of his early trade, Russell's works representing "legitimate concerns" never comprised a significant portion of his sales. More important to his profitability were his almanacs by authors like Benjamin West, Nathaniel Ames, Daniel George, and Abraham Weatherwise. Almanacs were important publications and it is quite likely that Russell derived most of his business from their sales. Those almanacs published by Benjamin West under the name Bickerstaff qualified as republican "best-sellers" since the astronomical data was considered accurate and many came adorned with illustrations. The popularity of the Bickerstaff almanacs attracted hordes of disreputable imitators and Russell was forced to suspend publication of them for a period of three years. Importantly, the Bickerstaff almanac for 1782 (the year in which Russell renewed publication of West's almanacs) carried a portrait of Phillis Wheatley on the cover indicating a subtle and important shift in Wheatley's public recognition and potential audience.

Assisted by his wife, Russell invented a logo consisting of a row of coffins and, at the height of his trade, Russell published in 1792 *A True and Particular Narrative of the Late Tremendous Tornado, or Hurricane* , decorated as Benjamin Franklin V tells us, "with no fewer than twenty coffins and nine exclamation marks on the title page" (441). Russell was therefore a purveyor of books with a strong popular demand and his trade was widely distributed—several of his publications advertise the fact that Russell would supply "Traveling Traders" at discount prices, "cheap by the quantity." While Russell appeared to have been interested in Wheatley's poems for their curious marketability, his enterprise seemed quite unlikely to be the mechanism by which Wheatley would launch the African-American women's literary tradition. While Benjamin Franklin V would allow that Russell's work reflected "certain eighteenth-century tastes," his main concern was for producing "interesting" but not "memorable" work that would ensure his own financial stability (Franklin 438-42). The failure of Wheatley's first proposal necessitated a second campaign involving English patrons and publishers.

Wheatley's volume, when it finally appeared in print in 1773, was the product of a transatlantic book trade financed, published, and marketed principally in England for English audiences. The transmission of Wheatley's poetry to New England was accomplished more by the exchange of personal correspondences than through direct commercial exportation. As the repeated failure of Boston-based publishing initiatives shows, the entrepreneurial incentives to publish Wheatley's poetry were exceedingly small. Consequently, the successful publication of Wheatley's poetry depended upon intricate personal and ideological alliances. When viewed in concert, the combined efforts of Wheatley's patrons amply illustrate Cathy Davidson's point, in *Revolution and the Word*, that beneath every text lies a variegated ideology: "An overt and covert cultural agenda, an ideological subtext, is encoded in the writing, publishing, reprinting, binding, titling, retitling, pictorializing, advertising, distributing, marketing, selling, buying, reading, interpreting, and, finally, the institutionalizing (within literary criticism and historiography) of any text" (7).

There are six principal figures responsible for the first publication of *Poems on Various Subjects*. The central American figure was Susanna Wheatley, the mistress whom Phillis Wheatley described as "my best friend" (Mason, Introduction 12-13). Susanna Wheatley was active in religious, humanitarian enterprises, and she maintained a wide correspondence with philanthropic persons in England. A deeply religious woman, Susanna Wheatley was profoundly influenced by the Great Awakening and George Whitefield. Along with Whitefield, Susanna shared an interest in Eleazar Wheelock's Indian Charity School (later to become Dartmouth College) and Samson Occom, a Native American preacher trained at the school who was an early advocate for the conditions of African-Americans and his fellow Native Americans. In 1748, Whitefield was appointed the domestic chaplain for the Countess of Huntingdon, who had used her wealth to found a seminary for the advancement of Calvinistic Methodism. Susanna Wheatley knew Whitefield and Occom; entertained members of Huntingdon's "connexion" in her home; and corresponded with the Countess and John Thornton, the English treasurer of the fund raised for the Indian Charity School.

On the English side, the Countess of Huntingdon's circle included Lord Dartmouth, a trustee of the fund dedicated to the Indian Charity School and, in 1772, the secretary of state for the colonies. Susanna Wheatley, acting in the capacity of an amanuensis, saw to it that Wheatley's proposed volume contained poems dedicated to each of the author's patrons.[11] A letter from Thomas Woolridge to Lord Dartmouth illustrates the degree to which Phillis Wheatley's reputation circulated among this group:

> While in Boston, I heard of a very extraordinary female slave, who had made some verses on our mutually deceased friend [Whitefield]: I visited her mistress, and found by conversing with this African, that she was no Impostor; I asked if she could write on any subject; she said yes; we had just heard of your lordship's appointment; I gave her your name, which she was well acquainted with. She immediately wrote a rough copy of the enclosed address and Letter, which I promised to convey and deliver. I was astonished and could hardly believe my own Eyes. I was present while she wrote, and can attest that it is her

own production; she shew'd me her letter to Lady Huntingdon, which I dare say, Your Lordship has seen; I send you an account signed by her master of her Importation, Education, &c. They are all wrote in her own hand. (Mason, "Letters and Proposals" 149n)

Susanna Wheatley's relationship with John Thornton, a London merchant who promoted such causes as the Society for the Propagation of the Gospel in Foreign Parts, the Clapham Sect of proto-abolitionists, and Wheelock's Indian School, led to his correspondence with Phillis Wheatley. Thornton was one of those who felt that Phillis Wheatley's vulnerable social position might make her into the tool of those who promoted her work. In a telling letter, Thornton writes, "Your present situation, and the kindness you meet with from many good people, and the respect that is paid to your uncommon genius, extort this friendly hint from me. I have no reason to charge you with any indiscretion of this kind, I mean only to apprise you of the danger I feared for you when you were here, lest the notice many took of you should prove to be a snare" (qtd. in Rawley 672). Following Wheatley's release from slavery, Thornton proposed that the writer return to Africa as the wife of either Bristol Yamma or John Quamine, African-American members of the Newport, Rhode Island congregation of Samuel Hopkins who had formulated a plan to return to Africa and proselytize. Phillis Wheatley, interestingly, deflected Thornton's proposal, writing "Upon my arrival how like a Barbarian shou'd I look to the natives; I can promise that my tongue shall be quiet, for a strong reason indeed, being an utter stranger to the Language of Anamaboe. Now to be serious, this undertaking appears to be hazardous, and not sufficiently eligible to go—and leave my British and American friends" (qtd. in Rawley 674).

Wheatley's second proposed publisher, Cox & Berry (and the one designated by Archibald Bell to receive subscriptions on his behalf), ran a more diversified business than Ezekiel Russell and maintained a decidedly royalist trade. The address of Cox & Berry, opposite Brattle Street Church and two doors above the British Coffee House, makes plain that the majority of their trade depended heavily on maintaining the standards of a thoroughly Anglicized culture. While little of substance is known about the extent of Cox & Berry's Boston business, the firm published a separate catalogue in 1772. The entire catalogue lists 1,148 titles so that Cox & Berry, while not very active as a publisher, nevertheless was an extremely credit-worthy enterprise well stocked with imported texts. Additionally, the range of their catalogue suggests that the bulk of Cox & Berry's business was conducted among members of the colonial gentry distinguished by wealth, family, and education.

About December 1772, a London printer, Archibald Bell at 8 Aldgate-Street, visited the Countess of Huntingdon with a manuscript brought to him by the master of the ship *London*, Captain Calef, who frequently carried correspondence between Susanna Wheatley and her English correspondents. Bell read the poems to the Countess, who found it hard to believe the works were genuine. Bell convinced the Countess of their originality by emphasizing Susanna Wheatley's connection and the Countess, taken with the idea of the volume being dedicated to her, asked to have an engraving of Phillis Wheatley as the book's frontispiece.

The Countess of Huntingdon saw Phillis Wheatley as an opportunity for the advancement of evangelical piety, and an American friend of the Countess, Richard Cary of Charlestown, underscored the appeal of the poetry for Huntingdon's circle. In a letter praising the writer as a "Christian Poetess, who continues in well doing," Cary wrote, "I hope she will continue an ornament to the Christian name and profession, as she grows older and has more experience, I doubt not her writings will run in a more Evangelicall Strain. I think your Ladyship will be pleas'd with her" (Mason, "Letters and Proposals" 186n). The Countess of Huntingdon viewed Wheatley principally as an opportunity to challenge the religious diminuendo of New England described by Richard Hofstadter as "conventional and formal . . . evident in a lack of interest in worship, a want of warm conviction" (220). The fact that Whitefield, the Countess's chaplain, showed little concern for the requirements either of consistent doctrine or of institutions tended to heighten Wheatley's own potent but vaguely defined piety.

It was during a visit to London in 1773 that Wheatley was given editorial access to the poems that had been in the printing process for some months before she arrived.[12] A letter of Israel Andrews, a Boston merchant, explains why the book, originally planned for publication in Boston, was to be published in London.

> In regard to Phillis's poems they will originate from a London press, as she was blam'd by her friends for print'g them here & made to expect a large emolument if she sent ye copy home, which induced her to remand it of ye printer & deliver in Capt. Calef who could not sell it by reason of their not crediting ye performance to be by a Negro, Since which she has had a paper drawn up & sign'd by the Gov. Council, Ministers & most of ye people of note in this place, certifying the authenticity of it, which paper Capt. Calef carried last fall, therefore we may expect it in print by the Spring ships, it is supos'd the copy will sell for £100 Sterl'g. (Israel Andrews to William Burrell, 24 February 1773)

Andrews's letter clarifies some important details about the publication of the *Poems*. Though Boston was initially considered as the place of publication, the prospect of larger financial rewards dictated that the book be published in London, where diversified dealers like Bell combined many of the roles we now associate with both publishing and wholesaling. Archibald Bell owned fractions of copyright on Wheatley's book and also presumably kept extensive stock. Bell acted in the capacity of wholesaler to Cox & Berry, who acted in turn as a distribution point to other port cities like New York and Philadelphia.

Stating that Calef was unsuccessful in trying to sell the volume without an attestation regarding its authenticity well before Bell's interview with the Countess, Andrews's letter tends to prove that Wheatley's manuscript was stale on arrival. The letter shows that while Archibald Bell agreed to publish the book, he was not a major exporter of such books to the colonies. Too risky a venture for the major "insider" firms like Dilly, Longman, Rivington,[13] Wheatley's book found a home with a secondary figure in the English book trade. The fact that Bell was not a large-scale businessman engaged in exploiting a peripheral market no doubt made the securing of credit from the Countess of Huntingdon and the promise of a fixed return vital preconditions for publication. In a letter a year later, Andrews, himself a shrewd businessman, claims that the volume of poems that was eventually published shortly after Wheatley's departure from England was a compromised edition for which further sales were anticipated. In a surprising comment, Andrews suggests that Wheatley herself may have manipulated the publication process so as to secure for herself potential future income as a freed slave. "After so long a time, have at last got Phillis's poems in print, which will be [delivered] you by Capt Dunn, in a brig Ben has the care of, these don't seem to be near all her productions, she's an artful jade, I believe, & intends to have ye benefit of another volume" (Israel Andrews to William Burrell, 28 January 1774).

Even as she was an icon of experimental republican values, Wheatley was forced to become her own entrepreneur in response to a lukewarm and confusing business climate. In what remained a relatively unspecialized trade, Wheatley concentrated on arranging for the coordination of production and commercial activities and the securing of the credit necessary to bring her book to the public. Anticipating in many respects the operation of vanity presses in our own day, she held a professional literary status always qualified by her necessary participation in the book trade.[14]

Wheatley's book was marketed principally as a literature for "extensive" reading and sold principally in urban port cities (most notably Boston) that dominated long-distance communications.[15] The precise cultural character of communications and commerce in Northern Ports is important for understanding the reception of Wheatley's work. The Wheatleys were among that group described by David Hall as "beginning to withdraw from [the] common world into a new gentility. The coming of gentlemen's libraries, together with dancing assemblies, the tea ceremony, and the theater, were steps in the making of a cosmopolitan alternative to the culture of traditional literacy" ("The Uses of Literacy in New England" 45). Wheatley's *Poems on Various Subjects* was originally intended to circulate in this world, and so it was important to the Countess of Huntingdon that the book contain a fine engraving. The engraving was only the most obvious example of a textual feature designed to convince purchasers that Wheatley's poems were more than a "book"; these poems were "literature." *Poems on Various Subjects* was intended for a fashion-minded clientele prepared to buy the book on "impulse."

Silent reading, as Roger Chartier says, permits a free and secretive intercourse with the written word.[16] However,

Wheatley's text was, from its very inception, designed to highlight the differential uses possible for the same book. Because the
volume so evenly split the opinions of readers like Jefferson and
Washington, Wheatley's poetry uncovers the central contradiction inherent in any history of reading. The history of reading,
Chartier points out,

> is informed by an apparent contradiction: either it
> affirms the total control of the text in its power to con-
> strain the reader (but then reading can no longer be
> considered an autonomous practice, and its variations
> lose their significance) or else it postulates the reader's
> liberty to produce his own unique sense beyond the
> text itself. . . . It seeks to identify for each period and
> each milieu the shared modes of reading that the
> model individual gestures, and it places the processes
> by which a reader or group of readers produce their
> own meaning of a text at the center of its interroga-
> tion. The construction of meaning, which varies his-
> torically and socially, is thus understood to be at the
> intersection of, on the one hand, the particularities of
> readers endowed with specific competencies, identi-
> fied by their social position and their cultural disposi-
> tions (as characterized by their practice of reading),
> and, on the other hand, the textual and physical forms
> of those texts appropriated by reading. (18-19)

Consequently, those who wish to teach Wheatley's poetry must read her text as being embedded in and interpenetrating
many other discourses in the early Republic. Wheatley's own
poetry attempts incompletely to control the centrifugal forces of
loyalist and republican politics, African-American and democratic notions of individuality, and masculine and feminine modes
of expression. Her poetry demands that readers attend to issues
of authorship, the permeability of writing to its controlling context, and the various "extensions" coded in the mixture of events
and meanings.

    In an effort to overcome the limited market for Wheatley's
work, Cox & Berry followed a commonly accepted distribution
practice of exchanging book lists with other publishers. This early
form of what, in the nineteenth century, was called "courtesy of the
trade" gave rise to a standard set of procedures that regulated the
rights of publishers to reprint in America the uncopyrighted works

of foreign authors (Winship 155-56). English publishers relied heavily on this convention as their book sales in America were frequently seen as the exploitation of a peripheral market not worth intense efforts at controlling distribution or satisfying customer demands that were hard to determine in the first place. As Wheatley was quick to point out in her 1773 letter to Colonel David Wooster of New Haven, "courtesy of the trade" worked to the decided disadvantage of those who create literary materials. The cover of the Bickerstaff almanac, while it signals a shift in the size and composition of Wheatley's audience, was probably an "unlicensed" use of material from the edition published by Archibald Bell. In an effort to counter "courtesy of the trade," Wheatley relates "if any should be so ungenerous as to reprint them the Genuine copy may be known, for it is sign'd in my own handwriting" (Isani 256-59). Wheatley's letter to Wooster is interesting because it indicates a sea change in printing ideology, according to which varieties of printing (signed originals versus reprints, for example) were perceived and used and played an active role in the constitution of power. The self-image of publishing as an enterprise exerted powerful inhibitions and encouragements for Wheatley (Winship 164-65). These forces were, in turn, related to general New England mercantile ideology and the specifically political context of Boston publishing. The rise of merchants to social, economic, political, and intellectual leadership in the last quarter of the eighteenth century did not place the Wheatley family in a position of secure and stable pre-eminence. Merchants like the Wheatleys faced more than the external challenges to their achievement of pre-eminence. They also needed an answer to a set of internal challenges. Peter Hall describes the internal challenges faced by the Wheatleys and others of their class as going

> beyond the need to elaborate on older forms of partnership to broaden the capital and manpower bases of business. They went beyond the need to expand patterns of human alliances through partnership and marriage. They even went beyond the use of the corporation as a legal device. [These challenges] posed a fundamental question about the relation between family, capital, and accountability. (69)

The Wheatleys' patronage of Phillis Wheatley was a key part of their strategic anticipation of a post-revolutionary commerce. And Phillis Wheatley's acquisition of her freedom was a direct consequence of John Wheatley's need to separate his private and public commitments. Participating in a pattern that increased steadily from the 1760s to the 1780s, the Wheatleys increased their direct involvement in charitable benevolence in an effort to diversify their public image through character-forming involvements that separated their "diffuse and particular private interests from their specialized and more formally institutionalized public ones" (Peter Hall 70). Like many of his friends, John Wheatley was caught at an inopportune moment by the revolution, and before the Wheatleys had adequately composed a set of answers to their internal challenges, he was forced to remove to Chelsea, and he died in 1787. His son had become a permanent resident of London the same year Wheatley's verse was published.

Many scholars have erroneously overemphasized the role played by newspapers in the advertising and marketing of Wheatley's volume.[17] The commercial and communications network of Wheatley's Boston depended overwhelmingly on the speed and privacy of face-to-face communication. Because of the size and complexity of the Boston community, the channels Wheatley's volume took (especially at the time of first publication) were highly specialized by class, neighborhood, and activity of the reader.[18] While valuable for genteel entertainment and reference, newspapers were considered by most to contain stale news, details, and irrelevant commercial notices that, in a much smaller community, would have traveled more efficiently by word of mouth (Brown 128). While it is true that Northern ports were information "hothouses" containing a dense variety of occasions for exchanging information and enriching the public at large, Wheatley sensed that her work operated primarily in a more insulated sphere, and she seems to have anticipated a specialized market characterized more by private enclaves than by public declarations.

II.

To this point, I have been describing the publishing networks through which Wheatley's poetry passed; it remains to be said what social consequences *Poems on Various Subjects* exerted upon the culture that received it. Naturally, the investigation has two possible forms: the consideration of individual readers or communities of readers as sites for cultural reception or the cultural definition of the individual author. Because of the scope of this essay, I will focus on Wheatley and the ways in which her authorship was formulated as a result of republican publishing objectives.

The status of authorship was a decidedly contradictory affair in 1773. On the one hand, authorship was seen as embodying legitimate power to influence cultural tastes and ideology. On the other, it was the task of an efficient republicanism to take legitimacy in cultural affairs out of the hands of persons. The central paradox of republican government was its need to adhere to a principle of liberty that was, in practice, impossible to fix. Historians familiar with American culture in the last half of the eighteenth-century are well aware of the absence of a conceptual framework that adequately explains the complex mingling of traditional and modern attitudes and behavior patterns which characterize the era. One has only to remember the activities of Phillis Wheatley's masters who, in purchasing and boarding and eventually freeing an indentured servant, satisfied their complex desire to be seen as the natural embodiment of affluence and superiority and of beneficent kindness in colonial society.

The efforts of the Wheatleys to balance a liberal concept of possessive individualism with civic humanism was mirrored by many of their contemporaries. However, in the years following the revolution, the displacement of persons such as the Wheatleys from positions of social stature was a consequence of political life assuming the characteristics of the economic marketplace. As Robert Shalhope warns, the attempt to separate out the individual threads of liberalism and republicanism is a distorting trait of recent scholars that ought to be abandoned since "Americans living in the eighteenth century could, quite unselfconsciously, believe simultaneously in the promotion of their own individual socioeconomic and political prospects, as well as in the distinct possibility that their liberty might be endangered by the corrupt forces of power within their governments" (xii). The presence of an African-American writer among the Boston literati implied an end to the idea that the principal activity of management was directed towards the control of the individual. Wheatley's *Poems* marked one boundary of a larger extradiscursive transformation in American society.

In the case of Wheatley's book, the ideological contradiction between liberalism and publishing is brought forward in the prefatory material—the title-page, the engraving, the dedication to the Countess of Huntingdon, the standard protesting preface arguing that the poems are written originally for the "amusement of the author" in her "leisure moments," the letter of John Wheatley to the publisher, and the attestation of authenticity signed by eighteen prominent male citizens. Two of these items bear special consideration. The engraving and the attestation have long been singled out as important loci for Wheatley's definition as author of her own poetry. "The attestation is one of the oddest oral examinations on record . . . an event unique in the history of literature," and the portrait is "a singular and almost revolutionary signature on the scroll of American history" (Gates 7,10). They contextualize the author's literary life as the object of cultural design. The engraving was so crucial to the marketing and reception of the book that it was offered for separate sale (Mason, "A Note on the Text" 38). The very image rendered in the portrait of Wheatley—that of a contemplative African-American female secure in both finances and intellect in the act of composing—is calculated to juxtapose the specific practices of New England print culture with shifting contexts of political discourse. That Wheatley was probably used as a tool of political containment by her white friends was not lost on the black English writer Ignatius Sancho, who reacted more to the attestation in Wheatley's volume than to the poetry itself:

> Phillis's poems do credit to nature—and put art—
> merely as art—to the blush.—It reflects nothing
> either to the glory or generosity of her master—if
> she is still his slave—except he glories in the low
> vanity of having in his wanton power a mind ani-
> mated by Heaven—a genius superior to himself. The
> list of splendid, titled, learned names, in confirmation
> of her being the real authoress, alas! shows how very
> poor the acquisition of wealth and knowledge are—
> without generosity—feeling—and humanity. These
> good great folks all knew—and perhaps admired—
> nay praised Genius in bondage—and then, like the
> Priests and the Levites in sacred writ, passed by—
> not one good Samaritan amongst them. (Crew 175-
> 176)

The clear message to readers of Wheatley's volume was that the governmentality of New England culture was marked by a critical shift in the arena of power from town meetings and market street conversations to a public realm constituted in writing and print. The portrait's framing of an African-American writer and a bound (but undifferentiated) volume signaled that the accidental substance of bound-over bodies and books was infused with the plenary meanings of spirituality and texts. This use of textual technology effectively sought to transform the contents of Wheatley's book into "literature" and to define Wheatley as a profoundly heterotopic personality.

The printing considerations that brought Wheatley's poetry to the public's attention also gave a shape to her life and career. As the trajectory of her career after her freedom attests, the print ideology Wheatley negotiated presumed a blending of the contradictory impulses to be self-repudiating and self-validating. The intense desire Wheatley held for publication ensured that she would become a focal point for the juxtaposition of several coded elements of republican thinking that, superficially at least, seemed incompatible with each other. The portrait placed at the beginning of *Poems on Various Subjects* represents the exchanging of one Wheatley identity with another. The "genuineness" of Wheatley the poet, eloquently argued by Sancho, becomes indistinguishable from the "genuineness" of the Bickerstaff almanac.

Throughout this essay, I have been discussing a purely textual feature, but the heterotopic personality I have described can also be explained in the manner in which republicanism epitomized the concept of personal liberty. In its fully articulated form, republican political theory assumes that the government of individuals requires the activity and freedom of the governed. The citizens of the republic, in acting and aligning themselves with needs and opportunities made possible by their society, will exercise their particular will in accordance with the ends imposed upon them by the culture. Phillis Wheatley exchanged a legalistic captivity for a commercial one.

Because Wheatley's work illustrates so clearly the influence of patronage, the economics of the transatlantic book trade, and the desire to construct a sufficient and sympathetic readership, the actual end the book accomplishes is dependent upon the constraints and facilitating choices of each aspect of the book's printing. When we make this argument, the question becomes: What conception of individual liberty is possible and necessary when Wheatley's work has been targeted by a printing venture whose objective is simultaneously to augment and to secure the reputation of the state and the success of its subjects? Firmly linked to the unstable and mercantilist gentry who clustered on Boston's King Street, Wheatley probably constructed a vision of her social situation according to vertical lines of dependency in much the same way Condorcet summarily described the means by which governmentality targets the individual:

> How, in this astonishing variety of labors and products, of needs and resources; in this alarming complication of interests, which connects the subsistence and well-being of an isolated individual with the whole system of society; which makes him dependent upon all the accidents of nature and every political event; which extends in a way to the entirety of his capacity to experience either enjoyment or privation; how, in this apparent chaos, do we nonetheless see . . . the common interest requiring that each should be able to understand their own interest and freely pursue it?
>
> (Condorcet 209)

Foucault characterizes the situation described by Condorcet as I have done, by explaining that the relationship of the individual to a social governmentality is, in the final analysis, a "local situation where the author is fixed in a doubly involuntary world of dependence and productivity" (qtd. in Burchell 133). Wheatley's power in her own culture (and perhaps ours) is generated by her reliance on an extrinsic network of patronage, profit, and literacy, as well as an intrinsic (and perhaps romantic) conceit of "genius," inspiration, or gifted talent. Roger Chartier views the tendency I have just described as the essence of popular reading:

> This popular reading requires explicit and repeated signs, numerous titles and headings, frequent summaries and images. It is only at ease with brief, complete sequences, seems to require only minimal coherence, and proceeds by the association of textual unities (chapters, fragments, paragraphs), which are themselves disconnected. Discontinuous, approximate, hesitant: this way of reading guides editorial strategies in giving form to the printed objects offered

> to the largest numbers, and guides the work of adaptation. . . . This other manner of reading also defines a specific relationship to print culture, a specific mode of comprehension that creates a cultural frontier based on the varying uses made by different classes of readers of the same texts rather than on the unequal distribution of texts in society. (30)

Our own culture shares with Wheatley's contemporaries a need to reconstitute the works of others in ways that reinforce our own social and cultural positions. Consequently, Wheatley's reputation is celebrated today because she enables our own secondary readings of what personal liberty means in the context of debates about political correctness and canonicity. Paradoxically, our "scholarly" editions with their extensive glosses, summaries, and indices provide a reconstituted reading at variance with the reading of the proper virtuosi of Wheatley's original volume. Only by completing the "arc" of our understanding with the knowledge of Wheatley's historically situated audience can we hope to reconnect the discourse of the text with the authority of her contexts.

The doubled world of dependence and productivity was clearly manifested in concrete social rituals. William Piersen comments on the fact that Wheatley, when offered a distinguishing seat at the homes of important whites, repeatedly requested that she be seated at a separate side table. Piersen locates in Wheatley's behavior the locus of a complex and contradictory fabric in the relations between Yankee whites and blacks "interweaving formal expectations of social roles with coarser strands of racial prejudice and finer strands of human affection" (31-32). Wheatley's power, textual or otherwise, exists by contrivance and artifice. Wheatley's ambition as a writer of belletristic poetry was not so much provided for by the republican culture of New England as it was directed within a calculated and contingent combinatory scheme dedicated to the convergence of private initiative and public advantage.

Acting invisibly, print ideology circulates around an "invisible center" designating the local conditions of Wheatley's art.[19] Regardless of whether we celebrate Wheatley ultimately as a marginal, revolutionary, or conservative representative of literary tradition, her publication objectives converge with others' only on the condition that her exercise of personal liberty escapes her personal knowledge and will.[20] In fact, the very stability of New England culture depended upon Wheatley's simultaneous inclusion and exclusion from the activities of republican polity because "entrepreneurial impulses [had] helped transform American society from one in which men and women assumed a fixed place . . . to a fluid one where individuals employed their property and wealth" within a liberal environment favoring "the clever, the artful, the ambitious, and the capable—those most skilled in the newly emerging world of market relations" (Shalhope 124-25). Significantly, Wheatley and her growing circle of marginal acquaintances insisting on power—persons like Samson Occom, a Mohegan Indian and Presbyterian minister; Obour Tanner, a fellow-slave and communicant in Samuel Hopkins's church engaged in efforts to recolonize Africa, and John Peters, who attempted to break into the retail trade shortly after his marriage to Wheatley as a purveyor of "Spirituous Liquors," began to challenge seriously the organization and continuity of the "invisible center" from which the Wheatley family profited.

In her description of the cultural function of early American novels in *Revolution and the Word*, Cathy Davidson argues the potency of "minor" texts when she claims that "literature is both an artificially framed world with an organized structure governing its interpretation and a part of a larger structure determined by economic, institutional, and ideological forces that govern its composition, its publication, its circulation, its reading, and the end—canonization or obscurity—to which it is read" (260). While the analysis I have made here goes a long way towards establishing a resonance between Wheatley's text and context, it does not preclude the fact that her poetry may have taken an intimate and possibly subversive shape in the minds of individual readers.

More important, however, is the realization that historical forces in 1773 demanded that Wheatley's poetry happen in the way it did because Boston was one significant place in American society where the issue of freedom and personal liberty was fundamentally unresolved. Wheatley's work, as briefly considered in Jefferson's and Washington's reader responses, bridged the interstices between public rhetoric and private expression and invited "forays into alternative possibilities of meaning where readers might not willingly venture on their own" (Davidson 260). Her poetry, whatever its literary merit might be for us, was a profoundly thick piece of propaganda in the eighteenth century whose range and power fundamentally depends on the historically governed context of book production and reception.

In grounding Wheatley's importance in terms of the specifics of publication, one is able to see the significance of a canonical work as both a literary achievement and as an important moment in the history of the book in America. Wheatley's sense of history was, first and foremost, intended to create in her audiences a profound sense of the "constructedness" inherent in self and society. After the publication of Wheatley's poetry, her view took on a new force and importance as a number of New England writers sought to anchor their examinations of liberal democracy in the "authenticity" of their writing. These writers knew, as Jefferson did, that histories were written less to glorify God than to transform an audience's conception of their social world. Wheatley revised the project of Revolution in terms of her own humanity. She did so for two reasons: to accommodate radical cultural, social, political, and religious change and to alter her readers' conception of the meaning of Republicanism, directing them to act and think and see in such a way that their reconstructed vision of America's critical mission would, through the audience's reception of the text, duplicate many of the insights Wheatley herself held to be essential to the expression of progressive government.

The markers of social disruption evinced in the several editions of the *Poems* are signs that are, according to Voloshinov, "multiaccentual":

> The social *multiaccentuality* of the ideological sign is a very crucial aspect [of an arena for class struggle] . . . the very same thing that makes the ideological sign vital and mutable is also, that which makes it a refracting and distorting medium. . . . In actual fact, each ideological sign has two faces, like Janus. Any current curse word can become a word of praise, any current truth must inevitably sound to many other people as the greatest lie. This inner dialectic quality of the sign comes out fully in the open only in times of social crises or revolutionary changes. (23)

If Wheatley's experience as an African-American immersed in debates about the limits of liberty functioned in some capacity as a master-text controlling and organizing her selection of poems, she was able to incorporate political accents into narrative centers, keywords, and plot formulae that foreground places of active meaning-struggle. The presence of these accents (which is especially pronounced in her shifting dedications) argues that we see her choices not as one-to-one correspondences between personages and thematic arguments but rather as the means by which Wheatley attempted to manage the legacy of patronage in deciding her literary success. In the eighteenth-century context, her task of management was an entrepreneurial exercise that extended to issues of publication and preservation, the reform of reading habits, and the act of reading itself.

Phillis Wheatley's *Poems on Various Subjects* is a fine exercise in pedagogical hermeneutics. Wheatley's republican text, because it makes plain the transformation of the literary figure into an agent of socialization, has infinite usefulness in the literature classroom. Since *Poems on Various Subjects* focusses and enforces our attention on the various cultural antinomies surrounding authorship in the republican era, Wheatley's work is a meetingplace for critical dissidents in my literature classes. Using the history of the book (or, more properly, the history of reading), I ask my students to understand both the nature of republican publishing ideology and some of the more important cultural correlates gestured in Wheatley's *Poems*. New Historicism is a necessary tool of such inquiry because the volume's publishing history reveals the inescapably "American" conclusion that culture, nature, and the self are granted power only by the limitations and accidents of history. Wheatley's text is complex enough that it requires two separate discussions. The first discussion concerns the fact that partial and personal interpretations of Wheatley polarize into symbolic oppositions, like liberty and equality, freedom and concealment, identity and politics. The symbolic polarities are never a source for oppositional conflict, but they are a dramatic revelation that, in the republican era, fragmentation is a necessary consequence of consensus. The second discussion concerns the issue of "ownership" of the poetry and republican notions of individual liberty.

In my teaching, I try to implement an "arc" from practice to theory and back. When teaching literature, I ask students to engage those fundamental, constituent processes and activities that underlie an academic appreciation of Phillis Wheatley: close readings of the work itself and a consideration of the several forms of the book itself. In order to understand both the unusual accomplishment of an African-American poetess and the variety of voices within individual poems, the class is moved to consider the underlying conceptual schemes controlling the expression of art in the early republic. Of necessity, my teaching and the students' range of inquiry become highly interdisciplinary as we draw from basic research in history, sociology, and anthropology. Ultimately, critical theories are brought into a more comprehensive network of meaning of both the text and context surrounding Wheatley's literary legacy. At this point, it is often the case that students are able to see that many of the theoretical frameworks themselves have effected radical changes in the ways literary history is practiced.

The text and context of *Poems on Various Subjects* are fully reciprocal concepts that were culturally imaged not at the level of symbolism but in the governmentality of the printing trade. Given the tactics of her culture affording her equality of opportunity but not equality of social or economic conditions, Wheatley was allowed to negotiate her publication and freedom. Wheatley's claim to the Countess of Huntingdon that the "Tongues of the learned are insufficient" presumes her involvement with an ideology construed as a network of complex reciprocities between social construction and textual creation (Mason, "Letters and Proposals" 149n).[21] In coining this deceptively simple phrase, Wheatley manages to situate herself favorably in the eyes of those reader's who wanted a glimpse of her simple piety and her ideological engagement with republican governmentality. Whatever else may be said of Wheatley's persistently ambiguous status within her culture, we should appreciate her trope of "insufficient tongues" as a commentary on cultural and authorial anxieties brought about by the local circumstances of republican publishing.

Appendix 1

Phillis Wheatley's Proposal, *Boston Censor*
Saturday, 29 February 1772[22]

PROPOSALS
For Printing By Subscription,

A Collection of POEMS, wrote at several times, and upon various occasions, by PHILLIS, a Negro Girl, from the strength of her own Genius, it being but a few Years since she came to this Town an uncultivated Barbarian from *Africa.* The Poems having been seen and read by the best judges, who think them well worthy of the Publick View; and upon critical examination, they find that the declared Author was capable of writing them. The Order in which they were penned, together with the Occasion, are as follows;

On the Death of the Rev. Dr. *Sewell,* when sick, 1765—On Virtue, 166 [sic]—On two Friends, who were cast away, do. To the University of Cambridge, 1767.—An Address to the Atheist, do.—An Address to the Deist, do.—On America, 1768—On the King, do.—On Friendship, do.—Thoughts on being brought from Africa to America, do.—On the Nuptials of Mr. *Spence* to Miss *Hooper,* do.—On the Hon. Commodore Hood, on his pardoning a Deserter, 1769.—On the Death of the Reverend Dr. *Sewell,* do.—On the Death of Master *Seider,* who was killed by *Ebenezer Richardson,* 1770.—On the Death of the Rev. *George Whitefield,* do.—On the Death of a young Miss, aged 5 years, do. On the Arrival of Ships of War, and landing of the Troops.—On the Affray in King-Street, on the Evening of the 5th of March.—On the death of a young Gentleman.—To Samuel Quincy, Esq; a Panegyrick.—To a Lady on her coming to America for her Health.—To Mrs. *Leonard,* on the Death of her Husband.—To Mrs. Boylston and Children, on the Death of her Son and their Brother.—To a Gentleman and Lady on the Death of their Son, aged 9 Months.—To a Lady on her remarkable Deliverance in a Hurricane.—To *James Sullivan,* Esq; and Lady on the Death of Her Brother and Sister, and a Child *Avis,* aged 12 Months.—*Goliah* [sic] of Gath.—On the Death of Dr. *Samuel* Marshall.

It is supposed they will make one small Octavo Volume, and

will contain about 200 Pages.

They will be printed on Demy Paper, and beautiful Types.
The Price to Subscribers, handsomely bound and lettered, will be Four Shillings.—Stitched in Blue, Three Shillings.

It is hoped Encouragement will be given to this Publication, as a reward to a very uncommon genius, at present a Slave.

This Work will be put to the Press as soon as three Hundred Copies are subscribed for, and and [sic] shall be published with all Speed.

Subscriptions are taken in by E. Russell, in Marlborough Street.

Appendix 2

Phillis Wheatley's Proposal, *Massachusetts Gazette and the Boston News-Letter*
Friday, 16 April 1773[23]

PROPOSALS
For Printing in *London* By SUBSCRIPTION,
A Volume of POEMS,
Dedicated by Permission to the Right Hon. the
Countess of Huntingdon.
Written by PHILLIS,
A Negro Servant to Mr. Wheatley of *Boston*
in New-England.
Terms of Subscription.

I. The Book to be neatly printed in 12 mo. on a new
Type and a fine Paper, adorned with an elegant
Frontispiece, representing the Author.
II. That the Price to Subscribers shall be Two Shillings
Sewed or Two Shillings and Six-pence neatly bound.
II. [sic] That every Subscriber deposit One Shilling at the
Time of Subscribing; and the remainder to be paid
on the Delivery of the Book.

Subscriptions are received by Cox & Berry,
in *Boston.*

Appendix 3

Phillis Wheatley's Proposal, *Boston Evening Post; and the General Advertiser*
Saturday, 30 October 1779[24]

PROPOSALS,
FOR PRINTING,
BY SUBSCRIPTION
A VOLUME OF POEMS
AND LETTERS,
ON VARIOUS SUBJECTS,
Dedicated to the Right Honorable,
BENJAMIN FRANKLIN, Esq;
One of the Ambassadors of the United States, at
the Court of France, By PHILLIS PETERS.

POEMS.
Thoughts on the Times.
On the Capture of General Lee, to I. B. Esq;
To his Excellency General Washington.
On the death of General Wooster.
An Address to Dr.—— ——
To Lt. R—— of the Royal Navy.
To the same.
To T. M. Esq; of Granada.
To Sophia of South Carolina.
To Mr. A. M'B—— of the Navy
To Lt. R—— D—— of the Navy.
Ocean.
The choice and advantages of a Friend to Mr. T. M.
Farewell to England. 1773.
To Mrs. W——ms on Anna Eliza.
To Mr. A. McB——d.
Epithalamium to Mrs. H—— ——.
To P. N. S. and Lady on the death of their infant son.
To Mr. El——, on the death of his Lady.
On the death of Lt. L——ds.
To Penelope.
To Mr. & Mrs. L—— on the death of their daughter
A Complaint.

To Mr. A.I.M. on Virtue.

To Dr. L——d and Lady on the death of their son aged 5 years.

To Mr. L——g on the death of his son.

To Capt F——: on the death of his granddaughter.

To Philandra an Elegy.

Niagara.

Chloe to Calliope.

To Musidora on Florello.

To Sir E. L——. Esq.

To the Hon. John Montague Esq; Rear Admiral
of the Blue.

LETTERS

1 To the Right Honorable William E. of Dartmouth Secretary of
State for N. America.

2 To the Rev. Mr. T. P. Farmington.

3 To Mr. T. W.——Dartmouth College.

4 To the Hon. T. H. Esq;

5 To Dr. B. Rush, Philadelphia.

6 To the Rev. Dr. Thomas, London.

7 To the Rt. Honorable the Countess of H——.

8 To I. M——Esq; London.

9 To Mrs. W——e in the County of Surry.

10 To Mr. T. M. Homerton, near London.

11 To Mrs. S.W——.

12 To the Rt. Hon. the Countess of H——.

13 To the Same.

Messieurs PRINTERS,

The above collection of Poems and Letters was put into my hands by the desire of the ingenious author in order to be introduced to public View.

The subjects are various and curious, and the author a *Female African*, whose lot it was to fall into the hands of a *generous* master and *great* benefactor. The learned and ingenious as well as those who are pleased with novelty, are invited to encourage the publication, by a generous subscription—the former, that they may fan the sacred fire which, is self enkindled in the breast of this *young* African—The ingenious that they may by reading this collection, have a large play for their imaginations, and be

ex[c]ited to please and benefit mankind, by some brilliant production of their own pens—Those who are always in search of
some *new* thing, that they may obtain a sight of this *rara avis in
terra*—And every one, that the ingenious author may be encouraged to improve her own mind, benefit and please mankind.

CONDITIONS.
They will be printed on good paper and a neat Type; and will
Contain about 300 pages in Octavo.
The price to Subscribers will be *Twelve Pounds*, neatly Bound
and Lettered, and *Nine Pounds* sew'd in blue paper, one half to be
paid on Subscribing, the other Half, on Delivery of the Books.
The Work will be put to the Press as soon as a sufficient
Number of Encouragers offer.
Those who subscribe for Six, will have a Seventh Gratis.
Subscriptions are taken by White and Adams, the Publishers,
in School Street, *Boston.*

Appendix 4

Phillis Wheatley's Proposal, *Boston Magazine*
September 1784[25]

The Poem, in page 488, of this Number, was selected from a manuscript Volume of Poems, written by PHILLIS PETERS, formerly
Phillis Wheatly [sic]—and is inserted as a Specimen of her Work:
should this gain the Approbation of the Publick, and sufficient
encouragement be given, a Volume will be shortly Published, by
the Printers hereof [Greenleaf and Freeman], who receive subscriptions for said Work.

NOTES

[1]For contemporaneous reviews, see *London Magazine: Or Gentleman's Monthly Intelligencer* September 1773: 456; *Monthly Review* (London) December 1773: 457-59.

[2]Jefferson's allusion to *The Dunciad* is an incisive reference because it cuts to the bone of republican uneasiness about the work of Phillis Wheatley. Pope's famous poem indicated that printing was a scourge to the learned and that the frequency with which new authors had gained access to the press was ushering in an "age of lead." In a supreme example of parody, Pope's variorum edition of 1735 used annotation as a burlesque of eighteenth-century printing, and his copious classical references were meant to criticize the gimmicks of marketing, the undue influence of patrons, the ignorance of his readers, and the commodification of taste, which he attributed to his age. Jefferson's reference brings these criticisms to bear on America, where the ascendancy of a print culture producing Phillis Wheatley threatens to displace the "purity" of some forms of literature by the promotion of works that suffuse poetry with additional meanings and directions. Jefferson's comment is a satiric response to his culture's celebration of an elaborately technologized text that presumes a great deal of readerly engagement.

[3]See Piersen 27 and 147-50. Even this fact, however, is a striking example of how Wheatley commonly turned what appears to be a limitation into a multivalenced appreciation of cultural tradition and her involvement in it. While on the one hand, the sun image is identified as a residual remnant of Lucumi Yoruba culture in the New World, it also links Wheatley to the Puritan cosmology of Mather Byles, one of those who attested to Wheatley's originality and, according to John Shields, stood foremost in Wheatley's literary relationships. The simple image, then, is capable of framing a profound inversion in literary authority and the genuineness of colonial tradition. See Shields, "Phillis Wheatley and Mather Byles: A Study in Literary Relationship."

[4]To see the ways in which the concept of literary "reterritorializations" assist and even become the precondition of revolutionary expressions of resistance, assertion, and development, see Deleuze and Guattari 60-61.

[5]For a fairly complete assessment of Wheatley and her poetry according to this "standard" view, see Albertha Sistrunk and

Benjamin Brawley.

⁶Houston Baker cites Wheatley as evidence refuting the notion that all African-Americans as far back as the eighteenth century perpetually spent their days in gross manual labor and their nights shuffling to the sound of exotic banjos (6).

⁷See works by Baym, Herrnstein Smith, Jameson, Kolodny, Lauter, Tompkins, and Wald.

⁸As William Charvat and others have argued, print culture is not a dyadic model constituted by producers and consumers; rather it is a combination of writers and readers who act upon the book trade and the publishers, printers, and booksellers who interpret and transmute the received influence of artists and audiences. See Charvat 74-75.

⁹As Michael Schudson notes, poetry and news stories both "reproduce" the real world by imaging themselves against the mental worlds of their readers:

> A news story is an account of the "real world," just as a rumor is another kind of account of the real world, and a historical novel is another sort of account of the real world. It is not reality itself (as if any sequence of words and sentences could be) but a transcription, and any transcription is a transformation, a simplification, and a reduction. The newspaper, as the carrier of news stories, participates in the construction of the mental worlds in which we live rather than in the reproduction of the "real world" we live in relation to. (423)

¹⁰The 1773 proposal was probably written by someone working for the Boston publisher Cox & Berry, and the 1784 proposal was probably written by an editor for the "Poetical Essays" section of the *Boston Magazine*.

¹¹"On the Death of the Rev. Mr. George Whitefield"; "To the Right Honorable William, Earl of Dartmouth, His Majesty's Principal Secretary of State for North America, &c."; "An Elegiac Poem on the Death of George Whitefield"(variant); "An Ode of Verses on the Death of George Whitefield" (variant); "To the Right Honl. William Earl of Dartmouth" (variant). A great many poems (including those listed here) were written after the publication of her 1772 Proposals. Attributions are determined from a copy of Wheatley's book at the American Antiquarian Society

which has a number of notes written in it.

[12]For a detailed account of Wheatley's trip to London, where she visited with and was visited by curious English nobility, gentry, and ministers, and distinguished Americans, see Robinson, "Phillis Wheatley in London."

[13]For an excellent survey of this topic, see Botein.

[14]Publishing, like filmmaking, is actually an arrangement of several distinct sets of activities. Robert Darnton has conceived of a model of the book trade that divides the several activities into horizontal and vertical axes. Along the horizontal axis are arranged "Creation," the activities of authors; "Publishing," the editors, annotators, illustrators, and designers; "Manufacturing," comprising composition, platemaking, printing, and binding; and "Supply" involving dealers of paper, ink, and type, as well as press manufacturers and die cutters. On the vertical axis, "Financing" is that function involving bankers or silent partners providing risk capital necessary for publishing firms; "Publishing" appears again; and "Distribution" includes the activities of book shops, jobbers, auction houses, and libraries. Finally the "Audience" represents the ultimate consumer in the book trade: those individual readers or purchasers who employ texts in a variety of ways for many different purposes (which do not always involve reading). See Winship 137–38.

[15]It is helpful when considering the overall impact of Wheatley's volume on the Boston of 1773 to bear in mind several issues. First, Americans at this time were exceedingly dependent on imported books. Second, the press was in the service of utilitarian needs. In general, fine books, fine bindings, and first editions did not loom as consequential. According to David Hall, "Only incidentally were printers and booksellers responsive to any other patronage than that of the marketplace, or of institutions such as schools, churches, and political parties" ("On Native Ground" 328). Third, literacy was widely diffused among the white population of the Anglo-American colonies. In New England, with its Puritan heritage, more than 80 percent of the men could sign their names in the early eighteenth century. That figure approached 90 percent in the early nineteenth century.

[16]Chartier states, "Silent reading does in fact establish a freer, more secret, and totally private intercourse with the written word. It permits more rapid reading, which is not impeded by the complexities of the book's organization and the relationships

established between the discourse and the glosses, the quotations and the comments, the text and the index. It also permits differential uses of the same book: given the social or ritual context, it can be read aloud for others or with others, or else it can be silently read for oneself in the retreat of the study, the library, or the oratory" (18-19.)

[17]See, for instance, Robinson, *Black New England Letters* 50-51, and 55.

[18]Because it provides significant insights into information networks, the methodology of the history of the book can revalue the ways in which we consider the governmentality of the state. As Roger Chartier says,

> From this perspective [of viewing the private sphere as separated from the public irrespective of national contexts], the aim of a history of reading is to trace a mobile and unstable frontier between private and public and also to offer a definition of the different forms of interlocking and competitive privacy: individual intimacy, familial intimacy, and convivial sociability. But the practices of reading are also at the center of a process that sees the emergence of a new public space confronting the authority of the State. (29)

[19]I borrow freely the term "invisible center" from Russell Ferguson, who uses it to describe the process by which historically marginalized groups challenge the hegemony of a dominant ideology. In Ferguson's view, "the power of a center" such as republican notions about personal liberty depend on a relatively unchallenged authority. Mainstream culture exists because of this omnipresent center, "which claims universality without ever defining itself, and which exiles to its margins those who cannot or will not pay allegiance to the standards which it sets or the limits it imposes" (10-13).

[20]Although I have not taken it as a direct subject of this essay, the details of Wheatley's biography after her publication were probably viewed in her own time as a perfect unfolding of republican notions of personal liberty. Wheatley, because of her unusual connection with Anglo-American society, presented the citizens of Boston with the practical problem of integrating persons with different particular interests, needs, aptitudes, and abilities. Republicans presupposed that a person like Phillis Wheatley

would consistently act in her own best interest as a rational interest-motivated economic agent. Her failure to succeed in a harsh marriage and rise above her poverty are secondary effects of her release from slavery—effects that rendered her governable. In the few glimpses of anxiety we see in Wheatley's letters and occasional writings, her situation reflects the change brought about by those who are made examples of liberal political thought: "It is when we are called upon to change our relation to government that we are also required to change our relation to ourselves, to change our subjective self-identity, and it is then that we become aware of the ways in which the political power of the state impinges on our individual lives, that we *feel* it" (Foucault, "Social Security," 163).

[21]For a discussion of ideology in this context, see Bercovitch, xviii-xxii.

[22]This proposal was also published in the *Boston Censor* of 14 March 1772 and 11 April 1772. See also Mason, "Letters and Proposals" 186-88.

[23]This proposal was also published in the *Massachusetts Gazette and Advertiser* of 19 April 1773 and 22 April 1773. See also Mason, "Letters and Proposals" 193.

[24]This proposal was also published in the *Boston Evening Post; and the General Advertiser* of 6 November 1779, 27 November 1779, and 4 December 1779, 11 December 1779, and 18 December 1779. See also Mason, "Letters and Proposals" 212-15.

[25]See Mason, "Letters and Proposals" 179n.

WORKS CITED

Andrews, Israel. Letter to William Burrell, Philadelphia, 24 February 1773. Massachusetts Historical Society, Boston.

_____. Letter to William Burrell, Philadelphia, 28 January 1774. Massachusetts Historical Society, Boston.

Baker, Houston. *The Journey Back: Issues in Black Literature and Criticism.* Chicago: U of Chicago P, 1980.

Baym, Nina. *Novels, Readers, and Reviewers: Responses to Fiction in Antebellum America.* Ithaca: Cornell UP, 1984.

Bercovitch, Sacvan. *The Office of the Scarlet Letter.* Baltimore: Johns Hopkins UP, 1991.

Botein, Stephen. "The Anglo-American Book Trade before 1776:
    Personnel and Strategies." In Joyce, Hall, and Brown, et
    al. 48-82.

Brawley, Benjamin. *Early Negro American Writers: Selections with
    Biographical and Critical Introductions.* 1935. Rpt. New
    York: Books for Libraries Press, 1968.

Brown, Richard. *Knowledge Is Power: The Diffusion of Information in
    Early America, 1700-1865.* New York: Oxford UP, 1989.

Burchell, Graham, Colin Gordon, and Peter Miller, eds. *The
    Foucault Effect.* Chicago: U of Chicago P, 1991.

Chartier, Roger. *Frenchness in the History of the Book: From the
    History of Publishing to the History of Reading.* Worcester,
    MA: American Antiquarian Society, 1988.

Charvat, William. "Literary Economics and Literary History."
    English Institute Essays. Ed. Alan S. Downer. 1949. Rpt.
    New York: AMS Presss, 1965.

Condorcet, Marquis de. *Esquisse d'un Tableau Historique des
    Progres de l'Espirit Humain.* 1793. Rpt. Paris:
    D'l'Imprimerie Nationale, 1971.

Crew, Francis, ed. *Letters of the Late Ignatius Sancho, an African.*
    London: J. Nichols and C. Dilly, 1782.

Darnton, Robert. "What Is the History of Books?" *Books and
    Society in History.* Ed. Kenneth Carpenter. New York:
    R. R. Bowker, 1983. 3-26.

Davidson, Cathy. *Revolution and the Word.* Oxford: Oxford UP,
    1986.

Deleuze, Gilles, and Felix Guattari. "What Is a Minor
    Literature?" In Ferguson, *Out There* 59-69.

Elliott, Emory. *Revolutionary Writers: Literature and Authority in
    the New Republic, 1725-1810.* New Haven: Yale UP, 1990.

Ferguson, Russell. "Introduction: Invisible Center." *Out There.*
    Ed. Russel Ferguson. 9-18.

_____, ed. *Out There: Marginalization and Contemporary Cultures.*
    Cambridge, MA: MIT P, 1990.

Foucault, Michel. "Of Other Spaces." *Diacritics* 16.1 (1986): 22-27.

_____. "Social Security." *Politics, Philosophy, Culture 1977-1984.*
    Tr. Alan Sheridan et al. Ed. Lawrence D. Kritzman. New
    York: Routledge, 1988. 183-97.

Franklin, Benjamin, V. *Boston Printers, Publishers, and Booksellers:
    1640-1800.* Boston: G.K. Hall, 1980.

Gates, Henry Louis. "In Her Own Write." In *The Collected Works
    of Phillis Wheatley.* Ed. John Shields. 7-26.

Hall, David. "On Native Ground: From the History of Printing to the History of the Book." *Proceedings of the American Antiquarian Society* 93 (1983): 313-36.

_____. "A Report on the 1984 Conference on Needs and Opportunities in the History of the Book in American Culture." *Proceedings of the American Antiquarian Society* 95. (1985): 101-12.

_____. "The Uses of Literacy in New England, 1600-1850." In Joyce, Hall, Brown, et al. 1-47.

Hall, Peter. *The Organization of American Culture, 1700-1900: Private Institutions, Elites and the Origins of American Nationality.* New York: New York UP, 1982.

Herrnstein Smith, Barbara. "Contingencies of Value." In *Canons.* Ed. Robert von Hallberg. Chicago: U of Chicago P, 1984. 5-40.

Hofstadter, Richard. *America at 1750.* New York: Knopf, 1973.

Isani, Mukhtar. "Phillis Wheatley in London: An Unpublished Letter to David Wooster." *American Literature* 51 (1979): 255-61.

Jameson, Fredric. *The Political Unconscious: Narrative as a Socially Symbolic Act.* Ithaca: Cornell UP, 1986.

_____. "Reification and Utopia in Mass Culture." *Social Text* 1 (1979): 130-48.

Jefferson, Thomas. *The Writings of Thomas Jefferson.* Ed. Albert Ellery Bergh. 2 vols. Washington, D.C.: Thomas Jefferson Memorial Association, 1905.

Joyce, William, David Hall, Richard Brown, et al., eds. *Printing and Society in Early America.* Worcester, MA: American Antiquarian Society, 1983.

Kolodny, Annette. "The Integrity of Memory: Creating a New Literary History of the United States." *American Literature* 57 (1985): 291-307.

Lauter, Paul. "Race and Gender in the Shaping of the American Literary Canon: A Case Study from the Twenties." *Feminist Studies* 9 (1983): 435-63.

Mason, Julian, ed. Introduction. *The Poems of Phillis Wheatley.* Ed. Julian Mason. 1-22.

_____. "A Note on the Text." *The Poems of Phillis Wheatley.* Ed. Julian Mason. 35-40

_____. "On the Reputation of Phillis Wheatley, Poet." *The Poems of Phillis Wheatley.* Ed. Julian Mason. 23-34.

_____, ed. "Letters and Proposals." *The Poems of Phillis Wheatley.* Ed. Julian Mason. 181-216

_____, ed. *The Poems of Phillis Wheatley.* Chapel Hill: U of North Carolina P, 1989.

Piersen, William. *Black Yankees: The Development of an Afro-American Subculture in Eighteenth-Century New England.* Amherst: U of Massachusetts P, 1988.

[Proposal for Printing.] *Boston Magazine.* September 1784. American Antiquarian Society, Worcester, MA.

"PROPOSALS for Printing in *London* By SUBSCRIPTION. . . ." *Massachusetts Gazette and the Boston News-Letter* 16 April 1773; *Massachusetts Gazette and Boston Post Boy and Advertiser* 19 April 1773 and 22 April 1773. American Antiquarian Society, Worcester, MA.

Rawley, James. "The World of Phillis Wheatley." *New England Quarterly* 50 (1977): 666-77.

Reed, William B., ed. *Reprint of the Original Letters from Washington to Joseph Reed, during the American Revolution.* Philadelphia: American Sunday School Union, 1852.

Robinson, William. *Black New England Letters: The Uses of Writing in Black New England.* Boston: Boston Public Library, 1977.

_____. "Phillis Wheatley in London." *CLA Journal* 21 (1977): 187-201.

Schudson, Michael. "Preparing the Minds of the People: Three Hundred Years of the American Newspaper." *Three Hundred Years of the American Newspaper.* Ed. John B. Hench. Worcester, MA: American Antiquarian Society, 1991. 421-43.

Shalhope, Robert. *The Roots of Democracy: American Thought and Culture 1760-1800.* Boston: Twayne, 1990.

Shields, John. "Phillis Wheatley and Mather Byles: A Study in Literary Relationship." *CLA Journal* 23 (1980): 377-90.

_____. Preface. *The Collected Works of Phillis Wheatley.* Ed. John Shields 27-32.

_____, ed. *The Collected Works of Phillis Wheatley.* New York: Oxford UP, 1988.

Sistrunk, Albertha. "Phillis Wheatley: An Eighteenth-Century Black American Poet Revisited," *CLA Journal* 23 (1980): 391-98.

Tanselle, G. Thomas. "The Bibliography and Textual Study of

American Books." *Proceedings of the American Antiquarian Society* 95 (1985): 113-59.

Tompkins, Jane. *Sensational Designs: The Cultural Work of American Fiction, 1790-1860.* Oxford: Oxford UP, 1985.

Voloshinov, V. N. *Marxism and the Philosophy of Language.* New York: Seminar Press, 1973.

Wald, Alan. "Hegemony and Literary Tradition in America." *Humanities in Society* 4 (1981): 419-30.

Washington, George. *The Writings of George Washington from the Original Manuscript Sources 1745-1799.* Ed. John C. Frederick. 39 vols. Washington, D.C.: Government Printing Office, 1931.

Wheatley, Phillis. "PROPOSALS for Printing By Subscription." *Boston Censor* 29 February 1772, 14 March 1772, 11 April 1772. American Antiquarian Society, Worcester, MA.

———. "PROPOSALS FOR PRINTING, BY SUBSCRIPTION. . . ." *Boston Evening Post; and the General Advertiser* 30 October 1779, 6 November 1779, 27 November 1779, 4 December 1779, 11 December 1779, and 18 December 1779. American Antiquarian Society, Worcester, MA.

Winship, Michael. "Publishing in America: Needs and Opportunities for Research," *Needs and Opportunities in the History of the Book: America, 1639-1876.* Ed. David Hall and John B. Hench. Worcester, MA: American Antiquarian Society, 1987. 61-102. Rpt. from *Proceedings of the American Antiquarian Society* 96 (1986): 133-74.

Ziff, Larzer. *Upon What Pretext?: The Book and Literary History.* Worcester, MA: American Antiquarian Society, 1986.

"Hideous Progenies":
Texts of *Frankenstein*[1]

Johanna M. Smith

My title pluralizes Mary Shelley's affectionate term for her novel to indicate that I want to address a variety of textual progenies here. And although I edited Bedford-St. Martin's *"Frankenstein": A Case Study in Contemporary Criticism*, I am writing here not as an editorial or textual specialist but as a feminist and teacher. When I look at written texts of *Frankenstein* as a materialist-feminist I am concerned with cultural production, with the changing conditions of feminine authorship in which Mary[2] wrote and rewrote the novel. When I turn to three movie reinventions of *Frankenstein*, I am concerned with historicizing the conditions of those reinventions. Situating *Son of Frankenstein* (1939), *Teenage Frankenstein* (1957), and *Frankenhooker* (1990) within cultural problematics, I also analyze how these movies address perceived audiences. By focusing throughout on textual instabilities and on the accompanying interpretive instabilities, I hope to suggest how gendering those instabilities could be a pedagogic tool.

I.

In this section I examine the manuscript and printed texts of Mary Shelley's novel. I begin with the textual situation of *Frankenstein*, noting the difficulties it poses for constructing a genealogy of the novel. As I then examine these difficulties in detail, I also address interpretive questions as well as several conditions of feminine authorship. As I do so, I also suggest strategies for teaching the textual, interpretive and gender issues raised by the several versions of *Frankenstein*.

In the Abinger Collection at Oxford's Bodleian Library reside the two surviving manuscripts of *Frankenstein*; both are incomplete, and neither is unadulterated Mary Shelley. One of these manuscripts is an intermediate draft which lacks Walton's initial letters; this draft is in Mary's hand, with interlinear and marginal additions and corrections by both her and Percy. The other is a fair copy of approximately the last twelve to fifteen percent of the draft; these pages are in Mary's hand except for the concluding section (from Victor's death on), which is in Percy's hand. Only tentative conclusions can be drawn from the Abinger MSS about *Frankenstein*'s progress from draft to fair copy, because the manuscripts are incomplete. Furthermore, Percy's presence—in the fair copy and in the extant draft—raises questions of authorial attribution.

These textual issues consequent on the lack of a single-author manuscript are further complicated by the three print versions of *Frankenstein*. The novel was first published anonymously in three volumes by Lackington in 1818. We do not have page proofs for this step from manuscript to print, so again we must be cautious in drawing conclusions about the novel's genealogy. That is, although we know from their letters that both Mary and Percy corrected proof, without the proof-sheets we cannot identify these corrections, let alone assign them to either Mary or Percy. In a copy of this 1818 edition which she gave to her friend Mrs. Thomas, Mary did make notes for additions and corrections, but these changes (known as the Thomas variants) were not incorporated in the next edition of the novel. That edition was published in 1823 by G. and W. B. Whittaker, under the supervision of Mary's father William Godwin; although it included 114 substantive changes from the 1818 edition, these alterations were made not by Mary but by Godwin or possibly by the compositor. Mary made no changes to the printed text of *Frankenstein* until 1831, when she revised the 1818 text and wrote an Introduction for the one-volume edition published by Colburn and Bentley in their Standard Novels series.

Although the 1831 text does not present the problems of attribution that the manuscripts do, Mary's revisions do raise the textual question of whether the 1818 or the 1831 text is the more authoritative. According to an Anglo-American tradition of privileging final authorial intentions, a critical edition of *Frankenstein* would use the later text as its copy-text if the author pervasively revised the 1818 text in accidentals and substantives for this 1831 edition. Dozens of popular reprints of the later text have been published since 1831, and it was given a scholarly imprimatur as copy-text with the M. K. Joseph edition published by Oxford in 1969. In 1974, however, James Rieger produced an edition using the 1818 version as copy-text; he incorporated the Thomas variants in the text, and he included an appendix collating the 1818 text and the 1831 substantive variants. Against the editorial convention that final authorial emendations have final authority, Rieger chose the 1818 version as copy-text for two reasons: because Percy's extensive revisions of manuscript and page-proof arguably entitled him to "a measure of final authority" (xliv), and because the novel's original conception was "radically" altered by the 1831 substantive variants (xliii). Rieger's rationale raises the textual question of whether there can be one definitive text of *Frankenstein* if there are two significantly different textual versions, and possibly two sources of final authority. In other words, if *Frankenstein* is not a single text but two different texts, one can argue that it is two different works.

This textual instability, however, is seldom evident in academic practice. Material conditions of production, most notably production in print, have tended to privilege the 1831 *Frankenstein* in the classroom. The Abinger manuscripts are the novel's earliest versions and are not available in print; in academic practice, then, the manuscripts' authority—in terms both of chronology and of material production—is insufficient to destabilize the 1831 version's preeminence. The 1818 work is the mama bear of this textual sequence, generally considered more authoritative than the MSS but less authoritative than the revised 1831 work; for this reason and because until recently it was available only in the pricey Rieger edition, the 1818 text was seldom taught. The 1823 text, I feel fairly safe in saying, has never been taught; it has long been out of print, and Woodstock's 1993 reprint is prohibitively priced at $65. In contrast, there are several cheap paperbacks of the 1831 text, and anecdotal evidence suggests that it is still more often taught than the 1818 text. Indeed, it may be more readily available *because* it is more often used in literature classes; as Katie King reminds us, "the apparatus of literary production, simultaneously *object* for analysis and *tool* of analysis, intersects in art, business, and technology," and this intersection "currently determin[es] 'literature,' both literary works and the academic disciplines of literature" (92). An example is my *Case Study* volume, which was designed for teaching purposes and includes the 1831 text: Bedford chose it over the 1818 text largely because of its frequent use in classrooms. When material production and academic considerations intersect, then, publishers and teachers mutually reinforce the final authority of the 1831 text. Furthermore, specialization of and within literature departments tends to authorize the written *Frankenstein* over versions in other media, so that only the written text becomes worthy of classroom study.

Against this institutionalization of the 1831 text, the different versions of *Frankenstein* could be used in a number of ways in the classroom. One could assign Rieger's edition and use the Thomas variants and the appendix to emphasize the *process* of textual production; or one could emphasize this process by assigning one of the reprints of the 1831 text along with Xeroxes of heavily revised portions of the 1818 text; or one could assign the 1831 novel and analyze another set of changes by also using a movie version. In these ways one could introduce students to textual scholarship—an area that many literature programs overlook—and to the issue of textual instability. Using such strategies should give students a sense that any "final" text is a *product*—not, or not just, of inspiration but of a complex of decisions and rethinkings and further decisions by the author or filmmaker, by the press or the studio. While such a focus on process would not necessarily improve students' writing, it might; and it might also expand the range of questions students ask of a text as they write about it.

As that last possibility suggests, teaching plural texts to introduce textual instability could also foreground interpretive instability. Textual comparisons between the 1818 and 1831 works might begin with the 1831 Introduction, where Mary characterized her revisions as "principally those of style" (24)[3] and added that she had not "introduced any new ideas or circumstances" or altered the story's "core and substance." An instructor might then adduce Mary Poovey's view (133-37) that the numerous references to Fate added in 1831 substantially diminish Victor's responsibility for his acts; s/he might also note the other added passages in which Victor expresses grief and remorse and warns Walton against repeating his own "madness" (35-36). One might then turn to James Whale's 1931 movie

Frankenstein, to pursue a related interpretive question raised by the novel: whether the monster's monstrosity is created by his maker Victor Frankenstein or by the community (frightened villagers, Felix de Lacey, the rustic) which attacks and ostracizes him. The movie leans toward the former interpretation by representing Victor as a Mad Scientist, but it also tempers his guilt by creating a new character, the Bad Scientist: it is the laboratory assistant whose bungling gives the creature a criminal's brain, and whose taunts turn a bewildered creature into a monster. And where both Victor and the movie Frankenstein fail to capture their monsters, the movie departs from the novel by having the villagers destroy the threat to their community; depending on the level of audience sympathy with the monster, their action might be seen as either just retribution or mob violence. By drawing attention to such differences in written and filmed versions of Victor's guilt, an instructor can emphasize for students the many avenues and difficulties of interpretation.

Another feminist entry into these issues of textual and interpretative instability is through the conditions of women's authorship. To illustrate, I return to the problems posed by the Abinger MSS and the lack of page proofs for the 1818 text. When Mary Shelley began *Frankenstein* in 1816, she was living with a published author who encouraged and oversaw her writing. Percy as well as Mary revised the extant draft and, although she corrected page proofs, for at least one set she gave him "carte blanche to make what alterations you please" (*Letters* 1.42). For these reasons, Rieger suggested that Percy was "more than an editor" of the 1818 text, possibly "a minor collaborator," perhaps even part-author with "a measure of 'final authority'" (xliv). Even though Rieger's suggestion has grounds in Anglo-American editorial theory, a feminist needs to question the gendering of such grounds: as editor of Percy's poetry after his death, for instance, Mary is seldom accorded "a measure of 'final authority.'"[4] Another textual question, which is also an interpretive question, is the extent to which Percy's fair copy of the conclusion revised the draft. Recall that the Abinger MSS are incomplete; furthermore, Percy's fair-copy conclusion differs from the extant draft in stressing Victor's noble qualities and hence tends to diminish his culpability for the monstrosity of the monster. Since Percy rewrote Mary's original conclusion, Anne K. Mellor's view that he "distorted the meaning of [Mary's] text" (62) may have some interpretive validity. Yet Mary accepted—perhaps welcomed—his rewriting, and this fact complicates the issue of distortion. For instance, Mary's 1831 revisions further reduce Victor's guilt: do those alterations constitute significant changes, as Poovey has argued, or do they merely clarify Mary's intentions in the 1818 text? More generally, is Percy to be seen as a meddler or as a collaborator?

Again using the textual and interpretive difficulties of attribution raised by the Abinger MSS, a feminist might analyze collaboration as a condition of feminine authorship. In the Abinger draft, for instance, similarities in Mary's and Percy's handwriting sometimes make it hard to attribute revisions; and even when we can identify Percy's revisions, we cannot know why Mary accepted them. An example: where Mary's draft had the monster ask simply, "Who was I? What was I?," Percy added, "Whence did I come? What was my destination?" (Abinger Dep.c.534, p.64). In an Anglo-American tradition of textual editing, revisions that do not originate with the author may nonetheless be regarded as representing final authorial intention if reviser and author are "voluntary collaborators" (Tanselle 190). For the 1818 text, then, Percy's revisions represent Mary's final intentions if she voluntarily accepted his collaboration, either directly or by giving him "carte blanche." But a feminist analyzing conditions of women's authorship will want to open up this issue. Was Mary struck by the aptness of Percy's queries, or did she accept them for the same reason that she gave him "carte blanche" over one set of proofs—because she was "tired and not very clear headed" (*Letters* 1.42)? In other words, was Mary cowed by her husband's greater experience as a writer into adopting his revisions, or did she welcome him as a collaborator? Mary later accepted an ideology of dependent femininity: in 1838 she described her 1823 self as having "the woman's love of looking up, and being guided" (*Journal* 554), and as unable "to put [her]self forward unless led, cherished and supported." If this retrospective view were also valid for the 1816 Mary writing her first novel, she might well have felt constrained to "look up and be guided" by her husband's suggestions. If so, revision urged by a more established writer on his less experienced and perhaps insecure writer-wife hardly constitutes voluntary collaboration. But it is equally possible that Mary freely accepted Percy's help. Having faced scandal in 1814 by eloping with the married Percy, two years later she might well have felt sufficiently confident to welcome collaboration with a fellow author. And if we read Victor as autochthonous "author"—of the monster (91), "unalterable evils" (84), and "[his] own speedy ruin" (92)[6]—then *Frankenstein* dramatizes the disastrous effects of self-sufficient creation and so may provide a brief for collaborative authorship. But even if Mary willingly accepted Percy as a collaborator, that very willingness might indicate her internalization of the putatively "feminine" need to be "guided" and "supported"; here again, "collaboration" would not accurately describe Mary's and Percy's literary relations.

And even if the 1818 *Frankenstein* were a collaborative effort of sorts, what about Mary's 1831 revisions? As an independent review of a perhaps collaborative text, the 1831 text suggests a new set of conditions of feminine authorship. One might analyze those conditions by using feminist textual scholar Brenda Silver's method of reading a woman's series of texts in reverse order.[7] That is, rather than reading *Frankenstein*'s drafts and early printed versions teleologically, as "moving inexorably toward some better end" of a final text (Silver 212), we might read backward from a final printed text to ask how a woman author is confronting and assessing her earlier work. In her 1831 Introduction, for instance, Mary insisted that "I certainly did not owe the suggestion of one incident, nor scarcely of one train of feeling, to my husband" (23). Does this assertion suggest that she saw the reissue of her novel as an opportunity to *make* it her own, to revise the product of a restrictive collaboration? Or do her revisions testify to a new set of restrictions; was she, as Poovey argues, bringing her younger and less orthodox author-self into line with an 1831 notion of the proper lady?[8] For example, in the 1831 text Mary omitted the passage in which Elizabeth denounces the judicial system for executing the innocent Justine (Rieger 83). Removing this single instance of Elizabeth's anger might be interpreted not only as muting the 1818 text's radical politics but also as rewriting Elizabeth in more conventionally feminine terms. Mary might then be repudiating a social critique which Percy, and her earlier self, had approved; but as she distanced herself from those politics she might also be aligning herself with an ideology of feminine propriety.

While such an analysis might seem to have achieved infinite regress, or even intentional fallacy, I have pushed the issue of collaboration into indeterminacy for a purpose. I mean to suggest how we can use such issues pedagogically—not to search for a single solution or to teach our students to do so, but to search for more, and more interesting, questions. By focusing on problematics in the process of Mary's authoring of *Frankenstein*s, we can suggest to students how cultural constraints operate on writers, how certain of them operate specifically on women writers, and how such gendered issues of literary production inflect our interpretations of texts.

II.

In this section my discussion of pedagogic tools turns to three movie versions of *Frankenstein: Son of Frankenstein, Teenage Frankenstein,* and *Frankenhooker.* As Chris Baldick has shown, nineteenth-century writers addressed contemporary issues by revising a myth of "Frankenstein"; similarly, these movies engage problematics of twentieth-century U.S. culture by reinventing the "Frankenstein" trope of Mad/Bad Scientist. With the new conditions and audiences for which each movie reworks gendered and other elements of the novel, new sets of textual and interpretive instabilities appear. Through filmed as through written texts, then, we can suggest to students that our task as interpreters is to ask not which text is a more accurate revision but what cultural work each text is doing.

Son of Frankenstein (1939) uses the Mad/Bad Scientist trope to rewrite the father-son relation between the novel's Victor and his creation. Since the eponymous hero is Baron von Frankenstein, ruler of the town of Frankenstein, the movie's father-son relations engage three interrelated projects of scientific, paternal, and political inheritance. Wolf von Frankenstein must vindicate his father Heinrich's scientific paternal creation of the monster and discredit the misuse of that creation by its bad father, the laboratory assistant Ygor; Wolf must also prove that he, not the monster, is the true son of Frankenstein; at issue in these two struggles is the Frankenstein family's fitness to rule the town. My materialist-feminist reading of these struggles addresses the family as an Ideological State Apparatus (ISA), one of the "distinct and specialized institutions" which are "not only the *stake* but also the *site* of class struggle" (Althusser 143, 147) and, I would add, of the gendering of that struggle. In other words, as the movie marginalizes women, its familial and political struggles, and what is at stake in them, are thereby masculinized. I begin with the workings of this marginalization. As the movie's opening scenes show the new Baron returning to the town of Frankenstein with his wife Elsa and son Peter, they also contrast Elsa's and the town's responses to Wolf's efforts to vindicate his father. Elsa listens without comment as Wolf insists, "it wasn't my father's fault that the being he created became a senseless murdering monster"; in contrast, when Wolf praises his progenitor at the train station, the assembled men—town council, burgomaster, and villagers—disperse in sullen resistance. And although Elsa is occasionally allowed to express fear, *Son of Frankenstein* lacks the usual scene in which a woman pleads with her scientist to cease his experiments (Ambrogio 37). Indeed, Elsa "never bother[s]" her husband in his laboratory, and the movie withholds from her the knowledge it gives the audience of Wolf's experiments on the monster; unlike Elizabeth, then, the movie wife is not endangered by science or by the monster. And although Elsa is represented as a good mother, the audience knows long before she does that the monster is lurking near her son Peter. Throughout, the movie excludes her from these problematics of the Frankenstein paternity, from a family ISA that then becomes the stake and site of father-son struggle.

Thus *Son of Frankenstein* focuses on the struggle among Wolf, the town's men, and Ygor to define and control the Frankenstein inheritance. The council defines this "heritage" as the town itself, "forsaken, desolate, shunned by every traveler . . . because of these Frankensteins," and as the havoc and fear created by the monster. Linked with this definition of the Frankenstein heritage, and with the town's helplessness against it, is the feral Ygor: a jury condemned him to death but the hanging failed, and Ygor now keeps the monster alive and uses him to kill off the jury-members. Thus as the council grumbles that Wolf will carry on the Frankenstein "heritage," Ygor and the new Baron become parallel threats to the community. Against this definition of his father's legacy, Wolf sneers that the villagers are "strange superstitious creatures" who do not understand the "miracle" his father created. Ygor then persuades him to treat the sick monster by saying "your father made him, and Heinrich Frankenstein was *your* father too"; by agreeing to doctor the creature, Wolf accepts Ygor's implication "that that is my brother." When he then alters the phrase "maker of monsters" on

Heinrich's tomb to "maker of men," he defines his father's true heritage and signals his filial allegiance to it rather than to the town. But since Ygor has replaced Heinrich by keeping the monster alive and killing, Wolf here commits himself not to Heinrich, the father of an innocent "being," but to Ygor, the father of the "senseless murdering monster." And although he comes to believe that the villagers' "fantastic tale[s]" about the monster are "absolutely true," he justifies himself as son and scientist for reanimating the comatose monster:

> I as a man should destroy him, but as a scientist I should do everything in my power to bring him back to conscious life, so that the world can study his abnormal functions. That would vindicate my father.

As the Baron thus endangers his town, the movie begins a critique of masculinist science that recalls the novel but also departs from it. In a shot of Wolf talking to Elsa before Heinrich's portrait, the movie is relatively faithful to the novel's representation of a Victor oscillating between his science and his devotion to Elizabeth. Wolf tries to convince Elsa that his "terrific experiment . . . could establish me and my [pause—both turn toward the portrait] my work as something outstanding in the world of science"; by substituting "my work" for "my father" and turning Elsa away from the portrait, Wolf acts as husband rather than son. When he then kills Ygor, he appears to be rejecting the bad father's legacy as well, but this seemingly principled act infuriates the monster, and here the movie glances at but significantly departs from the novel. When Victor killed the mate he had created for the monster, the monster retaliated by killing Victor's wife Elizabeth; when Wolf kills the monster's "father," the monster retaliates by abducting Wolf's son. As this act alludes to the murder of Victor's brother William in the novel, the movie reiterates the novel's focus on Victor's neglect of his family; but as the abduction of the son replaces the murder of Elizabeth, it also replaces the novel's emphasis on scientific victimization of women with a focus on endangered sons. And where Victor was unable to protect Elizabeth or to punish his monster, in another significant departure from the novel Wolf not only rescues his son but kills the monster. By saving his son from his monstrous "brother," Wolf proves himself the true son of Frankenstein, and he frees not only his family but the town from the Frankenstein "heritage." The latter liberation is completed in the movie's final scenes, which reverse its opening: as the Frankensteins board an outbound train surrounded by grateful villagers, Wolf cedes the castle and estate to the town. By first saving the town from Ygor and the monster and then rejecting his true father's legacy of feudal privilege, that is, Wolf leaves the town to self-government.

Unlike the novel's Elizabeth, the movie's Elsa survives, yet she is thoroughly marginalized as the movie creates a family ISA that privileges father and son. Where Elizabeth served to call into question a masculinist science, the movie undermines such a science only to replace it with a masculinist polity: baronial government is succeeded by a burgomaster and a town council composed entirely of men. One might interpret this conclusion culturally, as a critique of the decadent politics of 1939 wartime Europe made from the vantage point of a democratic and peace-loving U.S. In a feminist interpretation, however, the new masculine polity is no less inhospitable to women than the old. Finally, by teaching this movie with the novel and showing how a live but occluded Elsa is less central to the movie than a dead Elizabeth is to the novel, one might destabilize a reading of the 1831 work's gender ideology as conservative.

* * * * *

If my reading of *Son of Frankenstein* achieves a certain coherence, *Teenage Frankenstein*'s efforts to resolve its contradictions resist such interpretive stability, and I have tried to make my analysis suggestive rather than conclusive. Via Frankenstein, the movie attempts to displace uneasiness over U.S. atomic science onto Nazi medical experiments. As the movie then works to consolidate that displacement through the Mad/Bad Scientist's relations with an experimental son and a woman scientist, it engages with two additional cultural problematics. Like other 1957 movies such as *I was a Teenage Werewolf* and *Jailhouse Rock,* this one uses an uncontrollable son to address a fear of juvenile delinquency. By incorporating but rewriting the novel's concern with scientific victimization of women, *Teenage Frankenstein* also addresses contemporary uneasiness with the professional/domestic woman. Although these two figures destabilize a family ISA, through them U.S. science is shakily recuperated from the taint of Mad/Bad science.

I begin with the ways in which *Teenage Frankenstein* represents European science and contrasts it with U.S. science. The movie opens on an audience of U.S. scientists criticizing the British Dr. Frankenstein's plan to transplant the "healthy eyes" of dead criminals; "we're all men of science," says one listener, but this science is "beyond the pale of experimental medicine." The last phrase is important: "beyond the pale" alludes to European ghettoization of Jews, and joined to "experimental medicine" it suggests an equation between Nazi medical experiments and Frankenstein's transplants that U.S. science opposes. In a second such equation, Frankenstein's plan to breed new humans recalls Nazi efforts to create a master race. "If you breed morons you get morons," Frankenstein explains; in contrast, his experiments in "selective breeding . . . point the way toward perfection in the human race." In his later claim that these experiments "will determine the fate of the world," the movie alludes to Nazi attempts to similarly "determine the fate of the world" by exterminating Jews and creating a master race.

Although the evidence for this interpretation seems to me strong, I am not sure how to read the fact that Frankenstein is not German but British. A related problem of interpretation arises with the U.S. scientist Dr. Karlton: although he objects to Frankenstein's monomania and thereby continues the contrast between U.S. and European science, that contrast blurs when Frankenstein compels his assistance by threatening to reveal the earlier shady experiments they performed together. It seems to me that both problems may be connected with U.S. guilt over its own wartime extermination of Hiroshima and Nagasaki, with its response to the worldwide concern over U.S. atomic testing in the Marshall Islands in 1954, and with the domestic concern over national security evinced by McCarthyism and especially by the 1954 brouhaha over atomic scientist J. Robert Oppenheimer's security clearance. Launched in 1955, the Atoms for Peace project extended U.S. expertise in atomic energy first to European allies and by 1957 to Eastern bloc countries; as this cooperation attempted to rehabilitate the effects of the Manhattan Project and the Marshall Island testing, however, it also heightened fears that such collaboration with Europe might reduce U.S. science's preeminence and weaken national security. I would suggest very tentatively that Frankenstein's Britishness and Karlton's cooperation might be read in light of these fears. The problematic of

U.S.-European scientific collaboration is suggested by Frankenstein's nationality but then distanced and mystified as his work is equated with the discredited science of Nazi medical experimentation. Even though Karlton is forced into squeamish complicity with Frankenstein's theories, his condemnation of them effects a shaky distinction between national sciences.

In an effort to consolidate this distinction, the movie reworks both the novel's monstrous father-son relations and *Son of Frankenstein's* problematic of paternal science. This movie's Frankenstein consistently addresses his creation as "my boy," and like the novel's Victor he has grandiose notions of paternity: as Victor envisioned himself the "creator and source" of "a new species" and "many happy and excellent natures" (55), so Frankenstein cobbles together a teenager, for "only in youth is there any salvation for mankind." While this Frankenstein's scientific procedure is much like Victor's, the movie departs from the novel when the scientist/father does not flee his creature but instead works to perfect "a youth I shall instruct and control." And when the boy escapes from the laboratory and turns juvenile delinquent by killing a tarty blonde teenager, what was climactic in the novel—Elizabeth's murder—is made little more than an episode in father-son relations. That is, Frankenstein punishes the boy not for murder (teenage daughters are expendable) but for "disobeying me"; in effect, he grounds his son by refusing to give him a new face as an alibi.

Like the movie's representations of science, its father/son relationship contains contradictions, for as in *Son of Frankenstein* a family ISA is the site and stake of struggle. No doubt many 1950s parents fantasized about achieving Frankenstein's control over a delinquent son—despite the boy's behavioral lapses, his vocabulary is pretty much limited to "yes sir" and "I will obey you"—and such a fantasy of the family ISA may well have been shared by the filmmakers. Yet a movie entitled *Teenage Frankenstein* was surely aimed at teenagers, and to this audience Frankenstein may have seemed as much the heavy parent as the mad scientist. Indeed, the movie sometimes plays to this young American audience, as for instance in the pomposity of Frankenstein's "in England we have a little more respect for the older generation." Here as in the novel, then, we see an interpretive instability, a slippage between the movie's fear of juvenile delinquents (suggested by Frankenstein's effort to create a good teenager) and its appeal to a teenage audience (who might see that effort as tyrannical).

A similar interpretive instability appears in the figure of Frankenstein's assistant and fiancée Margaret. Unlike the woman scientists of such 1950s sci-fi movies as *The Thing* and *The Beast from 20,000 Fathoms*, Margaret is not actively engaged in the movie's science. But neither does she fade from narrative focus as the scientific women do; instead she interferes with Frankenstein's experiments. In thus refusing the passive romantic/professional role he assigns her, I suggest, she is both integral to the movie's project and punished by it.

Much as Frankenstein attempts to create and control the perfect teenager, he tries to create in Margaret the perfect combination of obedient assistant and wife. This combination of roles is Frankenstein's strategy for controlling Margaret: as he persuades her to work for him, for example, he clinches the deal by saying "I'm a man as well as a scientist" and proposing to her. And when she later complains that he neglects her for the experiments he conceals from her, he placates her first by adducing "the pure clear flame of science" and then by agreeing to her suggestion that they drive to a lover's lane and neck. It is important that the suggestion was hers, for through it and her complaints Margaret resists the gendered and professional subordination Frankenstein is imposing. In another act of dual resistance she later sneaks into his laboratory, and she justifies herself as both scientist and fiancée:

> I reasoned it out and I came to the conclusion you didn't want to marry a fool, a puppet who would simply obey you blindly. . . . I'm not brilliant but as your future wife I felt I should know—that I had a right to know what you were striving for, to help me to understand you better, perhaps to love you better.

Of course Frankenstein *does* want a "fool" and "puppet" wife, and he now replaces Margaret with the son who does "obey [him] blindly." He convinces his creature that Margaret prevented him from giving the boy a new face, and the obedient son kills the disobedient fiancée.

With this second allusion to Elizabeth's death, the movie again revises the novel in important ways. Where Victor was the unwitting cause of Elizabeth's murder, the movie's Frankenstein intends and orchestrates the murder of his fiancée. And where the novel represented Elizabeth as a passive victim, the movie positions an active Margaret as bringing her death on herself. In the novel, Elizabeth's passive feminine domesticity was made the necessary complement to Victor's active masculine science, so her death was a critique of that science. The meaning of Margaret's death is more complicated, for unlike Elizabeth she is a domestic *and* professional woman and in both roles she refuses to be passive. When she acts as a domestic woman, her resistance to passive femininity threatens a male-dominant family ISA; unlike Elsa, for instance, she is not a wife and mother expressing fear but a fiancée seeking access to her future husband's secrets. But because she is also acting as a professional woman, such behavior is necessary to the movie's critique of Frankenstein's Mad/Bad Science; in fact, Margaret as a U.S. woman challenges that science more frequently and doggedly than does Karlton as a U.S. scientist. This is crucial, for we have already seen that the movie's project of recuperating U.S.-European cooperation requires that Karlton resist Frankenstein but also collaborate with him; but the project also requires a resistance which refuses cooperation but must be defeated. Thus the movie both requires Margaret's resistance and punishes her for it. Like the novel, the movie needs a feminine victim of science, but unlike the novel it also needs to recuperate a masculine version of U.S. science. Margaret dies, then, because her professional resistance to Frankenstein's science is also a rejection of her womanly role.

Parallel to Margaret's, the teenager's resistance to a family ISA makes him another necessary victim to the recuperation of U.S. science. By obediently murdering Margaret, initially the boy replaces her: in a chilling allusion to the earlier shot of Frankenstein and Margaret driving to the lover's lane, father drives son on the same journey to obtain the boy's reward, a handsome new face. As the teenager then spends all his time at the mirror, once again he seems a parent's dream, for in this state of (feminized?) narcissism he is no threat. Although he resists parental authority when Frankenstein decides to vivisect him and take him to England as an exhibit, this parental misconduct all but excuses the boy's violent response and arguably he performs a service to humanity when he kills Frankenstein. As with Margaret, however, the movie both requires a counter to

Frankenstein's science and punishes resistance to a family ISA. Thus the boy dies because the movie cannot reward a juvenile-delinquent patricide, but it turns his death to account: while fleeing the police he falls against an instrument panel in the laboratory and is electrocuted, so it is Frankenstein's Bad/Mad Science that kills him. And since Karlton, who called the police, is the proximate cause of the boy's death, U.S. science is vindicated as more effectual than the U.S. woman against aberrant European science. If *Son of Frankenstein* replaced masculinist science with a masculinist polity, *Teenage Frankenstein* ultimately recuperates that science, and it does so through the agency but also at the expense of an unruly fiancée and a disobedient son.

                                    * * * * *

In the low-budget comedy *Frankenhooker* (1990), the gender questions I have teased out of the earlier movies are addressed directly but contradictorily. The Boy Genius/Mad Scientist's efforts to create the perfect woman are satirized as masculinist, and the feminine victims of his experimentation are avenged, but this drive-in movie also plays to a masculine gaze. While its conjunction of feminist politics and sexual titillation may well be a deliberate appeal to disparate audiences, the resulting contradictions create an interpretive instability particularly disturbing for a feminist.

After his fiancée Elizabeth (of course an allusion to the novel) is decapitated and dismembered by a lawnmower he invented, Jeffrey Franken preserves the head and becomes obsessed with creating a new body for it. But he decides to better the original by constructing "the centerfold goddess of the century" out of parts from prostitutes. Through this glance at the procedure of the novel's Frankenstein, the movie mocks Jeffrey's sexual/scientific desire to improve on nature; but it also positions the masculine gaze so that the spectator views with Jeffrey the centerfolds from which he chooses his favorite parts. In addition, the movie represents Elizabeth as complicit with Jeffrey's desire that she achieve a perfect body; she had earlier allowed him to staple her stomach, for instance, because "we're going to be married." With a characteristic duality, then, the movie satirizes Jeffrey's masculinist science but also gets laughs at Elizabeth's expense.

Similar contradictions appear as the movie uses Jeffrey's science to ridicule the anti-drug hysteria of the 1980s. To get parts from prostitutes for Elizabeth's new body, Jeffrey creates a designer-crack whose high will be literally explosive. As he does so he listens to a woman talk-show guest who advocates legalizing prostitution, and he agrees that "this crack shit's killing them." But he immediately adds that his supercrack "will do the job a lot faster," and he concludes that "if they don't want to do it they can just say no." The movie's position on crack and prostitution is made no clearer by the scene in which Jeffrey carries out his plan, for soft-core porn shots of scantily-clad prostitutes getting high and feeling each other up are designed to appeal to a masculine and prurient gaze rather than a just-say-no audience. While the latter is unlikely to attend a movie entitled *Frankenhooker*, still these contradictions destabilize any interpretation of the movie's gender politics.

The progress and outcome of Jeffrey's scheme seem designed to critique both johns who exploit prostitutes sexually and Jeffrey, who exploits them scientifically. From the parts of several crack-exploded prostitutes which he has stockpiled in an estrogen bath, Jeffrey constructs a body and attaches Elizabeth's head; in a nod to the 1931 James Whale movie, lightning animates the whole. In another allusion to that movie and to the novel, the result is not what Jeffrey expected: instead of his sweet fiancée, his creation is a brassy prostitute who escapes from his laboratory and terrorizes New York's 42nd Street. The fact that contact with her kills several potential johns might be seen both as a parody of the moralized horror of prostitutes and as a prostitute's revenge. The prostitute-victims of Jeffrey's experiment are also avenged when the leftover parts seize a pimp who has come to Jeffrey's laboratory and drag him into the estrogen bath. The movie then concludes with Elizabeth's revenge. After Jeffrey gives his botched creation a dose of electricity, she seems to become the Elizabeth he intended—"so proud" of him for the "miracle" by which he reanimated her. When she realizes why he constructed her new body, however, it becomes clear that Elizabeth is no longer the passive subject of his experiments. Using Jeffrey's notes she constructs an exaggeratedly voluptuous female body to which she attaches his head. She then repeats to him his own justification for experimenting on her: "Granted what I did may have been a bit unorthodox, but hey—you look great and you're alive and you're back with me and I love you." Her final words, heard over a shot of Jeffrey's horrified face, are "we're together again—all of us." By foisting on Jeffrey the body he had assembled as ideal for her, Elizabeth avenges all the feminine victims of his masculine science.

Yet I am not sure that punishing a man by giving him a woman's body is a feminist move. Clearly Jeffrey has been foiled by his own science, and the grotesquerie of Elizabeth's creation might prompt a spectator to share his horror; but in him and in the spectator, does that horror arise from what he has done, or from what has been done to him? In its conclusion as throughout, then, the indeterminacy of *Frankenhooker*'s gender politics is among the most extreme examples of interpretive instability in the texts of *Frankenstein*.

Some of the textual questions I have raised about *Frankenstein* remain unanswerable, but I hope I have indicated how we might use these issues of textual instability in the classroom. And although I have offered interpretations of the novel and the movies, I have tried to do so in ways that would open up rather than close down interpretive instability, that would suggest how indeterminacy can be a useful pedagogical tool. With such reading strategies, we can use *Frankenstein*'s many texts to help our students interrogate not only definitive texts but definitive interpretations.

NOTES

[1]For suggestions and timely aid, I thank Anthony Ambrogio, Cammy Thomas, David Ketterer, Philip Cohen and especially Charles E. Robinson, for generously sharing his encyclopedic knowledge of the Abinger MSS and thereby saving me from many egregious errors.

[2]Since I refer to both Shelleys, to avoid confusion I use their first names.

[3]References are to my edition unless otherwise noted.

[4]In his edition of Percy's poems, for instance, Thomas Hutchinson omits the grammatical corrections "introduced by Mrs. Shelley, apparently on her own authority, into the texts of 1839" (iii). For Mary's concern with what she called editorial "mutilation" of Percy's work, see *Letters* 2.301, 305, 326.

[6]Mellor 65 believes that all three uses of the word

"author" were introduced into the MS by Percy. Even if this is so, I think we still have to ask whether the word had precisely the same connotations for Mary as for Percy.

[7]See Friedman for a similar analysis of H.D.'s work, and Bennett on the need to read an author's text in the light of her full oeuvre. For discussions of some textual difficulties in editing women's writing, see Crane and Reiman.

[8]See Poovey chap. 4; Bennett 76-79 critiques this argument.

WORKS CITED

Althusser, Louis. "Ideology and Ideological State Apparatuses." *Lenin and Philosophy and Other Essays.* Trans. Ben Brewster. New York: Monthly Review, 1971. 127-86.

Ambrogio, Anthony. "*Frankenstein*—or 'My Heart Belongs to Daddy.'" Unpublished essay, 1979.

Baldick, Chris. *In Frankenstein's Shadow: Myth, Monstrosity, and Nineteenth-Century Writing.* Oxford: Clarendon, 1987.

Bennett, Betty T. "Feminism and Editing Mary Wollstonecraft Shelley: The Editor And?/Or? the Text." *Palimpsest: Editorial Theory in the Humanities.* Eds. George Bornstein and Ralph G. Williams. Ann Arbor: U of Michigan P, 1993. 67-96.

Crane, Elaine Forman. "Gender Consciousness in Editing: The Diary of Elizabeth Drinker." *TEXT* 4 (1988): 375-83.

Frankenhooker. Dir. Frank Hehenlotter. Shapiro Glickenhaus Entertainment, 1990.

Frankenstein. Dir. James Whale. Universal, 1931.

Friedman, Susan Stanford. "The Return of the Repressed in Women's Narrative." *Journal of Narrative Technique* 19 (Winter 1989): 141-56.

Hutchinson, Thomas. Preface. *The Complete Poetical Works of Percy Bysshe Shelley.* Ed. Thomas Hutchinson. 1905. London: Oxford UP, 1952.

King, Katie. "Bibliography and a Feminist Apparatus of Literary Production." *TEXT* 5 (1991): 91-103.

Mellor, Anne K. *Mary Shelley: Her Life, Her Fiction, Her Monsters.* New York: Routledge, 1988.

Poovey, Mary. *The Proper Lady and the Woman Writer: Ideology as Style in the Works of Mary Wollstonecraft, Mary Shelley, and Jane Austen.* Chicago: U of Chicago P, 1984.

Reiman, Donald H. "Gender and Documentary Editing: A Diachronic Perspective." *TEXT* 4 (1988): 351-59.

Rieger, James. Introduction. *Frankenstein; or, the Modern Prometheus* (The 1818 Text). By Mary Shelley. Ed. James Rieger. 1974. Rpt. Chicago: U of Chicago P, 1982. xi-xxxvii.

Shelley, Mary. *Frankenstein.* *"Frankenstein": A Case Study in Contemporary Criticism.* Ed. Johanna M. Smith. Boston: Bedford-St. Martin's, 1992.

_____. *The Journals of Mary Wollstonecraft Shelley.* Ed. Paula R. Feldman and Diana Kilvert Scott. Oxford: Clarendon, 1987.

_____. *The Letters of Mary Wollstonecraft Shelley.* Ed. Betty T. Bennett. 3 vols. Baltimore: Johns Hopkins UP, 1980-1988.

Silver, Brenda R. "Textual Criticism as Feminist Practice: Or, Who's Afraid of Virginia Woolf Part II." *Representing Modernist Texts: Editing as Interpretation.* Ed. George Bornstein. Ann Arbor: U of Michigan P, 1991. 193-222.

Son of Frankenstein. Dir. V. Lee. Universal, 1939.

Tanselle, G. Thomas. "The Editorial Problem of Final Authorial Intention." *Studies in Bibliography* 29 (1976): 167-211.

Teenage Frankenstein. Dir. Herbert L. Strock. Anglo American Film Distributors, 1957.

"My thought is undressed": Some Theoretical Implications of the Texts of Dickinson's Poems

Tim Morris

Emily Dickinson's publication history, which R. W. Franklin has characterized as a "bewildering series of editions" (xvi), is actually an exemplary model of scholarly progress toward the truth. The first editions, by the poet's friend Mabel Loomis Todd in the 1890s, are full of editorial interference. Subsequent editions by the poet's niece Martha Bianchi or by Todd's daughter Millicent Bingham, from 1914 to 1945, are far more diplomatic. In 1955, professional scholarship entered Dickinson studies with the minutely accurate variorum edition by Thomas H. Johnson. Franklin himself achieved the limit of this series by publishing facsimiles of Dickinson's own manuscript "books" in 1981. The history of Dickinson's text shows editors replacing received texts of the poems with successively closer approximations to the author's manuscripts. The case of Dickinson reflects a normal, and normative, process of seeking authoritative readings, of establishing texts that reflect the author's intentions rather than those of editors and publishers. Unfortunately, as Jo-Anne Cappeluti has remarked, all of this exemplary scholarship may have been undertaken in the service of "imposing final intentions on a body of work that intentionally resists being finalized" (101).

Even Cappeluti's neat deconstruction of the program of Dickinson textual scholarship depends on the notion that a text must have an informing intention—perhaps not authorial, but located somewhere in its coherence as *text*. The legacy of the New Criticism is, perhaps, to have relocated intentionality, to place it in the structural coherence of the text as closed aesthetic whole.

Poststructuralist concepts of textuality rely in turn on this formalist legacy: deconstructive explosions of textual pretension depend for their very existence on the assumption that texts indeed encode such intentional pretensions; non- or anti-deconstructive approaches, such as the neo-organicism that informs much recent feminist and psychoanalytic theory, reconstitute intentionality just below the level of authorial consciousness.

When we reach the level of Dickinson's manuscripts in search of the author's testamentary textual intentions, however, we find a textual situation that corresponds to none of these theoretical formulations. The manuscripts, as Franklin's facsimile edition shows, are in themselves indefinite; the final authorial state of many poems is itself a variorum. In poem after poem, Dickinson includes alternate readings in footnotes to her own fair copy manuscripts. Manuscripts which are not "drafts" are nevertheless radically unfinished. The author's intention, by any measure, is indeterminate. The text lacks formalist coherence; it also lacks deconstructable pretension. And by being located in uncertainty, a Dickinson manuscript begins in inorganicism; it proceeds not from a bodily chant but from substantive variant readings.

What *are* Dickinson's texts, then? They continue to be something other than any totalizing theory of textuality would have them be. This otherness is in one sense Dickinson's style. The uniqueness of her textual situation corresponds to so many other idiosyncrasies about her that make her work so personally identifiable. But at the same time, Dickinson's textual "otherness" is a warning to any criticism of any text that sees the ultimate purpose of reading as either the eliciting of authorial teleology or the reconstruction of an authorial persona. Feminist and cultural criticism (including Marxist and New Historicist criticism), which have by and large remained comfortable with intentionality and with the author behind the text, are faced in Dickinson with a text that abnegates authorially imposed closure.

One thing is inescapable: Dickinson's texts *"are,"* unavoidably, their own textual histories. Those histories include, of course, the continual rediscovery of the author's "true" legacy, after editions like those of 1955 and 1981, and subsequent impulses to erase previous historical strata of textual history and literary interpretation. It is easier to erase textual history than it ought to be; and literary scholars, who are more verbally conservative than any other group of people, are among the most blithe of historical erasers, in pursuit of a "more" historical, more authoritative, version of the basic material of their profession.

We can trace this pursuit of authorial intention in the publication history of a single Dickinson poem. The following text appears in the 1937 Little, Brown edition of *Poems by Emily Dickinson*; it is the one established by Mabel Loomis Todd's and T. W. Higginson's 1890 edition of *Poems*:

> The soul selects her own society,
> Then shuts the door:
> On her divine majority
> Obtrude no more.
>
> Unmoved, she notes the chariot's pausing
> At her low gate;
> Unmoved, an emperor is kneeling
> Upon her mat.
>
> I've known her from an ample nation
> Choose one;
> Then close the valves of her attention
> Like stone.

The 1960 *Complete Poems* published by Little, Brown prints a text slightly different in wording and very different in appearance; it is the one adopted by Thomas H. Johnson in his 1955 edition of *The Poems of Emily Dickinson*:

> The Soul selects her own Society—
> Then—shuts the Door—
> To her divine Majority—
> Present no more—
>
> Unmoved—she notes the Chariots—pausing—
> At her low Gate—
> Unmoved—an Emperor be kneeling
> Upon her Mat—
>
> I've known her—from an ample nation—
> Choose One—
> Then—close the Valves of her attention—
> Like Stone—

The 1955 Johnson edition provoked nothing short of a paradigm shift in the study of Dickinson; decorous Victorian punctuation and orthography poems suddenly exploded into a riot of dashes, capitals, and misspellings. The new presentation of the poems seemed to indicate an entirely different creative psychology at work. Many changes in wording in the 1955 edition were replacements of "improvements" that Todd and Higginson had made (like "chariot's" and "is kneeling" in this poem) with the readings of the manuscripts; in many cases poems changed quite radically from received versions that had become canonical.

The appearance of Franklin's 1981 facsimile edition, *The Manuscript Books of Emily Dickinson*, instigated subtler changes in how Dickinson poems looked. Critics began to suspect that "there may be no way to reproduce Dickinson in print—to publish her—without re-writing her at the same time" (Bennett, "'By a Mouth'" 85). Instead of citing the poem in Johnson's metrical lineation, for instance, critics in the 1980s began to use the lineation of Dickinson's narrow manuscript pages. They also began to include the alternative readings with the text. Paula Bennett has explained the critical principle behind such an approach. When confronted by a variant reading, "As readers, we are forced to hold both views simultaneously in mind since, unselected by Dickinson, her variants must have equal authorial status in our eyes" (*Woman Poet* 42). In this form, our example reads:

> The Soul selects her own Society—
> Then—shuts the Door—
> +To her Divine Majority—
> +Present no more—
>
> Unmoved—she notes the Chariots—pausing—
> At her low Gate—
> Unmoved—an Emperor be kneeling
> +Upon her Mat—
>
> Ive' known her—from an ample
> nation—
> Choose One—
> then—Close the +Valves of
> her attention—
> Like Stone
>
> +On +obtrude + On + Rush Mat + lids—
> (Manuscript Books 450)

Dickinson used the small crosses or plus signs to key words in her "adopted" text to variants at the bottom of her page—and not always unambiguously.

It is possible to go a step further. Since there are *no* authorized publications of Dickinson poems from her lifetime, one can only preserve her intentions by presenting all of her work exactly as she left it, in manuscript facsimile. Such a method would fail only the demand of easy legibility. But citing in facsimile would establish a text for some of Dickinson's poems that has nothing further "underneath" it. Interpretation could then proceed confidently in the assurance that we are finally in direct touch with the author's legacy.

Or could it? The limit of faithfulness to the text as Dickinson left it, or at least abandoned it, is to present her manuscripts directly, and hers is an unusually clean legacy, with no competing published versions to distract us from the manuscripts. But the result of this faithfulness is, as Franklin recognized, in no way an arrival at a basis for a definite and unequivocal authorial expression. "We lack . . . authorial final intention throughout the poems of Emily Dickinson" (Franklin, *Editing* 133). The problems of Dickinson's manuscripts are intractable, because many poems exist in different manuscript versions for different purposes and recipients and are often indeterminate even within single versions:

> "Those fair—fictitious People" (V499) exists in a semi-final draft with twenty-six suggestions that fit eleven places in the poem. From this, 7680 poems are possible—not versions but, according to our critical principles, poems. (*Editing* 142)

The form of those Dickinson manuscripts which include variants at the bottom of the manuscript text adds more uncertainty to the process of explication than any possible conflict between variant stages in the revision of poems from manuscript through different printed editions. "The Soul selects her own Society—," for instance, is a poem that has drawn a great amount of critical attention; while its referent remains a point of debate—love, religion, friendship, art have been adduced—there is a consensus that the poem is about determinate choice. Given the received text of the poem, that consensus is unescapable. Given the variants that Dickinson included with her text, the theme of determinacy is severely undercut.

> Ive' known her—from an ample
> nation— / Choose One—
> then—Close the +Valves of
> her attention—
> Like Stone
> + lids   (450)

is a vexing stanza in its manuscript version. It can be paraphrased: "I've seen certainty. I've seen someone's attention shut like a valve. Or maybe a lid. One of those two. I'm not certain which."

In a letter of 25 April 1862 to T. W. Higginson, Dickinson said of some poems she enclosed: "While my thought is undressed—I can make the distinction, but when I put them in the Gown,—they look alike, and numb" (*Selected Letters* 172). Since it's unclear just what "them" and "they" refer to, I want to propose less an explication than a parallel. Criticism, Dickinson's words suggest, depends on undressing language. The social mechanisms of textual transmission—anthologies, reviews, publication, printing, even (as here) making a fair copy of an indeterminate text in order to send it to a friend—interfere with the collaboration between text and reader which possibly, for Dickinson, constitutes literature. To "make the distinction" we must return to as naked a textual situation as possible, one where the sense of option is still as alive as possible.

Gary Stonum has characterized Dickinson's poetics as "an affective theory of literature" (50); I would agree and go further by suggesting that the reader of a truly indeterminate text like Dickinson's chooses the text itself from a set of alternatives—by improvising a melody over a ground bass of meter. Take, for example, a poem explicitly about affect, P-505:

> I would not paint—a picture—
> I'd rather be the One
> It's+bright impossibility
> To dwell—delicious—on—
> And wonder how the fingers feel

Whose rare—celestial—stir—
+Evokes so sweet a Torment—
Such sumptuous—Despair—

I would not talk, like Cornets—
I'd rather be the One
Raised softly to+the Ceilings—
And +out, and easy on—
Through Villages of Ether—
Myself + endued Balloon
By but a lip of Metal—
The pier to my Pontoon—

Nor would I be a Poet—
It's finer—own the Ear—
Enamored—impotent—content—
The License to revere,
A+privilege so awful
What would the Dower be,
Had I the Art to stun myself
With Bolts—of Melody!

+fair + Horizons + by—
+ upborne + upheld + sustained
+ luxury + provokes (*Manuscript Books* 357)

While the thought of this poem is "undressed"—not stark naked, but with its foundation garments on and a few possibilities laid out on the bed—the role of the reader becomes one of choosing the specific "Gown," the verbal finish that will complete the aesthetic experience. The alternatives are substantially metrical equivalents—"fair" and "bright," "the Ceilings" and "Horizons"—but can be distant in sense and connotation: "privilege" and "luxury," for example (especially for a nineteenth-century reader who might have a positive sense of "privilege" and would see "luxury" as a deadly sin).

The weakness of the affective aesthetics presented in the received text (1890-1937) of this poem is its internal self-contradiction. The poet disavows expression in favor of affect but does so by expressing herself. But the manuscript version is not as sharply self-consuming. By suspending the expression at an indeterminate stage, the poet allows herself the experience of affect by stopping short of finalizing her expression—and enjoys the added benefit of making the reader complicit in expression by leaving the poem "unfinished."

Of course I have no confidence that my "poet" in the previous paragraph is in any way similar to Emily Dickinson. I don't believe that the historical Dickinson looked at her manuscript page and said: "I have—suspended the Expression—at an—Indeterminate Stage." I'm using a misleading shorthand—"poet" for "the implications of a set of readings." In fact, I would disagree with Stonum when he goes so far as to call Dickinson an *articulator* of an affective aesthetics. Her *texts* articulate an affective aesthetic, by demanding the performance of such an aesthetic by the reader. My distinction is not trivial. Much recent debate over Dickinson has centered on readers' images of the poet; as Martha Nell Smith observes, "serious biographers and critics continue to shroud her in sentimental and exclusively heterosexual notions and see something of a weak, defeated damsel instead of a writer, strong and self-aware" (97). But there are dangers in the image of the poet as "self-aware" of everything the critic of the 1990s finds implicit in her texts, too. When we demand a coherent "strength" in an image of an artist as the validating presence behind a text, we fall back into the desire for a certain *type* of artist—a Romantic, self-justifying type, a Walt Whitman—as the only possible bearer of aesthetic value. Therefore, any writer we study tends to become this type.

If the form of the manuscripts serves to heighten the complications between affect and expression, then that is what it does, no matter what Dickinson intended. Thomas H. Johnson's ultimately subjective course of distinguishing more from less "finished" poems in the manuscripts grants more canonical status to those where Dickinson, by eliminating or by just not preserving alternative readings, left the impression of more "polished," "controlled" verse. But the texts are ultimately mute on the degree of control the author had over them. Now, they exist, like one of their protagonists, "in Silence" (P-338).

The aesthetic of Dickinson's manuscripts can even challenge the postmodern critic. In its received form, "I would not paint—a picture" is an ideal candidate for deconstructive reading—a reading that I have already sketched in capsule form above. There, writing stands as a Derridean "supplement" to reading; reading is valorized and offered as the ideal category of poetic experience. But to valorize reading, Dickinson must resort to writing. The received poem culminates in an exasperating, paradoxical wish for a poetic power strong enough to destroy its own wielder and reduce her to the status of passive recipient. In fact, one is tempted to read the received version as a disingenuous power game where the poet toys with the supposedly valorized reader: "It's far, far better to read than to be a poet like me. I'd like to be a reader, like you. How I wish I could. Because then I could zap myself all the time, like THIS" ("If I were an Oscar Meyer Wiener / Everyone would take a bite of me").

But when we encounter the text in its fascicle form, the poem has a participatory, bridging quality that—without erasing the disturbing paradox inherent in any definite version chosen from its options—brings the reader closer to the poet and the poet closer to the reader, helps to blur the role of each in the construction of aesthetic experience. The poem becomes, on one hand, harder to deconstruct. By surrendering some pretensions to textual closure, it exposes its own status as a contingent artifact; it is a step closer to a construction site where the scaffolding and the debris become part of the final building. On the other hand, the text disarms some of the motives for deconstruction: the desire of the deconstructor to show up pretense, the deconstructive critic's commitment to proving that the literary text is in the same ontological boat as the critical text. Quite right, says the Dickinson manuscript, let's share the experience. It will be a privilege—or will it be more like a luxury?

"I would not paint—a picture" is hardly a text that completely resists deconstructive readings or even limits them very much. It is still composed, like other texts, of traces; the participatory strategy I have tried to rehearse using the manuscript text is as amenable, in turn, to deconstruction as any reading based on a single version of the text. But an overtly indeterminate single text is a new object for criticism, an object which questions many of the assumptions of both traditional close reading and deconstructive reading.

Dickinson's texts in their manuscript form also resist—without rendering powerless—poststructuralist reading strategies that are not based on deconstruction. In *La révolution du langage poétique* (1974), Julia Kristeva critiques aspects of deconstruction and offers a new kind of organicist poetics, one based not on Romantic concepts of artistic unity but on Lacanian psychoanalysis and its positing of a subject *en procés*: a pun in French, the phrase can mean "in process" or "on trial." Language, for Kristeva, is not a unified phenomenon or activity; like the subject who speaks it, it is fluid and dynamic. Language is situated at the thetic boundary, where the speaking subject names and separates the world from itself, positing its own separation, always of course in the syntactic and symbolic terms that social language imposes on it and that pre-exist any individual. But the drives that impel a subject towards the acquisition of language arise in ontogeny before the establishment of the thetic boundary and therefore are anterior to any symbolic activity; these drives come from the earliest, most undifferentiated stage of bodily experience, which Kristeva calls the *chora*. The *chora* is not present in language—indeed the thetic boundary is necessary to convert the drives of the *chora* into language—but it is the source of *semeiosis*, which for Kristeva is not, or not simply, the production of signs, but is, for want of a better approximation, human nature. We are born semiotic, in Kristeva's thinking; the subject's unconscious drive economies are the organic foundation of the subject's nature of existing through the production of signs.

The *chora* is crucial to the concept of textual practice that Kristeva develops in *La révolution du langage poétique*; in her analysis, certain early modern poets, freed from the formal "fetishism" of traditional nineteenth-century verse but writing before Freudian insights made later modernists self-conscious about the role of dreams and drives in the creative process, exemplified a textual practice that made extraordinarily productive use of the irruptions of the *chora* into the realm of language. Kristeva's examples are Mallarmé and Lautréamont—significant for our purposes in that they present an analogy, in terms of their historical situation, to Emily Dickinson: late-19th-century poets who broke with conventional expression and influenced the modernist *avant-garde*.

I have characterized Kristeva's poetics—at least in this 1974 formulation—as a neo-organicism. Yet Dickinson's manuscript poems resist organic readings, both overtly and because of their textual situation as sets or kits of alternative readings. Poem 646 presents a disjuncture between textuality and bodily experience (or "Life," as the poem succinctly calls it). Here, experience—particularly erotic experience—is seen, and indeed realized, as dissevered from the poet's decision to "become" a text.

I think To Live—may be a
+Bliss
To those + who dare to try—
Beyond my limit to conceive—
My lip—to testify—

I think the Heart I former
wore
Could widen—till to me
The Other, like the little
Bank
Appear—unto the Sea—

I think the Days—could
every one
In Ordination stand—
And Majesty—be easier—
Than an inferior kind—

No numb alarm—lest Difference
come—
No Goblin—on the Bloom—
No + start in Apprehension's Ear,
No + Bankruptcy—no Doom—

But Certainties of +Sun—
+Midsummer—in the Mind—
A steadfast South—upon the Soul—
Her Polar+time—behind—

The Vision—pondered long—
So +plausible [appears] becomes
That I esteem the fiction—
+real—
The +Real—fictitious seems—

How bountiful the Dream—
What Plenty—it would be
Had all my Life+but been Mistake
Just +rectified—in Thee
+Life + allowed +Click + Sepulchre—
Wilderness + Noon + Meridian + Night + tangible—
positive+true+truth+ been One + bleak + qualified—

(*Manuscript Books* 814-815)

The ostensible theme of the poem is the speaker's regret that she hasn't been able to live with a loved one. In this way it fits into the general pattern of Dickinson's poetry of erotic renunciation, like "I cannot live with you." But the poem is so unenergetic in its erotic connotations that it slides into being "about" something quite different, into being "about" an inability to participate in the real life that lies outside of the text. The poem reads just as coherently if one takes it as being a poem addressed by a text to a reader as if one takes it as a communication between lovers.

But the text reverses some of the traditional Western commonplaces about fixed textual forms. The classical commonplace is that the text will outlive, and preserve the living lovers— as in Spenser:

> let baser things deuize
> to dy in dust, but you shall liue by fame:
> my verse your vertues rare shall eternize,
> and in the heuens wryte your glorious name.
> Where whenas death shall all the world subdew,
> our loue shall liue, and later life renew.
> (from *Amoretti* LXXV, *Poetical Works* 575)

In "I think To Live," by contrast, "Life" is something that the poem has not "dared to try"—though the reader's natural question, whether "daring" would be enough to bring a text to life, is anticipated by the variant "allowed to try," which suggests that the attempt to live may be impossible. The text itself, through its juxtaposition of "adopted" readings and variants, exposes the futility of claiming that a text can live or "conceive" life. "A Bliss / To those who dare to try" is the overt face of the poem, its concession to those who might prefer to maintain the fiction of a text's ability to live and elide the poem's concerns by accusing it of cowardice in the face of the challenge to live fully. "A Life / To those allowed to try" is the underside, the simple recognition that for the text "To Live—may be a Life" so tautologically expressed that it is truly beyond the "limit" of the page. "What is life? It's being alive. I can't understand this, I'm a poem. Next question."

The conception that the text here has of life is the reverse of the view held by classical texts. Organic life, beyond the text's limit, features "No numb alarm—lest Difference come"—precisely the opposite of classical commonplaces about bodily decay.

Spenser's assumption of poetic immortality finds no echo here; the text feels alarm about the coming, in its own textual realm, of "Difference." How can "Difference come" to a text? That's easy for a reader of Dickinson's manuscripts (or a post-Derridean reader, who would be well-prepared for *différance* to come). The metaphor that the text presents for its own fears about its limited condition is that of a "start in Apprehension's Ear," a "Bankruptcy." Or is that a "click in Apprehension's Ear," a "Sepulchre"? Or maybe "Wilderness"? Given the burgeoning of variants, the situation of mortality becomes *less* precarious than the indeterminate situation of textuality. The text copes with this doubt by taking refuge in its own imaginative powers: "I esteem the fiction—real— / The Real—fictitious seems," a neat paraphrase for the Spenserian insistence on the generative powers of fictive language. As in "I would not paint—a picture," the situations within and without the text become blurred, a blurring that continues in the poem's final stanza, which speculates on the existence the text could have had had its life been a "Mistake / Just rectified—in Thee"—or, "Just qualified—in Thee," suggesting (as do the variants to the first stanza) that becoming flesh was never one of the options that the words here had—that the best they ever could have hoped for would have been the "qualification" of an illusory embodiment in the reader.

 An organicist reading that attempts to define "I think To Live" as an example of textual practice runs up against the poem's striking hesitation to utter itself. If the *chora* is pressing urgently on the language of the poem, it is doing so with a profoundly ambivalent urgency. Instead of being forged by the pressure of the *chora* on symbolic language, a poem like "I think To Live" has an overdetermined quality that reflects the ambivalence of the poetic voice caught in a necessary condition of textuality—a realization of its own arbitrariness, a realization that it is turning into trace even as it is being uttered. Of course, like the deconstructive reader I postulated earlier, this organicist reader has moves available. The poem may be seen as reflecting neurosis rather than jouissance. And even its formal elements may support organicist readings. As in virtually every case in the fascicles, the variants that accompany the text are metrically equivalent to the words they can replace. Line 27, for instance, reads "Had all my Life but been Mistake"; its possible alternatives are "Had all my Life been one Mistake" and "Had all my Life been bleak Mistake." Since, in Kristeva's organicism, the irruption of the *chora* into textual practice creates *the bases pulsionelles* of rhythm, one could conceive of the "text" of the poem—admittedly at one degree of abstraction—as the metrical framework that is filled in by the verbal choices of the text, a framework set by the relentless characteristic hymn-meter of the Dickinson style. This deeper level of organicist reading brings us back to the paradox of Dickinson's style: how a poetry and poetics that cannot be considered traditional or "fetishistic" can express itself in a metrical form that is utterly conventional.

If Dickinson's confusing textual history poses problems at the level of the explication of individual poems, it poses even more complicated ones for the study of reception. When one tries to consider the reception of a given Dickinson poem diachronically, it often helps to treat the 1955 edition as a saltatory disruption in the criticism, as indeed it was perceived to be by critics in the 1950s. Dickinson criticism "held its breath" for the ten years 1945-55; very few items were published then, as critics were reluctant to base interpretations on soon-to-be-obsolete texts. They then moved quickly in 1955-65 to interpret the new versions that appeared at the beginning of that decade. In individual cases we can note the errors that critics made before 1955; as Jerome McGann has pointed out, Allen Tate's assessment of "Because I could not stop for Death" as "one of the greatest [poems] in the English language" (160) is based on a reading of a text that is very unlike what Dickinson actually wrote—Tate was using a text abridged and emended by Todd and Higginson. Of course, Tate was using what he had. He liked "The Chariot," Todd and Higginson's version of "Because I could not stop for Death"; he had no access to the manuscript; and his critical judgment on that particular text must stand even when the text has lost its authorial "signature" and its authoritative status.

The larger problem, however, is that Dickinson *as an author* became canonical in, and as a result of, the Todd-Higginson versions (and later, similarly flawed versions edited by Martha Dickinson Bianchi and Alfred Leete Hampson). Without the critical success of the flawed editions, there would have been no support for the editorial process which was to so radically revise them in the 1955 edition. To make a hypothetical analogy, there may very well be flaws in the editions of Adelaide Crapsey's poems that appeared after her death in 1914; but since

Crapsey shows no signs of attracting the interest of canonizers, any restoration of authorial readings in the Crapsey *oeuvre* would be greeted with petrifying indifference. The 1955 variorum did not *cause* scholarly interest in Dickinson; it was the *result* of scholarly interest in Dickinson.

Dickinson's reception from 1890 to 1945 created a literary personality, and critics became interested in establishing and preserving what that personality uttered, at whatever cost to the texts that had created the interest in the first place. I cannot follow all the details and implications of that phenomenon here; I simply want to consider it as an example of normative literary research. Despite the odd circumstances that surround Dickinson's reception—the facts that most of her work was published posthumously, that she was unusually withdrawn in her correspondence and social life, that possession of her poetic manuscripts was divided even before her death (between herself and Susan Gilbert Dickinson)—the research situation on Dickinson has fit a normal pattern. The poet's image was generated by a series of first publications and collections, and research became devoted to stripping away the tendentious manipulations of that image by intermediaries in order to restore the purity of the author's unmediated expression.

And Dickinson did have immediate readers during her lifetime, especially her sister-in-law Susan Gilbert Dickinson. The fullest picture that survives of Dickinson interacting with a critical reader and shaping her own (very local) reception is in the case of "Safe in their Alabaster Chambers." In about 1859, the poem appears in one of the fascicles:

> Safe in their Alabaster Chambers—
> Untouched by Morning—
> And untouched by Noon—
> Sleep the meek members of the Resurrection—
> Rafter of Satin—and Roof of Stone!
>
> Light laughs the breeze
> In her Castle above them—
> Babbles the Bee in a stolid Ear,
> Pipe the Sweet Birds in ignorant cadence—
> Ah, what sagacity perished here!
>
> (*Poems of Emily Dickinson* 151)

Sometime in 1861, Dickinson was discussing this poem with Sue, who apparently didn't like the second stanza. So the poet wrote a new one:

> Grand go the Years—in the Crescent—above them—
> Worlds scoop their Arcs—
> And Firmaments—row—
> Diadems—drop—and Doges—surrender—
> Soundless as dots—on a Disc of Snow—
>   (2b; *Poems of Emily Dickinson* 152)

Sue's response to this stanza survives: "I am not suited dear Emily with the second verse—It is remarkable as the chain lightening that blinds us hot nights in the Southern sky but it does not go with the ghostly shimmer of the first verse as well as the other one" (*Poems* 1955: 152). So Dickinson wrote a third:

> Springs—shake the Sills—
> But the Echoes—stiffen—
> Hoar—is the Window—and numb—the Door—
> Tribes of Eclipse—in Tents of Marble—
> Staples of Ages—have buckled there—
>   (*Poems of Emily Dickinson* 153)

She sent this to Susan with a comment: "Could I make you and Austin—proud—sometime—a great way off—'twould give me taller feet" (*Poems* 1955: 153). Susan's reply, if any, is lost.

There exists yet another possible second stanza:

> Springs—shake the Seals—
> But the silence—stiffens—
> Frosts unhook—in the Northern Zones—
> Icicles—crawl from Polar Caverns—
> Midnight in Marble—Refutes—the Suns—
>   (*Poems of Emily Dickinson* 153)

About 1861, Dickinson included this stanza and the previous two she had sent to Susan, along with the first stanza, in a fascicle manuscript. That manuscript therefore consists of four stanzas, three of which are alternative second stanzas to go with the first. The poem remained a radically indeterminate set of possibilities. Dickinson sent the "version of 1859" ("Light laughs the breeze") to Bowles, who printed it in the *Springfield Daily Republican* in

1862. She sent the "version of 1861" ("Grand go the Years") to Higginson, also in 1862.

A short article by Florence S. Hoyt in the *Congregationalist* for 2 March 1893 describes an "Emily Dickinson evening" held at the house of a minister in suburban Chicago:

> To each person were distributed two typewritten slips of paper, each slip bearing a half of a poem by Emily Dickinson. Each person was to find and claim the second half to complete the slip in his hand, which bore a title, so in time the company had been well shaken up and each person held one whole poem.
>
> (Buckingham 322)

It would be unwise for a literary scholar to dismiss this parlor game as naive. The example of "Safe in their alabaster chambers" shows that in certain textual situations the minister's guests were making the same textual choices that an editor or a critic either must—or cannot.

But "Safe in their Alabaster Chambers" is more than just a particularly colorful example of textual indeterminacy. It suggests layers of reception often overlooked in literary scholarship. "Safe in their Alabaster Chambers" shows a multiplicity of kinds of audience-directedness in its four versions. There is a version ("Light laughs the breeze") quite literally "for publication." There is another ("Grand go the Years") sent privately to a leading figure in the literary vanguard. Higginson preferred "Grand go the Years" to "Light laughs the breeze," but at least one public Victorian reader disagreed. *The Manchester Guardian* for 11 August 1891 would quote the stanza "Grand go the Years" and call it "more than almost drivelling" (Buckingham 162). There is another version ("Springs—shake the Sills") for the poet's most intimate friend, and a fourth ("Springs—shake the Seals") for nobody but herself. When we recover the manuscript, all four versions are equally authorial, reflect equally the author's "final intentions." And when we consider the version in which the poet became canonical, we find something she never contemplated, the poem that Mabel Loomis Todd put together in 1890 and that was the only version known before 1955:

> Safe in their alabaster chambers,
> Untouched by morning and untouched by noon,
> Sleep the meek members of the resurrection,
> Rafter of satin, and roof of stone.

Light laughs the breeze in her castle of sunshine;
Babbles the bee in a stolid ear;
Pipe the sweet birds in ignorant cadence,—
Ah, what sagacity perished here!

Grand go the years in the crescent above them;
Worlds scoop their arcs, and firmaments row,
Diadems drop and Doges surrender,
Soundless as dots on a disk of snow.

(Poems of Emily Dickinson 158)

Pace Jerome McGann and with a nod to the memory of Allen Tate, that is a great poem, too. The second stanza concludes with just the right false touch of epigrammatic presumption. "Her castle of sunshine," Loomis Todd's contribution, is just silly enough. The poem gains its tremendous unsettling effect from the contrast of the second stanza's slightly satiric mid-Victorian disdain of one's pious ancestors against the frightening images of eternity and "circumference" in the third. It's a great poem; the only problem with it is that Emily Dickinson didn't write it.

WORKS CITED

Bennett, Paula. *Emily Dickinson: Woman Poet*. Iowa City: U of Iowa P, 1990.

_____. "'By a Mouth That Cannot Speak': Spectral Presence in Emily Dickinson's Letters." *The Emily Dickinson Journal* 1.2 (1992): 76-99.

Buckingham, Willis J. *Emily Dickinson's Reception in the 1890s: A Documentary History*. Pittsburgh: U of Pittsburgh P, 1989.

Cappeluti, Jo-Anne. "Fading Ratios: Johnson's Variorum Edition of Emily Dickinson's Poetry." *The Emily Dickinson Journal* 1.2 (1992): 100-120.

Dickinson, Emily. *Poems by Emily Dickinson*. Eds. Martha Dickinson Bianchi and Alfred Leete Hampson. Boston: Little, Brown, 1937.

_____. *The Poems of Emily Dickinson*. Ed. Thomas H. Johnson. Cambridge, Massachusetts: Harvard UP, 1955.

_____. *The Complete Poems of Emily Dickinson*. Boston: Little, Brown, 1960.

_____. *Emily Dickinson: Selected Letters*. Cambridge, Massachusetts:

Harvard UP, 1971.

———. *The Manuscript Books of Emily Dickinson*. Ed. R. W. Franklin. Cambridge, Massachusetts: Harvard UP, 1981.

Franklin, R. W. *The Editing of Emily Dickinson: A Reconsideration*. Madison: U of Wisconsin P, 1967.

Kristeva, Julia. *La révolution du langage poétique: L'avant-garde á la fin du xixe siècle: Lautréamont et Mallarmé*. Paris: Seuil, 1974.

McGann, Jerome J. "The Text, the Poem, and the Problem of Historical Method." In *Literary Theories in Praxis*. Ed. Shirley Staton. Philadelphia: U of Pennsylvania P, 1987. 202-215.

Smith, Martha Nell. "Gender Issues in Textual Editing of Emily Dickinson." *Women's Studies Quarterly* 19.3-4 (1991): 78-111.

Spenser, Edmund. *Poetical Works*. London: Oxford UP, 1970.

Stonum, Gary Lee. *The Dickinson Sublime*. Madison: U of Wisconsin P, 1990.

Tate, Allen. "Emily Dickinson." In *The Recognition of Emily Dickinson: Selected Criticism Since 1890*. Caesar R. Blake and Carlton F. Wells, eds. Ann Arbor: U of Michigan P, 1964. 153-167.

Multiple Editorial Horizons of *Leaves of Grass*

Mike Feehan

What odd quirk of poetic temperament led Walt Whitman to use the same title for nine books over the thirty-seven years from 1855 to 1892? Could he never quite get it right? Was he merely embellishing a project that had actually been completed on its first (second, third) appearance? Did he change his mind nine times, taking nine distinct directions, all somehow encompassed by the one title *Leaves of Grass*? The various versions include quite different contents: some versions contain only poems; some contain poems and prose. Some versions add new poems while deleting older ones. Long poems dissolve into new, shorter ones that may be scattered through the book. Titles of poems change from version to version. Poems are shuffled and reshuffled. Tables of contents change radically through the years. The first *Leaves* had fewer than one hundred pages while the ninth had nearly four hundred. In order to make some sense of "Walt Whitman's poetry," every reader, whether novice or specialist, must make some judgment about which poems and how many poems constitute the governing concept, *Leaves of Grass*.

The dominant editorial approach to *Leaves*, from the time of Whitman's death to the present, has promoted the ninth, 1891-92 version, the last one Whitman actually saw. Since the centennial of *Leaves* in 1955, however, an alternative approach has emerged: promote one of the early versions while describing the subsequent history of *Leaves* as a devolution. We now have four such arguments exemplifying this approach, one argument each for the first, second, third and fourth versions.[1] Yet all these arguments share one crucial belief: that Whitman was always writing and rewriting just one work, under the guidance of "evolution," whether upward or downward: the argument for the first *Leaves* sees Whitman as revealing his vision in 1855, a vision which, for thirty-seven years, is evolving. Each of the arguments for the second, third, and fourth versions sees Whitman as attempting to reveal his vision in early versions, but completing the project only in the given editor's preferred version, which thereafter devolves. The argument for the ninth *Leaves* sees Whitman as struggling for thirty-seven years to complete his original vision, achieving completion only at the very end of his life.

A very different view of textual choices for *Leaves of Grass* arises if we suppose, for the sake of argument, that the one title, *Leaves of Grass*, actually covers more than one poetic work— perhaps as many as nine, depending on how we choose to sub-categorize. But to suggest multiple *Leaves* could well put us in the position of arguing that two versions of the book count as different works merely because the arrangement of entries in the two tables of contents differ. Happily, an argument leading in that direction is proposed by Jerome McGann in a discussion of Arnold's "Empedocles on Etna." McGann begins by noting that the first and second editions of the poems exhibit only minimal differences in wording:

> In fact, however, the Empedocles of 1852 and the Empedocles of 1867, though linguistically congruent represent radically different texts. It seems to me the business of critical editing to make those differences clear. (*Textual Condition* 51)

The poems differ because of their differing contexts, their differing placements within differing collections of Arnold's poems. McGann congratulates H. S. Milford for having made his readers aware of this difference by including, in his 1909 edition of Arnold's poems, the tables of contents for both 1852 and 1867. (Thus the editors of the NYU Variorum *Leaves of Grass* are also to be congratulated for including the tables of contents of all the eight *Leaves* that have such tables.) McGann does not, however, argue that the different placements of "Empedocles" constitute different poetic acts, different works. The differing placements merely create distinct texts, each of them demanding independent interpretive attention, though both contributing to just one poem.

Leaves of Grass demands that we go farther, that we

examine the possibility that Whitman's many manipulations of his texts actually create new works, however stable his title. The present essay will attempt to construct a methodology for an examination of this possibility. First, we will look at another argument of McGann's, an argument for seeing all texts as composed of two codes: the linguistic and the bibliographical. Then, we will add the concept of time to McGann's bifurcated text by introducing Kenneth Burke's concept, "Circumference," Burke's calculus of perspectives, his interpretive schema for examining transformations of value. Together, McGann and Burke will allow us a dual view of the nine *Leaves*—they are nine separate, distinct texts and nine participants in a thirty-seven-year drama. We will not reach a final, definitive pronouncement about the nature and number of *Leaves of Grass*, but we will construct a comprehensive framework for investigating permanence and change in Walt Whitman's poetic career.

McGann's approach begins with a bifurcation of the concept of text itself, "calling attention to the text as a laced network of linguistic and bibliographical codes . . . a distinction that licenses a more comprehensive study of textuality. . .[to] explore such matters as ink, typeface, paper, and various other phenomena which are crucial to the understanding of textuality" (*Textual Condition* 13). McGann argues that:

> [A] careful distinction must be drawn between the linguistic and the bibliographical features of the text. The distinction is important because it highlights the interactive nature of textuality as such. So far as editors are concerned, the chief (but not sole) authority over the linguistic text is the author, whereas the chief (but not sole) authority over the bibliographical text normally falls to the publishing institution within which an author is working. (*Textual Condition* 66-67)

The words that make up the substance of the work constitute only one part of the text; attention must be paid also to the material aspects of publication. This dualistic approach allows McGann to study the social context through which a text emerges (say, the price of a book as a measure of author-audience relations) without losing contact with the language of the text. Implicitly, authorial intention loses its primacy, becoming one of among many considerations: "'[The] author's intentions,' first or final, has to be one among several criteria we use in trying to edit" (*Textual Condition* 64). Authorial intentions will continue to play a role in textual studies, but only in relation to other people's contributions, in relation to the bibliographical code of the text. McGann sees the bifurcation of texts as a foundational aspect of a project for rethinking what editors should be doing, rethinking the relationships between documents and their contexts, and rethinking the possibility of a "definitive" edition.

All texts emerge through some human situation—in McGann's Jaussian metaphor, "an editorial horizon (the horizon of their production and reproduction)": "Briefly, the editorial horizon forces one to reimagine the theory of texts—and, ultimately, theory of literature—as a specific set of social operations" ("Literary Pragmatics" 3). Writers work in a given time and place, drawing on their tribe's store of language. Manuscripts move beyond their authors to be read, judged, commented on, reproduced, even altered by various hands. Editors must take cognizance of the ensemble qualities of printed texts. This approach implies a surrendering of the concept of "definitive text" and of its grounding in "correctness":

> Correlative with this position is the argument that no single editorial procedure—no single "text" of a particular work—can be imagined or hypothesized as the "correct" one, that there are many mansions in the house of editorial choices. The indeterminacy of the textual situation fluctuates in relation to the size and complexity of the surviving body of textual materials: the larger the archive, the greater the room for indeterminacy. (*Textual Condition* 62)

McGann includes in the textual archive "manuscripts, proofs and editions, [and] all the subsequent textual constitutions which the work undergoes in its historical passage" (62). For *Leaves of Grass,* we would have not only the nine versions but all the documents leading up to each of them, including the various chapbooks and broadsides that were absorbed into *Leaves.* In addition, editors must investigate the meaning of McGann's "subsequent textual constitution," since all nine versions purport to be *Leaves of Grass.* Given nine texts, what work, how many works, are constituted under Whitman's recurrent title?

In sorting through the enormous bulk of the Whitman

"archives," we begin with eighteen categories: nine linguistic and nine bibliographical. For each version, we must first distinguish those aspects of the text that emerged during the composing process from those that emerged during the publication process. This act of distinguishing has particular relevance to *Leaves of Grass* because Whitman was often personally involved in designing new versions of the book. For instance, we know that Whitman himself participated in setting type for the first 1855 *Leaves*, though we cannot be sure of the extent of his contribution. Unfortunately, we lack the manuscript, so we do not know whether Whitman designed the book while he was writing it or later on, after consultation with his publishers. In contrast, the fourth, 1867 *Leaves*, provides, in the form of Golden's "manuscript" facsimile, abundant evidence about Whitman's textual practice. It seems that Whitman prepared the fourth *Leaves* by working through a copy of the third version, penciling revisions in the margins and between lines, pasting in slips of paper containing new lines or even whole poems. In McGann's terminology, the bibliographical code of the third *Leaves* becomes an active participant in the emerging linguistic code of the fourth. When the ninth version was prepared, 1890-91, Whitman was paralyzed, sick, near death, still writing poems, but cut off from the actual making of the book, cut off from direct contributions to the bibliographical code of *Leaves*.

The process of sorting out the two codes within each version, of course, merely begins the process of sorting out a full, textual history of *Leaves*. Nine linguistic codes paired with nine bibliographical codes give us nine distinct *Leaves*. Yet all nine were composed by the same man, and all nine bear the same title. We require some rationale for examining the relations across time of the nine *Leaves*. Such a rationale may be found in a concept of Kenneth Burke's "watershed moments":

> [W]e should watch for "critical points" within the work, as well as at beginnings and endings. There are often "watershed moments," changes of slope, where some new quality enters. (*Philosophy* 78)

Burke enrolls the Aristotelian notion of peripeteia, moments of recognition or turning, as the key to studying textual change across time. We should treat a writer's texts as aspects of the full dramatic development of the writer's life, but we will not be concerned with the whole biography. Textual "watershed moments" include only those experiences which bring the writer to the act of writing. This is not to say that all "watershed moments" will be objectively verifiable or conclusively determinable. Scholars will disagree over which moments count as "watersheds," over the relative importance of any given "watershed," and over the scope of each "watershed." For *Leaves of Grass*, for instance, some scholars see the crucial watershed moment as occurring before the first *Leaves* was written, others point to the death of Whitman's father just after the first *Leaves* appeared, still others propose a love affair, variously dated as 1848, 1850-52, 1858-59. Most often, "watershed" arguments about *Leaves* take the form of arguments about the "true" *Leaves*, along the following lines, "The true *Leaves* appears only in version [1,2, 3, 4, or 9], because his (definitive or culminative) watershed moment occurred in (1855, 1856, 1860, 1867 or 1881)." Regarding the present argument, that we are dealing with several quite different works, we would translate the argument thus: "There are [either 1, 2, 3, 4, or 9] *Leaves* because Whitman experienced [either 1, 2, 3, 4, or 9] watershed moments." Which of these options we choose will depend on how we evaluate the importance to *Leaves* of various events and experiences in Whitman's life. As we differ over "watershed moment," we will differ over the number of works constituted under the title, *Leaves of Grass*. We are not here concerned to choose among these alternatives; the goal here is merely to describe a methodology for a three-way sorting among "codes": textual, bibliographical and temporal.

If we now translate McGann's vocabulary into Burke's dramatistic terminology, it will be possible to comprehend all three codes under Burke's more general concept, "circumference": "The word reminds us that, when 'defining by location,' one may place the object's definition in contexts of varying scope" (*Grammar* 77). That is, for any given situation, there are numerous possible perspectives, some of them closer to the action, some farther away. The observer's distance from the action will influence interpretation because each wider concentric circle includes new and different contents. Up close, we see the central action clearly, but we cannot see much of the periphery. As we move back, the center becomes less clear, but we see more of the surrounding activities. Using the idea of drama, for instance, we may study the characters as they move across the stage or we may narrow our focus to study the sentences they use, their words, their pronunciations. Or we might step back to study the actors in relation to their dramatic characters. We might widen our focus even further to study the audience's expectations about the drama, or we might even step outside the theater to study the background knowledge that members of the audience bring with them to the theater. Any two observers, on leaving the theater, may find themselves in utter disagreement over what they saw because they have viewed the drama from different stances, with different circumferences, different contents, different values.

McGann's dualistic theory of text describes the boundaries between two circumferences: the "linguistic code," which focuses narrowly on the words on the page, and the "bibliographical code," which focuses more widely on the "physique" of the document as a whole, including, of course, the linguistic code. Here we should recall McGann's argument, cited above, that linguistic codes tend to link editors and authors, while bibliographical codes tend to link editors and printers. What Burke adds is an explicit logic of these linkages. From the perspective of linguistic code, the social conditions of production all but disappear as the editor focuses on what the writer has inscribed. From the perspective of bibliographical code, social conditions dominate the editor's concerns, directing attention to materials available to and economic pressures upon publishers. From the perspective of an added code, the temporal, suggested by Burke's "watershed moment," a turning point in the author's life (caused by sociohistorical context) may also shape the text to a greater or lesser degree.

The three codes, then, can be understood as three circumferences, three concentric circles encompassing the printed page.[2] In line with Burke's dramatistic emphasis, I propose a translation of McGann's terminology: McGann's linguistic code becomes "the workshop," and his bibliographical code becomes "the printshop." This translation implies a widening of focus in textual study from examinations of material objects to interpretive explorations of the human dramas that surround and include those objects. Where McGann's "horizon" focuses on the boundary line between aspects of a text, Burke's "circumference" accounts for all the elements within each arena or venue: actors, events, settings, props, themes, values (*Grammar* 231). We have, then, three scenes of production and reproduction.

At the narrowest focus, "the workshop horizon or venue," the writer sits alone facing the blank page, drawing on internal needs and hopes, drawing from the situation that has led to this writing, and aiming toward some public, "finished" version. Though clock-time may pass, we are concerned with a single "moment" in the sense that documents are emerging through the writer's own self-dialogue, attempts to capture as fully as possible some personal sense of achievement. Whether and to what extent the rest of the world may impinge on the workshop can be determined only by a close study of the composing processes of individual writers.

At a next wider focus, "the printshop horizon or venue," we now move to documents that have been produced during or as the result of interactions with other people. The writer leaves the workshop to present a set of documents to some reader for the purpose of publication. The documents will necessarily undergo change. The impact of the author's intentions will differ for every author-publisher relationship, regardless of whether the text at issue is a new or revised work.

At the next wider focus, "the watershed moment" or "watershed horizon," we look at the situations that led the writer into the workshop. We will not be concerned with every event in the writer's life but only with those that directly affect the making of the text. Of course, any two scholars may disagree vehemently about which events have stimulated composition and about the importance of that stimulation. We should also note that there may well be more than one watershed moment for any given text. Indeed, it might be argued that, for writers like Joyce and Faulkner, the output of the printshop is itself a watershed moment. That is, the very act of seeing typed versions of their work might well drive authors back into the workshop, to make corrections, change directions, or add new, unexpected passages. For *Leaves of Grass*, there will be at least nine watershed moments—at least one for each version—though investigations of Whitman's composing habits across thirty-seven years might well evince more than nine.

The three circumferences and their relations provide a reasoned pattern for sorting through a writer's archive, a methodology for "staging" the drama of production and reproduction. When we examine the six mathematically possible hierarchies among these circumferences, we will begin to see how various scholars, all looking at the same texts, can arrive at quite different judgments about editorial practice. Some editors will believe that the composing process always takes pride of place in interpretation, the complexities of biography or publication serving only to corrupt the text. Some editors will argue that the work of publishing a book so changes the author's relation to the work that the printshop must be recognized as the dominant circumference. Some editors will insist on the dominance of social context. The methodology proposed here will provide a format both for sorting among these different perspectives and for recognizing their inevitability:

1. Workshop, watershed, printshop. The process of composition generates the text; social-historical context plays the secondary role in providing content, a background across which the poetic impulse moves; the demands of publication may have some tertiary impact.[3]

2. Workshop, printshop, watershed. The process of composition generates the text; the demands of publication, house style, serializations, book design, etc, cause alterations in the manuscripts; social-historical context may play some tertiary role.

3. Watershed, workshop, printshop. The social-historical context impels the writer to plan a new work; the process of composition alters the plan, perhaps a great deal, perhaps only slightly; the demands of publication may play some tertiary role.

4. Watershed, printshop, workshop. The social-historical context impels the writer to plan a new work; the demands of publication alter the plan, perhaps a great deal, perhaps only slightly; the process of composition may play some tertiary role.

5. Printshop, workshop, watershed. The technology of publication makes some new work possible; the composing process attempts to realize that possibility; the social-historical context may play some tertiary role.

6. Printshop, watershed, workshop. The technology of publication makes some new work possible; the social-historical context suggests a particular content for that new work; the composing process may play some tertiary role.

For *Leaves of Grass*, a workshop approach would give focal attention to Whitman's habits of composition, his notetaking, the manuscript form, and the types and levels of revision. A watershed approach would focus on Whitman's biography, on his personal experiences, the development of his ideas about poetry and the connections between those ideas and the growth of America. A printshop approach would look most closely at the "physique" of each of the nine versions, at their shape and size, at the appearance of the poems on the page. These three circumferences make possible a rereading of various editors' arguments about *Leaves*, arguments about the number of "editions" of *Leaves*, about Whitman's final intentions, and about the identification of a "best" *Leaves*.

Though nine versions of *Leaves of Grass* appeared during Whitman's lifetime, the editors of the monumental NYU Variorum *Leaves* do not count all nine as "editions": "Actually, there are not nine editions of *Leaves of Grass*, but only six" (Bradley 1: xxi). Employing arguments from McKerrow and Bowers, the editors of the Variorum employ the title "edition" only where the plates have been altered: McKerrow stipulates, "one setting-up of type"; Bowers requires, "a complete resetting of the type" (Bradley 1: xx). According to this approach, the fifth and sixth versions of *Leaves* (1871 and 1876) together comprise one edition, and the seventh, eighth and ninth versions (1881, 1888, 1891-92) together count as one edition. The first, second, third, fourth, fifth and seventh versions (1855, 1856, 1860, 1867, 1871 and 1881) all count as separate editions, because "each was printed from one setting-up of type, each contained new material, differently arranged, and the format of each book was wholly new" (Bradley 1: xxi). The sixth, eighth and ninth versions will be demoted to "impression," a new issue without the resetting of plates. The distinction between edition and impression allows the Variorum editors to distinguish further between *Leaves*-proper and *Leaves*-plus-ancillary materials. In the view of the Variorum editors, Whitman completed *Leaves*-proper in 1881; therefore, the poems added in appendices in 1888 and 1891-92 cannot be taken as parts of "the perfected *Leaves of Grass*" (Bradley 1: xxv).

From the perspective of the three circumferences, however, it appears that the approach to "editions" evident in the Variorum *Leaves* illegally crosses a textual boundary. The editors tell us, "The 1881 edition finally conformed to his conception of his book as a 'single poem'" (Bradley 1: xviii). The 1881 edition is "final" because Whitman did not reset the plates after that date. The editors, following McKerrow and Bowers, have crossed the boundary between workshop and printshop: author's intentions have been reduced to printer's plates. The editors can situate Whitman's final thoughts about *Leaves* in 1881 because the poet did not thereafter reset the plates. The author's ideas about his life's work can be adequately explained on the basis of the negative fact of his not making new demands on his printers.

An attempt to avoid the improper crossing of boundaries appears in Hans Walter Gabler's controversial edition of *Ulysses*. Gabler begins by recognizing that Joyce himself continually crossed the boundary between workshop and printshop:

> The composition of *Ulysses* was directed towards publication. It advanced from notes and draft via final draft, fair copy, typescript and extensive revisions on the typescripts and multiple proofs to its culmination in the first edition of February 1922. (1891)

Each time Joyce handed a portion of his manuscript to someone, he found that the resulting document, whether typescript or proof, demanded further work—additions, deletions, permutations. Then, shortly prior to February 1922, someone decided to start the presses, and Joyce's chances for continued tinkering simply ended. Unfortunately, the resulting document, the first edition, cannot be used as copy-text because "it does not present the text as he wrote it" (1891). The output of the printshop venue differs significantly from the output of the workshop venue. The first edition contains a "high incidence of corruption" (1892). In place of the first edition, Gabler proposes as his copy-text an ideal intermediate text, the Continuous Manuscript Text, "freed of the errors with which *Ulysses* was first published" (1892). Because the printers have sinned against authorial intention, the editor attempts to identify, within the near chaos of intersections between workshop and printshop, the precise state of the text at the moment the presses began to run, the moment when all workshop activity ended and printshop activity swerved off on its own "corrupt" course.

A circumferential, multiple texts approach would begin by thanking Gabler for his work toward identifying the boundary between workshop and printshop in the making of *Ulysses*. The idea of a Continuous Manuscript Text provides a textual focus for any editor dealing with a writer like Joyce, who characteristically responds to the printer's texts by making another new text. For instance, as Gabler points out, there are times when Joyce himself, acts merely as "scribe," introducing nonauthorial changes—times, that is, when the author becomes merely one of the printer's agents (1892). Gabler's invention of a new kind of copy-text shows a strong insistence on the primacy of the author's workshop. The contributions of the printshop are seen as secondary and intrinsically problematic: a first printed text introduces errors; the next printing corrects some of those errors while introducing new ones; and so on. Gabler treats the watershed horizon as wholly destructive: temporal distance from composition deprives even the author of "authorial intention." Gabler must create his new kind of copy-text, because he espouses a workshop, printshop, watershed approach. The present discussion does not suppose that Gabler's approach is definitive, only that it identifies a crucial moment in the development of a text. Nine published versions and nine Continuous Manuscript Texts would give us eighteen possible *Leaves*. Future editors will employ Gabler's Continuous Manuscript model if and only if their interpretive stances rank the workshop venue above both the printshop and the watershed moment. If we look at the McKerrow-Bowers orientation we see that the choice of first edition as copy-text arises as the text most relevant to their interpretive stance: printshop (primacy of plates), watershed (final, postpublication authorial corrections), workshop (some manuscript emendations allowed).

If we turn now to the question of a copy-text for *Leaves*, we find that most editors prefer the ninth "deathbed" edition, usually because of an argument similar to that of the editors of NYU Variorum:

> The 1891-92 *Leaves of Grass* was approved by Whitman "for future printings, if there should be any," and represented the culmination of his effort, begun in 1855, to construct a unified "poem," *Leaves of Grass*. (Bradley 1: xv)

The Variorum editors do not subscribe to the simplistic view that Whitman's final plan "had been prefigured from the start." On the contrary, they insist, "Quite simply, Whitman altered *Leaves of Grass* from edition to edition as his own views changed" (Bradley 1: xi). Still, Whitman produced *Leaves* as a single, perfected poem. For all the changes in Whitman and his book, there was always one conclusive *Leaves* toward which all the others evolved. The editors argue that Whitman actually completed the perfect *Leaves* in the seventh, 1881 version, but subsequent authorial corrections to that version require the choice of the ninth version as copy-text. Thus we have a printshop (1881 plates, as corrected), watershed (Whitman's deathbed note) orientation. Whitman's workshop is here explicitly rejected. The editors seem to state, "Although we choose the 1891-92 version as copy-text, we exclude any poems written after 1881, because Whitman did not place any of them inside the plates of *Leaves*-proper."

The very different, multiple works, view of *Leaves* might begin with the kind of argument employed by Leslie Fiedler in his centennial essay, "Images of Walt Whitman":

> Even his face changed, along with his stance and costume, as he willed himself from photograph to photograph into the image of the Rowdy, the Christ, the Workman's Friend, the Beard and the Butterfly, the Good Grey Poet. (57)

These six images of the poet (and numerous others, i.e., the Nurse, the Gay Lover) have all appeared in literary critical studies of *Leaves of Grass*, the poem. In each case, the given critic has proposed one or the other image of Whitman as the one and only unifying image for the whole work. A multiple works approach would ask whether each of these images might not characterize one of the many *Leaves*. The Whitman of 1855, the Rowdy, created poems out of the experience of New York City and its environs. The Whitman of 1864, the Nurse, created battlefield poems. The 1865 Whitman, the Mourning Patriot, grieved for Lincoln. The Whitman of 1871, the Good Grey Poet, wrote poems of the reconciliation of the states. The 1881 Whitman wrote Old Age poems.

The poet of 1855 could not have written the battlefield or the Lincoln poems. Even the 1856 poet, writing about Death, was not writing poems about the physical agonies of old-age infirmities. A circumferential approach to *Leaves* would begin by looking at each of the nine versions as though they were wholly unrelated—as if they were nine works by different authors—works that happen to share the same title. For each of the nine versions, we would attempt to determine the scope and contents of the workshop, printshop, and watershed. (Scholars would, of course, disagree about the relative importance of each of these horizons to the given *Leaves*.) Only with such individual analysis completed would we begin to ask about interrelations. (Any disagreements that have already arisen about the interpretation of a given version will, of course, carry over to and color our attempts to construct linkages among the nine *Leaves*.) For the present argument, we can make only a cursory survey of the nine versions of *Leaves* and suggest some of the ways in which the horizons approach can help to sort through various editorial arguments.

Whitman's activities through the years preceding the composition of the first *Leaves*, "the long foreground," have received more scholarly attention than any other aspect of Whitman's career. Virtually all of Whitman's pre-*Leaves* writings have been reproduced, and various claims have been made about the events that transformed a rather unexceptional journalist into Walt Whitman. Unfortunately, for all the mass of early texts we possess, it is not possible to describe clearly the watershed moment because most of the manuscript has disappeared. Whitman probably distributed manuscript pages among the typesetters and then retrieved them and used the reverse sides for other writing projects. We cannot compare Whitman's pre-*Leaves* work with the manuscripts of the first *Leaves* to see how the events of composition contributed to the new poetry. We do possess, however, the printed text of Whitman's first *Leaves of Grass*, the output of the first printshop horizon.

Malcolm Cowley gives an efficient summary of the unusual appearance of that first sortie:

> The original work is a thin folio about the size and shape of a block of typewriting paper. The binding is of dark-green pebbled cloth, and the title is stamped in gold, with the rustic letters sending down roots and sprouting above into *Leaves*. Inside the binding are ninety-five pages, numbered iv-xii and 14-95. A prose introduction is set in double columns on the roman-numeraled pages, and the remaining text consists of twelve poems, as compared with 383 in the final or

> "Deathbed" edition. The first poem, later called "Song of Myself," is longer than the other eleven together. There is no table of contents, and none of the poems has a title. (vii)

When we look at the "facsimile" edition that Cowley actually published, however, we can see how an editor's preferred orientation can color his textual judgments. Cowley reduces the page size, reduces the type size, removes the double-columns from the prose opening, adds a table of contents and gives all the poems the titles of their last published version. For Cowley, despite Whitman's personal role in creating its striking appearance, the "physique" of the first *Leaves of Grass* need not be part of the process of reading the book.

The printshop horizon, then, plays only a minor role in Cowley's estimation of Whitman's achievement. Surprisingly, the workshop horizon plays an even lesser role. Cowley situates the key poetic quality of the work not in the writing act but somewhere in the fields of rural Long Island, in the watershed moment: "What it must have been was a mystical experience in the proper sense of the word" (xii). Cowley then suggests, in line with Whitman's disciple Dr. Bucke, that the experience in question occurred "on a June morning in 1853 or 1854" (xii). After this experience, having pondered its significance, Whitman inscribed a report in verse. Cowley's hierarchy is clearly watershed, printshop, workshop. Many of the scholars who have written about the first *Leaves* employ this same general schema; differences arise only in choosing a date for the watershed "experience."

The 1855 *Leaves of Grass*, as it came to the hands of its first readers, not only hides its generic identity but refuses to explain its own internal structure. The title page announces *Leaves of Grass* but names no author. The prose opening has no title, and its presentation, in long double columns with small, rather muddy type, virtually demands that the reader pass by. The title *Leaves of Grass* reappears, in large type, at the head of the first page following the prose opening, introducing a text in large type that might be anything from lax verse to notes to aphorisms. The title *Leaves of Grass* appears again and again throughout the book, as a header to all eighty-one pages of text, and as a spacer between six of the following eleven sections. Each of the twelve subsections of might-be-verse exhibits a distinct thematic focus and something like a formal development of theme, yet the text gives no clues about the possible interrelations of the subsections. Might not this first *Leaves* actually form one complex event, ensemble, a sort of sonata form—overture (untitled prose opening); first movement, forty-three pages, full range of themes; second movement, twenty-eight pages, five short, alternative perspectives (in some distinct tempo?); third movement, ten pages, a summative passing through of themes (in some third tempo?). Or are these varied elements just the collected jottings of a rambling mind whose overall mood is called *"Leaves of Grass"*?

If we had only the first *Leaves*, we would still be wondering just what kind of document Whitman had produced. Indeed, the book might be a miscellany, an anthology exhibiting a collection of lyric outbursts related only by their having been written at about the same time. Cowley designs his "facsimile" by looking backwards from 1892 to 1855, a move characteristic of scholars who assume that Whitman produced only one *Leaves*. If we reject such an anachronistic view, we see Whitman's first *Leaves* as questioning, by its very physical appearance, the idea of a "book," the idea of unity and the idea of genre. Only with the second version does *Leaves* take on a more recognizable, "Collected Poems," appearance.

Where the first *Leaves* is tall and skinny, the second, published about a year after the first, is short and fat, about the size and shape of an English grammar handbook. This book does not stick its head up above the crowd as the first one does; this stubby creature would hardly be noticed on a bookshelf and its bulk would probably seem quite forbidding to a reader of newspapers, the audience Whitman had been addressing for the preceding quarter century. Because the pages are now so small, the long lines look even longer than they did in the first version, as though they are whole paragraphs. More important is the fact that Whitman provided this second *Leaves* with a table of contents, listing thirty-two items numbered consecutively. The prose passage has been removed, though much of it now appears as verse, and the book contains twenty new items, scattered among the original twelve. Furthermore, Whitman gave each of the entries an individual title, identifying each of them as "Poem."

The first *Leaves* had been a complete flop: it died without a whimper, except for Emerson's laudatory response. Of the very few readers, most simply did not know what to make of the book; even the anchor of genre proved elusive: Emerson employed the noncommital epithet, "extraordinary piece of wit and wisdom." In addition, Whitman's father died just as the first *Leaves* was published. Whitman's response: reuse the same title along with Emerson's recommendation; add more pages and identify the genre as unequivocally poetry. Again, we lack manuscript materials, but the published text of the second *Leaves* gives us: (1) "Crossing Brooklyn Ferry," which critics have seen as a tightened version of the poems of the first edition, an attempt in verse to confront the death of the father, and (2) "Poem of Many in One," a verse rewriting of the prose opening from the first *Leaves,* in itself a portrait of the boundary between verse and prose for Whitman. Study of the second workshop, though possible, has received little attention. The intriguing printshop question has not even been asked: why has the bold broadside of the first version become, in the second, such an undistinguished, huddled mass?

The third, 1860 version, looks a good deal more like the second version than the first, a few centimeters taller but considerably thicker. Significantly, the book now exhibits an extensive and complex internal articulation. For this third *Leaves,* Whitman invents the concept, "cluster," a concept he associated with sonnet cycle, a group of short poems more or less connected by theme. Each cluster is given a title. Within clusters, some sections have numbers, and some have individual titles. Some of the poems are themselves divided into numbered subsections: "Walt Whitman," for instance, has 372 sections (its 1892 cognate poem, "Song of Myself," has fifty-two sections). The table of contents has become so convoluted that it is difficult to tell how Whitman wants his readers to understand the internal shape of the book. There are thirty-one main entries, five of these listing numbered subsections, one of these five having fifteen individually titled subsections. Several different typefaces are used: bold caps, small caps, initial caps with small letters, and italics. One of the main entries is called *"Leaves of Grass"* and it has twenty-four subentries. Nothing in the contents and no statement in the book tell readers how to understand these convolutions. While the first *Leaves* virtually denies all internal articulation and the second rather sniffs at articulation with its bare list of titles, this third *Leaves* assaults us with a bewildering swarm of coordinations and subordinations. Fredson Bowers has provided a vivid picture of this workshop activity for this third version in his *Whitman's Manuscripts*: *"Leaves of Grass" (1860)*. Bowers shows clearly that Whitman's monumental redesigning of *Leaves* developed in the workshop, as did his composing of new poems, long before the book went to the printers.

As we saw above, Arthur Golden's edition of *Walt Whitman's Blue Book* shows that the poet created his fourth *Leaves* by intersecting the printshop and workshop, by composing the new *Leaves* directly on the printed pages of the previous version. With this fourth, 1867 *Leaves*, Whitman also created an important new complication for *Leaves*: the addition of two appendices, "Drum-Taps" and "Songs of Parting." Four years later, in the fifth *Leaves*, both of these appendices have been situated within the text of *Leaves*-proper. To understand the process by which these first two appendices became absorbed into *Leaves* we must step back to 1865, to the publication of *Drum-Taps* as a separate volume. Whitman wrote about this new book to his friend Nellie O'Connor:

> It is in my opinion superior to *Leaves of Grass*—certainly more perfect as a work of art, being adjusted in all its proportions and its passion having the indispensible [sic] merit that though to the ordinary reader let loose with wildest abandon, the true artist can see that it is yet under control. . . . Still *Leaves of Grass* is dear to me, always dearest to me as my first-born, as daughter of my life's first hopes, doubts, and the putting in form of those days [sic] efforts and aspirations. (qtd in Miller xxviii-xxix)

In 1865, Whitman sees *Leaves* as appropriate to an era now concluded. The coming of the Civil War demanded a new poetic, one which expressed

> the pending action of this Time and Land we swim in, with all their large conflicting fluctuations of despair and hope, the shiftings, masses, and the whirl and deafening din. (qtd in Miller xxix)

Leaves of Grass cannot contain this new poetic. Yet, just two years later, "Drum Taps" can appear as an appendix to *Leaves*; in another four years, "Drum-Taps" can be rethought as an integral part of the first-born. Nor is "Drum-Taps" simply dropped into *Leaves*. The cluster, "Drum-Taps," retaining many of its poems, has been placed just beyond the halfway point of *Leaves*. However, more than a dozen poems from the volume *Drum-Taps* now appear in other, newly created clusters, such "Marches Now The War Is Over" and "Bathed In War's Perfume." Several other *Drum-Taps* poems, including all of the Lincoln elegies, fail to appear in this fifth *Leaves* at all, having been removed to the separate volume *Passage To India*. Later, of course, in 1881, that volume will also be absorbed into *Leaves*, its contents scattered, rearranged, and revised.

Then what are we to make of Whitman's 1865 claim that *Leaves* had been completed, that a new poetic begins with *Drum-Taps*? If we see all nine *Leaves* as constituting just one work, we must argue that the Whitman of 1865 misunderstood his own Civil War poems, that even Whitman did not realize the elasticity of the concept, *Leaves of Grass*. From a multiple-horizons perspective, it might be argued that the Whitman of 1865 correctly understood the radical disjuncture between the poems of the third *Leaves* and the new poems of *Drum-Taps*. By 1871, however, the nature of *Leaves of Grass* itself had changed, with the emergence of the Good Grey Poet, the poet of a reconstituted America, an America now reconciled to the Civil War but not yet reconciled to the death of Lincoln.

We begin to see a complex process in which Whitman tried to escape from *Leaves of Grass* by simply declaring victory. In composing *Drum-Taps*, the workshop activity of 1861-65, Whitman has created a new kind of poem, a new set of themes, a whole new direction for his poetry. When the next *Leaves* was issued, in 1867, Whitman could highlight the differences between his older and newer poetry through juxtaposition, by binding the two works together. Then, four years later, Whitman created a new *Leaves* that could incorporate the new and the old poems in one arena. From a multiple-horizons perspective we must ask about the venues of the changes: did the new poetic of 1865 assault Whitman as a "mystical" experience on the battlefield, or did Whitman, in struggling over a blank page, find that his battlefield experiences could emerge only as some new, unexpected kind of poem? Did the absorption of *Drum-Taps* into *Leaves* arise through some conversation or correspondence with readers, or did the absorption begin in the workshop as Whitman rethought the nature of *Leaves*; or did the absorption arise in the printshop where Whitman could see the scattered plates and envision a new kind of incorporation? A process of absorption occurred, too, with the Lincoln poems and "Passage to India," which first entered *Leaves* in an appendix and later became integrated into the whole.

These processes of absorption suggest that we should take with some skepticism Whitman's deathbed insistence that the ninth, 1891-92 version constitutes the final, unalterable *Leaves of Grass*. In the spring of 1892, Whitman's closest friends brought a proof copy of the ninth *Leaves* to his sickbed. There Whitman wrote and signed a note recommending this version, "complete, for future printings, if there should be any" (Bradley et al I, xxv). At this point, Whitman was almost completely paralyzed and near death. He had not altered the plates of *Leaves* proper for ten years, though *Leaves* did appear, in several different bindings, in 1888 and 1889. He did add two clusters, "Sands at Seventy" (1888) and "Good-Bye My Fancy" (1891) and a prose reprise, "A Backward Glance O'er Travelled Roads." Still, Whitman continued to write poems, fifty-eight for "Sands at Seventy," bound in as an appendix in 1888 and another thirty-two for "Good-Bye My Fancy," bound in as a second appendix in 1891. Several new poems, along with some old rejected pieces, would be collected by Whitman's friends and bound into a tenth (1892) *Leaves* as the appendix, "Old Age Echoes."

Because Whitman did not situate the last three clusters within *Leaves*, the editors of the Variorum conclude that the poems contained in them do not belong in the canon of *Leaves of Grass*. A multiple-horizons approach would take a quite different line: Whitman did not simply drop appendices into *Leaves*. And placing a new cluster within the text demanded serious poetic work: reconsidering of the shape of the work as whole, reshaping the new cluster, bringing in poems from other clusters, removing some poems to other clusters, dropping some poems completely. Though Whitman could still compose individual poems, he did not, in his final days, possess the strength for the monumental task of reconceiving *Leaves of Grass*. Accordingly, the three appendices may indeed be considered part of the project *Leaves of Grass*; the workshop need not be neglected.

Certainly Whitman carried a single image, *Leaves of Grass*, across thirty-seven years, but we would be poor readers of poetry if we took that image to be univocal. *Leaves of Grass* may make up a green field or, once mown, may fly off on the wind or be baled as hay. Or we may leave grass behind, or the grass may leave us, or Whitman may admonish us to leave off undervaluing the grass: a flag of disposition, a handkerchief of the Lord, a child, a sign, the uncut hair of graves. Reading the arguments favoring one or the other version of *Leaves* and recognizing in each of them an important insight into Whitman's achievement, we might posit that each argument accurately illuminates one of the many *Leaves*. Then a choice of copy-text will depend on how many distinct *Leaves* we identify. From the list of printed texts, the Variorum editors list six as distinct. The multiple-horizons approach might ultimately take all nine published versions as distinct. Hans Walter Gabler's Continuous Manuscript concept would create either six or nine more texts, six or nine pre-publication *Leaves*. Then, if Gabler can invent an ideal text at the boundary between workshop and printshop, is it not possible that someone might invent an ideal text between the watershed and the workshop, thus providing us with as many as nine more *Leaves*, for a total of twenty-seven? An ideal tenth *Leaves*, with the published tenth *Leaves* and the Continuous Manuscript tenth *Leaves*, would raise the total number of defensible texts to thirty.

NOTES

[1]For the first (1855) version, see Cowley; for the second (1856), see Goodson; for the third (1860), see Pearce; for the fourth (1867), see Moon, chapter 5.

[2]Though the range of circumferences must be infinite, reaching, in Burke's vocabulary, to "god terms," the study of versions of *Leaves of Grass* requires only that we account for the three perspectives proposed here.

[3]The first term identifies the dominant focus, followed by the secondary and tertiary. The numbers 1-6 serve as reference points only, implying no priorities. I proceed from the smallest circumference to the largest.

182   Mike Feehan

WORKS CITED

Bowers, Fredson, ed. *Whitman's Manuscripts: "Leaves of Grass"
   (1860), A Parallel Text*. Chicago: U of Chicago P, 1955.
Bradley, Sculley, et al., eds. *"Leaves of Grass": A Textual Variorum
   of the Printed Poems*. By Walt Whitman. 3 vols. New York:
   New York UP, 1980.
Burke, Kenneth. *A Grammar of Motives*. 3rd ed. Berkeley: U of
   California P, 1969.
_____. *The Philosophy of Literary Form: Studies in Symbolic Action*.
   3rd ed. Berkeley: U of California P, 1974.
Cowley, Malcolm. Introduction. *Walt Whitman's "Leaves of
   Grass"; The First (1855) Edition*. New York: Viking, 1959.
Emerson, Ralph Waldo. Letter to Walt Whitman. Concord, 21
   July 1855. In *Leaves of Grass*, By Walt Whitman. Bound in
   before frontispiece. Brooklyn: [Rome Brothers], 1855.
   (Second issue).
Fiedler, Leslie A. "Images of Walt Whitman." *"Leaves of Grass":
   One Hundred Years After*. Ed. Milton Hindus. Palo Alto:
   Stanford UP, 1955. 55-73.
Gabler, Hans Walter. Afterword. In *"Ulysses": A Critical and
   Synoptic Edition*. By James Joyce. Eds. Hans Walter
   Gabler with Wolfhard Steppe and Claus Melchior. 3
   vols. New York: Garland, 1984. 1859-1907.
Golden, Arthur. *Walt Whitman's Blue Book: The 1860-61 "Leaves of
   Grass" Containing His Manuscript Additions and Revisions*.
   2 vols. New York: New York Public Library, 1968.
Goodson, Lester. "The Second *Leaves of Grass* (1856): A
   Revaluation." *Papers on Walt Whitman*. The University of
   Tulsa Monograph Series 11. Ed. Lester Zimmerman and
   Winston Weathers. Tulsa: U of Tulsa P, 1970. 6-34.
McGann, Jerome. "Literary Pragmatics and the Editorial
   Horizon." *Devils and Angels: Textual Editing and Literary
   Theory*. Ed. Philip Cohen. Charlottesville: UP of Virginia,
   1991. 1-21.
_____. *The Textual Condition*. Princeton: Princeton UP, 1991.
Miller, F. DeWolfe. Introduction. *Walt Whitman's "Drum-Taps"
   (1865) and "Sequel to Drum-Taps" (1865-6)*. Ed. F. DeWolfe
   Miller. Gainesville, FL: Scholars' Facsimiles & Reprints,
   1959. vii-lix.
Moon, Michael. *Disseminating Whitman: Revision and Corporeality
   in "Leaves of Grass."* Cambridge: Harvard UP, 1991.
Pearce, Roy Harvey. *Leaves of Grass (Facsimile Edition of the 1860
   Text)*. Ithaca, NY: Great Seal Books, 1961.

A "Very Different Dance": Intention, Technique, and Revision in Henry James's New York Edition

James Murphy

The revisions Henry James made for his New York Edition continue to spark critical debate, principally over which versions to prefer, to read, to canonize. The history of this long debate is beyond the scope of this essay, which wishes just to offer another way of understanding the relation of intention to text and to find the place revision has in that relation. However, limited by a concern with this relation, we can summarize the debate by briefly describing the choices theoretically available. Currently a reader or an editor is faced with but two ways of understanding authorial changes: either they are the product of a new vision, a new comprehensive intention, or they are further developments of the original unifying vision, the original comprehensive intention. G. Thomas Tanselle, in his influential "The Editorial Problem of Final Authorial Intention," calls the first type of revision "vertical" and the second type "horizontal" (193). Changes understood to be part of a vertical revision, because they are the fruit of a new intention, are said to result in a "new work" if they are sufficiently numerous, leaving us with two separate works to be edited independently. Changes seen as part of a horizontal revision because they are the fruit of the original intention should be adopted since failing to adopt them constitutes a violation of authorial intention and no grounds for rejection exist other than an aesthetic disagreement with the author, a disagreement that no properly humble editor ought to presume to offer. Our decision, then, should be determined by how we understand the "source" of the changes: if there is no new unifying vision, then there is no new work, so we humbly accept all authorial changes. Because this view is so pervasive and because most simply assume it, I will call it the conventional view.

Most critical commentaries on James's revisions are not primarily theoretical but aesthetic, so they do not address the source of the revisions directly. The authors of these commentaries simply assume the conventional view that James's changes were expressions of his original intentions, and they content themselves with celebrating the increased artistic sophistication of these changes—an assumption and a tendency Hershel Parker shows decisively in his review of such commentaries in his *Flawed Texts and Verbal Icons* (chapter 4). Since Parker's 1984 work, Philip Horne has published the most extensive expression of the conventional view in his *Henry James and Revision: The New York Edition* (1990). Horne succeeds in showing that if we compare single original passages to single revised passages, we will find a marked increase in artistic sophistication, and he would have us understand that increase as a "precise readjustment on behalf of an ideal vision" (98). In spite of the extent of the James canon he treats—the whole New York Edition—Horne remains conventional in that he sees each work individually; in doing so, he is assuming that there is an "ideal vision" of each work and that it is this vision that unifies the revisions and the unchanged passages within that work.

There are two assumptions here that I should like to challenge. First, by finding a marked similarity among the revisions regardless of the works in the New York Edition, I question whether the revisions made for that edition address a vision of each individual work. Second, by finding in a new understanding of technique an alternative source for those words, I question whether some prior vision is the source for either the words originally composed or the revisions. Once relieved of these two assumptions, we may want to question whether we should continue to accept the New York revisions into our most commonly read texts.

For the evidence necessary for a complete investigation of the first assumption, we would need complete collations of all of the New York changes. We haven't such, so I will rely upon the collations available to me, those of the first four novels James revised for the Edition, the ones on which he spent the most time and which he most extensively revised: *Roderick Hudson, The*

American, The Princess Casamassima, and *The Portrait of a Lady* (Murphy).

Moreover, we can, I think, summarize the commonality of the changes by considering the distinction James made between the romantic and realistic principles of art, a largely technical distinction called to his mind by his attempt to make his most romantic novel, *The American*, a realistic one: "The only general attribute of projected romance that I can see, the only one that fits all its cases, is the fact of the kind of experience with which it deals—experience liberated, so to speak; experience disengaged, disembroiled, disencumbered, exempt from the conditions that we usually know to attach to it and, if we wish so to put the matter, drag upon it, and operating in a medium which relieves, in a particular interest, of the inconvenience of a related, a measurable state, a state subject to all our vulgar communities" (1907, 2:xvii). As we can see, for James an element of a fiction was romantic if it was offered as sufficient unto itself, if it was not measured by something outside of itself, if it was not related to "the conditions we know to attach to it," if it was offered as independent of some engagement to a community. The romantic, then, is the opposite of the connected, the related. For James, only the rigorously connected "artistically counted"; only such material contributed to his goal of complete "pictorial fusion"; only such work evinced an "organic form." He tried to accomplish his purpose of connectedness by attaching whatever element struck his mind as "loose" or "arbitrary" to something else within the fiction, by increasing the degree of that element's dependence on something else within the fiction or by exchanging for the loose element something that offered a greater sense of relatedness, of connection. James's revising for connectedness, for the sake of the realistic principle of art, may be seen in the aforementioned four novels.

For example, to James's mind, the ideas of "happiness" and "discontent"—in order to be artistically intelligible—apparently needed to be made subject to something that revealed their connection to something else. In *Princess Casamassima*, James changed his remark about the poverty-stricken Hyacinth from "reading was his happiness, and the absence of any direct contact with a library his principal source of discontent" (1886, 1:94) to "reading was his extravagance, while the absence of any direct contact with a library represented for him mainly the hard shock of the real" (1908, 1: 101). With this revision, James changed two romantically loose words to more realistically connected ones: "happiness," which is given in terms of (i.e., is attached to, is measured by) Hyacinth's usual parsimony; and "discontent," which is given in terms of his usual avoidance of any contact with the real world. In place of the unsecured originals, a web of relationships is given to the reader, a context—Hyacinth's usual behavior—through which the reader could understand the text.

We can see the commonality we are seeking in the shift to greater connectedness throughout the revisions of his earliest works, although space permits only a few examples. The revisions range from changing how a character is identified (from merely giving the character's name to giving that character's relation to someone else: e.g., from "Pansy" to "her companion") to an addition of self-consciousness to a character (from a character's sense of self being unconnected to the people in his or her social context to having a character define him- or herself by the way he or she fits within that context). The latter type of revision may be illustrated by two versions of a passage from *The American*:

> (Newman speaks first, then Valentin)
> "Is she clever?"
> "She is the most intelligent woman I know. Try her, some day, with something difficult, and you will see."
> "Is she fond of admiration?" (*Atlantic Monthly*, September 1876, 311; 1883, 1: 117)
>
> "Is she clever?" he then asked.
> "Try her with something you think so yourself and you'll see."
> "Oh, how can I try her?" Newman sighed with a lapse. But he picked himself up. "Is she fond of admiration?" (Facsimile, 117; "then" substituted for "and" in 1907, 2: 150)

In the original, Newman is essentially romantic, for he shows no consciousness of how he stands in relation to the other characters; he simply goes from question to question. As is customary in the original, the reader is uncertain whether Newman failed to note the challenge in Valentin's answer or he simply did not mind it. The New York Newman, on the other hand, captures that challenge (which is emphasized by the deletion of Valentin's declaration of Claire's intelligence, which is itself romantic because it is unattached to anything else) and responds by reflecting on himself, on how he stands in relation to Claire. And he finds himself wanting. As was one of his most frequent practices throughout all four revised novels, James used the *turn ancillaries* (those little pieces of narration accompanying dialogue; here, the "sigh," the "lapse," and the "picked himself up") to make what had been loose conversation reflect each character's position relative to the other characters.

James more closely attached Roderick to Rowland and Cecilia in *Roderick Hudson* when he changed the dialogue and the *turn ancillaries* of "Hudson gave a vigorous nod. 'Aye, poor fellow, he's thirsty!' And on this he cried good night, and bounded down the garden path" (1879, 1: 42) to

> Hudson gave an approving nod. "Well, poor wretch, you wouldn't have him die of thirst, would you?" But without awaiting a reply he called good night from the garden-path and lost himself in the darkness.
>
> (1907, 1: 27)

Here James accomplished a tighter connection among the elements of the immediate context in four ways at once. First, he exchanged for the vague "vigorous" the more direct reaction to something someone else had said that is reflected in "approving." Second, James changed the words Roderick speaks from a simple agreement to a rejoinder; third, he changed the way he had described Roderick's departure from a simple indication that leaving was the next action—"and on this"—to a phrase that built upon an expectation of a reply from the others—"but without awaiting a reply." And last, James changed the description of Roderick's action from its simple location—"bounded down the garden path"—to his relation to the others—"lost."

James could accomplish his purpose with a minimal number of words. In the following example from *The Princess Casamassima*, a single word elicits a new, tighter connectedness:

> "Bless my soul, you must be the little 'Enning!" Miss Pynsent exclaimed, planted before her and going now into every detail.

"Well, I'm glad you have made up your
mind. I thought you'd know me directly. I had a call
to make in this part, and it came into my 'ead to look
you up. I don't like to lose sight of old friends."

"I never knew you—you've improved so,"
Miss Pynsent rejoined, with a candour justified by her
age and her consciousness of respectability. (1886, 1:
56)

"Bless my soul, you must be the awful little
'Enning!" Miss Pynsent exclaimed, planted before her
and going now into every detail.

"Well, I'm glad you've made up your mind.
I thought you'd know me directly and I dare say I was
awful. But I ain't so bad now, hey?" the young woman
went on with confidence. "I had a call to make in this
part, and it came into my 'ead to look you up. I don't
like to lose sight of old friends."

"I never knew you—you've improved as I
couldn't have believed," Miss Pynsent returned with
a candour justified by her age and her consciousness
of respectability. (1908, 5: 60)

Here James created a tighter connection between Miss Pynsent
and Miss Henning by adding to Pinnie's statement the opinion
"awful," an opinion Pinnie had, now apparently, held from the
time Miss Henning was a child. This insertion has given Miss
Henning an excuse to ask for a new opinion, one based on her
current appearance, something that Pinnie had given in the earlier version anyway. However, by making Miss Henning ask for
that opinion, James also created a new context within which the
reader understands her; the reader is forewarned that her
improvement is only superficial, a conclusion the reader of the
earlier version has to arrive at with less guidance—if indeed, he
or she is to arrive at this conclusion at all. James emphasized her
superficiality by changing Pinnie's words from "improved so" to
"improved as I couldn't have believed." Because the context
within which the reader has understood Pinnie, almost from the
first page of the novel, had emphasized the limits of "this
artist's" mind, the improvement in Miss Henning becomes by
this change even more directly ironic.

But Miss Pynsent and Miss Henning were characters in
conflict; therefore, it is not surprising to see them engage in what

James's brother William called "fencing in dialogue" (William James to Henry James, ? November 1905, Parker, "Henry James 'In the Wood'" 496). But James also made sympathetic characters duel orally, in an apparent attempt to relieve the looseness of a conversation. For example, after Cecilia had asked Rowland what he thought of Roderick, both Rowland and Cecilia had simply commented upon Roderick:

> "I confess I like him," said Rowland. "He's crude and immature—but there's stuff in him."
> "He's a strange being," said Cecilia musingly.
> (*Roderick* 1879, 1: 42)

James revised this to

> Rowland replied after a little by a question of his own. "Isn't he a case of what's called the artistic temperament? That's interesting to see, for the 'likes' of us."
> "Speak for your own temperament! But he's a very odd creature," Cecilia conceded. (1907, 1: 27)

Again James sought a new coherency by adding narrative commentary before the dialogue, and, as he had with the conversation between Pinnie and Miss Henning, he added to a character's words in order to elicit a new response. Cecilia's reply became in the revision so connected to Rowland's words that she must make a concession, another added tightness, in order to agree.

Since characters act as well as speak, James changed how a character acted after a conversation in ways that create a new closer connection, as in changing

> "My dear Lord Warburton," she [Isabel] said, smiling, "you may do, as far as I am concerned, whatever comes into your head."
> And with this she got up, and wandered into the adjoining room, where she encountered several acquaintances. (*Portrait* 1881, 390)

to

> "My dear Lord Warburton," she said, smiling, "you may do, so far as I'm concerned, whatever comes into your head."

> And with this she got up and wandered into
> the adjoining room, where, within her companion's
> view, she was immediately addressed by a pair of
> gentlemen, high personages in the Roman world, who
> met her as if they had been looking for her. (1908, 4:
> 221)

Here James has made what had been the simple action of leaving the room into an opportunity for giving the scene in that other room a new, closer relation to Warburton and to the social circle he shares with Isabel.

Comparisons were one means James used to subject unattached ideas to measurements outside of themselves. For example, when James reread "she sounded the letter r peculiarly" (*Princess* 1886, 1: 115), he found the same kind of disengaged description—"peculiarly"—that his mature terms of cognition demanded that he make intelligible. In order to make dependent the disengaged "peculiarly," James compared Lady Aurora's pronunciation of "r" to something within the community; in this case, he changed the language to "she sounded the letter r as a w" (1908, 5: 123). His purpose—to relieve an element of looseness by making it dependent upon something else—was the source of James's propensity, in his revisions, for using comparisons, including more "imagery." Style is, as we always say, not a mere matter of expression or ornament; it is part and parcel of the way an author thinks. James did not choose to include a greater number of comparisons in his revisions because they create a prettier style. He used them because they were an effective means toward his artistic goal: to make his work coherent by offering conditions for whatever appeared to him disengaged. James's comparisons—imagistic or not (as in the case above)—were but one way of taking a disengaged word or phrase and attaching it to something outside of itself; in this case, "peculiarly" gave way to how a "w" is usually pronounced. To write "as a w" is not especially fanciful stylistically, but it met, as "peculiarly" did not, James's idea of the artistically meaningful.

My next examples illustrate the similarity of purpose between the addition of a simple comparison (as in my last example) and the revising to include an image. The word "pretty" is the same kind of general word we have seen James connect with common expectations and standards above; when James read "through the open door it looked very pretty" (*Portrait* 1881, 324), the final phrase must have offered to his mind the same kind of question we have seen him face earlier: "Pretty in relation to what." In the revised comment—"through the open door it looked the very temple of authorised love" (1908, 4: 109)—James subjected the idea of "pretty" to the conditions of community by bringing into the description the idea of community sanction with the word "authorised" and the community ideal of a bridal bower. And when James changed "but the Marquis seemed neither more nor less frigidly grand than usual" (*American* 1883, 1: 180) to "but if the Marquis had been ruffled he stepped all the more like some high-crested though distinctly domestic fowl who had always the alternative of the perch" (1907 2: 232), he made the description of the Marquis' attitude subject to something the reader, and any member of the community, has probably seen. For James, the idea of "frigidly grand" is now artistically intelligible because it is now measured by something within the context of the community. This is not, of course, to say that the idea survives the measurement without change, only that the revision, unlike the disengaged original, met James's mature standards of coherency and realism.

James could make his comparisons serve two purposes at once: to offer the conditions to which the idea was subject (as we have been seeing) and to tighten the connection between characters in the immediate context. James attempted to achieve these purposes by making more intelligible the idea of "primness" when he substituted for the uncontrolled attitude in "she received his good wishes with a touch of primness" (*Roderick* 1879, 3: 27) the posturing of "she received his good wishes as if he had been a servant, at dinner, presenting the potatoes to her elbow. She helped herself in moderation, but also all in profile" (1907, 1: 372). How "primness" looks, and thereby Miss Blanchard's attitude toward Rowland, is now dependent upon the reader's knowing how a lady receives food from a servant. James intended to create closer connections between his characters, and one of the ways he did so was with imagery.

We can see the same two layers of connections working in another example. When James changed his account of Poupin's act from "the latter merely gazed at him a while" (*Princess* 1886, 1: 108) to "the latter merely viewed him a little as if he were a pleasing object" (1908, 5: 116), he was attempting to make Poupin's gaze intelligible by giving the reader the conditions within which the relation between Poupin and Hyacinth is most meaningful. And that relation's meaningfulness depends upon the conditions of community in that the reader needs to know how one looks at a pleasing object. To render meaningful was the intent governing the images, however fanciful, that James imposed upon the looseness of the earlier versions. James attempted to make meaningful Madame Merle's former and present relation to Osmond and Isabel when he replaced "he seldom spoke of Madame Merle, and when his wife alluded to her he usually let the allusion drop" (*Portrait* 1881, 353) with "he seldom consented to finger, in talk, this roundest and smoothest bead of their social rosary" (1908, 4: 158). The imposed image highlights Madame Merle's relation to Osmond and Isabel (that she had been Osmond's and Isabel's most important social link) and emphasizes that Osmond now preferred to leave that link unstroked. Also, the relation between Miss Henning and Hyacinth, the attraction he had for her, was the focus of the change from "he was exceedingly 'rum,' but this quality took her fancy" (*Princess* 1886, 1: 72) to "he was exceedingly 'rum,' but he had a stamp as sharp for her as that of a new coin and which also agreeably suggested value" (1908, 5: 77). With this change, James took the disengaged idea of catching one's fancy and placed it within the conditions of what would be most attractive to this fashion-conscious and upwardly mobile young lady: a new coin, with both its up-to-the-minute appearance and its purchasing power.

In another example, the notions of intensity and tint offered in "Mary had a brilliant eye and a deep colour in her cheek" (*Roderick* 1879, 3: 34) were unconnected to anything else, so James changed the sentence to "Mary looked a little as if she had just jumped, rather dangerously, to save her life or her honour, from some great height" (1907, 1: 377). Not only does the revision make the notions more conditional by giving a comparison, but it also tightens the immediate context by suggesting Mary's reputation with the word "honour." The tightening is appropriate because in this scene Christina had come to a party just to see Mary, a woman whose honor she has been challenging by dallying with Mary's fiance, Roderick. In *The American*, James replaced the unattached "disagreeable" of "it was useless [for Newman] to shut his eyes to the fact that the Marquis was pro-

foundly disagreeable to him" (1883, 1: 170) with the more appre-
hensible comparison (provided, of course, the reader has seen
human-like apes): "it was useless to shut his eyes to the fact that
the Marquis was as disagreeable to him as some queer, rare, possible dangerous biped, perturbingly akin to humanity, in one of
the cages of a 'show'" (1907, 2: 219). The distance Newman felt
between himself and Urbain is captured by the image, as is the
degree of Urbain's disagreeableness. Notably, in the earlier version of the novel, the character M. Nioche had been Newman's
friend, a fact which is clear in that as Newman watched M.
Nioche trying to live on pennies, he had found an "ungrudging
entertainment" (1883, 1: 55). But James must have considered
both "ungrudging" and "entertainment" unattached, because he
substituted a "diversion akin to the watching of ants" (1907, 2:
69). James gave "entertainment" an attachment when he used in
its stead "diversion," a word that focuses on the relation of the
action to one's usual activities; his use of the word "ants" was a
way of emphasizing the distance between M. Nioche and
Newman, a distance not captured (and perhaps not intended) by
the open-ended "ungrudging." Here, as we saw when James
made Rowland duel verbally with Cecilia, the original empathy
between two characters did not prevent James from making the
same kind of revision to a passage concerning them that he made
to a passage concerning characters originally more in conflict.

James also used the animal kingdom to render comparative the relationship between Isabel and her sister Lilian in *The
Portrait of a Lady* when he changed, "'I have never felt like Isabel's
sister, and I am sure I never shall' she had said to an intimate
friend; a declaration which made it all the more creditable that
she had been prolific in sisterly office" (1881, 24) to "'I've never
kept up with Isabel—it would have taken all my time,' she had
often remarked; in spite of which, however, she held her rather
wistfully in sight; watching her as a motherly spaniel might
watch a free greyhound" (1908, 3: 39). James imposed a connection upon both the idea of how, for Lilian, it should feel to be a
sister (one should be able to keep up with her) and the idea of
how Lilian might see her connection to an unsister-like sibling,
whom she cannot keep up with (she can only watch the much
speedier animal wistfully).

We can summarize the kind of revision James performed
when he decided in 1905-7 that an element needed to be made

related, to be connected, with the next example. When Roderick had not responded to Rowland's compliment on a sculpture, Rowland considered that the "oversight was a sign of the natural self-sufficiency of genius" (*Roderick* 1879, 1: 40). As the more complete collations show, and as I have tried here to demonstrate, nothing for the mature James was self-sufficient; everything could be understood only in relation to something else. Therefore, the bald objective statement concerning Roderick's oversight had to be made to fit within James's mature terms of cognition. Accordingly, James changed the passage: Roderick's oversight became "a sign of the indifference of conscious power" (1907, 1: 25). An indifferent person, one conscious of his power, is at least aware of his relation to the community around him. James did not leave loose or self-sufficient whatever he noticed as unattached. Again the connections between things, here between a character's consciousness and the rest of the world, were his sine qua non of artistic intelligibility.

The most striking thing that the collations reveal is the similarity of the changes James made regardless of the work that lay before him. It is to their similarity, then, that we must turn. That similarity means that it cannot be the life within any particular work that elicited those changes; we have isolated not so much James's "vision" of any particular work, but his mature technique, his "late style." This conclusion, however, calls into question the way we are used to understanding the notion of "technique."

Technique is usually understood as the means of expressing the theme, the vision, or the idea. In thinking of literature, we tend to assume a rather logical relation among an author's vision, technique, and words on the page. Authors conceive an intention (theme, vision, purpose, idea, etc.) that they wish to see fulfilled on the page. In order to realize that vision, authors create (refine, copy, develop) techniques that are more or less felicitous as these techniques are more or less successful at embodying the original vision in words on the page. The realization of the vision (intention, purpose, idea), then, is the end toward which the techniques are the means. The words on the page are understood as illustrations of, or instances of, the unifying theme. A work is assumed to be unified by this theme, this vision, which must exist before the application of technique.

This means/end relation is assumed so universally, I think, because it is so natural; it describes the vast majority of our language acts: we have a meaning in mind, however vaguely; then we try to express that meaning in words. Indeed, I have not been able to find any rhetorician or language theorist who makes any other assumption. I wish to argue here that a distinction between natural and creative language acts is fundamental; in natural language acts, we have a meaning that seeks a technical expression. In creative language acts, the artist works without that prior "meaning." How he or she does so is the subject of the rest of this paper.

Even our careful qualifications in specific cases usually evince the centrality of the assumed means/end relation. Confronted by an absence of a presumed unity of vision in a specific case, we speak of "changes of mind" (i.e., shifting visions or the discovery of new visions or of a work's "real theme") and/or of techniques that proved "inadequate" to the realization of the presumed unifying vision. Our search for authorial intention, then, has focused upon the discovery of the unifying vision, the "meaning" of which the words are an expression.

The assumed relation among idea, technique, and words can be seen clearly in the work of E.D. Hirsch, Jr. In his *Validity in Interpretation*, Hirsch makes two related claims. First, he argues that a logical hierarchy of meaning is necessary for our intuitions to achieve the status of knowledge; he thus makes explicit what almost everyone else seems merely to assume. Second, he claims that this hierarchy can accurately reflect the author's intentions. For Hirsch, we can intuit an intrinsic genre, a broad statement of authorial intention for the work as a whole. The intuition becomes a hypothesis by being placed at the highest level on a rational hierarchy. From that intuition, according to the implications of Hirsch's view, we can understand the relations among the words on the page, relations that are essentially logical in that they are exemplifications or illustrations or implications of the intrinsic genre. The intuition, then, becomes a hypothesis, which is tested against its ability to render felicitously meaningful at least most of the words on the page.

Nor has the fact that many have abandoned the search for "authorial" intention altered the presumed means/end structure. Our presumed structure persists no matter what we see as the source (i.e., history or culture or economics or gender or any unconscious poststructural "system," or all of these) of the unifying theme; we still tend to see the work as unified by a preexisting and logically broader vision.

We can see that it is this logical assumption that governs the way revisions are understood. To join Hirsch with Tanselle, "vertical" revisions are governed by a new intrinsic genre, a new hierarchy of meaning, and are, therefore, foreign to the original text. "Horizontal" revisions continue to be governed by the original hierarchy, so they are simply new instances or illustrations or implications of that original vision.

In order to escape this false dichotomy, we must come to a better understanding of the relations among an author's intentions, his or her technique, and the actual words on the page, relations called into question by the similarity among the New York changes. Currently, as mentioned, the words are seen as instances or illustrations of a governing intention; technique is merely the means by which that intention is realized in words. The way out is to take a closer look at intention, a scrutiny which then allows us to see technique in a more realistic light.

For this closer look, I will use, quite loosely, John Searle's discussion of intention, contained most completely in his *Intentionality: An Essay in the Philosophy of Mind.* Generally, Searle discusses intentionality from two perspectives: prior intentions and intentions in action. Prior intentions are our plans, wishes, the direction in which we intend to move. In contrast, intentions in action are the specific acts we perform in moving in the direction intended. The contents of each kind of intention is that intention's "conditions of satisfaction," those things that must happen in order for either kind of intention to be successful. The contents of a prior intention, its conditions of satisfaction, are characteristically vague, but usually verbal. The contents of an intention in action arise out of the immediate acting situation, not a prior vision, and are rarely verbal.

To take an example loosely from Searle: We can form the prior intention to drive home. The specific acts we perform while actually moving toward home are the intentions in action. The prior intention is vague and merely directional, and it is fulfilled if we get home; that prior intention, however, cannot account for all the acts we perform in getting home because it does not contain the conditions of satisfaction for those specific acts. Within the loose constraint of getting home, we can drive at almost any speed, and the specific speed we choose will have more to do with our habitual way of driving as it responds to the particular situation than it will with the plan. The conditions of satisfaction of the intention in action will grow out of a specific set of external conditions (traffic, weather, etc.) or out of varying internal conditions (mood, attentiveness, etc.); the "reasons" for the actions themselves we usually have not verbalized and often could not verbalize. In other words, the general direction is set by the prior intention, but the actual acts grow out of techniques, defined as habitual ways of moving, and a concrete situation. Those acts that feel utterly right can be said to resonate with and within their context. In other words, we know that an act is right, that it fulfills the conditions of satisfaction for the intention in action, when performing it creates a resonance between our normal, habitual ways of acting and the demands of the concrete situation. Our specific actions are given a direction by a prior intention, but they are not illustrations or instances of that wish. The wish is prior to the act, but is not a category of actions or of meaning. We can see the fairly independent status of intentions in action by noting that we are likely to respond to a similar concrete situation, say someone cutting us off in traffic, in a similar way regardless of whether we're heading home or to the store. And any difference in our response will more likely arise out of some unnoticed difference in the situation than out of the direction in which we're heading.

Nor can we say that any unforeseen actions constitute, at some level, a new plan; most of our responses to concrete situations are conscious but nonverbal. We may deliberately speed up at any moment, but we do not plan to press harder on the gas pedal—we just do. If asked later why we pressed harder at that particular moment, we probably couldn't answer, for the "why" was never verbal, although the act was, in this view, certainly intentional. The closest we can come to understanding why we responded as we did, other than to say merely that our response felt right at the moment, is to discuss our habits, our driving techniques, in general, separate from any particular act. Of course, concrete situations that would lead to what may be called a new direction can arise. Faced with a blocked road, or a new road, or a sudden whim, we may make a turn and head in an entirely new direction, but we will have adopted a new direction, not a new detailed plan, for that new direction as a new prior intention will

remain as unspecified in the concrete sense of specific actions as
the old prior intention had been.

Prior intentions can, of course, vary in their degree of
specificity; the only possible theoretical limit to their specificity is
that they must be possible within the conventions of the language, for, according to this constrained view, we must be able
to formulate them verbally. Prior intentions do, however, have a
practical limit to their specificity. If we add to our simple prior
intention to drive home the more specific conditions to use a certain path and to get home as quickly as possible, there lurks a
potential, even probable, conflict among these now more specific conditions. A concrete situation, say traffic, may force us to
choose between the planned path and the desired speed. In short,
prior intentions contain a direction and only the vaguest of conditions of satisfaction, or they often fail.

We can extend this description to the act of fiction writing, something Searle does not do, for he assumes the natural
language relation of meaning prior to expression and therefore
makes no radical distinction between natural language and creating (see his *Expression and Meaning*). In my view, and speaking
generally, an author sets out with a mere prior intention, having
only a direction and his or her habitual, technical conditions of
satisfaction. The act of writing down actual words, the intentions
in action, will at least start off in that prior direction. But each
word written creates a concrete artistic situation, one that will
give rise to specific decisions that must be made at that time,
decisions the prior intention did not contain within its vague
conditions of satisfaction. What is written will not be merely an
expression of the prior intention, but will be more a response to
the immediate context, a response governed largely by the confluence of two things: the author's technique, his or her usual
way of adding word to word, and the "resonance" he or she will
feel between the words added and the words already written.

Writing fiction is, of course, vastly more complicated
than driving. The most important source of the complication is
the presence of various characters. In good fiction, the characters
act on their own; they are in a very real sense independent persons, each with his or her own characteristic ways of being, of
moving about, in the world. Artists must create characters and at
the same time preserve these characters' independence. Artists,
according to this view, must create a characteristic, a habitual

way of moving for each character, one unplanned in the same way that any human's movement is unplanned. Thereafter, each specific action by the character must maintain a harmony between that character's habitual way of moving and the specific concrete situation, an individual and local resonance. Each of the characters will have his or her own typical ways of speaking, and an author will often revise to maintain the consistency of that individual's voice, a task made difficult by the likely and subtle intrusion of the author's own voice. I would argue, however, that the author discovers the consistency of each character's voice most likely by writing, by moving in that voice, not by planning. Once the consistency has been created, the author may revise to increase the consistency. The revisions often center upon replacing the intrusive authorial voice with the more authentic voice of the character, be that a dramatic voice or a narrative one.

It is important to recall both that the consistency we feel as we follow a character is the resonance between the character's individual voice and the concrete situation and that the character is not constrained by any *a priori* idea, an idea that would make that character and his or her work allegorical, representative (except in the case of intentional allegory). We and the author may be surprised by what the character does, but we will feel that, somehow, what the character does is harmonious with who he or she is. Of course, authors may revise for other reasons; they may discover other harmonies in writing that they can then revise to make more extensive. Authors can even revise in the way Hirsch would have them compose, by increasing the logical consistency of the work. But authorial feelings of harmony, of the rightness of this or that change, are not limited to a mere logical consistency, a logical unfolding of what the character must do given the constraints of the idea represented; these feelings of harmony are more likely and more often an at-the-moment resonance.

Deconstructionists have, of course, made a living debunking unity by finding and emphasizing discontinuity, disruption, rupture, but they have looked only for a superficial logical consistency, hardly the unity we find in fiction (or in life for that matter). A text's unity is built moment by moment by the creation of resonances only one of whose many sources is the logical consistency deconstructionists insist upon and then find absent. Their rejection of unity as a characteristic of texts is, according to this view, rendered pointless by their use of a radically impertinent standard for unity.

Searle, I think, can help us understand James, both the similarity among the revisions and the process of revision itself. In his account of the writing of *Portrait*, James explicitly drew a distinction between general, prior intentions and the actual writing of the novel. Recalling that the only direction he had given himself originally was to make Isabel "complex," James writes this about the actual words:

> It [*Portrait*] went, however, but a certain way, and other lights, contending, conflicting lights, and of as many different colours, if possible, as the rockets, the Roman candles and Catherine-wheels of a "pyrotechnic display," would be employable to attest that she was [complex]. I had, no doubt, a groping instinct for the right complications, since I am quite unable to track the footsteps of those that constitute, as the case stands, the general situation exhibited. They are there, for what they are worth, and as numerous as might be; but my memory, I confess, is a blank as to how and whence they came. (1908, xvii)

James draws here a distinction between two kinds of intention that correspond closely to the two kinds of intention we have been discussing. James parallels a prior intention with his vague plan to make Isabel "complex"; and he parallels intentions in action with his technique, his "groping instinct" for the "footsteps" that produced the "right complications." That he could remember the plan—to make her complex—but not the source of the footsteps reflects the difference between verbal and nonverbal conditions of satisfaction.

James drew the distinction between prior intentions and intentions in action a dozen or so times in his early prefaces, always separating his plans from the actual words, the prior intention from the intentions in action. Space demands that I limit myself to one more instance of his making the distinction from the same preface: "I do at least seem to catch the key to a part of this abundance of small anxious, ingenious illustration as I recollect putting my finger, in my young woman's interest, on the most obvious of her predicates. 'What will she "do"?'" (xix-xx). James recalls having answered that question with a merely directional intention: he would send Isabel to Europe. What she did when she got there, the vast majority of the words of the novel, was called into being by his technique—his "groping instinct"— as it responded to the particular, immediate situation in which he found himself at any given moment, a response that is governed by nothing more explicitly "meaningful" than a felt resonance between the technique and the specific situation. His words were not "planned," nor were they illustrations or instances of some higher level abstraction, some "theme." Nor could James remember why they were there.

It is both interesting and important that James could remember his prior intentions but not his intentions in action. This fact is exactly what Searle's distinction would have us expect; we can easily remember the intention to go home quickly, but we almost never remember when or why we shifted or accelerated or changed lanes or any of the other specific actions we actually took. Well, how did we get home? James answers by mentioning his "groping instinct" for the right words. This instinct parallels driving: we do not have to stop and plan every time we act; we have a habitual way of driving, a technique. We can remember our plan, for it had to be consciously formulated; our actions we did not have to formulate in this way, so tied were they to habit and to the immediate situation.

While an author's actual words are so tied to the technical response to a particular context that their appearance cannot be exactly verbalized, technique considered on its own—something we have already seen as unifying the New York revisions—can be so verbalized. So, just as we can describe our characteristic way of driving, say offensively or defensively, writers can and do discuss their techniques. James discusses at length, in his preface to *The Golden Bowl*, precisely the notion of a habitual way of moving. First, he mentions his relationship to his late work:

> To re-read in their order my final things, all of comparatively recent date, has been to become aware of my putting the process through, for the latter end of my series (as well as, throughout, for most of its later constituents) quite in the same terms as the apparent and the actual, the contemporary terms; to become aware in other words that the march of my present intention coincides sufficiently with the march of my original expression; that my apprehension fits, more

> concretely stated, without an effort or struggle, cer-
> tainly without bewilderment or anguish, into the
> innumerable places prepared for it. (xiii)

James here claims that the "march of [his] present intention"
coincides with the original expression; his present way of moving, his march, fits without a struggle with his earlier habits.

There was no such harmony between his earliest works
and his current mind, but, rather, a contrast that James describes
in his next sentences:

> This truth throws into relief for me the very different
> dance that the taking in hand of my earlier produc-
> tions was to lead me; the quite other kind of con-
> sciousness proceeding from that return. Nothing in
> my whole renewal of attention to these things, to
> almost any instance of my work previous to some
> dozen years ago, was more evident than that no such
> active, appreciative process could take place on the
> mere palpable lines of expression—thanks to the so
> frequent lapse of harmony between my present mode
> of motion and that to which the existing footprints
> were due. (xiii)

James draws here a distinction between the habitual way his
mind now operates (its "mode of motion," his technique) and the
way it had operated at the time of his earliest compositions (that
mode of motion that had produced the existing footprints), a difference that precludes any deliberate harmony between his present intentions in action and his original ones. James describes
the "very different dance," the bewilderment and the anguish
that had been his relation with his earliest works, in a striking
image: "It was, all sensibly, as if the clear matter being still there,
even as a shining expanse of snow spread over a plain, my
exploring tread, for application to it, had quite unlearned the old
pace and found itself naturally falling into another, which might
sometimes indeed more or less agree with the original tracks, but
might most often, or very nearly, break the surface in other
places" (xiii-xiv). James admits here that he has developed, over
the intervening years, new habits of moving, ones that do not
coincide with his earlier modes of motion. He is, in our analogy,
a new kind of driver, one who has "unlearned" the habitual way

he had moved some years earlier. While technique can be considered in isolation, technique in action is nonverbal, for it is largely automatic, something James notes when he goes on to claim that the words created by his new mode of motion seemed to him "inevitable," that he seemed compelled, without having a conscious verbal intention, to write those new words, for they now seemed his "very terms of cognition."

We can now account for the similarity among the changes: they were essentially technical, not thematic, something Leon Edel noted some thirty years ago when he said that James's "late revisions [were] extremely artificial. James reexperiences in them questions of his craft rather than the life within the work" (333). We can say, then, that James was neither writing from a new plan, a new intrinsic genre or theme, a new prior intention, nor better expressing his original intentions. Rather, he was doing what he says he was doing: imposing his new mode of motion upon the footsteps, the words, that had originated in a radically different mode of motion, an imposition that was spontaneous, inevitable, and largely unconscious, happening, as he said it did, "in a fiftieth of a second."

In order to understand James, then, we have had to come to a new understanding of technique, at least for James: that technique is not the expression of an *a priori* "vision," but is James's way of adding word to word, his way of creating a vision, one that did not exist until his technique combined with the concrete artistic situations that had created it. The unity of a work is not therefore a function of a theme, a prior intention, but the product of an author's careful movement, word to word, incident to incident, chapter to chapter, of his or her intentions in action, that confluence of technique and resonance. Regarding technique, James could see the radical disjunction between the old and the new. But resonance, the conditions of satisfaction that govern the original choice of actual words, arises out of the pressure a concrete situation places upon that technique, and James never discusses the disjunction between the original pressure and the later one or the dissonance his revisions created. His authorial voice, his mature technique acting without the pressure of the concrete situation of new composing, imposes itself upon his characters and his original narrative voice: in the revised passages only, Newman sounds like Isabel who sounds like Hyacinth who sounds like Roderick who sounds like Osmond, and all the narrators sound like each other. Instead of revising to remove the intrusion of his own voice, as is more common in revisions made when the life of the individual work still resonates, James has veneered his early works with his craft, with technique alone.

Unity is not something an author begins with and then succeeds or fails to keep but, rather, something that an author creates as he or she adds word to word. What came before elicits what comes next. The relation among the words of the work is not their logical relation to an overarching theme, but their temporal relation to what has been said, a relation I have called "resonance," the confluence of technique with concrete situation. And, because that relation is temporal, because the resonance is felt but not articulated at the moment of the composition, and because the unity of a work as a whole is the product of countless inarticulate moments of felt resonance, going back to an earlier work is more likely than not to introduce dissonance. James noticed the differences between his early technique and his late technique; in fact, he discussed his works according to the harmony or disharmony, not between their themes, but between their modes of motion. That is, he did not say a particular theme or vision now bored him and so was left out of the Edition; he said that his current way of moving was so different from his early one that no appreciable process was possible on "mere palpable lines of expression."

We should conclude by returning to our original debate. Horne, as our representative of the conventional view (see Parker, *Flawed Texts*), succeeds in showing that if we compare single original passages to single revised passages, we will find a marked increase in artistic sophistication. But we cannot agree with him any further, for he sees in that increased complexity, as mentioned, "precise readjustment on behalf of an ideal vision" (98). James's revisions, inevitable and spontaneous and sophisticated as they are, embody his mature technique, his late style, and not any "ideal vision" of any specific work. And set side by side with unrevised passages, they are profoundly dissonant; characters blur into characters, losing their individuality, their "life." Technique governs without the felt pressure of the concrete situation, which is why the single revisions often are so brilliant even as they are so wrong.

Again, as Edel said, the New York changes are "interesting to study for the light they shed on the novelist's creative process"; they do give us considerable insight into James's mature technique; they can help us understand the creation of an organic form—they reveal that James's late technique was to leave no actions loose and unrelated to something else. But the revisions are intrusions upon the early works, each of which is the fruit of its own technical drive toward a complete resonance, a unity.

WORKS CITED

Edel, Leon. Afterword. *The American*. By Henry James. New York: Signet, 1963. 326-33.

Hirsch, E.D., Jr. *Validity in Interpretation*. New Haven: Yale UP, 1967.

Horne, Philip. *Henry James and Revision: The New York Edition*. New York: Oxford UP, 1990.

James, Henry, Jr. "The American." *Atlantic Monthly* Sept. 1876:310-29.

_____. *The American*. 2 vols. London: Macmillan, 1883.

_____. *The American*. Vol. 2 of *The Novels and Tales of Henry James*. 1907.

_____. *The Golden Bowl*. Vols. 23 and 24 of *The Novels and Tales of Henry James*. 1909.

_____. Henry James, *"The American"*: *The Version of 1877 Revised in Autograph and Typescript for the New York Edition of 1907*. Ed. Rodney G. Dennis. Houghton Library Manuscripts 1. London: Scolar Press, 1976.

_____. *The Novels and Tales of Henry James*. 26 vols. New York: Scribner's, 1907-1917.

_____. *The Portrait of a Lady*. Boston: Houghton Mifflin, 1881.

_____. *The Portrait of a Lady*. Vols. 3 and 4 of *The Novels and Tales of Henry James*. 1908.

_____. *The Princess Casamassima*. 3 vols. London: Macmillan, 1886.

_____. *The Princess Casamassima*. Vols. 5 and 6 of *The Novels and Tales of Henry James*. 1908.

_____. *Roderick Hudson*. 3 vols. London: Macmillan, 1879.

_____. *Roderick Hudson*. Vol. 1 of *The Novels and Tales of Henry James*. 1907.

Murphy, James. "An Analysis of Henry James's Revisions of the First Four Novels of the New York Edition." Diss. U of Delaware, 1987.

Parker, Hershel. *Flawed Texts and Verbal Icons: Literary Authority in American Fiction.* Evanston, IL: Northwestern UP, 1984.

_____. "Henry James 'In the Wood': Sequences and Significances of his Literary Labors, 1905-1907." *Nineteenth-Century Fiction* 38 (March 1984): 492-513.

Searle, John. *Expression and Meaning: Studies in the Theory of Speech Acts.* New York: Cambridge UP, 1979.

_____. *Intentionality: An Essay in the Philosophy of Mind.* New York: Cambridge UP, 1983.

Tanselle, G. Thomas. "The Editorial Problem of Final Authorial Intention." *Studies in Bibliography* 29 (1976): 167-211.

Discourse versus Authorship: The Baedeker Travel Guide and D. H. Lawrence's *Twilight in Italy*

Paul Eggert

In the last chapter of *Twilight in Italy*, D. H. Lawrence's first travel book published in 1916, he narrates his walking tour of 1913 through Switzerland. He comes across only one Englishman, "a tall thin young man, whose face was red and inflamed from the sun" (209-10). The man is "sick with fatigue and over-exhaustion" (210), but Lawrence coaxes him into conversation:

> Then he began, like a general explaining his plan. . . .
> He had walked round over the Furka Pass, had been
> on foot four or five days. He had walked tremen-
> dously. Knowing no German, and nothing of the
> mountains, he had set off alone on this tour: he had a
> fortnight's holiday. So he had come over the Rhone
> Glacier across the Furka and down from Andermatt to
> the Lake. On this last day he had walked about thirty
> mountain miles. . . . The way he sank on the table in
> exhaustion, drinking his milk, his will, nevertheless,
> so perfect and unblemished, triumphant, though his
> body was broken and in anguish, was almost too
> much to bear. (210, 212)

Packed into a fortnight, the man's holiday "plans" would have necessitated very detailed information. Unsurprisingly, he soon pulls out "a guide-book with a timetable" to answer a question of Lawrence's about the departure of the next steamer (211). As Lawrence and every other European traveller knew, the famous Baedeker series of travel guides had all the information this "perishingly victorious" Englishman needed (210).

Considering the two forms of travel writing together— the travel book traditionally thought of as authored, the guide not—prompts questions of authorship as both biographical fact and explanatory paradigm. A peculiarly restrictive French form of the latter lay behind Barthes's and Foucault's essays of the late sixties, "The Death of the Author" and "What Is an Author?" Since then, whether in the service of Foucauldian, Derridean, New Historical, Feminist or other approaches, discursive forms of analysis have gradually come to predominate in literary and cultural studies, and authorship has found little theoretical support—despite its ongoing usefulness in citations and library catalogues, its central relevance for biographies of authors, interviews with them, creative writing classes, and for critical editions which appeal to authorial intention.

Contradiction between theory and practice is no new thing of course. But when left unexamined, as in this case it has been, it tends to quarantine the two kinds of interest when they could, I will argue, profitably be seen as alternatives. In the Anglo-American tradition, interest in authorship had already been weakened by the unintended alliance of New Criticism and Leavisism on the question of authorial intention. Lawrence's dictum to trust the tale rather than the teller was frequently cited by Leavis and others; there was a common preference expressed, especially in criticism of the novel, for "showing" rather than "telling"; and practical criticism helped to give impetus to the New Critical idea that a poem could be studied more or less independently of its originating contexts (which would at best provide "background information" rather than be seen as in any way continuous with the work). Authorship, admittedly, was still the rhetorical sanction and personal location of claims for the moral intelligence evinced in great works, but they themselves were clearly the centre of the enterprise. They possessed a pseudo-objectivity (hence the possibility of definitive editions): they were a communication across time of whose meanings even the author might not have been fully aware.

Thus the empirical and pragmatic strands of the Anglo-American tradition hardly required a thoroughgoing dislodgement of authorship given that it was, in practice, already in question (except in some areas of literary scholarship, including editing). But the 1970s and 1980s deconstruction of the subject as a unified consciousness and the attack on personal agency as a liberal-humanist illusion finished the job: literary works could henceforth be seen as essentially or most interestingly authored by the circulating discourses which traversed their textual space, regardless of what the ostensible author thought he or she was doing.

This essay argues that there is a need to revisit authorship and to re-figure it for the needs of the present: it offers a beginning for such a venture. I first develop a discursive approach to the Baedeker guides but then attempt to put some boundaries around its explanatory capacities by looking carefully, by way of contrast, at the biographical locatedness—the *authorial* intertextuality—of Lawrence's writing and revision of his travel book. Breaking down the boundary lines between Lawrence's works and their versions challenges the 1950s and 1960s positivist separation of the work from its authorial contexts as much as it does the bibliographic timidity of post-structuralist thought. It allows one to trace the contours of an evolving intellectual project—an ambitious rewriting of nineteenth-century history and of a wartime present, evidence of the operation of a culturally buffeted (and therefore non-autonomous, non-unitary, non-self-identical) but nevertheless highly intelligent and compelling personal agency. The discursive and the (re-imagined) authorial emerge as differently useful explanatory paradigms.

I.

The "FOURTEENTH REMODELLED EDITION" of the Baedeker travel guide, *Northern Italy* of 1913 ([iii]), deals with the same area at the same time that most of *Twilight in Italy* does. The author is given on the titlepage as Karl Baedeker. However, he had died in 1859. Whoever was actually responsible can at best have provided an overview given the number and complexity of the travel guides which came out under the same name. For us now, the authorship here is only a bibliographical convenience. This is not a piece of creative writing; it is a commercial production, a workshop compilation, probably incorporating the contributions of many Baedeker employees. So I will refer to it as "the Baedeker" rather than as a text written by Karl Baedeker.

The Baedekers date from the late 1820s. Baedeker himself originally aimed to give the traveller enough information to dispense with paid guides. He checked the information about hotels by personal, incognito visits, and he devised a system to asterisk hotels and "objects of special interest" for particular commendation (vi). He was phenomenally successful. By the time of his death, most of Europe was covered by his various travel guides. Translations had begun to appear in French in 1846 and would begin in English in 1861. They appealed to the rapidly expanding class of moneyed, middle-class people who formed the bulk of the travelling classes in the nineteenth century and whose numbers were much increased, at the lower end of the scale, as a result of the general introduction of paid annual holidays around the turn of the century in Britain.

The Baedeker was meticulously detailed and scrupulously edited. Indeed the editing has almost a rhetoric of its own—a severely factual flavour. There is an extensive use of hiccuping abbreviations, scrupulously punctuated lists, packed but always grammatical sentences—no mean feat, given that these English-language books were produced in Leipzig (from 1872). There is a discriminating use of typographical styles (italics, boldface, small capitals and up to three font sizes creating a complex but exact hierarchy of importance, in use on virtually every page), as well as extensive cross-referencing within the volume. The maps, printed in three subdued colours, have a Germanic rigour and consistency, reflecting the age of scientific progress from which they sprang. A vast amount of work has gone into each one. Thus the maps, too, have their rhetoric, a cartographic one: these are maps one feels one can trust; they contain everything one needs to know.

All this implies a clear and confident conception of audience: someone in the party of travellers, or the self-reliant individual traveller, would have had to be able to become proficient with these codes—quickly. In order to use a Baedeker to its potential, one would have needed to have been able to read both textually and visually, closely *and* pertinaciously. One would have been someone who was better trained and more experienced in the complexities of a print culture than is today's average user of travel guides.

The audience must have been considered to contain a good number of amateur botanists—and, after the mania for collecting and classifying natural specimens in the nineteenth century, this is understandable. The Latin names are given for the dominant and rarer species in each area. Convalescents must have figured prominently in the readership too. Sirmione, for example, is described as "not for consumptives," but it has "a hot sulphur spring (149° Fahr.)" (*Northern Italy* 281). This is no accidental reference. In the *Eastern Alps* volume (1911) every Alpine resort is graded by altitude together with the sorts of bacteria which cannot survive that altitude, and each resort's appropriateness for certain kinds of convalescence is given.

For any town, lake or river, the audience wanted to know—or the compilers of the *Northern Italy* guide *believed* the audience wanted to know—some basic geographical facts, preferably with its classical history and any cultural references attached. So we read of "The *Lago di Garda (210 ft.), the *Lacus Benácus* of the Romans" (279); we hear that Virgil remarked on its rough water, and are provided with the reference to the *Georgics* and the first line in Latin. For the town of Sirmione, the ruins of Catullus's country home are noted, and Tennyson's enchantingly rhythmical poem in octameters about the same spot, "Frater Ave Atque Vale," is not overlooked. A Public School education is assumed, with an ability either to read or to have read Latin poetry or at least to identify socially with its use.

One begins to sense a discursive alliance, usually unspoken, between compilers and the middle-class audience. Horse and donkey hirers who were in the habit of beating their beasts are mentioned on occasions in the Baedekers, and the traveller is given guidance in how to treat such miscreants. Advice is also provided for dealing with beggars: as their "profits . . . too frequently go for the support of able-bodied loafers, travellers should either give nothing, or restrict their charity to the obviously infirm. Gratuities to children are entirely reprehensible" (*Northern Italy* xv-xvi). In Venice there were other problems: "The insolence of some gondoliers towards visitors who do not know the language, and especially towards ladies unaccompanied by a gentleman, has long been a matter of complaint" (343). Two avenues of redress are mentioned, but by and large the expectation of the Baedeker is that the traveller will not be visiting Italy for the purposes of changing it or getting involved in its politics. A middle-class morality rarely surfaces as plainly as it does in these examples, but its evaluative categories are nevertheless enforced through the unquestioning transmission of its idiom: whether the pensions are "unpretending," or "very fair," whether "respectable, clean, reasonable, and fairly well provided with the comforts and conveniences expected in an up-to-date establishment" (341, vi). Expected by whom? It is unnecessary to reply. The compilers are blind to the cultural relativities embodied in class: in this sense, the Baedeker can be said to have been partially constructed by the discourse of class, even as it contributed to its wider construction.

The same kind of observation can be made about aesthetic and racial or national discourses. If the compilers' gaze is other-directed towards Italy, it is securely one-way. What travellers will be helped to see will extend and please and even make them healthier, but their existing ways of understanding the foreign will be confirmed rather than challenged. The English-language Baedeker's whole business was to act as intermediary between the British traveller and the foreignness of northern Italy, but the Baedeker is hardly interested at all in the northern Italians themselves, except as irritants. They are the most notable absence.

The foreign place is nearly always distanced by the rhetoric of aesthetic and other appreciation. The aesthetic is known by its non-utility, whereas the middle class prided itself on its practicality (Mr. Meagles' catchcry and Daniel Doyce's practice in *Little Dorrit*). However the paradox is readily explained: by not entering into the political arena where money-making might be vulnerable to principled criticism, the aesthetic elevates or sanctifies the pursuits of those people capable of rising to its level. If their middle-class life was of the plain, then the Baedeker specialised in the valleys and mountains, in the geographic and cultural sublime.

Travel writing was a thriving genre in the late nineteenth century, and very many books about travelling in the Alps were produced. The delectation of Alpine views had almost reached the status of a science (as in Conway's *The Alps from End to End*), and others indulged to the full in the hyperbolic language and religiose gestures of the transcendently picturesque. James Blake's *Joy of Tyrol* (1910), for instance, uses the emotions stirred by the afterglow of Alpine sunsets to confirm the efficacy of the blood of Jesus. German romantic paintings of mountain scenery infused with spiritual meaning, sometimes complete with crucifixes on the mountain peaks (*Gipfelkreuze*) must have been influential in establishing the taste. The Aesthetic movement and

Henry James's novels among others, must have played their part in the creation of a shared climate of interest and expectation.

The superbly competent specificity of the Baedeker, the sheer busy-ness of its "cultural" appreciation, witnessed and confirmed by the physical layout of the page, are constantly reminding the audience that the aesthetic level of engagement is hard enough if it is to be done properly without bothering their minds about anything else—especially when there were the (multitudinous) details of food, lodging, and transport to be attended to. Baedeker divides Northern Italy into seventy-three routes. All of those routes painstakingly recount the Roman remains, the Renaissance and later paintings, murals, and architecture, both sacred and secular. A vocabulary of aesthetic appreciation enacts the drama not of personal participation but one seen, as it were, through the proscenium arch: witness "the picturesque plateau," the "fine Gothic cloisters," the "impressive" "precipitous cliffs" (285). The traveller comes upon the unknown or previously unexperienced already pre-digested by reference to an existing aesthetic discourse. The discursive loop is completed, text and audience made continuous.

II.

Having made this case, I now wish to question its capacities, partly because I find it all too easy to cross the border from description of a class's travelling habits and inferable blindnesses, as witnessed in its travel gospel, the Baedeker, to implications about its unspoken conspiracy to shape one part of the world— northern Italy—to its convenience by turning it into an object of aesthetic-historical appreciation. I find it faintly condescending—a touch self-congratulatory, indeed—to point at as I have done, if not exactly demonstrate, the complicity of such structures of understanding or knowledge with power. The argument virtually writes itself, and the discourse of discursivity confirms itself.

Cultural discourse as a notion enshrines a rhetorical generality which, once accepted, is well-nigh impossible to refute at the level of the individual case. If one answers with a different modelling of the discourses at work, one merely confirms the practice while disputing the details—even though individual cases may have been what initiated one's sense of the existence

of the discourse in the first place. Some New Historicists pride
themselves on such anecdotalism. My worry is *not* that history is
thereby eclipsed, because history is inevitably written, known
and contested in the present, and even earlier historians' understanding of history only exists for us now in our understanding
of theirs. There seems to me to be little point in contesting the
post-structuralist conclusion that history is irremediably textual.
Yet if, in this textual sense, the people of earlier times are our creations, the documents they left behind are not. *They* have a physical existence that is essentially independent of our understanding of them.

The force of this distinction is not often taken by those
who wish to pursue discourse as an interpretative method.
"Discourse" runs together document (taken as, say, ink on paper,
paint on canvas, a building) and text (*what* we read from the document, *how* we read the document) in order to demonstrate intertextual circulation of meanings. But the documentary level, once
distinguished from the textual, creates an explanatory obligation
on anyone wishing to interpret the past: an obligation to explain
the very existence of the document, and the individual agencies
of its textual markings. Editors are in the business of doing this.
They deal all the time with the documentary results of the physical inscription of textuality. They seek to attribute the textual
markings to persons identified, by name preferably or, if not, by
function.

In other words, they attempt, at every possible point, to
tie textuality to personal agency rather than to discourses imagined as being in circulation or under negotiation.[1] It can be
argued that awareness of personal agency in the author creates
an ethical obligation for the reader which rules certain interpretations out of court on the grounds of eccentric impressionism or
willfulness (see Hirsch). The argument opens up larger ones
about whether works are essentially communications between
individuals or whether they can function in the absence of the
author and all readers and so can be seen as authorised by imper-
sonal discourses or power structures (see Derrida). I do not enter
into that debate other than to observe that personal agency can
be admitted without the authorial subject being regarded as self-
identical, autonomous or in full conscious control of the work,
taken as an intended communication. The author "responsible"
for the text I am reading—the set of attributes which I attach in

my reading to the name—is inescapably an imaginative creation of mine, but one for which, at my leisure, I can find thousands of textual and contextual stimuli and delimiters with which my "creation" needs sorting. Awareness of my self-involvement in the positing of personal agency does not reduce this intellectual (and probably ethical) obligation: I grant the author an otherness, including a historical otherness from myself because the documents, as distinguished from the texts they bear, continuously oblige me to do so if I am to explain their existence (the editorial question of textual transmission becomes important here).

Keeping explanation at the level of discourse relativises knowledge by defusing this sense of obligation. Personal agency on the other hand, as witnessed by the physical document, grounds it. Furthermore, because editors are interested in the transmission of text from one document to another over time, they must practise a diachronic and causal kind of history. The limitation of discursive explanations, from this point of view, is the constant temptation to occlude personal agency in favour of epistemic or synchronic or circulatory modes of thinking.

It must be granted, nevertheless, that much of the time personal agency is not of special importance. When I chose not to treat Karl Baedeker as an author, I ran "him" together with his compilers as a middle-class voice. This was necessary if I was to tease out the elements of the cultural discourse of the turn-of-century travel guide. It also corresponded to the function of the title-page's author-statement in that case—a form of trademark or shopkeeperly endorsement of the reliability of his wares, in his case travel information. But if I wanted to particularise the discourses at the level of personal agency, then detailed historical work on the professional relations within the firm of Karl Baedeker in Leipzig would be necessary: statements by Baedeker and his sons about how they saw their publishing function and audience, what training they had had; the activities of their competitors; how they organised the collection of information for the guides; the print runs in the various languages and the effect of the Franco-Prussian and First World Wars on them; and the division of the publishing, cartographic, and printing functions. By means of this information and some well-chosen optical collations of texts and maps in various editions of the same guide, my account of the cultural discourses talking through the Baedeker might be particularised at the personal and trade levels. I doubt however that it would be entirely overturned: I suspect that a closer understanding of the personal agencies would, in this case, provide only a moderate resistance to discursive analysis. Further, if I were to restrict my analysis entirely to what I discovered of those collaborative personal agencies within the firm of Baedeker I may have had little of general interest to report.

But when it comes to a writer of Lawrence's ability, authorship as an explanatory device has potentially far more to yield. Undoubtedly the notion of authorship has been freighted with ideological cargo it would be better off without, for example, the author as inspired discoverer of universal truths about human experience (see Section III below). Nevertheless, at the basic level of the initiating physical inscription, it is unavoidable. The critical editor who must explain the provenance of textual markings which witness the passage of the work from its writer and producers through generations of readers usually wants to retain authorship as a working tool. But can a more active concept of it be defined for the present? To do that, its past must first be put into perspective.

III.

Authorship in its modern guise was largely constructed by the print-culture of the eighteenth century, metaphysically deepened by Romantic doctrines and metaphors of individual creativity, and fortified by Victorian veneration for the writer-sage and by the tradition of dilettantish biographical criticism in the newly institutionalised discipline of English in the universities in the first half of the twentieth century.[2] In the first half of the nineteenth century not all writers of imaginative or discursive prose thought of themselves as authors: that was a special distinction one might feel chary of claiming. Take the case of the Utilitarian, John Bowring; he was also a writer of moral tales for children and of devotional poetry. In his *Matins and Vespers: with Hymns and Occasional Pieces,* which I consulted in its third edition, altered and enlarged, of 1841, he remarks:

> These Hymns were not written in the pursuit of fame or literary triumph. They are full of borrowed images, of thoughts and feelings excited less by my own contemplations than by the writings of others. I have not sought to be original. To be useful is my

first ambition—that obtained, I am indifferent to the rest. (vi)

Stephen Drew, who died about 1826, makes a similar statement in his *Principles of Self-Knowledge: or, an Attempt to demonstrate the Truth of Christianity, and the Efficacy of Experimental Religion, against the Cavils of the Infidel, and the Objections of the Formalist* (1828):

> In executing this, I have not scrupled to make use of the thoughts and words of any man, when I found they could be pressed into the service of God; and I have often done this, without acknowledging, or perhaps knowing, or even being able now to discover, the sources from whence I took them. But for this I make no apology; because I have no vain desire of being thought an author.

Of the opposite inclination was a Victorian versifier named Mrs. Edward Caudle, whose one very slim volume celebrates the opening of a charity bazaar in 1850: *Poems, Written by Mrs Edward Caudle, Authoress of "Ah! Lady Why upon thy Brow?" and Dedicated by Permission to Lady Molesworth.* This is the only thing of hers known to the catalogue of the British Library. Her printer, J. Kent of Bishopsgate Without, evidently did not feel it came under the law requiring publishers to give copies of all books they produced to the British libraries of deposit. She was preserved for posterity only because a contemporary collector of fugitive verse by women bound up her pamphlet with other ephemeral publications, the volume (entitled in holograph, "A Poetical Seraglio") finally making its way into the collection of the British Library. In her address "To Messrs. the Public," she refers to herself as an "authoress" (5). She is invoking what was already the social prestige of authorship: she was writing to an audience of other ladies, among whom she fondly hoped would be numbered Queen Victoria. But of course the primary meaning of authorship she was invoking, not a little vainly in her case, was originality.

Mircea Eliade commented in 1963 in *Myth and Reality* that "the prestige of origins" runs deep in our culture (21). Nowadays, we are perhaps more attuned to the exceptions to this truism. Authorship does not (and probably never did) function in popular culture: the success of, say, a Hollywood movie is more likely to be identified with the leading actor than the director or producer; electronic mixing of singing and music may mean that the performers in front of the camera in a video-clip are not in fact the people we are hearing (as in the recent case of Milli Vanilli); and best-selling novels, as Jack Stillinger has recently shown, are almost invariably collaborative, their author-statement functioning more as a sales pitch than biographical fact. And in the thriving if less popular realm of Postmodernist writing and art, the habit of cultural quotation (rather than origination) is the *sine qua non.*

Biographical authorship is teasingly elusive. Our own enquiries are conducted in the present, and we do not so much recover as create: the textuality of a dead author's existence, conveyed to us in other texts, is therefore inescapable. If we participate in what we know, then no completely secure objective knowledge is available. Yet this post-structuralist conclusion is not the end of the story; it merely puts more pressure on the need to arrive at self-consciously pragmatic solutions. Our "creations" of text from the past *can* be entirely free-floating, responsive only to the needs of the present. Alternatively, we can choose to constrain them by empirical appeals to a multitude of documents that can be shown, at least within the pragmatics of historical bibliography, to have been physically inscribed in the past. The question of why we should so choose engages the larger ethical question I mentioned before; suffice it to say here that although authorship may not be graspable or securely knowable, it is no less important for that when the rest of the past is in the same boat. Authorship as an explanatory paradigm is richly disputable, if the old idea of the author as possessing an unchanging and always already-formed essence (e.g., Shakespeare as the man for all time) manifested in the isolated mountain peaks of his works is replaced by that of a subterranean intelligence at the service of an ongoing intellectual project manifested in a series of making-present ideas in the act of writing. While always in one (very undiscriminating) sense culturally "given," the ideas are provisionally reformulated and complexly intertwined in a variety of related writings.

IV.

The available archive becomes a matter of importance here. The existence of pre-publication versions of a literary or other work raises questions which discursive analysis is ill-equipped to answer. In theory, an enterprising historian of discourses could trace those which so multiply positioned the author-as-subject as to produce the major and minor changes in the extant documents. But could that historian so explain the thousands of minute changes in expression, organisation, and punctuation commonly found by critical editors of novels? It is hard to imagine. The likelier conclusion is that the discursive and authorial paradigms have different capacities or answer overlapping questions differently.

Authorial intention can only be postulated: it is a literary critical interpretation, so there is no point pretending it has objective status against which the success of the text can be measured. The more important question is on what archival basis the postulation—inevitably provisional—is done. Versions of works inhabit a world of other texts: yet some speak more clearly (and nearly) to one another than do others, and so pragmatically a line can be drawn around them identifying them as "versions." Biographical location of textual changes from version to version becomes crucial if the matter is pursued. And so, gradually, a form of authorship is re-figured, one which links the textual and the biographical-historical. My example is Lawrence's revision in 1915 of his travel essays of 1912–13. The case is a particularly good one for, by the time he carried out the revision, the meaning of the War had come home to him and he was a changed man.

* * * * *

In early 1915, with interest in England running high in the wartime fighting on the relatively successful Italian front, the publisher Gerald Duckworth asked Lawrence to write a travel book on Italy for him. Lawrence complied, thinking it an easy job to gather up the ten essays he had written when he first travelled to the Continent in May 1912 with Frieda Weekley. They spent the Northern winter of 1912–13 at Gargnano on Lake Garda in northern Italy. He was not able to lay his hands on some of those essays in 1915: two had not been published; another two were lost; and two did not quite fit the bill. So in the end he radically revised four (the first four in the volume) and wrote six more, including "The Return Journey" which describes a later walking tour of September 1913 and from which I quoted at the beginning.[3]

As a would-be travel writer in 1912, Lawrence made it hard for himself by going in the off-season to a place like Gargnano which was but poorly endowed culturally and historically. What art objects were there (something on which the Baedeker is informative) Lawrence largely ignores: he discusses a nearby church, but for its secludedness and animal darkness rather than for its eighteenth-century architecture, sixteenth-century fresco, baroque chapel or its Byzantine style mosaic. But he does provide some superb nature descriptions (expected in the Alpine travel book), including a sunrise over Monte Baldo on the other side of the lake, and this description gets into the 1915 version of "The Lemon Gardens" almost unchanged (*Twilight* 128). And he evinces a very acceptable botanical curiosity in seeking out Christmas roses and snowdrops in a gully behind that church. But his main interest was in the social life of the Garda, particularly the peasant life he saw going on around him. The three Garda essays (all written in early 1913) are centred around a dramatised incident in which he appears as participant and on which he offers thoughtful but usually rather tame interpretations.

A discourse which feeds into the essays is the longstanding racial and cultural opposition of the southern European nations as sun-drenched sites of unselfconscious and sensuous ease, from the northern as cold places of intellectual consistency and industrial achievement. Lawrence was well aware of it, as witnessed by (amongst much other evidence) a letter dating from early 1913 and written in Gargnano. He recalls

> that beastly, tight, Sunday feeling which is so blighting in England. I like Italy, which takes no thought for the morrow, neither fear nor pride. The English are "good" because they are afraid . . . and the Italians forget to be afraid, so they're neither good nor wicked, but just natural. (i. 548–9)[4]

Lawrence adapts the racial discourse in the 1913 and 1915 versions of the Garda essays (all in *Twilight*) in, for instance, the Spinner's uninquiring self-enclosure as she spins wool ("The Spinner and the Monks"); in Signor di Paoli's anxiety about having had no children ("The Lemon Gardens"); in the compelling account of the incongruities of an Italian peasant performance of

Hamlet ("The Theatre"); and in the stormily sensual relationship of Paolo and Maria in "San Gaudenzio," first written in 1915— significantly after the completion of *The Rainbow*. And the racial discourse is a small part of the explanation for the shockingly frank evocation of the principle of the Tiger in the 1915 version of "The Lemon Gardens":

> So the Italian, through centuries, has avoided our Northern purposive industry, because it has seemed to him a form of nothingness.
> It is the spirit of the tiger. The tiger is the supreme manifestation of the senses made absolute. This is the
> Tiger, tiger, burning bright,
> In the forests of the night
> of Blake. It does indeed burn within the darkness. But the *essential* fire of the tiger is cold and white, a white ecstasy. It is seen in the white eyes of the blazing cat. This is the supremacy of the flesh, which devours all. . . . So the Italian, so the soldier. . . . The will of the soldier is the will of the great cats, the will to ecstasy in destruction, in absorbing life into his own life, always his own life supreme, till the ecstasy burst into the white, eternal flame, the Infinite, the Flame of the Infinite. Then he is satisfied, he has been consummated in the Infinite.
> This is the true soldier, this is the immortal climax of the senses. This is the acme of the flesh, the one superb tiger who has devoured all living flesh, and now paces backwards and forwards in the cage of its own infinite, glaring with blind, fierce, absorbed eyes at that which is nothingness to it.
> The eyes of the tiger cannot see, except with the light from within itself, by the light of its own desire. . . . So the white eyes of the tiger gleam to a point of concentrated vision, upon that which does not exist. Hence its terrifying sightlessness. The something which I know I am is hollow space to its vision, offers no resistance to the tiger's looking. It can only see of me that which it knows I am, a scent, a resistance, a voluptuous solid, a struggling warm violence that it holds overcome, a running of hot blood between its jaws, a delicious pang of live flesh in the mouth. This it sees. The rest is not. (117–18)

This account does not exist in the early version; in fact, the 1913 essays betray no interest in extreme states of being. What had happened? The discursive explanation does not take us far enough with the substance nor capture the idiosyncratic urgency of the 1915 writing. Inevitably one turns to the authorial paradigm for explanation, and here one has means of getting very detailed.[5]

V.

Preparing a travel book about foreign places must have seemed an easy prospect to Lawrence. But his attempts to come to grips with what he had been coming to see as his culture's deathwish—the War—inevitably intruded. His partial rewriting of his philosophy from 2 March–9 July 1915 (ii. 300, 362) had no doubt engaged with this theme (cf. ii. 318, 331, 340); and it is possible that some of that writing was only slightly adapted for interpolation into the published Garda essays of 1913—after he had completely rewritten in late July 1915 an essay first written in September 1912, "Christs in the Tyrol" (in *Twilight*). Newly entitled "The Crucifix Across the Mountains," it became the first essay in *Twilight in Italy*. After next revising the proofs of *The Rainbow* by mid-August, Lawrence sent the second essay rewritten for *Twilight*, "The Spinner and the Monks," for typing on 20 August 1915, and "The Lemon Gardens" on 24 August. On 1 September, he sent his typist the first half of "The Theatre" and on the 5th, having read the typescript of the new version of "The Lemon Gardens," he must have been dissatisfied with it for he asked to have seven pages of it replaced with new material he had just written and which was considerably longer. The superseded version of these pages is lost; the retyped version (also lost but it served as copy for the first edition) is a philosophical meditation which includes the account of the tiger. Lawrence had also extensively rewritten another two pages of the essay (part of a second philosophical meditation), on both the ribbon and carbon copies. He did not ask for these pages to be retyped, probably thinking the copies neat enough for submission to Duckworth and magazines as they stood.[6] Nevertheless his typist took it upon himself to retype from the revised ribbon copy, and retained the revised carbon copy, furnishing Lawrence with retyped duplicates and probably the (now-lost) revised ribbon copy to check them against. The revised carbon copy (TCC) which the typist kept is extant among the typist's papers in the Nottinghamshire Archives.

The possibility that Lawrence had, at first, simply inserted philosophical material in the "Lemon Gardens" essay would offer one explanation for his replacement in typescript of the two meditations in "The Lemon Gardens": upon reading them in context he may immediately have felt they did not cast sufficient light on the Italian spiritual condition. But it is more likely that his understanding of the cultural crisis and its historical roots changed while he was writing the magnificently ambitious account of *Hamlet* in "The Theatre"—the bulk of which was written 1–6 September and did *not* need immediate revision. (He returned "The Lemon Gardens" for retyping on the 5th.)

Comparison of the typed version on TCC against its holograph revision reveals a major shift.[7] Its significance can be appreciated only when seen against the background of Lawrence's previous twelve months. Writing to Lady Cynthia Asquith, also on 5 September 1915, he expressed a newfound, almost furious determination to use the rewriting of the sketches to diagnose the present:

> The persistent nothingness of the war makes me feel like a paralytic convulsed with rage. Meanwhile I am writing a book of sketches, or preparing a book of sketches, about the nations, Italian German and English, full of philosophising and struggling to show things real. My head feels like a hammer that keeps hammering on a nail. The only thing I know is, that the hammer is tougher than the nail, in the long run. It is not I who will break. (ii. 386)

The 1914–15 winter had been a bad one for Lawrence. His confiding in January 1915 that "The War finished me: it was the spear through the side of all sorrows and hopes" (ii. 268) might be thought a posture were it not for abundant evidence of the depth of his shock. On 25 August 1914 he had confided: "The war is just hell for me. I don't see why I should be so disturbed—but I am. I can't get away from it for a minute: live in a sort of coma, like one of those nightmares when you can't move." But, he added, "I've whitewashed the house" (ii. 211 and cf. ii. 339).

The counterbalancing sanity of that last sentence is typical: he would try to deal with the personal predicament in his writing but with a doubled sense of responsibility that he was writing also for his civilisation: "A man must now needs know himself as his whole people . . . each work of art that is true, now, must give expression to the great collective experience, not to the individual" (ii. 300–1). This sense of mission, expressed in March 1915, was, in its substance, less a sudden new departure than an extension of a position he had already taken in a well known letter of 5 June 1914 from Fiascherino, rejecting the novel's "old-fashioned human element—which causes one to conceive a character in a certain moral scheme and make him consistent" (ii. 182). In his characterisations Lawrence said he was looking to tap the underlying force "according to whose action the individual is unrecognisable" (ii. 183); and on 21 September 1914, from having seen Egyptian and Assyrian sculpture at the British Museum, he took away a sense of "the tremendous *non-human* quality of life. . . . It is not the emotions, nor the personal feelings and attachments, that matter" (ii. 218). He was registering the need to engage with life at the level of fundamental principles. He had made early attempts in the first travel essay he wrote (in May 1912—and not published till 1994 in *Twilight*), "The Germans and the English," and in his "Foreword to *Sons and Lovers*." But now the history of those underlying forces might, if he could only grasp them, make sense of the War; he might get perspective on the profoundly disorienting present. In a letter of 5 September 1914 he had written: "What colossal idiocy, this war. Out of sheer rage I've begun my book about Thomas Hardy. It will be about anything but" (ii. 212). He made repeated attempts to write the needful history in 1915—each of them ambitious, provisional, responding to new influences and opportunities, but all conditioned by the overriding fact of the War. The intellectual project crosses the boundaries of the novel (particularly in his revisions to the typescript of *The Rainbow* from mid-March till 31 May and to the proofs from 9 July to mid-August), the short story (writing "England, My England" by 6 June and "The Thimble" by 29 October), the private letter and travel essay, and the philosophical essay (he turned to another version of his philosophy—"The Crown"—from *c.* 11 September to 2 October).[8]

The extant carbon-copy pages of "The Lemon Gardens" (TCC) exemplify the provisionality and demonstrate the intertwining of ideas. As typed, TCC extends the line of thought first voiced in the "Foreword to *Sons and Lovers*" about the relative sources of knowledge: the Flesh and the Word. In "Study of Thomas Hardy" (completed by 5 December 1914) Lawrence had developed the idea of historical shifts growing out of a never-ending process of conflict, within the self, between the expressions of God the Father (Flesh, Female, Being) and God the Son (Word, Male, Knowing); but then, crucially, he localises the process in his discussions of paintings and novels. While he admits the terms are "arbitrary, for the purpose of thought" (60), they nevertheless nominate for him an eternal opposition which, in its shifting balances, affords opportunities for the self's leap into the unknown—the Holy Ghost, which emerges from the opposition. Lawrence's analysis is essentially benign at this stage; there is process without polarisation.

Reading Mrs. Henry Jenner's *Christian Symbolism* (1910) later in December 1914 he wrote: "It is necessary to grasp the Whole. At last I have got it." The medieval church symbolism he found in the book suggested another "form of expression" in which the grand, extra-human narrative of "Egotism" in opposition to spirituality could be told. "The old symbols," he wrote, were "a great attempt at formulating the whole history of the Soul of Man" (ii. 247-9). Lawrence continued to depend on Christian terms in his thinking, admitting in February 1915 to E. M. Forster (whom he charged with confusing the opposite principles embodied in Pan and Christ in his Pan stories): "I use old terms . . . because I am not inventive or creative enough" (ii. 276). Nevertheless the Christian story of rebirth, reinforced by the coming of spring in 1915, gave him heart to provide *The Rainbow* with a hopeful ending (completed 2 March). The action of acorn kernels breaking forth in February (456) becomes a type of a new life for Ursula, and—proclaimed by the rainbow—a new covenant for the people of Beldover; the hope echoes Lawrence's feelings expressed in letters of that same February (ii. 269, 276).

But in his revisions to the typescript in March-May the relationships of Will and Anna, and Ursula and Skrebensky are put under a strain not present in the manuscript.[9] In the cathedral scene (chap. vii), for instance, a greatly increased tension is figured in Will and Anna's dispute over the significance of the ceiling bosses, and Lawrence is at pains to balance responsibilities for their marital stalemate by taking their responses to the cathedral to opposite near-extremes. Their sexual relationship, after Will's flirtation with the girl in Nottingham, issues in "a sensuality violent and extreme as death" but also in an "Absolute Beauty" (219-20); there is liberation sensed in the extremes but, crucially, they do not get reconciled within a synthesising understanding. Assertion of self entails destructiveness, most obviously in Ursula's case; and it is she who, in her Botany classes (but not until the proof revisions), comes to an understanding of "Self" as "a supreme, gleaming triumph of infinity" (409).

Meanwhile, by 24 March 1915, Lawrence had read *The Idiot*. While he claimed to dislike Dostoevsky ("He is again like the rat, slithering along in hate, in the shadows, and, in order to belong to the light, professing love, all love"; ii. 311), he must have found that novel's structural opposition of the all-forgiving Myshkin and the obsessively passionate Rogozhin an endorsement of his own intellectual direction. In the novel's devastating finale, after Rogozhin has raped Nastasya—whom Myshkin, trapped by his own compassion, had been just about to marry out of pity—and killed her, and become demented, the two men spend the night together tenderly, side by side, a grotesque parody of two lovers. In the manuscript of *The Rainbow* Lawrence had written: "If the lamb might lie down with the lion, it would be a great honor to the lamb, but the lion's powerful heart would suffer no diminishing" (317-18, 634). Although Lawrence allowed this sentiment of Ursula's to stand in typescript and proofs, the pressures that would cause its disavowal (see below) were building up.

So we find him saying on 8 April: "This is the very worst wickedness, that we refuse to acknowledge the passionate evil that is in us. This makes us secret and rotten" (ii. 315), as if the Dostoevskian denouement—where the polarity of lion and lamb is defused, catastrophically for both men—had foretold the contemporary situation. Letters give a sense of the considerable strain Lawrence was under at this time after having been shocked by the "triumphant decay" he sensed at Cambridge in early March (based on a sudden awareness of homosexuality in acquaintances, ii. 319-21). And in *Rainbow* proof revisions, he went on to lay new emphasis on the fixed rigidity of the spirit of life in the industrial town, Wiggiston (321-3); and that of the people of Beldover changed from one of "self-care and self-greed" to "disintegration" (459). Nevertheless Lawrence persevered with the metaphor of a new covenant; but on the proofs, in a more desperate hope than that typified by the kernels of the acorn in

February, he has Ursula foresee "the world built up in a living fabric of Truth, fitting to the over-arching heaven" (459). The corruption beneath (in Uncle Tom Brangwen, Winifred Inger, Skrebensky's ethic of public service, and the "stiffened bodies of the colliers," 458) is accommodated in the vision—but only by Ursula's rising above it. Newly awakened, innocent, feeling a "poignant affection" for the man whose spirit she has destroyed (457), her new outlook has little substance other than violent rejection and pious hope. Her goal (added in proof) is "to create a new knowledge of Eternity in the flux of Time" (456). This wish echoes the terms Lawrence adumbrated for joint social action (in a plan he was developing with Bertrand Russell in response to the War) on 20 June 1915: "We must centre in the Knowledge of the Infinite, of God. Then from this Centre each one of us must work to put the temporal things of our own natures . . . in accord with the Eternal God we know" (ii. 359).

TCC as typed is similar. Our direction is said to have been (like Ursula's) back to the flesh and beyond "to the Original Creation," a journey in which scientific research has (somehow) assisted. With sermonising earnestness Lawrence exhorts us to look outwards towards a "golden" future, "a new world" which we can create once we have removed the "great stumbling-blocks, immense falsities that we have gropingly reared against ourselves . . . it is our business to set the whole living world into relation to the eternal truth. When we have done that we shall have re-created Paradise."

Submitting relationships to increasingly pressured and destructive stresses while simultaneously insisting on the possibility of an eternal utopia may help explain the relief Lawrence evidently felt when, by 14 July, he came upon the writings of Herakleitos, as expounded in John Burnet's *Early Greek Philosophy* : "I have dropped writing my philosophy. . . . I have been wrong, much too Christian in my philosophy. These early Greeks have clarified my soul . . . my christian religiosity . . . was only a muddiness" (ii. 364–5). His belief in the efficacy of a "spirit of unanimity in truth" (ii. 380) seems to have been sapped during a bruising day's arguing the point with Russell, Lady Ottoline Morrell and Frieda on ?7 August (ii. 377). This argument marks a falling out with Russell, but the letter of 16 August when Lawrence reflects on the argument suggests it stung him into self-criticism. It may have sent him back to Burnet, beyond the

third chapter (on Herakleitos) to consider, or reconsider, the fifth
on Empedokles, for by the time he rewrote the TCC fragment (by
5 September) he seems to have accepted the thrust of
Empedokles' doctrines; and a few weeks later when writing "The
Crown" he was actively adapting them.

Although in his letter about Herakleitos Lawrence
quotes mainly the anti-democratic fragments (in the context of
his disagreements with Russell about a new political order), he
would have found the whole project of the early Greek philosophers inspiriting. For Burnet, the writings manifest a progression
in empirical inductive reasoning towards the more genuinely scientific, later Greek philosophy. Serenely ignoring this valuation,
Lawrence must have welcomed the ancient accounts of cosmo-
genesis arrived at without resort to the idea of a God of creation—for he had been trying to do an allied, if somewhat less
ambitious, sort of thing himself. He would have found that
Herakleitos' notions chimed with his own in the "Study of
Thomas Hardy": "what is at variance agrees with itself. It is an
attunement of opposite tensions" (Burnet 150), the indispensable
opposites having originally flowed from the one source, divert-
ing into two streams. "All things are flowing" is usually attributed to Herakleitos (162); Lawrence would soon write in "The
Crown": "Matter is a very slow flux" (302). Burnet quotes Plato
on the teachings of Herakleitos and Empedokles: "It was safest . . .
to say that reality is both many and one, and is kept together by
Hate and Love" (159). According to Herakleitos this process was
"eternal and simultaneous" (159). But Empedokles, as Burnet
explains it (231-44), introduced the notion of stages whereby one
tendency (Strife, making for complete differentiation, or Love,
for reconciliation and togetherness) would gradually gain ascen-
dency, but in reaching its climax would give way to its opposite—whereupon the reverse movement would occur, and so on.
In the first installment of "The Crown," submitted on 20
September 1915, Lawrence wrote: "Love and hate, light and
darkness, these are the temporary conquest of the one infinite by
the other. . . . But when the opposite is complete on either side,
then there is perfection."[10]

In Lawrence's thinking the liberation had been effected;
he would henceforth feel free to explore the fundamental principles to their extreme extensions (and thus to tap a new kind of
explanatory potential) without the capping of tensions by

appeals to Eternal Truth and unanimity in action. Process could become polarisation, and only a vague theoretical frame for the eternal action and counteraction need be posited: the Holy Ghost, whom he now saw, in revised TCC, as the "relation between" the two extremes. Lawrence's *tour de force* in "The Theatre"—the historical essay, centering on *Hamlet*, on the expression and then abandonment of the position of "King, Father, in the Self supreme" (146)—and the remarkable meditation in "The Lemon Gardens" on the tiger are the first fruits; in revising the second meditation in that essay (i.e. TCC) he wrote:

> The lion shall never lie down with the lamb. The lion eternally shall devour the lamb, the lamb eternally shall be devoured of the lion. Man knows the great consummation in the flesh, the sensual ecstasy, and that is eternal. Also the spiritual ecstasy of unanimity, that is eternal. But the two are separate and never to be confused.

For Lawrence the War was the prime confusion: after a century of commitment to a principle of selflessness his culture had reached the Empedoklean climax and was turning back on itself. But in perversely attempting to arrest an (inevitably changing) present under its longstanding banner of selflessness it was becoming fiendish. In Lawrence's tiger there is no gap between volition and violent action; no instrumentality intervenes. But, as he now saw it, a century of scientific analysis of the world outside the self and of the development of machines and weapons (which act instead of the self) had made the new stirrings of the tiger-principle horrific: "Confusion," he wrote in the TCC revision, "is horror and nothingness." He himself had, in the first version as typed, run the two principles together in a last, opaque expression of end-of-*Rainbow* hopefulness; but in the revision "There are two ways, there is not only One."

Given Lawrence's sense of how his world had changed since 1913 and his new crystallisation of its direction over the previous century, it was inevitable that the more innocent surface observation of the 1913 essays and their chatty and anecdotal elements would be subjected to a new, polarising intellectual tension. With a secure agreement with Duckworth, Lawrence was not under the constraints of 1913 when he was submitting his work to magazines; he could now afford to strike out. The ener-

gy and ambitiousness of the experiment began to pay off the further into the volume he went, and it laid the intellectual foundations for both "The Crown" where he analyses the spiritual corruption caused by the present impasse and *Women in Love*—
where he peoples it (the Criches, Hermione, the mechanised min-
ers) and explores the extreme expressions the responses would
necessarily take (in the principal characters and Loerke). What
saves Lawrence's interpretations of the Italians in *Twilight in Italy*
from a codifying rigidity and gives them boldness is his ability,
after *The Rainbow*, to follow the opposite tendencies to their
extreme psychological and spiritual roots.

This brings us back to the "perishingly victorious"
Englishman. Lawrence did not usually have a serene distance
from what and whom he chose to describe in his writings. And
there are few accidents, even in his travel prose. Nearly everything links. His fascination with the wayside crucifixes in the first
essay in *Twilight in Italy* (and its early version of 1912) is linked,
though not reducible, to his guilt at having destroyed Ernest
Weekley's marriage with Frieda (see *Twilight* xxxiii-xxxiv). His
depiction of the Alpine Christs' desolating awareness of death in
the flesh without the compensating awareness of heavenly
release shockingly located, for Lawrence, the consequences of
extreme self-abnegation in the service of a spiritual ideal. He had
already been identifying this condition as essentially English (see
"The English and the Germans" in *Twilight*). He would later
identify it as the root cause of the guiltily philanthropic Mr.
Crich's moral sickness in *Women in Love*. His son Gerald's death
in the Alps, just after having seen a mountain crucifix, was one of
Lawrence's—Lawrence the novelist's—alternative extreme fates:
the victorious Englishman is the rather surprising link.

In *Twilight*, Lawrence notes from the hotel register that
the man has a "fair, clerkly hand"—just as Lawrence did (212).
He himself had been a clerk in a Nottingham factory and habitually wrote "fair." Moreover there is sufficient evidence from
Lawrence's letters and other sources to show that the
Englishman's exhausting "thirty mountain miles" of walking
(210)—a crucial detail in Lawrence's account—was replicated the
next day by Lawrence, but *up* the valley instead of down. The
day before, Lawrence had in fact walked for eight and a half
hours; the day before that he had covered perhaps 26 miles; and
two days after meeting the Englishman (if Lawrence's memory

of a train fare—recently worked out against distance—can be trusted) he walked an impressive 38 miles, almost 15 of which were very steep.[11] Like the Englishman his purse was "definitely limited" (211)—to 3 shillings a day (ii. 76)—and a comparison Lawrence made to himself in a letter he wrote during his next walk through the Alps in 1914 (ii. 186) was transferred to the Englishman in 1915: "So he had walked on and on, like one possessed, ever forward. His name might have been Excelsior, indeed" (211). The Englishman's failure to break out of the industrial "machine" (211) to which he was returning connects with the racial discourse of Northern and Southern nations: he "reached his Furka [Pass, to the south], only to walk along the ridge and to descend on the same side! My God it was killing to the soul" (211).

Gerald Crich would find the courage not to go back to the machine existence; instead he would perish in the snow. But, like the Englishman, he would not go South:

> [The Englishman's] eyes were dark and deep with unfathomable courage. Yet he was going back in the morning. He was going back. All he had courage for was to go back. He would go back, though he died by inches. Why not? It was killing him, it was like living loaded with irons. But he had the courage to submit, to die that way, since it was the way allotted to him. . . . His body must pay whatever his will demanded, though it were torture. (212)

* * * * *

Discourses traverse this textual space but discursive analysis is extremely unlikely to locate its tensions and *frissons*. Recourse to the authorially-focussed intertextual flow is necessary, as is the opening up of the author's writings to reveal how their versions relate to one another. Setting boundaries around a literary work to distinguish it from all others is resisted just as steadily by the authorial paradigm I am working within here as it is by the discursive. While Lawrence's problem was to identify the underlying forces (differently from Freud) that would deconstruct the liberal tradition of individuality he had inherited, our problem now is to reconstruct *his* (at least his as an author) in a way that will respect the historicity of his ongoing cultural and intellectual project—rather than to keep on recruiting him, as in the 1950s and 1960s, as the profoundly intelligent prophet of Life or, as commonly in the 1970s and after, as misogynist and fascist. The "Author"-figure to which Barthes and others objected was a prior, unifying consciousness exhibited equally in the personal life and in the writings; the meaning of the works could therefore, as it were, be read off the life. My proposal is for a paradigm of authorship where the reverse is the case and where an attentiveness to provisionality and experiment replaces the temptation toward interpretative closure.

NOTES

[1]But cf. McGann's attempt to redefine the object of editorial attention as the social production of text. For a discussion, see Eggert.

[2]See Eagleton, Eisenstein, Foucault, Myers and Harris (the eighteenth-century chapters), Saunders and Hunter, Williamson, and Woodmansee.

[3]For uncited factual assertions, see the detailed account of the composition, revision and production of the essays in the Introduction to *Twilight*, from which the present essay incorporates some material.

[4]*Letters*, vols. 1 and 2, are abbreviated thus throughout.

[5]For further influences at work in the Tiger passage—Exodus, Isaiah, Blake, Rilke, Banquo's ghost—see the Explanatory notes for 117-18 in *Twilight*.

[6]He was hoping for dual publication (hence the need for ribbon and carbon copies), but nothing came of it.

[7]A facsimile of TCC appears in *Twilight*; it corresponds to *Twilight* 125–6. Quotations of TCC refer to the facsimile.

[8]"The Thimble" is in *England, My England*; "The Crown" is in *Reflections*.

[9] See *Rainbow* xxxviii-xlii; the changes are in its textual apparatus.

[10]*Reflections* 258 and (for 1915 wording) 469.

[11]See Explanatory note on 210: 27 in *Twilight*.

WORKS CITED

Baedeker, Karl. *Northern Italy.* 14th ed. Leipzig: Baedeker, 1913.
_____. *The Eastern Alps.* 12th ed. Leipzig: Baedeker, 1911.

Barthes, Roland. "The Death of the Author." 1968. In *The Rustle of Language.* Ed. Richard Howard. New York: Hill and Wang, 1986. 49-55.

Blake, James M., ed. *Joy of Tyrol: A Human Revelation.* London: Stanley Paul, 1910.

Bowring, John. *Matins and Vespers: with Hymns and Occasional Pieces.* London: J. Green, 1841.

Burnet, John. *Early Greek Philosophy.* 2nd ed. Edinburgh: Black, 1908.

Caudle, A. (Mrs. Edward). *Poems.* N. pub.: n.d. [1850]. Printer: J. Kent.

Conway, William M. *The Alps from End to End.* London: Constable, 1895.

Derrida, Jacques. "Signature, Event, Context." 1972. In *A Derrida Reader.* Ed. Peggy Kamuf. Harvester: New York, 1991. 80-111.

Dickens, Charles. *Little Dorrit.* London: Chapman and Hall, 1857.

Drew, Stephen. *Principles of Self-Knowledge.* London: Longman, 1828.

Eagleton, Terry. *Literary Theory: An Introduction.* Oxford: Oxford UP, 1985.

Eggert, Paul. "Document and Text: The 'Life' of the Literary Work and the Capacities of Editing." *Text* 7 (1995): 1-24.

Eisenstein, E. L. *The Printing Revolution in Early Modern Europe.* Cambridge: Cambridge UP, 1983.

Eliade, Mircea. *Myth and Reality.* London: Allen and Unwin, 1963.

Foucault, Michel. "What Is an Author." 1969; in English 1979. In *The Foucault Reader.* Ed. Paul Rabinow. London: Penguin, 1986. 101-20.

Hirsch, E. D. *Validity in Interpretation.* New Haven: Yale UP, 1967.

Jenner, Mrs. Henry. *Christian Symbolism.* London: Methuen, 1910.

Lawrence, D. H. *England, My England and Other Stories.* Ed. Bruce Steele. Cambridge: Cambridge UP, 1990.
_____. *The Letters of D. H. Lawrence.* Vol. 1. Ed. James T. Boulton. Vol. 2. Ed. George J. Zytaruk and James T. Boulton. Cambridge: Cambridge UP, 1979, 1981.
_____. *The Rainbow.* Ed. Mark Kinkead-Weekes. Cambridge:

Cambridge UP, 1989.

_____. *Reflections on the Death of a Porcupine and Other Essays.* Ed. Michael Herbert. Cambridge: Cambridge UP, 1988.

_____. *Sons and Lovers.* Eds. Helen and Carl Baron. Cambridge: Cambridge UP, 1992.

_____. *The Study of Thomas Hardy and Other Essays.* Ed. Bruce Steele. Cambridge: Cambridge UP, 1985.

_____. *Twilight in Italy and Other Essays.* Ed. Paul Eggert. Cambridge: Cambridge UP, 1994.

_____. *Women in Love.* Ed. David Farmer, Lindeth Vasey, and John Worthen. Cambridge: Cambridge UP, 1987.

McGann, Jerome. *The Textual Condition.* Princeton: Princeton UP, 1991.

Myers, Robin, and Michael Harris. *Fakes and Frauds: Varieties of Deception in Print and Manuscript.* St. Paul's Bibliographies: Winchester, 1989.

Saunders, David, and Ian Hunter. "Lessons from the 'Literary': How to Historicise Authorship." *Critical Inquiry.* 17 (1991): 479-509.

Stillinger, Jack. *Multiple Authorship and the Myth of Solitary Genius.* New York: Oxford UP, 1991.

Williamson, Dugald. *Authorship and Criticism.* Local Consumption: Sydney, 1989.

Woodmansee, Martha. "The Genius and the Copyright: Economic and Legal Conditions of the Emergence of the Author." *Eighteenth Century Studies* 17 (1984): 425-48.

"The Key to the Whole Book": Faulkner's *The Sound and the Fury*, the Compson Appendix, and Textual Instability

Philip Cohen

In 1929, William Faulkner published *The Sound and the Fury*, his example *par excellence* of modernist American fiction. Sixteen years later in 1945, he wrote what is known as his Compson Appendix for inclusion in Malcolm Cowley's *Portable Faulkner*, which Viking published in 1946. What had begun as a brief synopsis of the novel soon turned into a superb extended genealogy that referred to much of Faulkner's post-1929 work and reassured him that writing screenplays in Hollywood had not destroyed his talent.[1] At the author's insistence, this discursive history of the Compson family also appeared at the front of Random House's 1946 Modern Library dual edition of *The Sound and the Fury* and *As I Lay Dying*. Since that time, the Appendix has appeared, sometimes with Faulkner's approval, at the front or the back of various editions of the novel or been omitted altogether. Understandably, Faulkner scholars have been divided over whether the Appendix constitutes a part of the novel or a separate entity and over where, if at all, it ought to appear in an edition of *The Sound and the Fury*. That this debate has significant consequences is illustrated by the effect that the Appendix with its substantial if often unremarked differences from the 1929 text of the novel has had on criticism of *The Sound and the Fury*.[2] My interest here is less in championing one of the authorized existing or possible texts of *The Sound and the Fury* than in discussing some of the consequences that the work's textual instability has had both for understanding it and for illustrating several theoretical concerns currently bedeviling editorial theory. As an authorial genetic critic, I hope to shed some light on how Faulkner's inclusion of the Appendix in the text of *The Sound and the Fury* re-contextualizes and so re-ontologizes, however intentionally or unintentionally, the novel, thus creating a new version or perhaps even a new and separate work. More simply put, the textual instability of *The Sound and the Fury* illustrates how an author can re-write a novel merely by framing an earlier version rather than re-writing it. While skepticism about the empirical evidence available prevents me from developing a sociology of the common reader of *The Sound and the Fury*, one documentary record does exist: the published record of scholarly responses to the novel. In much of what follows, I document both some of the ways in which Faulkner's Appendix frames as well as clashes with the 1929 *Sound and the Fury* and how it helped shape the contours of the novel's critical reception.

In the mid-1940s, *The Sound and the Fury*, which originally had been met with good reviews but poor sales, was out of print like most of Faulkner's other works. In thrall to Hollywood during much of the decade, Faulkner quickly agreed to help Malcolm Cowley in 1944 when the latter proposed writing an essay on the former's fiction. As this collaboration led to their work on the *Portable Faulkner,* their correspondence grew in warmth although it also reveals the strains produced by the different conceptions and estimates the two men had of Faulkner's literary corpus. Consequently, James Meriwether has cautioned us not to take all of Faulkner's comments about the Appendix at face value ("Textual" 27).

Cowley planned to arrange the anthology selections chronologically to represent Yoknapatawpha County's evolution from the time of the Indians to World War II.[3] The main problem, Cowley noted, was what to include from *The Sound and the Fury* (FCF 23). While Faulkner's response was unequivocally positive, he too wanted the collection to contain an excerpt from *The Sound and the Fury*, preferably Jason's monologue. Although Cowley concurred that Jason's section was the one most capable of standing on its own, the two men settled on an excerpt from the final section preceded by a brief synopsis of the first three sections of the novel. Written by Faulkner, this note would tell "why and when . . . and how a 17 year old girl [Miss Quentin] robbed a bureau drawer of hoarded money and climbed down a drain pipe and ran off with a carnival pitchman" (SL 202). While it seems likely that Faulkner originally conceived of his Appendix as something akin to the brief genealogy and chronology he had produced nine years earlier for *Absalom, Absalom!* (1936), he soon surpassed that earlier effort.[4] In early October of 1945, for example, he wrote Cowley that the synopsis should be "an induction, I think, not a mere directive" (SL 204). Faulkner subsequently wrote nearly thirty pages of Compson family history stretching back in time to 1699 and forward to 1943. He emphasized the 1929 novel's two generations of Compsons but also extended their stories beyond the earlier time limits. As he wrote, Faulkner invented new characters and events and drew on stories and novels he had written after 1929.

Faulkner triumphantly announced the Appendix's completion to Cowley in October of 1945: "I should have done this when I wrote the book. Then the whole thing would have fallen into pattern like a jigsaw puzzle when the magician's wand touched it" (SL 205). The Appendix was, he thought, "really pretty good, to stand as it is, as a piece without implications" (SL 205). By this time, it had clearly become more of an evaluative history of the Compson family than an introduction to the excerpt. Whatever else Faulkner was up to in writing the Appendix—introducing an excerpt for Cowley's *Portable*, writing a new and separate fiction, responding to the unintentionally reductive and unflattering conception of his life's work implied by Cowley's design for the *Portable*—his remarks suggest that he was also trying to explain what he often called his favorite novel yet one more time to a readership that originally had neither understood nor admired it.

Cowley admired the Appendix, but was puzzled by the various discrepancies between it and the 1929 *Sound and Fury*.[5] He went so far as to send Faulkner a carbon of the *Portable*'s excerpt from the novel to aid him in revising the Appendix (FCF 48, SL 209). The author probably ignored it, however, since he later told Cowley that he had no plans to eliminate the discrepancies between the Appendix and the novel.[6] Cowley did not notice any of the more glaring differences between the 1929 novel and the Appendix. Confronting Jason with a color photograph of Caddy and a Nazi general on the French Riviera clipped from a slick magazine, librarian Melissa Meek suddenly realizes in the Appendix what Dilsey had intuited years earlier: that

Jason was blackmailing Caddy into never returning to Jefferson and into "appointing him sole unchallengeable trustee of the money she would send for the child's maintenance" (ML 340). Although this alleged knowledge on Dilsey's part in the Appendix explains why Jason did not commit Benjy to an asylum until after his mother's death in 1933, I can find no evidence in the 1929 novel that Dilsey knows Jason may be blackmailing Caddy or that he is afraid of the Compson servant. In the Appendix, we also learn that he submits "annual reports . . to the district Chancellor, as required of him as guardian and trustee by his bondsmen" (ML 344), but again no evidence of this appears in the 1929 novel. Regarding the aftermath of Miss Quentin's theft, moreover, the Appendix tells us that Jason

> couldn't even report it; he could not only never receive justification . . . he couldn't even demand help in recovering it. Because he had lost four thousand dollars which did not belong to him, he couldn't even recover the three thousand. (ML 346-47)

Jason cannot report the theft, that is, because the first four thousand dollars sent by Caddy for Miss Quentin were "officially recorded as expended and consumed" (ML 347). He "couldn't even go to the police for help . . . he didn't dare pursue the girl himself because he might catch her and she would talk" (ML 347). In the 1929 novel, however, Jason *does* go to the sheriff and he *does* pursue Miss Quentin until he realizes the chase is futile.

Despite the occasional strained moment, Faulkner appeared genuinely pleased with the *Portable* when it appeared in April of 1946. He told his agent Harold Ober that "Malcolm Cowley has done a fine job in Spoonrivering my apocryphal county. . . . Be sure to see it" (SL 218), and in May he wrote Robert Haas, his publisher at Random House, that the volume pleased him very much (SL 234). True, Cowley and Faulkner were often at loggerheads as the novelist kept pressuring the editor to remove biographical information about Faulkner's military experience in World War I without telling him that it was inaccurate. Nor was Faulkner receptive to Cowley's notion that his work as a whole formed a symbolic parable about the rise and fall of the Old South's aristocratic planter class. Cowley's introduction describes Faulkner as an epic poet or bard in prose who invented "a Mississippi county that was like a mythical kingdom but was complete and living in all its details" and then made "his story of Yoknapatawpha County stand as a parable or legend of the Deep South" (2). "I'm inclined to think that my material, the South," he wrote Cowley in an oft-quoted letter, "is not very important to me. I just happen to know it, and dont [sic] have time in one life to learn another one and write it at the same time" (SL 185). Nonetheless, when Faulkner received an advance copy of the volume, he wrote Cowley jubilantly: "The job is splendid. Damn you to hell anyway" (SL 233).

Well before the *Portable*'s appearance, Robert Linscott, Random House's new senior editor, requested an introduction from Faulkner for the forthcoming Modern Library dual edition of *The Sound and the Fury* and *As I Lay Dying*. Meriwether has suggested that Faulkner's subsequent desire to include the Appendix at the front of the dual edition may have been an attempt to get out of writing an introduction ("Textual" 29). For better or worse, however, it was Faulkner himself who insisted in a February 6th letter that Linscott include the Appendix not as an introduction but as a new first section of the novel:

> When you reprint THE SOUND AND THE FURY, I have a new section to go with it. I should have written this new section when I wrote the book itself. . . . By all means include this in the reprint. When you read it, you will see how it is the key to the whole book, and after reading it, the 4 sections as they stand now fall into clarity and place. . . . When you issue the book . . . print this Appendix first, and title it APPENDIX. . . . Then continue with the sections as they now are. . . . Be sure and print the Appendix *first*. (SL 220-21).

Faulkner also makes clear in the same letter that he did not consider the Appendix a substitute introduction: "I never read introductions either, and know little about them. . . . But I'll have to think about it, try to think up something" (SL 221). Although he never supplied Random House with an introduction, the dual edition with a paradoxical "New Appendix as a Foreword by the Author" appeared on December 20, 1946.

Faulkner's insistence that the Appendix appear as the first section of *The Sound and the Fury* in the new edition probably resulted, as Noel Polk claims, from his seeing the Appendix as making the novel more comprehensible and so more accessible to the reader (17-18). Indeed, his correspondence with Linscott indicates that he felt the genealogy could help counter the old charge of obscurity which had originally been levelled against the 1929 *Sound and the Fury* in general and against Benjy's section in particular:

> As you will see, this Appendix is the key to the whole book; after reading this, any reader will understand all the other sections. That was the trouble before: the BENJY section, although the most obscure and troublesome one, had to come first because of chronology, the matter it told. (SL 228, also see SL 237)

For his part, Faulkner continued to insist that the Appendix was a crucial part of the novel. In 1955, he told Jean Stein that he wrote *The Sound and the Fury* "five separate times trying to tell the story" (*Lion* 244) and that the 1929 novel was "not complete, not until 15 years after the book was published when I wrote as an Appendix to another book the final effort to get the story told and off my mind" (*Lion* 245).

As a result of Faulkner's steadily increasing popularity, the 1946 Modern Library text of *The Sound and the Fury* with the Appendix at the front was reprinted and reissued frequently from 1954 to 1961 under the inexpensive paperback Modern Library and Vintage imprints (Meriwether, "Textual," 31).[7] At the same time, we must remember, that copies of Cape & Smith's 1929 *Sound and the Fury* and two more small printings issued in the wake of *Sanctuary*'s notoriety in 1931 had become exceedingly rare. During the 1960s, the Appendix appeared at the back of several reissues of the novel and some omitted it entirely.[8] The wheel came full circle when Polk omitted the Appendix from both his Random House corrected text of *The Sound and the Fury* in 1984 and his Vintage paperback of the same text in 1987. When David Minter reprinted this text in his 1987 and 1994 Norton Critical Editions of *The Sound and the Fury*, however, he included the Appendix in the "Backgrounds and Contexts" sections. Finally, Polk omitted the Appendix once more from a facsimile reprint of the 1984 text in a different format in a 1990 Vintage International volume, but included it accompanied by a brief explanatory note at the rear of another facsimile reprint, the 1992 Modern Library volume.

If the presence and position of the Appendix in texts of *The Sound and the Fury* have varied, its contents have remained relatively stable. The piece situates Faulkner's commentary on the immediate Compson family within the context of a lengthy genealogy of the generations that preceded them. Its broad scope extends backwards in time to the arrival of the first dispossessed Scottish Compson in America: one Quentin MacLachan Compson, who fled with his claymore and tartan from Culloden Moor and Bonnie Prince Charlie's unsuccessful attempt at the English throne in 1745. It also takes the family's history past the 1929 novel's conclusion on Easter Sunday, 1928, to Caddy's liaison with a German staff general in occupied France during World War II. Jason Compson IV, we learn, established his own business, committed Benjy to the state asylum in Jackson as soon as his mother died in 1933, fired the black servants, and ultimately partitioned the Compson house into apartments before selling it to a buyer who converted it into a boarding house. Unlike the psychological and emotional immediacy and intensity of the 1929 novel's stream-of-consciousness monologues, the genealogy showcases Faulkner's labyrinthine late expository prose style as it explains and assesses events and character motivation in the book. While it covers much of the same ground as the 1929 *Sound and the Fury*, the Appendix tells us less about what Faulkner once thought as he toiled at his fourth published novel in 1928 than about the man and author he had since become in 1945. His attempt to explain the book to his readers was done from the vantage point of over fifteen years of hindsight. Indeed, the Appendix, as Mary Jane Dickerson argues, is intimately connected to Faulkner's symbolic genealogical narrative techniques in *Absalom, Absalom!* (1936) and *Go Down, Moses* (1942) whose families "are twisted and sterile" and "finally unable to transcend the old sins" (327).

As with Faulkner's other great families, both high and low, the Compson record is one of shifty dealings, first to acquire Compson's Mile, the future site of Jefferson, from the Indians and then to found a line. The land becomes the Compson Domain, now "fit to breed princes, statesmen and generals and bishops" to avenge earlier dispossessions "from Culloden and Carolina and Kentucky" (ML 333). Just as Thomas Sutpen and Flem Snopes contain traces of each other, so the Compsons of the

Appendix suggest a composite of Sutpen and Snopes. Jason Lycurgus Compson, Quentin's great-great grandfather, is no aristocratic cavalier from the school of moonlight and magnolia but rather a gambler, a sharper, and an opportunist. He wins races and goods and land from the Indian chief Ikkemotubbe with "a small . . . mare which could do the first two furlongs in definitely under the halfminute and the next two in not appreciably more, though that was all" (ML 332). By limiting these races "to a quarter or at most three furlongs," Quentin's great-great-grandfather rose rapidly in Snopes-like fashion to become the half partner of the Chickasaw Agency's store (ML 332). From such humble origins, the family's fortunes grow to include a governor and a Civil War general, but their grand dreams of founding a dynasty all come to nought. Decline sets in and accelerates with the novel's Mr. Compson, a failed alcoholic lawyer, and his four children. It is Mr. Compson who sells "the last of the property, except that fragment containing the house and the kitchengarden and the collapsing stables and one servant's cabin" for Caddy's wedding and Quentin's lone year at Harvard (ML 334). The family line itself ends with Jason IV, a childless bachelor.

The rise and fall of the House of Compson described in the Appendix is reminiscent of similar parabolic trajectories traversed by the fictional Sutpen and McCaslin families. Understandably, some readers of texts of *The Sound and the Fury* that include the Appendix have taken the novel to be a mythologized representation of Southern deterioration: the Compsons yield to the Snopeses who take over Jefferson, leaving only Jason to hold his own with them. If the 1929 *Sound and the Fury* concentrates on a single Southern family in disarray, the Appendix clearly mythologizes through the declining Compson family fortunes Faulkner's historical sense of the white man's sojourn in the South and perhaps in America as well. The Appendix opens with the murderous Ikkemotubbe, who is dispossessed by Jason Lycurgus Compson, and ends with some of the black servants from the novel who "endured" (ML 348), suggesting by synecdoche the Scotch and English migration to America bracketed by the dispossession of the Indians and by the heritage of the curse of slavery.

Given the circumstances surrounding the genesis of the Compson Appendix, it should come as no surprise that it and the 1929 *Sound and the Fury* contradict each other in ways far more significant than the minor discrepancies readers have heretofore noticed. The motivations of the novel's primary characters in the genealogy clash repeatedly with their previous dramatization in the 1929 novel. Moreover, the characters in the Appendix suffer various psychological simplifications even as they gain from the historical and social contexts Faulkner provides. After reading the Appendix, for example, Cowley recalls telling Faulkner that Jason seemed "altogether repellent and hateful" in the novel, whereas the genealogy portrayed him "as having a certain redeeming doggedness and logic" (FCF 42). Indeed, Faulkner's entry for Jason ironically stresses his inhuman sanity several times, calling him "The first sane Compson since before Culloden. . . . Logical rational contained and even a philosopher in the old stoic tradition" (ML 342-43).[9] While Jason competes successfully with the Snopeses in the Appendix (ML 343), the 1929 *Sound and the Fury* depicts him as primarily motivated less by the inhuman and inhumane economic and materialist rationality of the Appendix than by the same irrational obsessions he shares with his two brothers. Throughout the 1929 novel, Jason generally remains unaware of his starved need for love and approval, his insecurities, his anxieties, and his resentment of his parents. More importantly, the disastrous failure of both Mr. and Mrs. Compson as parents is movingly dramatized in the 1929 novel, generating some small measure of sympathy for the young Jason as victim even though he becomes a monstrous victimizer as an adult. It is precisely this childhood that the Appendix elides in order to focus on its broader historical perspective. Recalling his father's funeral, Jason thinks in the 1929 novel how he "began to feel sort of funny" (232) and then remembers standing by the newly-filled grave with Caddy after everyone else has gone home,

> thinking about when we were little and one thing and another and I got to feeling funny again, kind of mad or something, thinking about now we'd have Uncle Maury around the house all the time. (233)

Neither the most introspective nor the most articulate of men, Jason's "funny" feelings may be construed as angry resentment of his alcoholic father for abandoning him both as a child and as a young man. Nevertheless, the authorial sanction of the

Appendix was such that the later "sane" Jason was often used to gloss the earlier obsessed one. In an influential 1959 discussion which quotes from the 1946 Modern Library edition, for example, Olga Vickery notes that "Jason operates in terms of a logic which informs the basis of social communication" (31).

The addition of Jason's post-1928 history to the Appendix is as troubling as what Faulkner omits from the genealogy. In the Appendix, curiously enough, Jason rises in the world. In Caddy's entry, we learn about "the farmers' supply store where Jason IV had started as a clerk and where he now owned his own business as a buyer of and dealer in cotton" (ML 338). More startling is the revelation that he

> used his own niggard savings out of his meagre wages as a storeclerk to send himself to a Memphis school where he learned to class and grade cotton, and so established his own business. (ML 343)

Thus Jason becomes relatively successful in business, rising from clerk to owner in a Horatio Alger narrative with Snopesian overtones: that is, he rises not only from greed and miserliness but from industriousness and application as well. But such an ascent seems implausible given Jason's character in the 1929 novel. The owner of the farmers' supply store where Jason works points out several times that Jason withdrew and spent the money his mother invested in the store to make him a partner. Rising by dint of his own strenuous efforts seems completely uncharacteristic of Jason whom the 1929 novel portrays as doing just about everything but putting in a hard day's work at the store. Rather he is obsessed with following, regulating, and reforming Miss Quentin; following his financial investments; and finding blank bank checks with which to continue deceiving his mother. Eventually, Jason's complex schemes all come to nought, concluding with his utter defeat on Easter Sunday at the hands of Miss Quentin. Such a portrait does not suggest a man capable of learning from his mistakes and experience, a man who could subsequently pull himself together, put himself through school, and become a successful businessman. Indeed, nothing in the 1929 novel suggests that Jason, as unaware and as conflicted as he is, can reform himself.

Although Faulkner believed that his attitude toward Benjy had not changed (SL 207), the Appendix's list of Benjy's three loves—"the pasture . . . his sister Candace, firelight" (ML 345)—omits Caddy's worn slipper, a significant token that others use to soothe and comfort him in the 1929 novel. A far more substantial discrepancy between Faulkner's two portraits of Benjy has gone unremarked: in describing Benjy's thwarted attack on the Burgess girl, the Appendix retreats from the 1929 *Sound and the Fury*'s daring suggestions not only of rape but also of unrepressed incestuous desire for Caddy, the latter paralleling Quentin's more self-consciously conflicted feelings for his sister. Accustomed to sleeping with Caddy even after it became inappropriate and to regulating his sister's sexuality by bellowing whenever he detects the smell of perfume on her, Benjy's loss of Caddy opens up a profound absence that he is unable to articulate let alone accept. After her departure, he routinely follows returning schoolgirls along the Compson fence each day at twilight, thinking perhaps, as T. P. observes, "*if he be down to the gate, Miss Caddy come back*" (V 59). The climax of Benjy's assault in the 1929 novel is conveyed in language that is sexually suggestive albeit ambiguous:

> the bright shapes were going again. They were going up the hill to where it fell away and I tried to cry. But when I breathed in, I couldn't breathe out again to cry, and try to keep from falling off the hill and I fell off the hill into the bright whirling shapes. (V 60-1)

Whether Benjy is experiencing an orgasm just as Mr. Burgess knocks him out or recalling how he was anesthetized before he was "gelded" as a result of this assult seems impossible to determine. Faulkner's language in the Appendix, however, simplifies Benjy's attempt, draining it of any incestuous implication or sexual menace:

> following a fumbling abortive attempt by his idiot brother on a passing female child, [Jason] had himself appointed the idiot's guardian . . . and so was able to have the creature castrated before the mother even knew it was out of the house. (ML 344)

Faulkner himself seemed to set his own seal of approval on this retroactive process of simplification of the assault when he commented to Cowley that Benjy was "gelded by process of law . . . since the little girl he scared probably made a good story out of it when she got over being scared" (SL 207). Thus the Appendix simplifies and sanitizes the very scene that might help a reader connect Quentin's conscious idealizations of Caddy and his unconscious desire for her to similar if less repressed impulses in Benjy. Emphasizing Benjy's innocence and his role as moral arbiter, especially where Caddy's sexual behavior is concerned, is, of course, a recurrent gesture in criticism of *The Sound and the Fury*, and one, I suspect, that the Appendix has supported. Thus Melvin Backman in *Faulkner: The Major Years* (1966) draws his quotations from the 1946 Modern Library edition as he repeatedly stresses Benjy's innocence, sexual and otherwise (17, 33-4).

Faulkner simplified and sanitized not only Benjy in the Appendix but also his complex and innovative presentation of Quentin's divided self in the 1929 novel. Perhaps the best example of this diminution is Faulkner's insistence in the Appendix that Quentin "loved not his sister's body but some concept of Compson honor" and "not the idea of the incest which he would not commit, but some presbyterian concept of its eternal punishment" (ML 335). Curiously, the Appendix remains silent on Benjy's and Quentin's parallel inner conflicts in the 1929 novel between conscious asexual and puritanical idealizations of Caddy as a substitute-mother on the one hand, and more or less repressed Oedipal desires for her as substitute-mother on the other. That Quentin's unconscious veneration of chaste womanhood masks an obsessive misogyny and a disgust with sexuality learned from Mr. Compson—Women *"have an affinity for evil for supplying whatever the evil lacks in itself"* (V110) and are "so delicate so mysterious . . . Delicate equilibrium of periodical filth between two moons balanced" (V147) he tells his son—and displayed in all its vitriolic harshness in Jason is a commonplace in recent discussions of the novel. Caddy's entry in the Appendix may refer to Quentin's perception of either her body or her maidenhead as "the foul instrument of [the family honor's] disgrace" (ML 336), but the genealogy as a whole elides the 1929 novel's emphasis on male Compson misogyny just as it evinces little or no interest in the unconscious desires of its characters.   In describing Quentin as someone "who loved death above all, who loved only death, loved, and lived in a deliberate and almost perverted anticipation of death" the Appendix strikingly ignores both his unconscious motivation and his tangled familial relationships in the 1929 *Sound and the Fury* (ML 335-36). Faulkner's eloquent thumbnail sketch of Quentin in the Appendix simply does not do justice to the richness of his earlier characterization. Although Faulkner may not have been deliberately closing off the dangerous pathways that he had explored earlier, the Appendix represents a deeply conservative re-reading or re-imagining of the 1929 *Sound and the Fury*.[10]

Faulkner's extensive comments on Quentin in the Appendix clearly had an impact upon critical discussion of the latter's motivation. Thus Vickery cites Faulkner on Quentin before writing that "Insofar as virginity is a concept, associated with virtue and honor, it becomes the center of Quentin's world" (37), and Dorothy Tuck refers to the same entry while arguing that Quentin makes "Caddy the repository of the Compson family honor" rather than the object of his incestuous desires (27). Richard Chase too notes that Quentin's incestuous fantasies represent only his desire to remove Caddy and himself "to a transcendent realm" and to immolate "their gross natural existence" (229). Faulkner's new conception of Quentin's character in the Appendix affected readers who used the 1946 dual edition such as Frederick Hoffman who approvingly echoes Faulkner when he underscores Quentin's desire to rescue the family's "'honor' by arresting time and thus force decay out of the Compson world. He is in love with stasis, represented . . . by Caddy's virginity, and eventually by death itself" (54-55). In his influential portrayal of Quentin as an incestuously chaste lover, Cleanth Brooks as well owes a significant debt to Faulkner's Appendix: "Quentin is not really in love with his sister's body, only in love with a notion of virginity that he associates with her" and ultimately "with death itself" (327).[11]

Significantly, critics pursuing psychological readings of the novel that stress Quentin's incestuous desire for his sister have felt constrained to interrogate relentlessly the Appendix's authority. Thus as early as 1954, Carvel Collins cautioned readers that Faulkner's "confusing" Appendix must not mislead them "into thinking that the feeling between Quentin and his sister Candace is entirely on some high moral or philosophical plane above the incestuous much as Quentin tries to put it there" (75).

In the essay in which this warning appeared, Collins was engaged in disputing the socio-historical view of the 1929 novel propounded by Cowley and his heirs and in setting forth his own ground-breaking psychoanalytical reading of Benjy, Quentin, and Jason as symbolic representations of Freud's id, ego, and superego. In discussing how Faulkner's "unrepressed and even undisguised" misogyny (109) manifests itself in the disturbing and forbidden incestuous games of some of his male characters, Albert Guerard too has questioned whether or not the 1929 novel bears out the Appendix's concern with Quentin's sense of honor: "His deepest concern would seem to be her loss of virginity *per se* rather than the loss of family honor" (118).

Like her siblings, Caddy also seems to have been reconceived somewhat in the Appendix. Faulkner writes movingly in Quentin's entry that she

> loved her brother despite him, loved not only him but loved in him that bitter prophet and inflexible corruptless judge of what he considered the family's honor and its doom, as he thought he loved but really hated in her what he considered the frail doomed vessel of its pride and the foul instrument of its disgrace; not only this, she loved him not only in spite of but because of the fact that he himself was incapable of love. (ML 336)

The emphasis here on Quentin's obsession with honor downplays his incestuous desire for her, a generally unconscious motivation that nevertheless permeates every aspect of his monologue. The passage raises other questions as well. Does the Caddy of the 1929 *Sound and the Fury* really love Quentin *because* he cannot love anyone? Does she really love masochistically "that bitter prophet and inflexible corruptless judge," or does she love and pity him as a brother and as a quasi-son? The passage seems impossible to reconcile with the Caddy of the 1929 novel who is tormented and torn by the obsessive, life-denying demands and desires of her three brothers. Together as strict monitors of her sexual behavior, Quentin and Benjy make Caddy's life impossible before she leaves home, and Jason takes over this function after she brings Miss Quentin back to Jefferson. While Caddy voices her resentment as well as pity over Quentin and Benjy's interventions on several occasions, the novel presents absolutely no evidence that she "loves" Quentin's constant puritanical interference.[12]

A number of Faulkner's critics have concerned themselves with the proper relationship of the Appendix to the 1929 novel. Cowley himself remained convinced that it was "an integral part of *The Sound and the Fury*" (FCF 37), and John Pilkington is "grateful for the enrichment . . . and the assistance [the Appendix] provides for the reader" (42). In 1962, however, Meriwether severely criticized Random House's placement of the Appendix at the front of the Modern Library edition, calling it "a negligible text" that performed a dubious service to unwary readers by presenting them "with what appears to be a five-part novel, the first part of which relieves them of the burdens which the second part was designed to impose upon them" ("Textual" 31, 29).[13] Conceding the superb quality of the Appendix and admitting that it appeared "at Faulkner's specific instructions, as part of two new editions of the novel after 1946," Noel Polk nevertheless argued that Faulkner added the Appendix to the Modern Library edition because the piece showed him that his creative powers had not deserted him entirely and then excluded the Appendix from three of his editions of the novel (16, 17). He too stresses the Appendix's unfortunate confounding of the book's "deliberately controlled revelation and concealment of the Compson family history" (Polk 19). Others have offered a more cautious defense of the value of the Appendix in relation to the novel. While rejecting the view of the novel as an allegorical representation of the Old South's decline, Perrin Lowery maintains that Faulkner sought to create a historical context for the novel and draw our attention to its "strong sense of historical time" by writing the Appendix (64).[14] More recently, however, Eric Sundquist has savaged the genealogy's "ponderous, often absurd prose" as a sign "that the muse of Yoknapatawpha was in decline" and noted only in passing that the Appendix "everywhere clashes with the novel" (4).

In a recent shrewd essay, Cheryl Lester discusses the Appendix as Faulkner's deliberate response to the conception of his work suggested by Cowley's introduction and selections for the *Portable*. Lester's Appendix aggressively refutes the anthologizer's characterization of Faulkner as an epic bard whose books in the aggregate constitute a coherent myth of the rise and fall of the South. There is much to admire in Lester's cogent arguments, and it is true that the initially friendly relationship between Cowley and Faulkner became somewhat strained as the two men danced gingerly around the author's alleged World War I experience and as Cowley tried in vain to reconcile inconsistencies within Faulkner's corpus and between *The Sound and the Fury* and the Appendix. Nevertheless, Faulkner's unstinting praise of the *Portable* seems genuine. More importantly, Lester implausibly reads Faulkner's claim that the Appendix was the key to the novel as a thoroughly outrageous and hence ironic assertion of "the impossibility of legitimating or countersigning his own desires" (389). That Faulkner insisted the Appendix appear in future editions of the novel itself does not suggest authorial irony. Given the state of his reputation at the time, I also have difficulty imagining Faulkner, generally the savvy professional writer, sabotaging a project designed to resurrect his reputation and that of his favorite creation. If the Appendix is, in part, a response to the assumptions underlying Cowley's *Portable*, it remains, as well, an attempt to explain once again his favorite novel, to win for it the audience Faulkner believed it deserved.

With its significant differences from the 1929 *Sound and the Fury*, the Appendix provides a splendid example of how a later authorially-produced frame can help re-contextualize a literary work, leading some readers to overlook or even smooth some of the over particularly egregious conflicts between the initial text and its subsequent frame. Indeed, the version of the text consulted in conjunction with the interpretive paradigm employed has often helped shape various premises, emphases, and conclusions concerning the novel. This situation is reminiscent of how Faulkner's *Sanctuary* was frequently read from the vantage point of *Requiem for a Nun* even though the latter appeared twenty years after the former. In all fairness, however, I should add that neither reliable biographical nor textual information was available to early critics. Of course, once the genesis of the Appendix was more accurately understood, some readers used the genealogy less to frame discussion of the 1929 novel than to explore how Faulkner attempted to revisit and revise the earlier novel or to answer Cowley's *Portable*. Consequently, this later use of the Appendix created yet another context and yet another interpretive re-contextualization of *The Sound and the Fury*.

Placing the Appendix at the front of the novel's 1929 text not only gives the game away, it gives it away *wrongly*, I think, by encouraging many readers to view the 1929 novel primarily as a study of "the decline and disappearance of the values of the Old Order," of the death agony of the patrician Old South played out against the backdrop of a diminished and alien New South (Taylor 51). Anachronistically deploying the Appendix as a heuristic tool in 1954, for example, William Van O'Connor summarizes the Compson history from the Appendix, notes that the "family is in an advanced state of decay," and then suggests that "Quentin's desire for incest with Caddy represents a social disorder," that of a narcissistic, enervated South living amid the ghosts and glories of the past (39). Three years later, Richard Chase quotes the Appendix on the eventual fate of the Compson house just after announcing that the novel's subject "is what happens to the last generation of the Compson family, a family whose ups and downs are representative of the experience of the South over the [past] two hundred years" (221).

Although the 1929 novel may offer little encouragement for foregrounding sociological or historical readings—its ostensible subjects, technical strategies, and language seem to resist doing so at every point—such readings of the later texts that include the Appendix seem more legitimate.[15] Indeed, they almost seem mandated by the social and historical re-contextualizing provided by the Appendix, regardless of the numerous inconsistencies and contradictions that pairing the 1929 novel with the genealogy creates. As a graduate student once told me, Faulkner's cursory treatment of Mr. and Mrs. Compson in the Appendix, two characters central to interpreting the novel as the tragedy of a dysfunctional family, assists in his work of recontextualization. Even Dickerson, herself well aware of the Appendix's problematic relationship to the 1929 novel, contends that its emphasis on Quentin's obsession with honor and glory and Jason's contrary sterile materialism and greed illuminate their characters in the larger work. They have inherited, she proposes, "[t]he absurd extremes" of their common ancestor Charles Stuart Compson, "who thought he wanted to be a teacher of classics rather than the soldier and opportunist he turned out to be" (326, 324).

More humanist New Critical readings of the 1929 *Sound and the Fury* have also been shaped by the Appendix. Cleanth Brooks provided an influential example of this in 1963 when he insisted that *The Sound and the Fury* be regarded not as a mythol-

ogized fable of Southern generational decline but rather "a parable of the disintegration of modern man" (342). This approach is,
of course, consistent both with Brooks's liberal humanism and
his attempt to raise Faulkner from the level of regional or local
author to that of universal artist.[16] Brooks's reading of the 1929
novel contrasts the different yet defective modern conceptions of
time and love that motivate the three Compson brothers with
Dilsey's almost religious conceptions of the same. His opposing
characterizations of Quentin and Jason often owe a significant if
occasionally unacknowledged debt to the Appendix: "Quentin is
not really in love with his sister's body, only in love with a notion
of virginity that he associates with her" and "Quentin is really, as
his sister knows, in love with death itself. In contrast with this
incestuously Platonic lover, Jason has no love for Caddy at all,
and no love for anyone else" (327).

More recently, other readers have deconstructed the disparate sections of the novel, so diverse in rhetoric, style, and concerns, only to reveal stunningly similar psychological assess-
ments of the three Compson brothers. This fictional strategy of
juxtaposed incongruities masking deeper parallels is central to
Faulkner's other work from the period including *Flags in the Dust*
and its shorter published version *Sartoris*, both versions of
Sanctuary, and *As I Lay Dying*, and is supported by Faulkner's
observation in 1933 that the novel had less to do with Southern
history than with his own projection of self-representations onto
the three Compson brothers (Cohen and Fowler 277). And what
do the three Compson brothers have in common? They share
anger and resentment over how their dysfunctional parents—a
drunken, disillusioned cynic of a father who has abdicated his
parental responsibility and a coldly selfish and hypochondriacal
mother—have failed them; an incestuous impotence and anguish
over the loss of their sister Caddy who has served as their substitute mother; and a misogynistic disgust with women and with
sexuality itself, a revulsion inherited from their cynical father
and from the Southern Protestant culture in which they live and
breathe.

In rejecting any change in their relationship with their
sister, all three male siblings refuse to acquiesce to the psychological and sexual changes that accompany the inevitable passage of time. A mental defective, Benjy never relaxes his hold
upon his experiential if not biological mother, bellowing inartic-

ulately and inconsolably when Caddy puts on perfume or loses her virginity or ultimately disappears. Similarly, the time-haunted Quentin tries to avoid accepting the painful fact of change in Caddy and in himself, first by destroying his watch and finally by drowning himself. Nostalgic for what he consciously takes to be an exclusive and intense asexual childhood relationship with Caddy that crumbled when she reached puberty, Quentin refuses to accept the possibility, suggested by his father, that some day he will no longer grieve over Caddy's fall. Although less articulate and introspective than Quentin, Jason is no more free from the past than his brothers: resenting the failure of his parents, he hoards his money and his anger over Caddy's betrayal: because Caddy married Sidney Herbert Head while pregnant with another man's child, Jason never received the precious bank job he so desired. Profoundly shattered by Caddy's departure from their lives, all three brothers are psychological cripples who remain unable to deal with their loss.

The Compson brothers also share a desire to regulate either the sexuality of their substitute-mother Caddy or that of her daughter Miss Quentin, a desire contradicted and undone by unconscious, displaced Oedipal desires to ravish that which they seek to protect. Benjy and Quentin not only stand guard obsessively as their sister's unwanted chaperones, they also play the roles of voyeur and vicarious participant. While Quentin's conscious mind only fleetingly acknowledges his unconscious incestuous desire for Caddy, his desire parallels Benjy's abortive sexual attack on the Burgess girl—one of several substitutes for Caddy—at the Compson fence where he used to wait for his sister to come home from school. As a boy, Jason is employed by Mrs. Compson to spy on Caddy's sexual entanglements. As an adult, his obsession with revenge over what Caddy's sexuality has cost him is displaced onto his policing of Miss Quentin's sexual behavior, a policing so constant as to suggest a more prurient and voyeuristic interest as well.

Viewing the 1929 *Sound and the Fury* as a sexually daring portrait of a disastrous Freudian family romance with all of its unacknowledged and displaced desires has been central to some recent criticism of the novel, especially André Bleikasten's influential *The Most Splendid Failure: Faulkner's "The Sound and the Fury."* Bleikasten's book is, among other things, an extended meditation on how all three Compson brothers are emotionally arrested children, similar "in their basic narcissism, their refusal of change, their denial of life's motion" (88-9). Tracing this narcissism to parental failure, Bleikasten details how Benjy and Quentin possessively turn to Caddy for the love their mother has denied them and how Jason's anger over the lost bank job is a more materialistic manifestation of his brothers' obsession with Caddy's lost purity. The three brothers may respond to loss differently—one bellows blindly, one commits suicide, and one seeks revenge—but dealing with loss remains their preoccupation. Knowing that the Appendix was "no organic part" of the 1929 novel may have helped Bleikasten focus his attention on the relationships and problems of the immediate Compson family (243).

Whether or not the Appendix bears some responsibility for obscuring the 1929 novel's delicate balance between Compson male difference and identity is impossible to determine conclusively. It surely helped shape Vickery's observation that Caddy means something different to each brother: "For Benjy she is the smell of trees; for Quentin, honor; and for Jason, money or at least the means of obtaining it" (30). Nevertheless, the Appendix's emphasis on difference can overshadow Faulkner's strategy in the 1929 novel of juxtaposing a baffling assortment of different character psychologies and expressive languages only to suggest through doubling, parallels, motifs, striking events, and symbolism a deeper identity among the three Compson brothers. The Appendix itself retreats from this most daring feature of the original novel, simplifying and sanitizing the 1929 novel's orchestration of image and word, of syntax and punctuation to manipulate a reader's responses to the Compson family story. Consequently, it may be said to obscure the 1929 novel's audacious portrait of three brothers who share strikingly similar conscious and unconscious obsessions.

Having no wish to load more weight onto Faulkner's Appendix than it can bear, I do not mean to suggest that the text of *The Sound and the Fury* one reads will determine whether one will produce a psychological or a socio-historical reading of Faulkner's novel. Because I believe that meaning arises out of the dialectical relationship between textual production and textual reception, I assume that other factors besides whether or not the text of *The Sound and the Fury* consulted has undergone an editorial appendectomy are also at work. Cowley's enormously influential introduction to the *Portable,* with its thesis that Faulkner's entire corpus relates an epic saga of Southern decline, also constrains the response of many an academic reader of *The Sound and the Fury.* Clearly, a critic's theoretical paradigm also shapes the contours of an interpretation of *The Sound and the Fury.* The rage for unity, coherence, and closure, for example, probably helped formalist critics overlook the numerous substantial discrepancies and inconsistencies between the novel and the Appendix, especially if they were viewing the former through the lens of the latter. More recent psychological readings of the novel may also be indebted to the surfeit of earlier socio-historical readings and to the loving resuscitation and revision of literary psychoanalysis by one wing of poststructuralism. In any case, psychological readings of the novel have noticeably downplayed the Appendix and stressed fraternal similarity while historical and social readings of the novel have emphasized both the Appendix and brotherly difference.[17] The Appendix, we should remember, probably also affected readers more in the 1950s and the 1960s because they were much more likely to encounter it at the front or the back of their copies of the novel. The perception of Faulkner scholars in those decades that the Compson brothers were essentially different was, it seems likely, supported by the Appendix with its attendant psychological simplifications and social and historical complications.

Whatever Faulkner's intentions may have been, his actions created a version of the novel so different from the original version as to raise the possibility that he had produced an entirely new work rather than a revised version that simply subsumed the earlier one. Some readers such as Polk and Dickerson even treat the Appendix as a separate, discrete work, thereby setting aside the author's own instructions. That *The Sound and the Fury*'s textual instability has had a significant impact on discussion of the novel makes the task of constructing a scholarly edition of it based on the available texts all the more crucial. Polk's decision to omit the Appendix from his 1984 Random House, 1987 Vintage, and 1990 Vintage International texts stemmed from his single-text and authorial orientations and his argument that the creative impulse that had originally produced the novel in 1929 had long since passed by 1945. Because Faulkner's insistence that the Appendix be included in any future edition of the novel only represented his extra-literary desire to render it more comprehensible to the general reader and thus resuscitate his nearly moribund reputation, Polk omits the piece in order to restore "the text of the novel as Faulkner wrote it in the first rush of his full genius and wanted it published in 1929" (19).[18] Relenting somewhat for the less widely circulated 1992 Modern Library trade edition of the novel, he included the genealogy along with a prefatory "Note to the Appendix" at the back of a volume. Given his interpretive designation of the Appendix as a separate literary work, Polk's eclectic construction of the text "that Faulkner would most like to have had in print in 1929 . . . a text that most nearly represents the author's 'final intentions'" (xiv) is well within the Anglo-American editorial tradition's theoretical emphasis upon a single, unified, authorially intended text and the stabilization of textual variation by purging transmissional corruption and critically emending a copytext with later authorial revisions.

Another way to approach the Appendix from within the Anglo-American editorial tradition might be to adopt G. Thomas Tanselle's influential distinction between vertical revision and horizontal revision: while the former "aims at altering the purpose, direction, or character of a work, thus attempting to make a different sort of work out of it," the latter "aims at intensifying, refining, or improving the work as then conceived . . . thus altering the work in degree but not in kind" (335). A prospective editor of *The Sound and the Fury* could thus argue that Faulkner's deliberate addition of the Appendix constituted either horizontal or vertical revision, creating either a revised *Sound and the Fury* or a new and different work. Such a provision for overruling an author's explicitly stated intention, however, may not be entirely consistent with the authorial orientation of Tanselle's overall rationale. More importantly, Tanselle's distinction between horizontal and vertical revision rests, as does the Anglo-American editorial tradition from whence it comes, on the contested New Critical assumption that a literary work and its text are best conceptualized spatially as solitary, self-contained well-wrought urns.

Such a Tansellian argument over the Appendix might well begin by recognizing that Faulkner initially wrote the Appendix for the *Portable Faulkner*, that he may not have had a copy of the novel when he did so, and that he had not completely thought through the unfortunate consequences of including the Appendix in an edition of the novel. One could respond, of course, that the extant correspondence shows Faulkner thinking through some of these consequences and that rendering the novel more accessible was simply more important to him at the time. One might also add that professional writers making their living by their pens usually prefer not to waste a single word. Students of Faulkner's work well know that he routinely salvaged rejected material, sometimes with little or no revision, for purposes other than those for which it had originally been conceived. He also habitually re-imagined and reworked earlier published material for use in new work, the most obvious consequence of this being the numerous inconsistencies and anomalies in much of his published Snopes material. In the act of solving some problems through revision, moreover, Faulkner, like most writers, often unintentionally created new problems. Consequently, an editor of *The Sound and the Fury* needs to decide whether or not an author has the right to ruin his own work as a textual scholar bluntly put it to me long ago in my first graduate course.

Such an actual web of inextricably interconnected texts, both published and unpublished, suggests a notion of textuality at odds with the stable, fixed, impermeable conception that underlies modern eclectic editing. Like some textual scholars in the 1980s, Paul Eggert has proposed alternatively that

> relationships within and between the author's writings form . . . an *authorial* intertextuality, a continuum of authorship, itself part of a larger biographical flux that takes its shape in response to the pressures of . . . social, cultural, and other environments. (66)[19]

It is thus only in the context of a particular theoretical framework or of particular commercial and scholarly publishing arrangements that we can think of published works as discrete entities.

None of Polk's editions of *The Sound and the Fury* for Random House are complete scholarly editions, of course, nor were they meant to be. They are texts prepared in a scholarly fashion by a scrupulous editor for a commercial publisher who may have been reluctant to include even the editor's short list of editorial notes. Combining Polk's edited text with his 1985 *Editorial Handbook* to the novel, however, will yield much of what a modern Anglo-American scholarly edition normally contains: a text accurately and consistently constructed according to an explicitly stated set of assumptions and procedures, textual and historical notes, tables of the variants derived from the collations, and a list of all emendations to the text accompanied by explanations. Polk's reluctance to include the Appendix in either the *Handbook* or some recent editions of *The Sound and the Fury* may also have been influenced by the earlier ahistorical reliance on it as an authorial *vade mecum* to the 1929 *Sound and the Fury*, a reliance that pre-supposed a stable and unified intention on Faulkner's part that survived the years separating the composition of the novel and the Appendix. While unity was a significant aesthetic criterion of modernist literature and criticism, however, postmodern readers are more likely to postulate Faulkner's intentions as unstable, conflicted, and possibly non-recuperable.

After detailing some of the consequences of the numerous clashes between the 1929 *Sound and the Fury* and the Appendix, it may seem paradoxical for me to be troubled by Polk's banishment of the genealogy not only from his most widely accessible paperback editions of the novel but also from his editorial handbook. The exigencies of commercial publishing and his decision to exclude the Appendix from these editions, however, combine to obscure the process of *The Sound and the Fury*'s textual production. At best, I would have preferred the Appendix to appear in Polk's first three edited texts of the novel and the *Handbook*, possibly set off with the type of qualifying introduction for the unwary reader that he includes in his 1992 Modern Library text. Including the piece would more easily enable scholars with other editorial or theoretical assumptions about literary texts and works to construct possible alternative texts of *The Sound and the Fury*.

One such alternative conception of textuality, for example, supplants the spatial metaphor with a temporal one, arguing that the authorially sanctioned appearance of the Appendix at the front and back of different editions of *The Sound and the Fury* created new and more conflicted authorial versions of the novel. Replacing singularity with multiplicity as a governing premise results thus in a work in progress, a dynamic series of inter-related and equally valid versions. Emphasizing inter-related versions and the temporal dimension of textual production and developing apparatuses to represent this dimension is a significant feature of much of the rethinking of the editorial function in the decade that followed the publication of Polk's edition of *The Sound and the Fury* in 1984. As Hans Walter Gabler writes in "Unsought Encounters," these premises are central to contemporary German editorial scholarship with its structuralist conception of the literary text:

> Superseded and superseding readings each stand in a relational context, and every antecedent text, just as every succeeding text, is to be regarded as a structural system of language. If these texts are successive synchronic structures, the work as a whole appears diachronically structured as a succession of such synchronic texts. (155-56)

This approach rejects stabilizing textual variation in the form of a single critical text by using the criterion of conscious authorial intention because the editor is no longer "the author's executor, but the historian of the text" (Gabler, "Textual Studies" 159). Such a conception of textuality argues that it is simply impossible to predict all the consequences a particular revision or group of revisions may have for a work. Thus the problem with the chronological breadth of the Appendix in later versions of *The Sound and the Fury* is not that it often caused readers to foreground Southern socio-historical decline, but that they retroactively projected this interest onto the 1929 *Sound and the Fury* with its ostensible emphasis on the disastrous consequences of a dysfunctional Freudian family romance. The *Sound and the Fury* such readers are examining is quite simply a late rather than early textual version of the work.

The distance between Polk's conception of the text and Gabler's delimits the broad range of choices that now confront an editor of *The Sound and the Fury*. Intentionalist Hershel Parker would use a notion of the determinate nature of the creative process to champion some early version of the text and thus avoid the sort of anomalous consequences that even the most deliberate authorial revisions of an original text might produce. Practitioners of French *critique génétique* and German textual criticism would present in an integral or synoptic apparatus much like Gabler's edition of *Ulysses* the transmissional record of *The Sound and the Fury* purged of indubitable errors. Using Peter Shillingsburg's arguments in *Scholarly Editing in the Computer*

Age, another possibility would be a historical edition that prints one historical text of the novel with only transmissional corruptions corrected and displays in appendices the development of the authoritative authorial texts of *The Sound and the Fury* through their variants (42). At the 1989 Society for the Study of Textual Scholarship, Jerome McGann even suggested publishing multiple historical rather than authorial versions of a text as a practical consequence of the social contract theory of textual criticism he enunciated in *A Critique of Modern Textual Criticism*.

As a Faulkner scholar, I have become less interested over the years in determining *the* text of a Faulkner work than in paying attention to *all* of the authorial textual versions of that work and their various relationships. Thus the task of a scholarly editor of *The Sound and the Fury*, for me, is to provide as many textual versions of the work as possible, with variants and their causes identified, so that readers may select or conflate or compile textual versions according to their own theoretical lights. Until electronic archives and editions become the scholarly norm, however, the economic realities of scholarly publishing ensure that one version will be presented, accompanied by tables of the relevant variants. The textual history of Faulkner's novel, suggests that editorial operations upon the historical reality of textual instability are interpretive acts that often implicitly and explicitly privilege one sort of textual orientation over others. These contests over the nature of text and work, as the case of *The Sound and the Fury* demonstrates, may and often do shape the parameters of interpretation. If we concede that there is no universal theory of textuality, then we cannot erase previous versions of Faulkner's novel, both commercial and scholarly, by omitting the Appendix. To do so is to make a part of the novel's literary and critical history more inaccessible in the name of a universal theory of textuality that may be little more than a chimera.

NOTES

My thanks to both Phillip Doss and Noel Polk for reading a draft of this essay and providing a number of invaluable suggestions.

[1]Blotner, *Selected Letters of William Faulkner*, 205. Hereafter cited parenthetically as "SL."

[2]The question of the Appendix is only one of several intractable problems that face editors of *The Sound and the Fury*, problems that become more pressing when one notes that Faulkner was a Modernist writer in nothing so much as in his attempt to shape expressively his novel's punctuation, typography, and layout. In this respect, he resembles many of his peers who sought to poeticize prose by exploiting the full expressive potential of the print medium. Although the manuscript and carbon typescript for the first edition of *The Sound and the Fury* (1929) survive, the setting copy and galleys that would help document the extensive copyediting of the novel do not. Noel Polk discusses the various issues involved in editing the novel in the introduction to his *Editorial Handbook for William Faulkner's "The Sound and the Fury"* (1-22).

[3]Cowley, *Faulkner-Cowley File*, 21-22. Hereafter cited parenthetically as "FCF."

[4]Within a year of *Absalom*'s publication, Faulkner also offered to produce but never wrote "a chronology and genealogy and explanation, etc." for Maurice Coindreau who was translating *The Sound and the Fury* into French (SL 99).

[5]While Jason kept his strongbox under a board in his clothes closet in the 1929 novel, for example, the Appendix locates it in a locked bureau drawer. In the 1929 novel, Miss Quentin escapes from her locked room by climbing down a pear tree, but the tree is replaced by a rainpipe in the Appendix (FCF 41-2). Cowley also observed that the 1929 novel suggests Miss Quentin stole $3000 from Jason while the Appendix asserts she stole $4000 that Jason had diverted from Caddy's support payments plus $2840.50 of his own savings. The passages Cowley refers to are on p. 352 of Polk's 1987 Vintage edition of the 1929 novel and on pp. 344, 346 of his 1992 Modern Library edition of the 1929 novel and the Appendix. Unless otherwise stated, quotations from the 1929 *Sound and the Fury* and from the Appendix are from these two editions.

[6]In February of 1946, Faulkner wrote Cowley that he wanted

> the Appendix [to] stand with inconsistencies, perhaps make a statement . . . viz: the inconsistencies in the Appendix prove that to me the book is still alive after

15 years, and being still alive is still growing, changing. (SL 222)

Although Faulkner went on to revise the Appendix somewhat
for Random House's Modern Library dual edition of *The Sound
and the Fury* and *As I Lay Dying*, his elaborate plea for respecting
the evolutionary nature of his creative imagination may strike
one as special pleading, as a plausible rationale to disguise his
unwillingness to re-read the novel. Thirteen years later, Faulkner
employed similar language in his author's note for *The Mansion*
to justify his refusal to eliminate the discrepancies between *The
Hamlet, The Town*, and the last volume of the Snopes trilogy.

[7]The text of the 1946 Modern Library edition was first
reprinted as a Modern Library paperback in 1954 and first published as a Vintage paperback in 1961. The 1946 Modern Library
text forms the basis for the text in Random House's *Faulkner
Reader* (1954) and for the 1959 New American Library Signet edition of the novel. The Appendix appears at the end of the novel
in both the 1954 *Reader* and its reprint in the Modern Library but
is located at the front of the 1959 New American Library Signet
edition. Most of the relevant bibliographical information on *The
Sound and the Fury* may be found in Meriwether's "Textual
History"; "The Books of William Faulkner," p. 419; and "The
Books of William Faulkner," pp. 268-69.

[8]In 1962, Vintage reissued the novel's 1929 text in paper
with "Appendix: Compson: 1699-1945" at the back of the volume
(Polk 18). In 1966, a Modern Library reissue of the 1946 text also
positioned the Appendix at the novel's rear, while Random
House reissued the 1929 text of *The Sound and the Fury* without it.
The next year saw the 1929 text reissued as a "Modern Library
College Edition" in paperback with the Appendix once again at
the rear.

[9]Jason is also called Miss Quentin's "last remaining sane
male relative" (ML 335) and "a sane man always" (ML 344).

[10]Alternatively, Dawn Trouard has recently examined
the "discrepancies and ruptures" (25) in the 1929 novel's representation of Caddy and the other Compson women, and argued
that the Appendix continues to present in the persons of Melissa
Meek and Caddy "a [feminist] model of the caring possibilities
yet to be realized" (57). Similarly, Susan Donaldson has contend-
ed that the Compson Appendix is Faulkner's self-reflexive cri-

tique of "the [patriarchal] structures of narrative, authority, and gender defining" the 1929 *Sound and the Fury* (27-8).

[11]Brooks's discussion of the novel in *William Faulkner: The Yoknapatawpha Country* (1963) draws its quotations from the 1946 Modern Library edition.

[12]Readers of Faulkner's entry for Caddy may also be puzzled by the absence of any mention of her intense love for Dalton Ames during the summer of 1909, a central episode in the 1929 *Sound and the Fury*.

[13]By 1971, however, Meriwether conceded reluctantly that Faulkner had "approved the inclusion of the Compson Appendix in the [Modern Library] volume"("Prefatory" 282). Believing that the Appendix sheds a great deal of light on the 1929 *Sound and the Fury* and "deserves more critical attention as a discrete piece of fiction," Dickerson also contends that placing the Appendix at the front of the novel was a commercial rather than authorial decision that obscured the Appendix's transcendence of its connections to the novel (316).

[14]Similarly disinclined to reduce the novel "to a socioeconomic study of the decline of a Southern family," Michael Millgate still believes that this aspect became more significant in the latter part of the novel and speculates that Faulkner presented the history of the Compson family in the Appendix because he felt "he had created the social context of the actions in insufficient detail" (99).

[15]Of course, these features were constructed by an author who was by no means in possession of a unified and unique self. Quite the contrary, Faulkner was a deeply conflicted subject. Moreover, his culture spoke through him to a certain extent, and he in turn constantly meditated on and modified this cultural expression.

[16]This New Critical or Modernist stance was quite deliberately intended to counter the view propounded first by George Marion O'Donnell's 1939 essay "Faulkner's Mythology" and then perpetuated by Cowley's *Portable* that Faulkner's work is fundamentally informed and unified by a tragic myth of Southern diminution.

[17]David Williams's conservative mythological reading of family relationships in the 1929 *Sound and the Fury*, for example, makes little use of the Appendix as it examines male Compson responses to Caddy's archetypal feminine, and David Minter's

"Faulkner, Childhood, and the Making of *The Sound and the Fury*" does not draw upon the Appendix as it outlines the deeply-rooted similarities among the three brothers such as the animosity and resentment they share as a consequence of parental inadequacy (117). Nor does Carolyn Porter consider "Faulkner's retrospective genealogizing of the Compson family" in the Appendix and its "myth of a patriarchal decline" relevant to her feminist Lacanian reading of *The Sound and the Fury* in her "Symbolic Fathers and Dead Mothers: A Feminist Approach to Faulkner" (85). One recent exception to this rule, John T. Matthews's *"The Sound and the Fury": Faulkner and the Lost Cause* (1991), develops a decentered reading of the 1929 text that is both socio-historical and psychological by reading between the lines of the novel rather than in terms of its ostensible subject. His Freudian-inflected New Historicist approach to the psychological problems of the three Compson brothers shrewdly examines how the 1929 novel represses its ideological contradictions by smoothing them over. From this perspective, the 1929 *Sound and the Fury* with its psychic dilemmas both represents and grapples with the decline of the white privileged class of Faulkner's south in the 1890s-1920s. Unlike some earlier discussions of the novel, however, Matthews is quick to note that Faulkner underscored in the Appendix what the 1929 novel only implied, that "the Compsons' brand of aristocratic honor and morality actually rested upon . . . financial, racial, and political opportunism" (124).

[18]For the most fully articulated exposition of the relationship between original creative impulses and later authorial revisions and its connection to editorial theory and practice, see Hershel Parker's provocative *Flawed Texts and Verbal Icons*.

[19]In his contribution to this volume, Professor Eggert discusses D. H. Lawrence's *Twilight in Italy* in relation to this notion of authorial intertextuality.

WORKS CITED

Backman, Melvin. *Faulkner: The Major Years: A Critical Study.* Bloomington: Indiana UP, 1966.

Bleikasten, André. *The Most Splendid Failure: Faulkner's "The Sound and the Fury."* Bloomington: Indiana UP, 1976.

Blotner, Joseph. *Faulkner: A Biography.* 2 vols. New York: Random

House, 1974.

_____, ed. *The Selected Letters of William Faulkner*. New York: Random House, 1977.

Brooks, Cleanth. *William Faulkner: The Yoknapatawpha Country*. 1963. Rpt. New Haven: Yale UP, 1966.

Chase, Richard. *The American Novel and Its Tradition*. 1957. Rpt. Baltimore: Johns Hopkins UP, 1980.

Cohen, Philip, ed. *Devils and Angels: Textual Editing and Literary Theory*. Charlottesville, UP of Virginia, 1991.

_____, and Doreen Fowler. "Faulkner's Introduction to *The Sound and the Fury*." *American Literature* 62 (June 1990): 262-83.

Collins, Carvel. "The Interior Monologues of *The Sound and the Fury*." *English Institute Essays*. Ed. Alan Downer. New York: Columbia UP, 1954. Rpt. and rev. in *The Merrill Studies in "The Sound and the Fury."* Comp. James B. Meriwether. Columbus, OH: Charles E. Merrill, 1970. 59-79.

Cowley, Malcolm. *The Faulkner-Cowley File: Letters and Memories, 1944-1962*. New York: Viking P, 1966.

_____, ed. *The Portable Faulkner*. New York, Viking P, 1946.

_____, ed. *The Portable Faulkner*. 1946. Rev. ed. New York, Viking P, 1967.

Dickerson, Mary Jane. "The Magician's Wand: Faulkner's Compson Appendix." *Mississippi Quarterly* 28 (1975): 317-37.

Donaldson, Susan V. "Reading Faulkner Reading Cowley Reading Faulkner: Authority and Gender in the Compson Appendix." *The Faulkner Journal* 7 (Fall 1991/Spring 1992): 27-41.

Faulkner, William. *Faulkner in the University*. Ed. Frederick L. Gwynn and Joseph L. Blotner. New York: Vintage, 1965.

_____. *The Faulkner Reader*. New York: Random House, 1954.

_____. *The Faulkner Reader*. 1954. Rpt. New York: Random House, Modern Library Giant, 1959.

_____. *Lion in the Garden: Interviews with William Faulkner 1926-62*. Ed. James B. Meriwether and Michael Millgate. New York: Random House, 1968; Rpt. in Lincoln: U of Nebraska P, 1980.

_____. *"The Sound and the Fury" & "As I Lay Dying."* New York: Random House, Modern Library, 1946. With "*The Sound and the Fury* Appendix / Compson: 1699-1945," pp. 3-22.

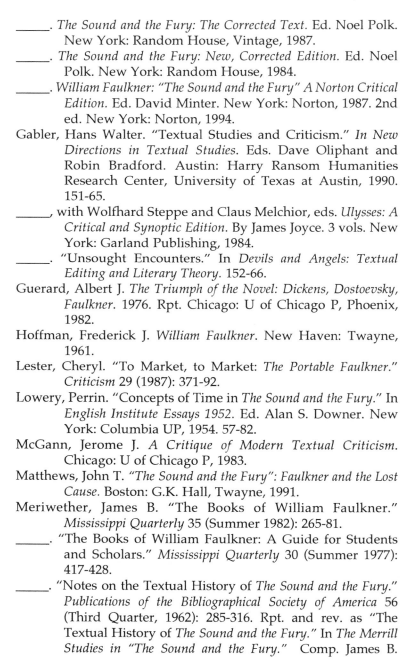

_____. *The Sound and the Fury: The Corrected Text.* Ed. Noel Polk. New York: Random House, Vintage, 1987.

_____. *The Sound and the Fury: New, Corrected Edition.* Ed. Noel Polk. New York: Random House, 1984.

_____. *William Faulkner: "The Sound and the Fury" A Norton Critical Edition.* Ed. David Minter. New York: Norton, 1987. 2nd ed. New York: Norton, 1994.

Gabler, Hans Walter. "Textual Studies and Criticism." In *New Directions in Textual Studies.* Eds. Dave Oliphant and Robin Bradford. Austin: Harry Ransom Humanities Research Center, University of Texas at Austin, 1990. 151-65.

_____, with Wolfhard Steppe and Claus Melchior, eds. *Ulysses: A Critical and Synoptic Edition.* By James Joyce. 3 vols. New York: Garland Publishing, 1984.

_____. "Unsought Encounters." In *Devils and Angels: Textual Editing and Literary Theory.* 152-66.

Guerard, Albert J. *The Triumph of the Novel: Dickens, Dostoevsky, Faulkner.* 1976. Rpt. Chicago: U of Chicago P, Phoenix, 1982.

Hoffman, Frederick J. *William Faulkner.* New Haven: Twayne, 1961.

Lester, Cheryl. "To Market, to Market: *The Portable Faulkner.*" *Criticism* 29 (1987): 371-92.

Lowery, Perrin. "Concepts of Time in *The Sound and the Fury.*" In *English Institute Essays 1952.* Ed. Alan S. Downer. New York: Columbia UP, 1954. 57-82.

McGann, Jerome J. *A Critique of Modern Textual Criticism.* Chicago: U of Chicago P, 1983.

Matthews, John T. *"The Sound and the Fury": Faulkner and the Lost Cause.* Boston: G.K. Hall, Twayne, 1991.

Meriwether, James B. "The Books of William Faulkner." *Mississippi Quarterly* 35 (Summer 1982): 265-81.

_____. "The Books of William Faulkner: A Guide for Students and Scholars." *Mississippi Quarterly* 30 (Summer 1977): 417-428.

_____. "Notes on the Textual History of *The Sound and the Fury.*" *Publications of the Bibliographical Society of America* 56 (Third Quarter, 1962): 285-316. Rpt. and rev. as "The Textual History of *The Sound and the Fury.*" In *The Merrill Studies in "The Sound and the Fury."* Comp. James B.

Meriwether. Columbus, OH: Charles E. Merrill, 1970. 1-32.

_____. "A Prefatory Note by Faulkner for the Compson Appendix." *American Literature* 43 (May 1971): 281-84.

Millgate, Michael. *The Achievement of William Faulkner.* 1966. Rpt. Lincoln: U of Nebraska P, 1978.

Minter, David. "Faulkner, Childhood, and the Making of *The Sound and the Fury.*" 1979. Rpt. in *On Faulkner: The Best From "American Literature."* Eds. Louis J. Budd and Edwin H. Cady. Durham: Duke UP, 1989. 110-27.

O'Connor, William Van. *The Tangled Fire of William Faulkner.* Minneapolis: U of Minnesota P, 1954.

O'Donnell, George Marion. "Faulkner's Mythology." 1939. Rpt. in *William Faulkner: Three Decades of Criticism.* Eds. Frederick J. Hoffman and Olga W. Vickery. 1960. Rpt. New York: Harcourt, Brace, & World, 1963. 82-93.

Parker, Hershel. *Flawed Texts and Verbal Icons: Literary Authority in American Fiction.* Evanston, IL: Northwestern UP, 1984.

Pilkington, John. *The Heart of Yoknapatawpha.* Jackson: UP of Mississippi, 1981.

Polk, Noel. *An Editorial Handbook to William Faulkner's "The Sound and the Fury."* New York: Garland, 1985.

Porter, Carolyn. "Symbolic Fathers and Dead Mothers: A Feminist Approach to Faulkner." In *Faulkner and Psychology: Faulkner and Yoknapatawpha 1991.* Eds. Donald M. Kartiganer and Ann J. Abadie. Jackson: U of Mississippi P, 1994. 78-122.

Shillingsburg, Peter. *Scholarly Editing in the Computer Age.* Athens: U of Georgia P, 1986.

Sundquist, Eric J. *Faulkner: The House Divided.* Baltimore: Johns Hopkins UP, 1983.

Tanselle, G. Thomas. "The Editorial Problem of Final Authorial Intention." *Studies in Bibliography* 29 (1976): 167-211. Rpt. in *Selected Studies in Bibliography.* Charlottesville: UP of Virginia, 1979. 309-53.

Taylor, Walter. *Faulkner's Search for a South.* Urbana: U of Illinois P, 1983.

Trouard, Dawn. "Faulkner's Text Which Is Not One." In *New Essays on "The Sound and the Fury."* Ed. Noel Polk. Cambridge: Cambridge UP, 1993. 23-69.

Tuck, Dorothy. *Apollo Handbook of Faulkner.* 1964. Rpt. New York: Thomas Y. Crowell, 1969.

Vickery, Olga. *The Novels of William Faulkner: A Critical Interpretation.* 1959. Rev. ed. Baton Rouge: Louisiana State UP, 1964.

Williams, David. *Faulkner's Women: The Myth and the Muse.* Montreal: McGill-Queen's UP, 1977.

The Rhetoric of Interactive Fiction

Jay David Bolter

In the last decade, the personal computer has given us a new form of writing. This electronic writing shares some qualities with its predecessor, the printed book, but it is also different in important ways. The text of a printed book exists in black and white; it remains the same text physically and visually for each new reader. A printed book is supposed to be a monument to its author, insuring that that author's words will pass on unchanged to new generations of readers. Admittedly, this is only an ideal: textual critics know that the author's revisions as well as printer's errors always undermine the stable transmission of printed texts. On the other hand, electronic writing does not convey a sense of monumentality even as an ideal. It is characterized instead by radical instability. In a word processor or textual database, the text remains only momentarily on the computer screen. The reader or user repeatedly scrolls up or calls up new text to take its place. In many forms of electronic writing, the reader of a text can intervene and change what he or she sees, and the changes can be saved for the next reader. In a form called *hypertext*, the reader determines the text in the act of reading. Each new screenful of text appears because of choices that the reader has made. The defining qualities of hypertextual writing are instability and interactivity.

Hypertext has already been put to a variety of uses. There are pedagogical hypertexts, read by students principally in the humanities and at the university level. Good examples are *Dickens Web* by George Landow and his students at Brown University and the Perseus Project at Harvard (Crane). The Perseus Project is in fact an example of hypermedia—a hypertext document that includes graphics and digital pictures as well as verbal text. In addition, thousands of presentation programs and textual databases in the academy and in business have some hypertextual capabilities. The electronic communication network called the Internet (which connects universities, research and government institutions, and some businesses) is being converted into a vast hypertext through the distribution of computer programs called the World Wide Web and Gopher. A reader on this net is able to mine bibliographic information from libraries, transport texts, and activate computer programs from sites around the world. Perhaps the most theoretically interesting hypertexts are the interactive fictions. A small number of fiction writers have begun to experiment with this new medium. Examples include *afternoon* and *WOE* by Michael Joyce, *Its Name Was Penelope* by Judy Malloy, and *Victory Garden* by Stuart Moulthrop. (See Coover "The End of Books" and "Hyperfiction.")

There is also a growing body of theory on the subject of electronic writing in general and interactive fiction in particular. (See Landow *Hypertext*, Bolter *Writing*, Joyce "Siren Shapes," Moulthrop "In the Zones," Douglas "Understanding the Act of Reading," and so on.) The provisional consensus is that hypertext embodies many of the insights of poststructuralist theory. What reader-response criticism, deconstruction, and semiotics as literary theory have had to say about texts in general seems to apply with particular appropriateness to hypertext in the computer. George Landow writes:

> Hypertext has much in common with some major points of contemporary literary and semiological theory; particularly with Derrida's emphasis on de-centering and with Barthes's conception of the readerly versus the writerly text. In fact, hypertext creates an almost embarrassingly literal embodiment of both concepts. (*Hypertext* 23-24)

The embarrassment comes in part from the fact that poststructuralists of the 1970s and early 1980s were not familiar with electronic writing. (There were only a few experimental hypertexts in existence, and they were certainly not widely known in European or even American literary circles.) These theorists were addressing our assumptions about stability and authority in printed texts. Yet poststructural theory seems to apply more obviously to electronic texts than to printed ones. In one sense hypertext validates poststructuralist strategies of reading. Yet hypertext also seems to undermine or bypass these strategies by its cheerful acquiescence in them (Bolter, *Writing* 164-166). Reader-response criticism, various methods of deconstruction, and to some extent critiques based on gender theory are by their nature subversive. They confront a text with its own inconsistencies and underlying assumptions regarding the truth value of language, the permanence and universal application of dominant cultural ideas, and so on. Such an assault works best upon a text that vigorously asserts its own independence, univocality, and permanence, as printed texts do by the nature of print technology. An electronic text, however, grants the poststructuralist critic all of his or her points in advance: an electronic texts admits its own impermanence and lack of unity and univocality. Hypertext comes to the critical reader already deconstructed.

Because hypertext enacts poststructuralist strategies of reading and interpretation, we can draw upon the body of this work to help us read hypertexts. Nevertheless, hypertext's playful acceptance of its own limitations also calls upon us to reconsider recent theory. An oppositional or subversive reading of hypertext threatens to become superfluous; we will need an affirmative rhetoric appropriate to this new form.

AN EXAMPLE OF HYPERTEXT

Hypertext does not yet have an established typography as the printed book does. However, the current generation of interactive fictions share some common elements. The text is typically presented in small units, which I will call episodes—often a few sentences or a traditional paragraph. An episode appears in a window on the computer screen, and the reader is invited to read in the conventional way. What is unconventional is the manner in which the next paragraph is determined and presented. A screen from Moulthrop's *Victory Garden* can serve as an illustration:

We stumbled from room to room flicking on TV's, radios, tape decks, VCR's. It was technological potlatch, an offering of power to the gods, conspicuous consumption of information on an epic scale.

While it was happening all we wanted was to be multiply channeled and networked. We needed to receive the event in black and white as well as full stereo surround. We yearned to hear all those voices around the dial, not out of distrust or skepticism so much as **a hunger for input**.

It was a reflex burned in **somewhere between Dallas and the Sea of Tranquility**. The event must be grasped in all its multiplicity, it must be broken down and remembered. We must **match the frequencies**, we must **get in tune**.

Four of the phrases in this episode are hot. (They appear in boldface type in the example above, although they are not boldfaced in the *Victory Garden* itself.) Each of these hot phrases is linked electronically to a different episode. If the reader selects a hot phrase with the mouse, a new episode will appear. There is also a default link, so that if the reader selects anything else on the screen, the default will take the reader to yet another episode. The process is iterative. Each episode that appears on the screen is linked electronically to one (usually several) other(s). *Victory Garden* is a vast network of about 990 episodes and more than 2800 links. The reader travels through his network by making a series of selections. The journey is not random. In this hypertext, the author has defined the links between textual elements. It is not possible to go just anywhere at all; the reader must follow paths that the author has already established. By following different paths, the reader creates and experiences a different text. And with so many paths, it is unlikely that any two readers (or the same reader on two days) will constitute the same text—that is, the same episodes in the same order.

Other hypertext and hypermedia systems offer their readers other means for traveling through the network. The reader may click on buttons, issue search commands, type answers to questions, and so on. The episodes called forth may consist of words on the computer screen, graphics, animation, or even video displayed on the screen or on an associated monitor. But all these systems present their materials in discrete units and require the reader somehow to participate in determining the order and character of the units presented.

ELECTRONIC RHETORIC

Authorship in print is a relatively rare and prized status: there are hundreds or thousands of readers for every author in print. Electronic technology tends to diminish the barrier between the author and the reader for two reasons. It is relatively easy and inexpensive to become an electronic author; one simply distributes a text on a diskette or over an electronic network. Furthermore, the hypertextual reader collaborates with the original author in the construction of the text. To read a hypertext is to write it, to put it together on the computer screen. In this way too, the distinction between authors and mere readers is undermined.

Both readers and writers of hypertext, therefore, need a rhetorical strategy. That strategy can derive in part from poststructuralist theory, but, as I have suggested, something more is needed. A rhetoric for electronic writing needs to address the characteristics of interaction that make electronic writing different from print. Those characteristics are curiously both postmodern and premodern. I am taking modernity to refer to the period dominated by print technology, and in particular the industrial age of print that began in the late eighteenth century and began to close with the introduction of electronic photocomposition in the mid-twentieth. (The premodern era therefore includes the complex history of earlier writing technologies: both the purely oral and the various combinations of oral and manuscripts technologies in the ancient world and the Middle Ages.) In *The Death of Literature*, Alvin Kernan has argued that modern concepts of authorship and literature developed in what I am calling the industrial age of print and are now threatened by electronic technology. Legal and aesthetic notions of copyright developed at roughly the same time. (See Woodmansee, "The Genius and the Copyright" and "On the Author Effect.") Postmodern literary theory itself can be seen as part of a historical process that closes off the modern era of print. Electronic writing still seems peculiar, because we are only slowly emerging from the late age of print. However, it may turn out to be the two hundred years of industrial printing with its emphasis on authority and fixity that is anomalous.

Electronic writing restores a balance between the production and the performance of the text, a balance that has been lost in the age of print. For that reason in trying to define an electronic rhetoric, we might look back to classical rhetorical theory to supplement what postmodern can offer. It may seem odd to try to measure hypertext by the standard of classical rhetoric. Yet there is a specific reason why the vocabulary of classical rhetoric may be well suited to describing the temporal relationships and paradoxes of electronic writing.

Rhetoric in the ancient world grew out of a rich oral tradition. It began as the study of speech making. Gradually its categories came to be applied to other forms, such as poetry and historical writing. Furthermore, oral performance in the ancient world dated back to Homer and continued to be a major feature of Greek poetry and of course drama down into the fourth century B.C. and beyond. Even ancient prose writers (especially historians but also philosophers) cared about the sound of their texts, for the ancients read texts aloud both in public performance and often to themselves. Clearly oral presentation is rigorously linear: each member of the audience must follow the text in the order and at the speed dictated by the author/performer. An individual reading alone, especially a modern silent reader, has much greater freedom to subvert the conventional order of the text to stop to consider arguments more closely or to skip over passages that promise little. Reading in the ancient world generally remained close to performance. And because oral performance was the paradigm, the ancients were inclined to assume that there was such a thing as the natural order for a text. They were very much interested in violations of the "natural" linear order of phrases and sentences for rhetorical effect.

The concern with linearity and its violations is an important common ground between ancient rhetoric and electronic writing. Hypertext, particularly hypertextual fiction, is quite self-conscious about the multiplicity of its presentation. The network of possibilities that constitutes a hypertext does not relieve the author (or reader as author) from worrying about linearity. On the contrary, the author must be aware of the relationship between pairs of episodes that the reader might activate as well as the longer narrative strands. In longer hypertexts, the number of different strands can be very large, and the author may not be able to keep track of all the narrative possibilities. Perhaps because the author must sacrifice this control, he or she becomes all the more sensitive to the variety of linearizations or readings that the text offers. In any case, in the early hypertext fictions now available, linearity (our moment-to-moment experience of reading the fiction) is itself a major theme.

MAPPING THE TEXT

Electronic writing brings the question of linearity to the forefront by forcing the reader to take account of his or her part in determining the order of presentation. Hypertext makes the order of presentation part of the presentation itself. One way to do this is to confront the author and the reader with the visualizations of possible orders. Here is such a visualization for Michael Joyce's *WOE*. (Figure 1.) The boxes represent episodes and the arrows possible links or paths through the episodes.[1] Such a map shows many possible linearizations, which are therefore violations of a single predictable course of events. The map is a spatial representation of the temporal relationships among episodes in the hypertext. The map is something like a musical notation in the sense that the patterns of links and episodes show us the rhythms of the hypertext; they indicate the parameters of allowed readings, what the reader as performer can and cannot do. Furthermore, recurring patterns within one hypertext or across many may provide us with a catalog of possible shapes.

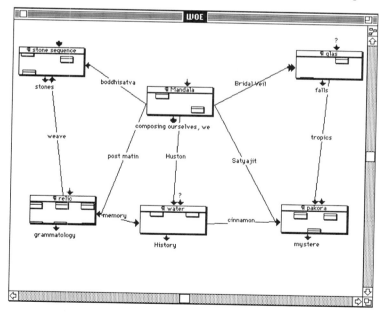

Figure 1. WOE Mandala

In a hypertext the patterns of episodes and links constitute verbal gestures. In a concept map these verbal gestures have shapes: there are both literal and figurative schema. *WOE*'s principal schema is the mandala, which is also the name of the central episode. The "mandala" episode serves as a hub connected to sets of episodes on the rim of the wheel. The reader starts in the center, travels out to the rim, and then returns to the center. But each return gives the central episode a different significance, precisely because the reader is returning from a different episode on the rim. Repeated visits to and from the rim cause the reader's possibilities to narrow; eventually, if read often enough, *WOE* resolves itself into a single linear narrative. That is, the hypertext is arranged so that after repeated readings its possible branches close down until the reader has only one choice leading from each episode. This kind of manipulation (narrowing or broadening) of the reader's choices can be done metaphorically in print. But it can only be realized operationally in presentation on the computer. (For a thorough and insightful reading of *WOE*, see Douglas. See also Bolter, "The Shapes of WOE.")

HYPERTEXT AND HYPERBATON

The word schema is doubly appropriate for describing the visualization of hypertext. It is a word sometimes used by computer scientists to refer to templates or data structures. The word also has an ancient pedigree: in later Greek, *schema* was the word for "rhetorical figure." It is in the theory of figures that classical rhetoric can be most helpful in understanding hypertext. Both modern and postmodern literary criticism do of course pay attention to figure—particularly to the two figures of metaphor and metonymy. (See Vickers; see also Genette.) But ancient rhetoricians and their Renaissance followers offered much more elaborate and subtle classifications. Most, if not all, of their figures concern displacement or departure from what is thought of as natural or clear exposition. Rhetoricians cultivated a sensitivity to classes of such violations of expected sound or sense. Of course we could not now accept a simple dichotomy between the natural and the artificial, between clarity and ornamentation, as Aristotle and others put it. The postmodern gesture would be to seek to subvert this dichotomy, to show how the natural is invaded by the artificial. (See Lanham, *Literacy and the Survival of Humanism.*) The ancient categories remain useful, in part, precisely because they give us a starting point for such a gesture of reversal.

One important class of ancient figures describes violations of the conventional order of words or ideas. Hyperbaton is the principal figure here; it is any departure from conventional order—in the first instance word order. The best-known modern example is perhaps Churchill's "This is the kind of impertinence up with which I will not put." (See Lanham, *Handlist* 86.) We can easily extend hyperbaton in a way that makes it applicable to hypertext. Electronic writing is the structuring not only of words but of larger units—verbal gestures that may be whole sentences, paragraphs or episodes. The reader of an electronic text becomes an author precisely because he or she is reordering the episodes of that text in the act of calling them on to the computer screen. Hyperbaton in an electronic text becomes any departure from or reversal of the conventional chronological order of episodes. In this sense hyperbaton is a defining quality of any hypertext, such as *Victory Garden* or *WOE*, that permits the reader to make significant choices in the order of presentation. If there is a narrative structure that extends across several episodes and if the reader is given choices, it must sometimes happen that the reader will choose paths in which the episodes are presented out of their chronological order. The very idea of natural order is what hypertexts call into question. An underlying chronological order to events is sometimes assumed by the plots of the hypertextual fictions, yet alternate orders invite or compel the reader to question that assumption.

Hyperbaton is what troubles readers of interactive fiction or electronic writing in general. For hyperbaton requires suspension: the reader must hold the displaced unit in mind while waiting for the rest of the syntax. Hyperbaton calls upon the reader to make a special effort at understanding. This is true even at the level of words: too much traditional hyperbaton wearies the reader or listener. When hyperbaton appears repeatedly at the level of episodes, the reader is asked to make a correspondingly greater effort. Ultimately, hyperbaton threatens the reader's faith that there is any conventional meaning to be gotten out of the text. The suspensions required by hyperbaton threaten never to be resolved.

VICTORY GARDEN *AND THE REMEDIES FOR HYPERBATON*

Let us consider how hyperbaton functions in *Victory Garden*. We must first understand something of the structure of this fiction. Most of the narrative takes place on the night the bombing began in the Persian Gulf War: January 17, 1991. Most of the scenes occur in a mythical town that is and is not Austin, Texas. The characters are academics—students, professors, or administrators—working at an institution called the University of Tara, and they all have their own (professional and psycho-sexual) problems. Each of these problems are connected in some way with the war. Characters constantly allude to the bombing in conversation, and above all they see it on television—in a bar, at a party, or in their bedrooms.

Television is an obsessive theme and at the same time the narrative engine for *Victory Garden*. It is not only that the charac-ters watch television. The reader also comes across quotations from Dan Rather or Peter Jennings, descriptions of the live cov-erage, passages from books on the impact of television, and mus-ings by one or more authorial voices on the TV coverage of the war. In *Victory Garden* the ubiquity of the televised reports and the fact that so much is happening more or less simultaneously on this night serve to relieve some of the reader's uneasiness with disruptions of the narrative. Wherever the reader branches in *Victory Garden*, the television is on, offering its version of the war. This helps to locate the reader in the narrative world and to com-bat the feeling of being uprooted by the hyperbaton of the fiction. Metaphorically, television provides a visual background against which the action occurs.

Victory Garden offers the reader a second way to visual-ize the narrative. With hundreds of episodes and thousands of interconnections, this hypertext constitutes a labyrinth of possi-ble reading paths. Appropriately it begins with a map. What the reader sees is a garden of intersecting paths and at each intersec-tion the name of an episode. The garden serves as a visual sym-bol for the whole fiction; it is also an allusion to Borges's story "The Garden of Forking Paths." What is most important is that the diagram functions operationally as well as metaphorically to control and organize the space of the fiction. The named inter-sections are linked to various episodes: by moving the cursor over a name and clicking twice with the mouse, the reader branches to that episode. Thus, the map is not ancillary, as are maps and diagrams in printed text: it is a part of the symbolic structure of *Victory Garden*. It functions both as a picture of the garden and as a set of symbols woven into the fabric of the text.

Hypertexts with such linked graphics remind us of medieval illuminated manuscripts. In such manuscripts the illuminated letters work simultaneously as abstract or figural art and as verbal elements in the text (Bolter, *Writing Space* 72-73). So too in *Victory Garden*, the map of the garden is part of the story.

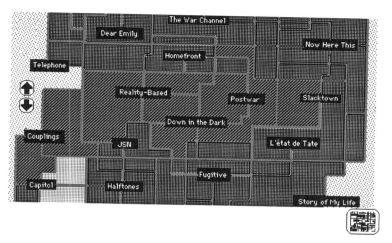

Figure 2. Middle map of *Victory Garden*

Because the map of the garden is too large to fit on one screen, it is divided into three parts: north, central, and south. As a reader, I might begin in the central part and click on the rectangle labeled "L'état de Tate." I will find myself thrust into a series of scenes involving characters named Tate, Madden and Urquhart. Who are these people and what are their relationships? I glean something from the episodes as I proceed, but there is much more that I can learn only later, if and when I return to this area of the garden after having visited others. On my return, I know that Urquhart is an unstable computer scientist and has just been chased across town by Madden, who is an FBI agent. The suspense of meaning, the hyperbaton, has to some degree been resolved. But when I first visit the scene, I am impatient to discover who Tate and Urquhart are and what brings them together. It is an apprehension that a reader may also feel with conventional literature: that the text is proceeding in a direction that will never satisfy a question that the reader may have. In a conventional text, however, the promise of closure is more likely to be kept. The printed book has a final page, which the reader can be sure of reaching. In a hypertext, the reader may never reach an episode that resolves the hyperbaton.

There are other traditional devices that help to give traditional coherence and sense of place to the narrative. For example, there are the allusions to Borges's "Garden of Forking Paths." The title *Victory Garden* is an explicit reference, and the text also includes quotations from Borges. There are numerous allusions: the scene in which Urquhart visits Tate in his tower alludes to the scene in which Yu Tsun visits the Sinologist Stephen Albert. Just as Yu Tsun has come to kill Albert, so Urquhart says at one point that he has come to kill Tate. Urquhart has also come to get "the answer," whereas Yu Tsun receives from Albert the unexpected answer to the mystery of the Chinese manuscript. In *Victory Garden*, Tate also reads to Urquhart from a lost oriental work. The reader who notices these allusions may also wonder whether Boris's action may be semiotic in the way that Yu Tsun's is. Could the killing of Tate be taken as a sign, and indeed does Urquhart kill Tate?

The allusive dialogue between *Victory Garden* and "Garden of Forking Paths" is a familiar device. Its familiarity helps to convince us that there is conventional meaning and intentionality in *Victory Garden*. There is, in fact, a tension between the hyperbaton and these devices of familiarization. Such devices give the reader a sense of place. The hyperbaton keeps pulling the reader out of place. In one sense, to read is to find one's place. This is certainly true of conventional reading of conventional linear fiction, where the voice of the text defines a perspective for the reader, a place from which to examine the events narrated. Hyperbaton in hypertext keeps wrenching us out of a comfortable or familiar perspective and putting us down somewhere else. That is what the discontinuities, the branches are about. So, after each branch, the reader must ask not only "what happens next?" but also "from what perspective am I to understand what happens next?"

Allusion in hypertext can be accomplished in two ways. One way is to create an explicit link between two passages. The other is to evoke the conventional, rhetorical power of language (similarities of phrase, sound, or context) to make the reader aware of the allusion. The explicit link is hypertext's realization of poststructural notion of intertextuality. A hypertext can point directly to the many sources upon which it draws in a larger body of literature; ultimately it could point to the whole of literature available in machine-readable form. However, explicit links can never explicitly achieve the subtle intertextuality imagined by Barthes or Derrida. However many links one inserts in a text, there must be indefinitely more that could be drawn. Each link itself opens up the possibility of a second link explaining why the first was made: each link fills one gap and creates another. Hypertext thus enacts the unending process of semiosis that the deconstructionists have invoked in their critique of structuralism. (See Harpold "The Contingencies of the Hypertext Link.") A hypertext such as *Victory Garden* has thousands of explicit links, and yet it continues to rely on (indeed cannot avoid) traditional linguistic and structural allusion. The links themselves often generate these traditional allusions.

Like other hypertexts (like portions of *afternoon* in particular), *Victory Garden* also relies on conventional narrative coherence. There are relatively long narrative strands (of four or five episodes) that do appear in chronological order. The reader enters one of these strands and may then continue in a linear fashion. But the reader can also branch willingly or inadvertently into another strand. Strands cross and recross, so that there is no certainty that a thread will continue. It is very seldom that a thread will continue to a decisive closure.

DISPLACEMENTS IN VICTORY GARDEN

Displacements in hypertext disrupt conventional meaning by setting one episode beside another, without allowing the reader to assume a simple or single relationship between the two episodes. Here is a particularly effective series of displacements in *Victory Garden*. The reader begins with a quotation from Neil Postman's *Amusing Ourselves to Death*. The relationship of this episode to the fiction is problematic. *Amusing Ourselves to Death* is not a book that any of the fictional characters is reading. It seems to be a gloss on the story:

> *It is conceivable to use television as a lamp, a surface for texts, a bookcase, even as radio. But it has not been so used and will not be so used, at least in America.*
> *Amusing Ourselves to Death*

By clicking on the appropriate word or phrase in this quotation, the reader can call any one of a number of different episodes onto the screen. As it turns out, each branch forces the reader into a different relationship with the original Postman quotation. Each new episode offers a somewhat different reading of the original.

Clicking on the word "lamp" leads to an episode that begins:

> Thea turned the TV to the wall, watching the auroras of living color that leaked from the edges of the tube and played across the wallpaper. She felt hollow, disconnected, almost viscerally shocked. She wanted another cigarette and she needed a drink.

This branch takes us back into the story, and the narrative immediately contradicts Postman's assertion: Thea does use the television as a lamp. She turns the TV to the wall so that it serves only to light the room. The party itself is part of the larger fabric of the narrative, into which the reader again enters.

Clicking on a "surface for texts" produces:

> *Constructive hypertexts require a capability to act: to create, to change, and to recover particular encounters within the developing body of knowledge. These encounters . . . are versions of what they are becoming, a structure for what does not yet exist. . . . A constructive hypertext should be a tool for inventing, discovering, viewing, and testing multiple, alternative, organizational structures.*
>
> Michael Joyce, "Siren Shapes"
>
> *There is no simple way to say this.*

This phrase "surface for texts" is read as inviting a comment on hypertext. We branch not back into the story but to an observation on hypertext from the theorist Michael Joyce. This episode again contradicts the Postman quotation—in practice as well as in theory. For at this moment, the reader's computer screen has become a surface for texts. *Victory Garden* is itself a text that plays across the surface of a videoscreen, as only hypertext can.

Clicking on "radio" presents an episode that includes the following passage:

> "I don't believe it," Veronica insisted. "What are we seeing? The same pictures over and over. Some suits talking. A lot of slick graphics, like this is some kind of warmup for the Superbowl. We might as well be getting this on the radio, like that *War of the Worlds* that fooled everybody in the fifties."
>
> "That was 1938, dear. Way before my time of course."
>
> "Whatever. It still seems wrong to me. Some kind of big show."

Again we are taken back into the story. The war is compared to the radio broadcast of War of the Worlds. Elsewhere, *Victory Garden* offers further comments on the reduction of television to radio in the war. Television became radio when CNN and other networks put the voices of their reporters on the air when they lacked video. So again this branch serves to contradict Postman's argument; television can be used as radio.

The words "bookcase" and "America" open other narrative lines. What might be called a "solipsistic narrator" intrudes. He sounds as if he were the author and he talks about himself. He is truly a solipsist, for in one thread leading from this episode he writes: "All that is really happening is happening to me. . . ." This authorial intrusion also provides several entry points into the fiction.

All the above branches can be regarded in some sense as hyperbaton. Beginning in the Postman quotation, each branch thrusts the reader into a different place in the narrative or the essay on media that *Victory Garden* seems to be. With each branch the reader has the opportunity to expand Postman's list in a different way. The original list seems to offer a way to encapsulate and to bring under control much of the story. The links attached to the items in the list can be read as elaborations (the classical figure is *epanodos*). They are elaborations, that is, if the reader happens to return to Postman's list. For with these digressions, return is not required. The list serves as a set of launching points and may send the reader on a variety of trajectories.

These examples of displacement or hyperbaton can also be analyzed under the larger category of substitution, namely metonymy. Richard Lanham has noted that figures of metonymy are instances of changes of scale (*Handlist* 102). All these branches substitute one verbal gesture for another: a different episode for the original Postman quotation. And each involves an enormous change in scale. The act of branching expands each of these elements into a narrative of indefinite size. Each branch says in effect to the reader: "if you are interested in this word, have I got a story for you!" and then proceeds to deliver that story, episode by episode.

The Postman quotation was arrived at by clicking through several other quotations about media or descriptions of or excerpts from Rather and other newscasters. From the perspective of the fiction in *Victory Garden* (the story of Thea, Boris, and the others), the Postman material seems to be a digression. In traditional fiction, the narrative is the center; whatever takes the reader away from the narrative is marginal, digressive. But as we travel back and forth through the Postman material, the priorities can come to be reversed. The whole of *Victory Garden* can be read as an essay on the American media and the Persian Gulf War. The narrative can be read as a fictional digression upon the reality of the war, as reflected in the prose excerpts. Or we can call it a fictional reaction to or explanation of the prose excerpts. What then displaces what? What comes first: the media or the story; the televised war offered to us as reality on CBS or Stuart Moulthrop's fictional account? The ambiguity works both ways: Postman and Rather threaten to become characters in the fiction, no more real than Thea or Emily. And in this way the rhetorical device of hyperbaton seems to deconstruct itself. The device of displacement is itself displaced. This is what we would expect: that hypertext would use the device until it "used it up" and end as a critique of the received rhetorical division between the center and the digression.

HYPERTEXT AS REPENTANCE

We have followed the figure of hyperbaton into its own dissolution. Let us start over with another class: figures of repetition. Anyone who reads such hypertexts as *WOE* or *Victory Garden* notices the repetitions. The reader often cycles around to the same place—either intentionally or inadvertently in an effort to get somewhere else in the text. In *Victory Garden*, for example, one can move in a circle sometimes simply by pressing the return key repeatedly. The Postman example contains no immediate cycles although there may be long-term ones. But the reader can always press the back icon on the control bar to create his or her own cycles.

Consider again what happens when I branch on the word "lamp" in the Postman episode. I find first that the Postman quotation is being used to introduce and at the same time to contextualize the story. I also find that the story serves to contradict the quotation. If I branch back, I read the Postman quotation differently. The quotation seems both more encompassing and more questionable. We have just considered the possibility that the quotation provides a frame for the story. Yet the story also refuses to be encompassed by the frame: it spills out beyond the frame and in a thoroughly postmodern fashion threatens to encompass the quotation and make it a part of the story. If I try each of the other words in the list, branching forward and then back in each case, then at each return my reading of the Postman quotation changes again.

So if repetition is a common feature of hypertexts like *Victory Garden*, it is repetition with a difference. The reader understands the repeated episode differently precisely because of the path he or she has traveled to get to that repetition. This is true of the experience of repetition in print as well. But current hypertexts exploit repetition to a far greater degree than conventional printed fiction—both because the text is divided into smaller units, which the reader is likely to encounter more than once, and because the repetition can be programmed into the link structure of the hypertext.

There are a couple of classic figures that express repetition with a difference. One is the little-known figure of *ploce* (Lanham, *Handlist* 116), which again in its strict form means repetition of a word in a different sense or grammatical function. In hypertext we could enlarge the term to mean any example of the thread: A -> B -> A, where episode A is now changed in some way as the result of the visit to episode B. Because our perception of episode A is always changed by visiting B, any round trip figure is ploce. Ploce is perhaps the dominant figure in Michael Joyce's *WOE*, in which the narrative voice repeatedly seeks to revisit memories and repeatedly fails.

These examples could be called *metanoia*, which is the repetition and improvement on a previous statement. Metanoia is also Greek for repentance; a palinode (a work in which the author recants an earlier position) is an instance of metanoia. Hypertextual fiction often seems to take the form of a palinode, in that it strives again and again to attempt to take back what has been said and replace it with something better. This quality may be due to the experimental nature of the early hypertexts. But the palinode functions differently in hypertext precisely because of evanescence of the electronic medium. In print it is hard (indeed impossible) to erase and correct a written idea. In the computer everything is a palinode, the hard (indeed impossible) task is achieving any fixity in writing.

DISRUPTING THE LINEAR

What we have been exploring in the hypertextual figures of hyperbaton, ploce, and metanoia are violations of linearity. The reader expects events to be narrated in a certain logical or chronological order, and that expectation is violated. All hypertexts must contend with their readers' desire for the linear. This desire may be more or less powerful in various cultures and at various times.[2] It is certainly still powerful at the end of the twentieth century in North America, where truly popular fiction, fictional bestsellers, are plot driven and linear. Hyperbaton works as an ornament for conventional spoken or written text because it successfully plays with the reader's expectation and desire for the linear. The difficulty with hypertext is that it does not offer alternative orders as mere ornamentation—that is, as exceptions to the "normal" practice of linear development. For hypertext, hyperbaton becomes the customary rhetorical strategy, while consecutive, chronological order is the exception. Hypertext reverses the relative values of ornamented and "clear" narrative.

This reversal is a noteworthy development in the history of rhetoric. As I mentioned earlier, the tension between clarity and ornamentation in rhetoric is one that we can trace back to Aristotle and Greek rhetorical theory. The Greek view, which we might be tempted to call naive, is that natural prose is clear, simple, and pure. An orator or writer ornaments a speech or narrative by violating in some sense the natural character of prose. Hypertext reverses our expectations of what is clear, transparent language and what is opaque or ornamental. When we read a hypertext we expect to jump around from one place and time to others. In *Victory Garden* it almost comes as a surprise how easily we can move along narrative threads in five or six screens. In hypertext clear narrative itself becomes ornamental. However, the turning of clarity into ornamentation is never likely to appeal to a large audience. Hypertexts of this kind may remain an esoteric practice among relatively few readers and writers.

One reason why hyperbaton in hypertext may remain esoteric is that it thwarts the reader's desire to be left alone with the story. The "naive" view is that prose should be transparent: the reader of a fiction should be able to believe that he or she is looking through a window onto a fictional world. Ornamentation threatens to interrupt the reader's gaze, making him or her aware of the prose as rhetoric, as a structure of verbal elements. The reader is suddenly looking *at* the prose rather than looking *through* it. Richard Lanham has argued that modern and postmodern art constantly plays with and upon the distinction between "looking at" and "looking through" (Lanham "The Electronic Word"). Hypertext does too. In exploring a hypertext, the reader oscillates between looking through the prose of each episode and looking at the junctures or links between episodes. Whenever the reader comes to a link and is forced to make a choice, the illusion of an imagined world must break down, at least momentarily as the reader recalls the technical circumstances of the electronic medium. It may be possible for the reader to ignore these circumstances if only a click is required to bring the next chronological episode onto the screen. After all, in a printed book the reader can turn pages without much conscious effort. But there is little point in transferring a printed text to the computer, if only to read it page by page at the click of a button. If a text is completely and irrevocably linear, then it belongs in the medium of print. The current interactive fictions all play the kind of rhetorical tricks (hyperbaton and metanoia) that we have been discussing, and every such rhetorical displacement draws attention to itself and therefore away from any simple illusion the narrative might create.

Herein lies the distinction between hypertext and computer-generated fiction. Some specialists in artificial intelligence have pursued the goal of programming the computer to generate coherent stories. Sometimes these stories are expressed in prose. Sometimes, however, the artificial intelligence programmers imagine a kind of 3D movie in Virtual Reality: the human user will tell the computer what characters and situations are desired and the computer will produce a stereoscope world into which the user can enter. This vision of artificial intelligence is naive in exactly the classical Greek sense. These programmers want a seamless world in prose or in video. They do not want interruptions that break the illusion. And they do not want a hypertext in which the reader is aware of and participates in the rhetorical structure of the illusory world. No AI programmer to my knowledge has developed a program for computer-generated hypertext. The goal instead is to permit the computer to instantiate the traditional printed notions of authority, linearity, and illusion.

Current hypertexts are generated by laborious human participation: both the original author and the subsequent readers do the work. In the future, artificial intelligence programs may be used to fashion new forms of hypertext. But the key to any electronic rhetoric will be its ability to manage the oscillation between traditional linear prose and the disruptive narrative techniques that have already characterized the modern and the postmodern.

NOTES

[1]Storyspace is a hypertext editing system developed by myself, Michael Joyce, and John B. Smith. It provides the original author of the hypertext with a map of the evolving structure of the document. It was used, for example, to create the structural map in *WOE*.

[2]I do not mean to suggest that the desire for linear narrative is in fact "natural"—i.e., innate in the human mind. It is hard to imagine how any psychological experiment could separate nature from culture in testing people's understanding and enjoyment of storytelling. I can only suggest that in many of the familiar periods of Western culture (Homeric Greece, classical antiquity, the Middle Ages, the Renaissance, the Industrial Age of print, and the twentieth century), linear narrative has been popular, perhaps more popular than more complex narrative forms.

WORKS CITED

Bolter, Jay David. "The Shapes of *WOE.*" *Writing on the Edge* 2 (Spring, 1991): 90-91.

_____. *Writing Space: The Computer, Hypertext, and the History of Writing.* Hillsdale, NJ: Erlbaum, 1991.

Bolter, Jay David, Michael Joyce, & J. B. Smith. *Storyspace.* Computer Software. Watertown, MA: Eastgate Systems, 1992.

Coover, Robert. "The End of Books." *The New York Times Book Review* (June 21, 1992): 1, 23-25.

_____. "Hyperfiction: Novels for the Computer." *The New York Times Book Review* (August 29, 1993): 1, 8-12.

Crane, Gregory. "Redefining the Book: Some Preliminary Problems." *Academic Computing* 2:5 (1988): 6-11, 36-41.

Douglas, Jane. "Understanding the Act of Reading: The WOE Beginner's Guide to Dissection." *Writing on the Edge* 2:2 (Spring, 1991): 112-125.

Genette, Gérard. "Rhetoric Restrained." In *Figures of Literary Discourse.* Trans. Alan Sheridan. New York: Columbia UP, 1982. 103-126.

Harpold, Terry. "The Contingencies of the Hypertext Link." *Writing on the Edge* 2:2 (Spring, 1991): 126-138.

Joyce, Michael. "Siren Shapes: Exploratory and Constructive Hypertexts." *Academic Computing* (November, 1988): 10-14, 37-42.

_____. *WOE.* Computer Software. *Writing on the Edge* 2:2 (Spring, 1991).

Kernan, Alvin. *The Death of Literature.* New Haven: Yale UP, 1990.

Landow, George P. *Dickens Web.* Computer Software. Watertown, MA: Eastgate Systems, 1992.

_____. *Hypertext: The Convergence of Contemporary Critical Theory and Technology.* Baltimore: Johns Hopkins UP, 1992.

Lanham, Richard. "The Electronic Word: Literary Study and the Digital Revolution." *New Literary History* 20 (Winter, 1989): 265-290.

_____. *A Handlist of Rhetorical Terms.* Berkeley: U of California P, 1991.

_____. *Literacy and the Survival of Humanism.* New Haven: Yale UP, 1984.

Moulthrop, Stuart. "In the Zones: Hypertext and the Politics of

Interpretation." *Writing on the Edge* 1:1 (1989) 18-27.

———. *Victory Garden*. Computer Software. Watertown, MA: Eastgate Systems, 1992.

Vickers, Brian. *In Defence of Rhetoric*. Oxford: Clarendon P, 1988.

Woodmansee, Martha. "The Genius and the Copyright: Economic and Legal Conditions of the Emergence of the Author." *Eighteenth Century Studies* 17 (1984): 425-448.

———. "On the Author Effect: Recovering Collectivity." *Cardozo Arts and Entertainment Law Journal* 10:2 (1992): 279-292.

Converging (or Colliding) Traditions: Integrating Hypertext into Literary Studies

Susan Lang

> By "hypertext," I mean *nonsequential writing*—text that branches and allows choices to the reader, best read at an interactive screen. As popularly conceived, this is a series of text chunks connected by links which offer the reader different pathways. (Theodor H. Nelson, in *Literary Machines*)

> . . . I leave it to be settled, by whomsoever it may concern, whether the tendency of this work be altogether to recommend parental tyranny, or reward filial disobedience. (Jane Austen, *Northanger Abbey* 212)

Although written over 150 years apart, both Ted Nelson's definition of hypertext and the concluding lines of Jane Austen's novel share an interest in the role of the interactive reader and in the notion of the indeterminate meaning of texts. However, Nelson, in describing hypertext, adds an overt method by which the reader may engage the "different pathways" offered by the text. As digital and electronic versions of texts become increasingly prevalent (witness the number of "books on disk" and "books on tape"), one question facing textual scholars is what may be gained or lost by the reader in this transformation from print to electronic format, particularly in the case of those lengthy texts like *Northanger Abbey* or Walter Scott's *Heart of Midlothian* that were written long before the digitalization of the word. We are beginning to ask what effect will the new technology have on the study of literature and what it is, exactly, that we

will do to these texts using Nelson's notion of multiple pathways. If hypertext is "nonsequential writing," does that mean
that a hypertextual reading of *Northanger Abbey* or any other
novel is a nonsequential reading, one that revises or undermines
the structure and unity of the text? In certain ways, elements of
the rapidly developing rhetoric of hypertext fit well with other
popular interpretive theories. We should inquire, though,
whether or not this "fit" justifies the inclusion of hypertextual
theory and application in courses devoted to pre-digitalized
texts.

       An examination of the 1990 Modern Language Association
(MLA) survey of English programs suggests that recent developments in critical theory have yet to gain a firm foothold in most
undergraduate literature classrooms; for the most part, members of
the profession still persist in teaching "the text" or "the texts."[1]
These individuals, though, may soon find themselves labeled a
dying breed. Theories of writing, of reading, of editing all refer
with increasing frequency to the various processes involved in
working with texts, while determinations of finite value become
less common. It seems appropriate, then, to give thought to the
ways in which we can negotiate boundaries between textual theories and textual study. In the pages that follow, I offer first a brief
overview of hypertext history as it crosses paths with literary theory. Hypertextual theory brings some unsettling issues to the forefront of literary studies, issues that must be considered as textual
scholars and instructors examine how this revolutionary change in
thought from "ideas of center, margin, hierarchy, and linearity" to
those of "multilinearity, nodes, links, and networks"(Landow 2)
may be applied to the ways in which we interpret and teach texts
written long before the digital age. I will then examine the convergence of linear printed texts and hypertext theory and technology
in the undergraduate classroom by focusing on how one nineteenth-century text, Jane Austen's *Northanger Abbey*, might be
taught by using such technology. Looking at Austen's text seems
particularly useful: since Austen's novels have long been praised
for their intricate structure, her work would seem especially ill-suit-
ed to the electronic platform. In the process, I will examine both the
interpretive implications—how this situation gives rise to different
readings of texts—and the pedagogical implications—how the converging technologies and conceptions of textuality alter the ways in
which the text is taught, or "encountered," in class.

RECENT DEVELOPMENTS IN HYPERTEXTUAL AND LITERARY THEORY

In the fifty years since Vannevar Bush first described his vision of an electronically-based information-retrieval system, the development of such "hypertextual" applications has progressed to the point that one needs to know nothing about computer programming in order to use them. Today a wide number of hypertext programs[2] are available to nontechnically-based fields, among them literary theory. During the past decade, an increasing number of literary theorists have explored and, to a surprisingly large extent, embraced hypertext. In "Literary Theory, Telecommunications, and the Making of History," J. Hillis Miller cites hypertext and the "digital revolution" in literary studies as one of the most significant developments in literary studies in recent years. Likewise, George P. Landow, in *Hypertext: The Convergence of Contemporary Critical Theory and Technology*, maintains that "hypertext promises to embody and thereby test aspects of theory, particularly those concerning textuality, narrative, and the roles or functions of reader and writer"(3), and Paul LeBlanc maintains that "more than any other technology, hypermedia authoring programs invite . . . teachers into the virtual age" (192). Even those who express reservations about the present state of hypertext agree that scholars must "assume responsibility for program design" to maintain "control over the modality of literary study" (Sosnoski 272-3).

If, as it appears, James Sosnoski and others are correct in assuming that the "electronic revolution is here and will continue to spread into every corner of our lives" (272), we must prepare to conduct our work, both research and teaching, in an increasingly digitalized environment. Before turning to a specific application of hypertext-based teaching, I want to reexamine the notion of hypertext to determine what this revolutionary medium entails and how it is presently used in the field of literary studies. Unlike the word processed document which may only enter the computer after being drafted elsewhere, the term "hypertext" signifies a text generated entirely within the electronic environment. The immediate differences one notes in hypertextual "documents" pertain to their appearance and their mutability at the reading level. As readers' interests or foci change, so can their reading paths, or threads, through the hypertext. The text's appearance differs as well; one recalls Barthes's notion of *lexias*, "a series of brief, contiguous fragments" (*S/Z* 13). In an electronic environment, though, the fragments do not require the permanent transitional devices associated with linear texts—the electronic environment enables the author and the reader to add these as warranted. In its format, then, a hypertext does represent a marked departure from the word processed document; one does not scroll down or page through a hypertext, one navigates the web of links or threads of the text. George Landow has focused much of his recent work on the links between hypertext applications and contemporary critical theory and suggests that

> [t]he many parallels between computer hypertext and critical theory have many points of interest, the most important of which, perhaps, lies in the fact that critical theory promises to theorize hypertext and hypertext promises to embody and thereby test aspects of theory, particularly those concerning textuality, narrative, and the roles or functions of reader and writer.
> (*Hypertext* 3)

Landow's hypotheses, while intriguing and useful, overly simplify the relationship between textual theory and composition. A hypertextual application such as HyperCard serves the same purpose as Microsoft Word or WordPerfect: it provides a platform on which to compose texts. The features of a hypertext program can be manipulated, as we shall see, in ways that support a number of types of textual theories.

Previously I discussed hypertexts in terms of text "chunks," Barthes's *lexias*, or "blocks," connected by various "links" or connections that enable a "user" (I resort to this term to hopefully avoid the multitude of connotations that surround the terms reader and author) to traverse a number of "paths" or "threads" through the text. These paths may differ with each new user or with each new encounter with the hypertext; in some cases, the user may also make new connections within elements of the existing document or even add new text(s). The hypertext components, then, do enable a different type of contact between the reader, text, and author than the printed, unchanging book, connections that might allow the reader to read and write differently. But if we continue this component-based examination of the hypertext, some new and potentially curious observations occur.

Consider first the web, or network, and the visualization of either as we understand them. Both consist of components, usually called "threads" or "lines." In the physical web, the individual threads do intersect with others a number of times within the structure; yet, each thread retains its integrity. To digress for a moment, the term "thread" also describes the organization of various network news groups. The tone and topics of any given news group may resemble in turn a "serious philosophical discussion" (whatever that may entail), a late-night phone-in talk show, or something in between. Regardless of topic, each subscriber can access a list of messages sorted by topic and follow each thread at will. Significantly, though, each thread of a news group follows a specific structure, usually in the form of a series of answers that are posed to a problem or question defined by a participant. If a user wants to change topics, he or she changes threads or begins to unwind, as it were, a new thread. When we examine each thread more closely, other surprises ensue. Each text chunk, or *lexia*, does not exist in some strange code; these components often look suspiciously similar to a sentence, paragraph, or page of text and read like them as well, although users might find "links" to other parts of the hypertext at any place in the text chunk.

And what about these links, these points in the text where one might find meaning deferred or redirected toward other topics that receive full treatment elsewhere in the document? Since these links are ostensibly one of the defining features of the environment of the electronic text, they deserve particular attention. Links between text chunks can revise the hierarchy of ideas of central text and citation as J. Hillis Miller discusses in "The Critic as Host." They can deconstruct, as it were, the hierarchy by allowing the two texts to co-exist in their entirety within the hypertext. Neither loses significance by being excerpted and taken out of its initial context. Links can also allow topics to be explored at length that might not be pursued in a printed text because of spatial or intellectual limitations; for these same reasons links promote collaboration in composing texts. The link, then, facilitates the multiplicity of readings so integral to Landow's conception of the electronic hypertext.

But, focusing even more closely on the link, we might find another more troubling function. What happens when we activate a link, not only in terms of electronics but in our thinking and reading processes? Hypertext's ability to represent theory comes into play.[3] Consider for a moment Jonathan Culler's summary in "Beyond Interpretation" of Stanley Fish's "Affective Stylistics." For Fish, "meaning lies not in the object but in the event or experience of reading. To ask about the meaning of a word or sentence is to ask what it *does* in the work, and to specify what it does one must analyze 'the developing responses to the words as they succeed each other in time'" (qtd. in Adams & Searle 326). What a link does in a hypertext is force a pause in the reading process, and, more importantly, force this pause at author-determined points throughout the document. Of course, users can always pause elsewhere in the text to contemplate what they have read, but judicious placement of the link can serve to highlight portions of the text that the link creator deems significant and worthy of additional space, both mental and electronic. Thus, hypertexts in which levels of interactivity remain low due to minimal user knowledge of either the subject matter or the hypertext system (one might term these content and form) may remain more in the realm of Barthes's readerly text, rather than the writerly text which "makes the reader no longer [merely] a consumer, but a producer of the text" (*S/Z* 4). The hypertext, then, apparently expands the realm of options available to its user rather than excluding any specific mode of textual production or reception. The label "authoring system" with all the implications of the term "author" is a particularly appropriate one for literary scholars and teachers to remember. The types of discourse created with hypertextual applications may be especially interactive, or not, and anyone who contemplates writing or teaching with hypertext must recognize its limitations as well as its potential.

DESIGNING A COURSE: PRIMARY CONSIDERATIONS

If hypertext can support multiple and contradictory ways of creating and viewing "texts" rather than simply adhere to one type of textual theory, using hypertext in the classroom becomes an even more complex matter. One cannot just decide to "teach hypertextually" and thus feel sufficiently avant-garde without considering the original aims of the course (if one is revising an old standby) or the goals of a newly-formulated class. While one could use hypertexts to explore new correlations between texts, James J. Sosnoski warns that a class could, if the instructor wished, "inculcate a structuralist or neo-formalist approach to literature" (274) by exploiting the sophisticated connective features of hypertext. Regardless of theoretical approach, though, one would be hard-put to find a course that did not focus on some specific texts as the set objects for study.

The above statement may strike most readers as a simplistic observation, yet in this case the obvious, that texts are set objects for study, merits further attention in our discussion of the effects of hypertext. William Paulson, in *The Noise of Culture*, writes that "[t]o some it may seem silly or tautological to observe that literature is literature because it is distinct from, among other things, psychology and biology, but the obvious is worth stating if it can help dislodge the prejudice that literature, as an object of study, has an almost natural existence" (3). Paulson's main question, which asks "what are the implications of *taking the literary text to be an object of knowledge*"(25),[4] may easily be extended to examining the intersection or collision of hypertext and printed texts. We need to ask ourselves how or if we can successfully teach the fixed or finite text with a medium that can so easily emphasize textual variance and instability given the present orientation of literary studies, since even postmodern theorists read a text as an object, albeit an object whose function seems impossible or ill-executed.

At this juncture, I would like to consider how hypertextual theory could change the way in which we present a particular text or course. Presently most of us rely on the notion of a course organized around a central text or texts although our treatment of those texts emphasizes some perceived relationships with other texts or events, rather than the isolated text. Such an approach allows the "text as discrete object" notion to remain prominent, but permits the introduction of hypertextual theory at the levels of both textual interpretation and presentation. Most English department offerings still fall into either the genre, period, or figure course and most likely exhibit a critical bias that the instructor is unwilling or unable to disregard completely.[5]

Let's consider how all of these observations might fit together in designing a course that would contain *Northanger Abbey*. For example, one course in which *Northanger Abbey* might appear would treat the nineteenth-century novel and emphasize its evolution as a genre throughout the century. Another might consider more specifically the genre of gothic fiction, either from the perspective of its place in eighteenth- and nineteenth-century fiction or in terms of its continuing social and literary significance. The novel may be found in a course dealing with women novelists or on narrative technique, or perhaps a course on Jane Austen. The rapid explosion in the field of literary studies allows for such diverse possibilities, yet they all rely on the existence of core texts that may be taught in order to illustrate a particular perspective or range of perspectives.[6] The emphasis remains on a closed transmission of information about selected texts.

Let us say, for example, that I have decided to again include *Northanger Abbey* in a course on Jane Austen. My brief course description might have previously read something like this:

> A study of Jane Austen in her social and cultural context through an examination of her six finished novels and other readings. Particular focus on evolution of narrative technique and issues of concern to the author throughout her life.

Such a course would probably have included lectures or discussions on each novel, some supplementary reading assignments, and a critical analysis of one or more works that required some outside research. The course has a clear plan of procession; indeed, anyone taking the course knows essentially how it will progress and how it will end. In the context of the course, *Northanger Abbey* would be analyzed as an "apprentice novel" (Monaghan 41), flawed because it lacks the structural unity of her later novels. Most of the scholarship written on *Northanger Abbey* has attempted to reconcile the diverse narrative threads and topics treated by Austen throughout the text, and even those scholars who defend the novel do so in ways that inadvertently reinforce notions of narrative fragmentation.[7] Critics who find *Northanger Abbey*'s various narrative threads incompatible and/or underdeveloped generally fault Austen for trying to accomplish too much or for simply not having a clear plan for developing her early text.[8] It seems that too often, regardless of the structural paradigm invoked, the prevailing critical tendency is to dismiss the novel as the roughly constructed work of a neophyte author who would refine her intentions and their execution in her subsequent works. If one designs a course to trace the development of the author and reads Austen's works in this chronological sense, no alternative exists but to see *Northanger Abbey* as flawed. Conventional conceptions of linear unity applied to the novel tend to limit themselves to a singular interpretation, with the remaining threads of meaning excluded or deemed inferior or irrelevant.

Given this linear and chronological approach to the text, how could one use either hypertextual theories or applications in the course? Even if one teaches the novel in the context of a "figure" course, the choice of whether or not to use hypertextual concepts may significantly alter the conduct of the course. The first potential role of hypertext in a course might be to provide a source of background and related texts. Perhaps the best-known application of such a hypertext is at Brown University, where students use hypertext webs to study English Literature from 1700-1900. The English 32 web integrates literary texts, related historical and literary documents, and materials that discuss matters of literary analysis.[9] Depending on one's own focus, an analogous web for *Northanger Abbey* might contain other fiction and prose by Austen, representative critical analyses of the novel, discussions of the gothic genre and of narrative strategy, and texts and analyses of other nineteenth-century novels and of other women writers. In the electronic environment, computer memory, not physical space, constrains the amount of texts one may compile for a course. Such a hypertext could be used to exemplify the concept of intertextuality in general and, specifically, to counter the conventional notions that Austen's work leads nowhere outside of the drawing room. Depending on the amount of student access to computer labs, one can either design a hypertext that illustrates the connections between Austen's text and other fiction or social documents for students to view at their leisure, or one might simply provide the documents in a hypertextual platform and ask the students to examine and mark interconnections. As the course progressed, students could add other texts to the document or add commentary to their own or to other students' intertextual links. The hypertext would then change from a "teaching tool" to a "learning tool."[10] Students would not only passively read the hypertextual links prepared by their instructor but would construct their own interpretations of how Austen's text related to other writings of the time. They would also, via the layering of hypertextual links, engage each other in conversation about their various readings of the texts, conversations that would transfer at times to the classroom or to any number of other course projects. Such interchanges allow a more equitable distribution of the discussion among class members and can be composed at the students' leisure.

Hypertext developers, beginning with Vannevar Bush and Ted Nelson, have long touted the ability of the systems to elicit active user participation.[11] In a traditional classroom context, the instructor has held the upper hand, both because of her position as more experienced reader and because of her position as evaluator. While the introduction of hypertext will not abolish either of these arrangements, using hypertext can certainly allow for the significant reconfiguration of them. If students spend class time at the keyboard reading and annotating links between *Northanger Abbey* and other texts, the traditional "class discussion" or lecture time obviously decreases. Furthermore, if students enter conversations with each other via the hypertext, the breadth of these exchanges may range from talk about the text as a parody of the gothic or as an early critique and problematization of social conventions to a discussion of Austen's commentary on the effects of reading. Throughout the term, students might refer to passages from the novel as evidence for their arguments about Austen's maturation as a writer, or they might create additional hypertextual documents that illustrate the ideological bases for the various readings of *Northanger Abbey*. While the instructor can and should participate in all of these activities, the focus of the hypertext document should remain on the student/text or student/student interactions. Learning becomes more a process of exploration and discovery that may occur during scheduled meetings or in the computer labs between classes than a cataloging of facts and details that students must recall on command. The instructor may see that the aspects of the novel that she had planned to emphasize have taken a backseat to other concerns that students find more interesting or relevant in their conversations. One may decide midway through a hypertextually-assisted course that the greatest difference comes in the form of apparent chaos. The course may have deviated from an "examination of Jane Austen's art through her six novels" to an apparently random look at various issues involving, to some degree, one or more of the texts, but also covering much unforeseen ground. The implications of that will occupy us in the next section, which considers how one might "read" *Northanger Abbey* hypertextually.

HYPERTEXTUALLY READING NORTHANGER ABBEY

Beyond providing visual examples of intertextuality, enabling far more extended discussions of the text, and encouraging a more "socialized" reading of texts than normally occurs in most undergraduate courses, what impact might a hypertextualized course have?[12] Not only could a hypertextually-assisted course facilitate discussing and coordinating the many existing interpretations of *Northanger Abbey*, applying principles of hypertext theory might shed new light on the text. By using elements of hypertextual theory and information theory, one can propose that the narrative patterns in the novel force the reader to adopt a different conceptual framework, one that defies conventional linear theories of structure and unity, and one that Austen employs in her subsequent works.[13] This paradigm, based on spatial rather than linear or even chronological relationships, allows the reader to recognize the interplay between Austen's topics without having to privilege one at the expense of the others. Michael Williams hints at such a reading of *Northanger Abbey* in *Jane Austen: Six Novels and Their Methods* :

> [W]e must establish a way in which the reader is able to respond simultaneously in different ways to the different elements, when they combine. Perhaps we need to think in terms of a continuum, one that will enable us to perceive a diversity of positions, and the complex interchange between the different positions that are reflected in the novel. . . . None of these possibilities is complete in itself; each exists and functions in combination with the others. (12-13)

If we approach the novel from the perspective of a hypertext, that is, a multiply-threaded text with a variety of connections between the individual topics ready for the reader to navigate, we might begin by examining how Catherine survives the confined and oppressive spaces of Bath and of the Abbey or the more relaxed area of Fullerton. The class might analyze how Catherine's perceptions of space change as she wanders from pump room to ballroom and back again in no sequential or linear fashion and then explore how her intellectual development becomes wrapped up in travel from one space to another. In hypertextual terms, how does she create links between the various nodes of her experience, whether those nodes be locations, like Blaize Castle, Bath or the Abbey, or her different sets of acquaintances, the Tilneys, Allens, and Thorpes? Indeed, how does Catherine revise her perceptions of herself, her friends, and her surroundings as they interact, connecting and reconnecting with different variables always at work? Catherine's social "text" functions much like a multiply-layered hypertext; even revisiting the same sites elicits different responses since others have also passed through those spaces and left their comments or actions.

Working from the paradigm of information theory, students might examine what constitutes information and noise for Catherine and how she resolves to comprehend the difference so that she may carry on the activities of perceiving, knowing, and speaking, all of which "take place through the integration of information and noise" (Paulson 49). Catherine's many conversations in *Northanger Abbey* treat a wide variety of topics from the place of the novel in education to the social rituals of Bath. These discussions bombard Catherine with a multitude of signals, both linguistic and otherwise. How she copes with these depends upon her perception of her own place within these physical and linguistic conversations. Paulson maintains that the

> link between language and the world passes through
> the body, the physical system in which perception and
> thought and speech take place. . . . In this view, we are
> capable of knowing what is around us not because we
> are separated from it, subjects facing objects, but
> because we are part of it, order amid disorder. What is
> noise, what is information depends on the position of
> the observer: information theory recognizes that it is
> itself caught up in systems of information. (49-50)

For example, Catherine's "visions of romance" seemingly end after Henry Tilney's lecture on "the country and the age in which we live." Tilney urges her to "[c]onsult your own understanding, your own sense of the probable, your own observation of what is passing around you" and ridicules her notion that such ideas [her vision of the relationship between Henry's parents] could flourish "in a country like this, where social and literary intercourse is on such a footing . . .where roads and newspapers lay everything open" (*Northanger Abbey* 165). Deferring to what she perceives as Henry's superior understanding, Catherine retires "with tears of shame" from the scene of her chastising, assuming that Henry's view of his parents and of society is correct.

Yet what has been resolved by Henry's speech? On certain levels, the mysteries of the text have been solved—General Tilney has not murdered his wife and stashed the corpse in an available vault, and the abbey contains no treasure but an old laundry list. But in other ways Henry's language is far from clear and his message sends contradictory signals, even though Catherine responds to his words as law. One might wonder if Henry realizes that in stating that "social and literary intercourse is on such a footing, where every man is surrounded by a neighbourhood of voluntary spies," he partially encourages the merging of the literary "voice" with the world at large through the shared discursive traditions even as he condemns Catherine for practicing that very activity. Henry recognizes that both traditions have the capability of making meaning and order[14] but ignores the fact that "they both complicate information with noise" and that "what is noise, what is information depends on the position of the observer" (Paulson 49-50). While "information theory recognizes that it is itself caught up in systems of information" (Paulson 50), Henry's words imply that he and the "voluntary spies" can remain the rational arbiters who distill the sense of language and, consequently, the order of his world. While Catherine acquiesces to his reading of society and those who inhabit it, Austen's readers may note the incompatibility of Henry's words with the actions of General Tilney, Isabella and John Thorpe, and Mrs. Allen. While an actual murder has not occurred, plenty of verbal deception has. Few of Austen's characters communicate translucently; all speech contains some degree of "noise" which impairs or prohibits its accurate reception.

While some readers of *Northanger Abbey* have noted the irony of Henry Tilney's words regarding his father and the multiple verbal deceptions of other characters throughout the novel, they still read this sequence as the culmination of a single narrative thread—Catherine's education by her future husband. Even if critics now judge *Northanger Abbey* as far more socially relevant than previously assumed,[15] they still insist on interpreting the novel as a series of discrete levels of meaning, some of which appear more compatible than others; in short, they analyze to seek unity in the static text. Paulson charges that this organic whole so sought after by Romanticists and their subsequent readers is "not a property of verbal architecture but a convention governing its reading and thereby determining its function as a dynamic system" (119). To read Austen's texts as dynamic systems by applying principles of hypertextual and information theory to the text allows readers to reexamine the possible connections Austen has made between writing and literature to larger social issues and situations. I use the term "possible" here because while the very existence of a text causes us to approach it as a unit, it "simultaneously reveals itself to belong to no totality that we can conceive" (Paulson 115). David Porush writes that the "literary text is best viewed as the result of the intersection of the author's mind with a very peculiar technology (a sort of antimechanistic technology) designed in its most advanced forms to capture the evanescent movements and fluctuations of the mind itself" (75-6). If we examine the structure of the novel as "*techniques at work*," whose operations are negotiated by reader, text, and author,[16] we abandon the concept of static unity for the amorphous "complex system"—one which contains "a discontinuity in knowledge between the parts and the whole" (Paulson 108). In doing so we accept that whatever "unity" that we recognize in the novel is dynamic, and cannot be continually read via a single paradigm. Both hypertextual theory and information theory liberate the reader from the binding singular interpretation and give the reader both the conceptual framework and electronic space to comprehend a text or texts based not on the sum of the parts but on the constant evaluation and re-envisioning of the various elements, either as a single reader or in collaboration with others.

WHAT NEXT?

We have seen that texts produced during the age of print technology can be examined via the lenses of hypertextual theory and information theory and that the undergraduate literature classroom can conduct productive analyses of texts using hypertextual technology. In fact, the new technologies appear to fit in quite smoothly to the field of textual studies, despite, or perhaps because of, their acknowledgment of linguistic complexity. To this end, witness Jacques Derrida's claim that our present awareness of both narrative structure and its limitations, combined with our consciousness of multiple critical paradigms, calls for a new nonlinear format of writing and reading, one that applies to texts both present and past: "one begins to reread past writing according to a different organization of space . . . .Because we are beginning to write differently, we must reread differently" (*Of Grammatology* 86-87). By applying hypertext technology to printed texts, we may continue to teach students to read and write more actively and more critically, thus making them more aware of the intricacies involved in the changing nature of texts. This is a laudable goal, but one that requires even more consideration than how we will read and write in and out of the classroom using the new theories and applications. Literary studies has long had the distinction of being the only field to confront the texts of the past on equal terms with those of the present, a trait that augments the impression of their timelessness and therefore their worthiness as objects of study. Michael Serres questions the viability of objective knowledge of any sort, noting that the observer or the learner has no special construction that enables her to separate herself from that which she seeks to know.[17] She constructs interpretations out of the same subjective system (language) that she seeks to definitively know through literature. The difficulty of this enterprise is self-evident; new theories for understanding texts appear every half-century or so, and scholars like Landow would have us believe that hypertextual theories are simply the next in a long line of interpretive strategies that enable us finally to "know the literary text" better.

Most advocates of hypertext have sought to soothe the collective anxiety of literary scholars by focusing on the compatibility of the new theories and existing practice. One might recall George Landow's assertion that "text-based computing in the humanities should be able to co-exist happily with more traditional modes of textuality" and Paul Delany's statement that "the arrival of hypertext causes the other occupants of the textual bus to shift position, but no one actually has to get off" (*Hypermedia and Literary Studies* 1). Three years ago, the bus was simply crowded, but the new occupant seems to have assumed more space and is now causing a seriously unbalanced load. What happens if the bus overturns as more and more textual practices take place in the electronic or hypertextual space? We now see hypertextual allusions everywhere, in mass-market magazines, on television commercials that use the familiar pull-down menus to deliver their information, and even in linear word-processing programs that now include such features as "annotation" or "bookmark," hypertextual in theory although labeled with more comforting names.

Whether we like it or not, hypertext and other facets of electronic textuality are not about to relinquish their seats on the bus. As advances in both hardware and software make hypertextual applications available to an increasing number of people, students will demand to be taught to use the new technology. English departments cannot deal with computers in the same ways that they have coped with the invasions of minority writers, radical theorists, and even composition by creating certain courses in which computer-assisted instruction is deemed appropriate, thus leaving the main body of teaching essentially as it had been. While the first courses to adapt computer-assisted instruction, such as composition, were often viewed as marginal, we have seen that the use of computers can go far beyond the word-processed text of the writing course and affect not only the methodology but the content of even the mainstream literature course.

Thus, integrating hypertextual theory into the field of literary studies by telling everyone how well it fits with contemporary theory (and then saying that the field has caught up to the rest of the world) negates the impact of electronic texts and hypertext and promotes the rather insular view of literature that has lead to charges of literature's irrelevance to the "real world." The type of activities discussed in this essay are only an initial step in the genuine integration of technology and accompanying theory to the field of English. The larger significance of hypertext lies somewhere in both the theoretical and practical aspects that enable us to see how these different types and theories of texts could build connections between English and other fields, and in doing so aid in their redefinition.[18]

In "Fictions as Dissipative Structures," David Porush maintains that literature "still breaks new ground in documenting our culture's understanding of itself, its relationship to individual imaginations, and the relationship between those imaginations and the universe that feeds it" (79). However, if literature is to continue to do so in our increasingly digitalized society, if it is to be, in the words of physicist Ilya Prigogine, a "model for a kind of knowing that best communicates the 'opacity'—or at least the complex unpredictability of the universe" (qtd. in Porush 80), it must confront and engage the new ways we have of creating texts and of thinking about the theoretical paradigms underlying the new methods. To read *Northanger Abbey* or any other predigitalized text hypertextually is not, then, to read non-sequentially, or nonsensically, as some might believe. Instead, reading and teaching hypertextually allows us to literally go above the individual text, to read and integrate both information and "noise" from many disciplines, and develop those complex and valuable ideas that are somehow more than the sum of their individual parts.[19]

NOTES

[1]In "Today's Literature Classroom: Findings from the MLA's 1990 Survey of Upper Division Courses," Bettina J. Huber summarizes the findings of the survey that delved into the classroom practices and orientation of upper-division literature courses. The MLA examined three particular areas: American literature from 1800 to 1865, the nineteenth-century British novel, and non-Shakespearean Renaissance literature. Huber posits that these "courses were selected because scholarly developments in these fields suggested that noncanonical writing and new approaches to the study of literature were likely to have influenced them" (36). Yet the results of this survey provide little evidence that "English faculty members have jettisoned traditional texts and teaching methods in their upper-division literature courses" (52). A vast majority of instructors in all three areas named works that fell within the canon as those "particularly

important" to the study of the period's literature. Additionally, most respondents in all course areas were most greatly influenced by "largely similar, and traditional, theoretical orientations in their teaching" (49), namely the New Criticism and the history of ideas. Traditional methods of teaching dominate classrooms, with nearly 97% using a combination of lectures and discussion, "each typically taking up about half the available class time" (50). Popular student evaluation methods remain the written examination and either long or short papers.

Instructional goals remain for the most part largely traditional. Huber states that "these aims revolve around providing students with the historical and intellectual background needed to understand the primary texts they are assigned and helping them to appreciate the merits of these texts" (52). Although instructors have adopted some goals that reflect scholarly changes in their fields, such as understanding the effects of race, class, and gender on literature, these goals are in addition to, rather than replacement for, the established goals of understanding historical background, comprehension of formal qualities, and textual explication.

[2]Programs currently available include *HyperCard* and *StorySpace* for the Macintosh and *Toolbook* for the IBM and compatibles.

[3]Finding an appropriate word to describe the relationship between hypertext and critical theory has proven difficult. Frequently used terms such as "physicalize" and "embody" seem especially inappropriate for an electronic representation of an abstraction, and words like "enact" or "execute" themselves counter the tenets of much contemporary theory.

[4]Italics here and elsewhere inserted by the original author, unless otherwise stated.

[5]Sosnoski's fears seem supported by the 1990 MLA survey. Bettina Huber's analysis of the MLA survey found that instructors rely on "well-established," if outdated, theoretical approaches. The vast majority purport to ascribe to either the History of Ideas or the New Criticism. Feminism is the most popular of the recent theoretical approaches; poststructuralist criticism are only "considered important by one in five respondents" (53). Most of the course readings consist of literary works and criticism of the period; few instructors devote more than a small

section of their reading lists to works in contemporary criticism, theory, historical background material, and biography (45).

[6]I use the term "core" rather than the problematic "canonical" since an increasing number of courses purport to teach texts that lie outside of the traditional cannon. Regardless of whether or not the works are canonized, they represent a finished entity.

[7]Defenders of the novel, like A. Walton Litz, have believed that the novel contains "detachable units" throughout. Those who perceive a unity include Katrin Ristok Burlin who argues that the novel is a "single, complex treatment of the theme of fiction"; Jan Fergus who claims that "the novel is about writing novels"; and Frank Kearful who writes that Austen combines "elements . . . in such fashion as to make us aware of the paradoxical nature of all illusion—even those illusions by which we master illusion."

[8]Ian Milligan finds *Northanger Abbey* "lacking in integration" and "marred by failures of serious purpose" (29-30), although he does label it "a kind of artistic manifesto" (30). David Monaghan reconciles the "chaotic surface" of the novel and defends Catherine Morland by focusing on the "prior invitation" pattern which "helps undo the impression, created accidentally by the anti-Gothic satire of the novel's opening chapters"(17-18), while Mary Evans finds *Northanger Abbey* "Austen's most imperfectly realized novel" (39).

[9]Mark Walter's "IRIS Intermedia: Pushing the Boundaries of Hypertext" describes the evolution of the Brown University computing project. George Landow discusses the use of Intermedia in detail in *Hypertext: The Convergence of Contemporary Critical Theory and Technology*, while James J. Sosnoski raises important concerns about the use of "formalistic" hypertexts in "Students as Theorists: Collaborative Hypertextbooks."

[10]See Phillipe C. Duchastel and Terry Mayes et al. in *Designing Hypertext/Hypermedia for Learning* (David H. Jonassen and Heinz Mandl, eds.).

[11]Among the increasingly abundant number of sources available on the topic, see Gary Marchionini, John L. Legett, and others in *Designing Hypertext/Hypermedia for Learning* (David H. Jonassen and Heinz Mandl, eds.) for discussions of the active learner in hypertextual systems. Also see George Landow's dis-

cussion of "Reconfiguring the Student" (126-30) in *Hypertext*.

¹²For arguments that texts themselves are social products, see Jerome McGann's *A Critique of Modern Textual Criticism* and *The Textual Condition*.

¹³The quantitative basis for information theory was developed in Bell Laboratories to maximize the efficiency of telecommunications. William Paulson approaches literary studies via information theory in *The Noise of Culture: Literary Texts in a World of Information*.

¹⁴Witness his preoccupation with "incorrectness of language" and Elinor's commentary on the issue; also his defense of history and historians, both in Chapter 14.

¹⁵See Monaghan's *Jane Austen: Structure and Social Vision*: "The well-being of the state is therefore directly related to the quality of the relationships that the individual is able to establish with his immediate family and community." By recognizing the importance of interpersonal relationships in society, Austen's novels become far more relevant than previously supposed (2-5). See also Marilyn Butler's *Jane Austen and the War of Ideas*.

¹⁶See Williams's *Jane Austen: Six Novels and Their Methods*.

¹⁷See Michael Serres's "The Origin of Language" in *Hermes: Literature, Science, Philosophy*.

¹⁸William Paulson calls for the breaking down of the traditional role of literature: "In suggesting that scientific concepts can and should be made a part of our thinking about literature, I am calling into question a romantic tradition of literature as a domain of protest against science's manipulative disenchantment of the world" (104).

¹⁹See Paulson: "complex [systems] have a discontinuity in knowledge between the parts and the whole" (104).

WORKS CITED

Adams, Hazard, and Leroy Searle, eds. *Critical Theory Since 1965*. Tallahassee: Florida State UP, 1986.

Austen, Jane. *Northanger Abbey*. New York: Signet Classic, 1965.

Barthes, Roland. *S/Z*. Trans. Richard Miller. New York: Farrar, Straus, and Giroux, 1974.

Burlin, Katrin Ristok. "The Pen of the Contriver: The Four Fictions of *Northanger Abbey*." In Halperin, 89-111.

Butler, Marilyn. *Jane Austen and the War of Ideas*. Oxford: Clarendon P, 1975.

Culler, Jonathan. "Beyond Interpretation." In Adams and Searle, 322-330.

Delany, Paul, and George P. Landow, eds. *Hypermedia and Literary Studies*. Cambridge: MIT P, 1991.

Derrida, Jacques. *Of Grammatology*. Trans. Gayatri Chakravorty Spivak. Baltimore: Johns Hopkins UP, 1976.

Evans, Mary. *Jane Austen and the State*. London: Tavistock Publications, 1987.

Fergus, Jan. *Jane Austen and the Didactic Novel: "Northanger Abbey," "Sense and Sensibility," and "Pride and Prejudice."* Totowa: Barnes & Noble, 1983.

Halperin, John, ed. *Jane Austen: Bicentenary Essays*. Cambridge: Cambridge UP, 1975.

Hayles, N. Katherine, ed. *Chaos and Order: Complex Dynamics in Literature and Science*. Chicago: U of Chicago P, 1991.

Huber, Bettina J. "Today's Literature Classroom: Findings from the MLA's 1990 Survey of Upper-Division Courses." *ADE Bulletin* 101 (1992) 36-60.

Jonassen, David H., and Heinz Mandl, eds. *Designing Hypertext/Hypermedia for Learning*. Heidelberg: Springer-Verlag, 1990.

Kaplan, Deborah. *Jane Austen Among Women*. Baltimore: Johns Hopkins UP, 1992.

Kearful, Frank J. "Satire and the Form of the Novel: The Problem of Aesthetic Unity in *Northanger Abbey*." *ELH* 32 (1965): 511-27.

Landow, George P. *Hypertext: The Convergence of Contemporary Critical Theory and Technology*. Baltimore: Johns Hopkins UP, 1992.

LeBlanc, Paul. "Ringing in the Virtual Age: Hypermedia Authoring Software and the Revival of Faculty-Based Software." In *Re-imagining Computers and Composition: Teaching and Research in the Virtual Age*. Gail Hawisher and Paul LeBlanc, eds. Portsmouth: Boynton/Cook, 1992. 191-206.

Litz, A. Walton. *Jane Austen: A Study of her Artistic Development*. New York: Oxford UP, 1965.

McGann, Jerome J. *A Critique of Modern Textual Criticism*. Charlottesville: UP of Virginia, 1983.

_____. *The Textual Condition*. Princeton: Princeton UP, 1991.

Miller, J. Hillis. "Literary Theory, Telecommunications, and the Making of History." *Conference Papers from the International Conference on Scholarship and Technology in the Humanities*. Sponsored by the British Library, the British Academy, and the American Council of Learned Societies, Elvetham Hall, England, May, 1990.

_____. "The Critic as Host." In Adams and Searle, 452-468.

Milligan, Ian B. *Studying Jane Austen*. Essex: Longman, 1988.

Monaghan, David. *Jane Austen: Structure and Social Vision*. London: Macmillan, 1980.

Nelson, Theodor H. *Literary Machines*. Swarthmore, PA: Self-published, 1981.

Paulson, William R. *The Noise of Culture: Literary Texts in a World of Information*. Ithaca: Cornell UP, 1988.

Porush, David. "Fictions as Dissipative Structures: Prigogine's Theory and Postmodernism's Roadshow." In Hayles, 54-84.

Serres, Michael. *Hermes: Literature, Science, Philosophy*. Eds. Josué V. Harari and David F. Bell. Baltimore: Johns Hopkins UP, 1982.

Sosnoski, James J. "Students as Theorists: Collaborative Hypertextbooks." In *Practicing Theory in Introductory College Literature Courses*. Eds. James B. Cahalan and David B. Downing. Urbana: NCTE P, 1991.

Walter, Mark. "IRIS Intermedia: Pushing the Boundaries of Hypertext." *The Seybold Report on Publishing Systems* 18:21 (1989): 21-32.

Williams, Michael. *Jane Austen: Six Novels and Their Methods*. London: Macmillan, 1986.

Notes on Contributors

Jay David Bolter, Professor of Literature, Communication, and Culture at the Georgia Institute of Technology, is the author of *Writing Space: The Computer, Hypertext, and the History of Writing* (Lawrence Erlbaum, 1991) and *Turing's Man: Western Culture in the Computer Age* (North Carolina, 1984).

Philip Cohen, Interim Chair and Associate Professor of English at The University of Texas at Arlington, has edited the collection *Devils and Angels: Textual Editing and Literary Theory* (Virginia, 1991) and published on literary and textual matters in such journals as *American Literature, American Literary History, Studies in American Fiction, Mississippi Quarterly, The Faulkner Journal,* and *TEXT.* He is currently writing the Faulkner chapter for the 1996 volume of *American Literary Scholarship* (Duke).

Paul Eggert, Senior Lecturer in English at University College, ADFA, Canberra, and Director of the Australian Scholarly Editions Centre, has edited D.H. Lawrence's *Twilight in Italy and Other Essays* (Cambridge, 1994), *The Boy in the Bush* (Cambridge, 1990) and *Editing in Australia* (New South Wales, 1990). His essays on Lawrence and textual scholarship have appeared in *Studies in Bibliography, Critical Quarterly, Southern Review,* and *D.H. Lawrence Review.*

James C. Faris, Professor of Anthropology at the University of Connecticut, is the author of *The Nightway: A History and a History of the Documentation of a Navajo Healing Ceremonial* (New Mexico, 1990) and *Southeast Nuba Social Relations* (Alano, 1989). His work has appeared in *American Anthropologist, Ethnology, History and Anthropology, Critique of Anthropology, Dialectical Anthropology,* and a variety of collections.

Mike Feehan, Independent Scholar, has published on Kenneth Burke, rhetoric, and composition in *Rhetoric '78, College English, Tennessee Linguistics, Pre-Text,* and *Semiotica.*

Christopher Felker, Research Analyst for Resource Development at the Massachusetts Institute of Technology, is the author of *A Puritan Invention: "Magnalia Christi Americana" and Democracy in the American Renaissance* (Northeastern, 1994) and essays on American literature in *New England Quarterly* and *Ellipsis.*

John Miles Foley, Professor of English and William H. Byler Distinguished Chair in the Humanities at the University of Missouri, is the author of *Immanent Art: From Structure to Meaning in Traditional Oral Epic* (Indiana, 1991), *Traditional Oral Epic* (California, 1990), and *The Oral Theory of Composition: History and Methodology* (Indiana, 1988). He is also the editor of the journal *Oral Tradition* and the *Encyclopedia of Oral Traditions*.

D. C. Greetham, Professor of English at the Graduate Center, City University of New York, is the Executive Director of the Society for Textual Scholarship. He is the author of *Textual Scholarship: An Introduction* (Garland, 1992) and the forthcoming *Theories of the Text* (Oxford). He has also edited the forthcoming *Scholarly Editing: A Guide to Research* (Modern Language Association), and his essays on editorial and literary theory have appeared in *Studies in Bibliography, Modern Philology,* and *Publications of the Bibliographical Society of America.*

Susan Lang, Visiting Assistant Professor at Wilkes University, has published on the practical and theoretical consequences of electronic information technology for English studies in ERIC/RCS and the *Proceedings of the 9th Annual Conference on Technology and Education.*

Tim Morris, Associate Professor of English at the University of Texas at Arlington, is the author of *Becoming Canonical in American Poetry* (Illinois, 1995) and essays on American writers in *Studies in American Fiction, Studies in the Novel, Essays in Literature,* and *American Literature.*

James Murphy, Associate Professor of English and Director of Writing Across the Curriculum at Carroll College, has presented papers on textual matters at MLA, SAMLA, and SCMLA. He is currently completing a book on Henry James's revisions for the New York Edition.

Johanna M. Smith, Associate Professor of English at the University of Texas at Arlington, is the editor of *"Frankenstein": A Case Study in Contemporary Criticism* (Bedford-St. Martin's, 1992). She has contributed to *Approaches to Teaching "Pride and Prejudice"* (Modern Language Association, 1992) and to *Critical Responses to Raymond Chandler* (Greenwood, 1992), and her essays on nineteenth-century and modern literature have appeared in *Emerson Society Quarterly, Studies in the Novel, Nineteenth-Century Contexts,* and *Texas Studies in Language and Literature.*

INDEX